virgin film

COMIC BOOK MOVIES

Other Virgin Film titles by the same author:

The Complete Kubrick
The Complete Lynch

COMIC BOOK MOVIES

virgin film

David Hughes

First published in Great Britain in 2003
by Virgin Books Ltd
Thames Wharf Studios
Rainville Road
London
W6 9HA

This book is an unofficial guide and should in no way be regarded as official merchandise.

A catalogue record for this book is available from the British Library.

ISBN 0 7535 0767 6

Typeset by TW Typesetting, Plymouth, Devon
Printed and bound in Great Britain by Mackays of Chatham PLC

Contents

For Ingrid, the harshest critic of all

Acknowledgements

While working on this book I had the benefit of a whole super-team backing me up. These unsung heroes include 'Captain Manga' (a.k.a. Jonathan Clements), who contributed the chapters on *Akira* and *Ghost in the Shell*; my researcher Rod Edgar, a.k.a. 'The Human Brain'; 'The Red Pencil' (a.k.a. editor Mark Wallace); and not-so-secret agent, Chelsey 'The Chelsea Fox' Fox.

Several interview subjects provided services above and beyond the call of duty, notably Max Allan Collins, Michael France, Todd McFarlane, David J Schow and Steven E De Souza. I'd also like to think my other interviewees, including Darren Aronofsky, Rick Baker, Chris Cunningham, Peter Deming, Chris Donaldson, Jack Epps Jr, the late Lee Falk, Kenneth Johnson, Nigel Phelps, John Shirley, Kevin Smith, Brian Singer, Barry Sonnenfield, Patrick Stewart, Wesley Strick, Kristy Swanson, Miles Teves, Adam West, Treat Williams, Simon Wincer, Billy Zane and Catherine Zeta-Jones.

Thanks are also due to David Willing, Dane McMaster, Gordon Dale, Dan Quinn, Angus Spottiswoode, Adam Newell, Lee Brimmicombe-Wood (for showing me there was more to comics than *Secret Wars*), Gail Stanley, Matt Barker, Ryan Poenisch at the WGA, Ken Reinstein, Brian Olson, Clare Macintosh, Michael Barrs, Bruce Craig, Alex and Nerissa, Paul Simpson, Soba, Starbucks . . . Zahida, Harry, Jenna, Liz, Mike and Jackie. As most of them know, I needed more support during the writing of *Comic Book Movies* than any of the other book, so . . . *thanks.*

And I said this one was going to be easy.

Picture Credits

Superman: Ronald Grant Archive
Batman: Ronald Grant Archive
Akira: Kobal Collection
Teenage Mutant Ninja Turtles trademark and copyright Mirage Studios 1984
The Crow: J. O'Barr
X-Men: Kobal Collection
Blade: Marvel Comics
From Hell: Eddie Campbell Comics
Dick Tracy: Kobal Collection
Ghost World: Fantagraphics Books
Road to Perdition: Paradox Press/DC Comics
Spider-Man: Ronald Grant Archive
The Hulk: Universal

Introduction

When Virgin approached me to write this guide to *Comic Book Movies*, I was initially sceptical, since the last two books I had written for this series – *The Complete Kubrick* and *The Complete Lynch* – were designed to be exhaustive; *Comic Book Movies*, on the other hand, would cover only twenty of the many movie adaptations of comics and graphic novels, spanning a quarter century, from 1978 to 2003 (i.e. *Superman* to *Hulk*). It soon became clear, however, that a great many comic-to-film adaptations have failed, at least artistically, for reasons that I was eager to discover. Why should this be, I wondered, when the two media seem to have so much in common? As comics legend Will Eisner (*The Spirit*) observed, 'Films were really nothing but frames on celluloid, which is really no different from frames on a piece of paper. Doing *The Spirit* was no different to making movies.' But was he right? 'A lot of people make this parallel between comics and film,' writer and artist Dave Gibbons (*Watchmen*) demurred, 'but I think it's a completely bogus comparison. A comic's script looks a bit like a film script and comic art looks a bit like storyboards, but there is no sound in a comic book and no movement. Also, with a comic book the reader can backtrack, you can reach page 20 and say, "Hey, that's what that was all about in that scene on page 3," and then nip back and have a look.'

Comic book movies have never been more popular. As this book went to press, no fewer than three Marvel-based properties were either in cinemas (*Daredevil*) or due for release (*X-Men 2*, *Hulk*); new films based on Superman, Batman, Ghost Rider, Judge Dredd, The Fantastic Four, Sandman, Dr Strange, Luke Cage, Iron Man, the League of Extraordinary Gentlemen and countless other comic book heroes are in production or advanced stages of development; and a comic book-inspired biography, *American Splendor*, had won prizes at the Sundance Film Festival. As Stephen Norrington, director of the comic book adaptations *Blade* and *The League of Extraordinary Gentlemen*, observed, 'The vibe feels much the same as when George Lucas and Steven Spielberg took black-and-white adventure serials and turned them into *Star Wars* and *Indiana Jones*. Now people take comics and turn them into big, A-class pictures like *X-Men* or *Hulk*.' Why this sudden fascination with comic book heroes? Perhaps because so many directors and studio executives grew up (as I did) on Marvel and DC comics – an entire generation learned about morality, heroism and the difficult choices faced by heroes not from the classics, but from *Spider-Man* and *The Hulk*, with mythologies as potent and powerful as those of the gods of ancient times. Whether the trend continues, as it did between the success of *Batman* in 1989 and the failure of *Batman and Robin* in 1997, remains to be seen.

Although limited to twenty titles, *Comic Book Movies* follows a format similar to the other books in the growing Virgin Film range, each chapter broken down into the following sections:

Title (Year of Release)

Running Time

Principal Credits

CAST: A list of cast members and characters credited on the film . . .

UNCREDITED CAST: . . . and those who weren't so lucky.

TITLE SEQUENCE: A brief description of the opening of the film.

SYNOPSIS: A plot synopsis of the film – complete with spoilers, so you might want to cover your eyes while you read this bit.

ORIGINS: A comprehensive look at the source material for the film – be it comic strip, comic book or graphic novel – including character description and development where appropriate.

PREVIOUS INCARNATIONS: An exploration of any previous appearances of the character on screen (i.e. film or television), from Saturday morning serials of the 1940s to Saturday morning cartoons of the 2000s.

DEVELOPMENT: Since the development of a comic book property is often a more exciting story than its eventual production, this section looks at the various attempts to bring the property to the big screen.

CASTING: The casting process, and – where applicable – actors who were auditioned or attached at earlier stages of production.

PRODUCTION: A look at the production process of each film, from ground zero to big-screen super hero, drawn from interviews with relevant sources where applicable.

COSTUME FITTING: Since costumes play such a major role in most comic book movies, it seems appropriate to have a separate section devoted to the costume designers who attempt to make what is *de rigeur* to comic book fans – men in tights, for example – acceptable to movie audiences.

MUSIC: Composer and, where applicable, soundtrack information.

CLASSIC QUOTES: A favourite quotation (or two) from the film.

DELETED SCENES: Those scenes which, for a variety of reasons, did not make it into the final cut of the film.

TRAILERS: From early 'teasers' to full-blown 'Winnebagos' (trailers with everything including the kitchen sink).

POSTERS: Don't know your 'one-sheet' from your 'quad'? It doesn't matter – most posters for comic book movies are as simple as they get.

TAG-LINE: 'You'll believe a man can fly' and other copywriting gems.

WHAT THE PAPERS SAID: Critical responses from the US and UK, drawn from three major publications: *Variety* (because it's the industry bible), *Chicago Sun-Times* (because Roger Ebert is a comic book aficionado) and *Time Out* (because they're brutally honest).

BOX OFFICE: Performance from both sides of the Atlantic.

AWARDS: Awards and nominations from around the world.

CONTROVERSY: Although mostly aimed at kids, comic book movies have had their share of controversy – so here are some of the terrifying true stories torn from the headlines of yesteryear.

TRIVIA: Frankly, all the stuff that wouldn't fit into any of the other sections.

APOCRYPHA: When you're fighting for truth and justice it helps to have the truth on your side – so here you might find a few myths exploded.

SEQUELS & SPIN-OFFS: A detailed look at the sequels, spin-offs and TV serials spawned by the film in question, if not directly, then as a result of the source material's new-found popularity.

FUTURE INCARNATIONS: A look at possible future incarnations of the character(s) in question, including sequels and series in development.

DVD AVAILABILITY: Information regarding the various DVD editions available in the UK (Region 2) and US (Region 1) complete with a breakdown of additional features where applicable.

FINAL ANALYSIS: My own two cents, for what it's worth (about 0.02 Euros).

EXPERT WITNESS: A summary quotation from one of the major players involved in the comic-to-film adaptation.

Superman: The Movie (1978)

143 mins (original version)/151 mins (2000 restored version)

Directed by Richard Donner
Produced by Pierre Spengler
Executive Producer Ilya Salkind
Associate Producer Charles F Greenlaw
Creative Consultant Tom Mankiewicz
Screenplay by Mario Puzo, David Newman, Leslie Newman and Robert Benton
Story by Mario Puzo
Superman Created by Jerry Siegel and Joe Shuster
Music by John Williams
Editor Stuart Baird
Director of Photography by Geoffrey Unsworth BSC
Production Designer John Barry

CAST: Marlon Brando (*Jor-El*), Gene Hackman (*Lex Luthor*), Christopher Reeve (*Kal-El/'Clark Kent'/'Superman'*), Ned Beatty (*Otis*), Jackie Cooper (*Perry White*), Glenn Ford (*Jonathan Kent*), Trevor Howard (*First Elder*), Margot Kidder (*Lois Lane*), Jack O'Halloran (*Non*), Valerie Perrine (*Eve Teschmacher*), Maria Schell (*Vond-Ah*), Terence Stamp (*General Zod*), Phyllis Thaxter (*Martha Clark Kent*), Susannah York (*Lara*), Jeff East (*Clark at eighteen*) Marc McClure (*Jimmy Olsen*), Sarah Douglas (*Ursa*), Harry Andrews, Vass Anderson, John Hollis, James Garbutt, Michael Gover, David Neal, William Russell, Penelope Lee, John Stuart, Alan Cullen (*Elders*), Lee Quigley (*baby Kal-El*), Aaron Smolinski (*baby Clark Kent*), Diane Sherry (*Lana Lang*), Jeff Atcheson (*coach*), Brad Flock (*football player*), David Petrou (*team manager*), Billy J Mitchell, Robert Henderson (*editors*), Larry Lamb, James Brockington, John Cassady, John F Parker, Antony Scott, Ray Evans, Sue Shifrin, Miquel Brown (*reporters*), Vincent Marzello, Benjamin Feitelson (*copy boys*), Lise Hilboldt, Leueen Willoughby (*secretaries*), Jill Ingham (*Perry's secretary*), Pieter Stuyck (*window cleaner*), Rex Reed (*himself*), Weston Gavin (*mugger*), Steve Kahan, Ray Hassett, Randy Jurgensen (*detectives*), Matt Russo (*news vendor*), Colin Skeaping (*pilot*), Bo Rucker (*pimp*), Paul Avery (*TV cameraman*), David Baxt (*burglar*), George Harris (*Mooney*), Michael Harrigan, John Cording, Raymond Thompson, Oz Clarke (*hoods*), Rex Everhart (*desk sergeant*), Jayne Tottman (*little girl*), Frank Lazarus (*Air Force One pilot*), Brian Protheroe (*Air Force One co-pilot*), Lawrence Trimble,

Robert Whelan, David Calder (*Air Force One crew*), Norwich Duff, Keith Alexander, Michael Ensign (*newscasters*), Larry Hagman (*major*), Paul Tuerpe (*Sergeant Hayley*), Graham McPherson (*lieutenant*), David Yorston (*petty officer*), Robert O'Neill (*admiral*), Robert MacLeod (*general*), John Ratzenberger, Alan Tilvern (*controllers*), Phil Brown, Bill Bailey (*senators*), Burnell Tucker (*agent*), Chief Tug Smith (*native American chief*), Norman Warwick (*superchief driver*), Chuck Julian (*assistant*), Colin Etherington (*power company driver*), Mark Wynter (*mate*), Roy Stevens (*warden*)

TITLE SEQUENCE: Black and white curtains open on to a simple caption – 'JUNE 1938' – which then dissolves through to the cover of *Action Comics* #1, the comic in which Superman first appeared. A young boy's hand turns the page as he reads aloud: 'In this decade of the 1930s, even the great city of Metropolis was not spared the ravages of the worldwide Depression. In the times of fear and confusion, informing the public was the job of *Daily Planet*, a great metropolitan newspaper whose reputation for clarity and truth had become a symbol of hope for the city of Metropolis.' As the unseen boy's voice echoes away, the last panel of the comic book image – depicting the offices of the *Daily Planet* – dissolves through to an identical live-action image. The camera tilts up towards the moon, and then continues out into space as the first titles fly toward us, in blue outline, except for the Superman 'S' logo which appears in its traditional red and yellow. The titles continue, now falling away from us as, the camera continues its journey through space, past the red outline of a boiling sun, we move towards the surface of the planet Krypton.

SYNOPSIS: On the planet Krypton, the Council sentences three insurrectionists – General Zod, Ursa and Non – to isolation in The Phantom Zone. Later, believing that the planet will shortly explode, Jor-El launches a spacecraft containing his infant son, Kal-El, towards Earth, a distant planet with a suitable atmosphere, and where his dense molecular structure will give him superhuman powers. Moments after launch, Jor-El's prediction comes true: Krypton is destroyed. The ship crashes in an American farming town, Smallville, where little Kal-El is found by Jonathan and Martha Kent and raised as their own son, Clark. Eighteen Earth years later, when Clark learns the truth about his heritage, he leaves the homestead and heads to the Arctic, where a vision of Jor-El appears before him, explaining his responsibilities on his adoptive planet. More years pass, and Clark Kent finds a job at the *Daily Planet*, where he meets and develops a crush upon fellow reporter Lois Lane, whom he later rescues from a helicopter accident – after switching his street clothes and glasses for a natty costume bearing his father's symbol. Later, he visits her at home, takes her for a flight over the city and allows her to interview him for a newspaper article in which she names him 'Superman'. Meanwhile, criminal genius Lex Luthor diverts two nuclear rockets from a missile testing site – one to Hackensack, New Jersey, the other to the San Andreas faultline, hoping that the latter will knock California into the sea, increasing the value of his real estate on what would become the new West Coast. To stop Superman from preventing the disaster, Luthor lures him to his underground hideaway, where he exposes him to Kryptonite, the only substance known to cause Superman harm. Superman escapes, in time to prevent the first impact but too late to stop the second; the missile explodes, and as a consequence, Lois Lane is killed. Unable to cope with her death, Superman ignores his father's warning not to interfere with human history, and spins the world back on its axis, effectively turning back the clock, and saving the woman he loves. While Lois is left to ponder why Clark Kent is never around when Superman shows up, Superman delivers Lex Luthor to his new home: prison.

ORIGINS: Cleveland-born Jerome 'Jerry' Siegel and Canadian-born Joe Shuster were classmates at Cleveland's Glenville High School when they created their first comic book hero, a Tarzan parody called 'Goober the Mighty', and started an amateur magazine, *Science Fiction*, the third issue of which, published in January 1933, contained a Siegel short story entitled 'The Reign of the Superman', about a super-powered megalomaniac. Siegel subsequently realised that Superman might work better as a hero than a villain, and came up with the concept of a superhero who hid his true identity under the guise of a mild-mannered reporter. Although Siegel and Shuster subsequently created such characters as 'Dr Occult' and detective Slam Bradley, it was four lean years before comic book publisher Detective Comics (later DC Comics) offered them $10 per page for a thirteen-page Superman story, which ultimately appeared in *Action Comics* #1, published in June 1938, with an ambitious coda: 'AND SO BEGINS THE STARTLING ADVENTURE OF THE MOST SENSATIONAL STRIP CHARACTER OF ALL TIME: SUPERMAN!' Although Siegel and Shuster were the only ones who truly believed this blurb, their words were prophetic: the adventures of Superman immediately gripped the nation, turning the newly launched *Action Comics* into an overnight success, and quickly becoming the most widely read character in popular fiction. By January of the following year, Superman had his own nationally syndicated newspaper strip, written and illustrated by Siegel and Shuster, running uninterrupted until May 1966. Much of the Superman myth, including his origin, came from the syndicated strips, which fed the public's appetite for superhero stories, of which Superman was undeniably the first. His popularity endures today.

PREVIOUS INCARNATIONS: The comic book Superman was barely two years old when he made his radio debut in *The Adventures of Superman*, broadcast in February 1940. A year later, Vienna-born cartoonists Max and Dave Fleischer (*Gulliver's Travels*) brought him to the screen in a series of fourteen animated shorts widely regarded as classics of the medium. Then, in 1948, Kirk Alyn donned the red and blue costume – albeit in black and white – for Superman's first live action incarnation, a fifteen-chapter 'Saturday morning' serial, subsequently reprising the role for a sequel, *Atom Man vs Superman* (1950). In 1951, thirteen years after his comic book debut, Superman became the star of another fledgling medium, as George Reeves made his first appearance in the TV series *The Adventures of Superman*, which ran until 1957. A decade later, Superman conquered yet another medium, as the star of a hit Broadway musical, *It's a Bird, It's a Plane, It's Superman*, with book by David Newman and Robert Benton, both of whom would go on to earn writing credits on *Superman: The Movie*. The stage show was adapted for television in 1975.

Just prior to the release of the film, Superman appeared with many other DC Comics heroes and villains in the William Hanna–Joseph Barbera animated series *Challenge of the Super-Friends* (1978), followed a year later by a series of half-hour shows entitled *The World's Greatest Super-Friends*.

DEVELOPMENT: Producers Alexander and Ilya Salkind (*The Three Musketeers*) originally optioned the film rights to Superman in the mid-1970s, signalling the seriousness of their intentions by signing two of the biggest stars of the time – *The Godfather*'s Marlon Brando and *The French Connection*'s Gene Hackman – and commissioning a screenplay from Mario Puzo, author of *The Godfather*. By 1977, however, *Superman: The Movie* had been in development for three years, and with barely three months to go before filming was due to begin – Brando was locked into an immutable start date – James Bond director Guy Hamilton (*Goldfinger*, *Diamonds Are Forever*) quit the project for tax reasons, leaving the film with two stars, a script and a start date, but no director – and, perhaps more importantly, no Superman. The Salkinds solved the first problem by hiring former television director Richard Donner, fresh from the success of *The Omen*. Donner immediately brought in a new writer, Tom Mankiewicz (*Diamonds Are Forever*, *Live and Let Die*), and a new production designer, John Barry (*Star Wars*), and effectively started from scratch. 'They had prepared the picture for a year,' he said, 'and not one bit of it was useful to me.'

Although Donner described Puzo's script as 'wonderful', he was afraid that, at 550 pages – which, although written to accommodate two films, was still more than twice the required length – it was impossibly ambitious; furthermore, rewrites by David and Leslie Newman and Robert Benton had let the story stray too often into the realm of camp, bordering on the over-the-top style of the *Batman* TV show. 'They had things in there like a scene where Superman is looking for Lex Luthor, and he sees a bald head on the street, so he flies down and grabs the guy. Well, the guy turns around and it's Kojak, and he says, "Who do ya love, baby?" ' Thus, he and Mankiewicz started from scratch, insisting that 'it had to be bigger than life, but, at the same time, it had to have some reality within the framework of the people'. For Donner, audiences had to believe not only that a man could fly – but that he was grounded in a living, breathing and largely realistic Metropolis, complete with *Daily Planet*, Lois Lane, Jimmy Olsen, Ma and Pa Kent, and the other trappings of the forty-year-old superhero saga. The most difficult task ahead was making Superman fly through a time warp from 1938 to 1978, where he would greet audiences who had just seen *Star Wars*.

CASTING: Marlon Brando and Gene Hackman had been signed to the project not just for their acting ability (both had just won Best Actor Oscars®, for *The Godfather* and *The French Connection* respectively) but for their box office clout (both films had been huge hits). Brando received an unprecedented salary – $3.7 million for two weeks' work, resulting in barely ten minutes of screen time – yet, for the Salkinds, it was money well spent, as Donner explained: 'They didn't buy Marlon Brando the actor; they bought Marlon Brando the name. They bought him to back up their investment, and once he agreed to do the picture, they were able to raise the money on his name.'

The search for someone to play Superman became one of the most famous casting calls in history, with every actor from Robert Redford to Bruce Jenner linked to the role at one time or another. At one point, John Wayne's son Patrick was signed, but when his father was diagnosed with cancer, he was released from his contract. When Richard Donner came aboard the project in early 1977, he hired casting director Lynn Stalmaster and immediately began auditioning would-be Supermen, including a tall young actor named Christopher Reeve, whose sole film credit was *Gray Lady Down*. 'I thought he was a little young for it . . . and he was a little skinny,' Donner recalled. Nevertheless, Stalmaster kept putting Reeve's headshot to the top of the pile, and Donner eventually brought him to London for a screen test with each of the actresses shortlisted for the role of Lois Lane: Stockard Channing (*Grease*), Anne Archer (future screen wife of Jack Ryan), Lesley Ann Warren (Lois Lane in the TV adaptation of the stage musical *It's a Bird, It's a Plane, It's Superman*), Holly Palance (daughter of future *Batman* co-star Jack Palance) and the successful candidate, Margot Kidder (*The*

Great Waldo Pepper). 'The minute he put on the costume, this tall, skinny kid just decided that he could do it,' said Donner. In addition, 'He really felt that he could put on the weight and build up.' With the help of fitness instructor and actor David Prowse – Darth Vader in the *Star Wars* films – he did, in three months. Nevertheless, said Donner, 'When I go back now and look at the tests – those old stills of Chris – I tell you, it was just blind faith.'

Keenan Wynn (*Dr Strangelove*) was originally cast as Perry White. When he flew into New York to begin shooting, however, he began having heart trouble, and was replaced by Jackie Cooper. Goldie Hawn and Ann-Margaret were the first two choices for the role of Eve Teschmacher, but the Salkinds refused to meet their salary demands.

PRODUCTION: Donner joined the production the first week in January 1977. Eleven weeks later, unable to move the start date due to Brando's limited availability, filming began on John Barry's crystal-inspired Krypton sets. When these scenes were in the can, the production was put on hiatus while pre-production chores such as casting, location scouting, construction and special effects trials – notably the all-important flying tests, which took eight months to achieve – were completed. Donner's visual effects team tried skydiving, suspending stuntmen from cranes, back projection and travelling mattes – until they finally hit upon the idea of a front projection system, which hung a projector and camera from a skyhook, while Reeve was suspended from wires, cables and pole arms invisible to the camera. 'It was the blind leading the blind,' said Donner, 'all experimentation. But I was very fortunate. I was surrounded by a terribly talented group of dedicated film-makers, and somehow or other, we pulled it off.'

COSTUME FITTING: Superman's costume had changed little in the years since he first appeared, and costume designers Jerry R Allen and Yvonne Blake matched the look of the comic book perfectly. So keen was Donner to ground the Superman myth in reality, he and writer Tom Mankiewicz even addressed the question of why Superman, whose real name was Kal-El, would wear a costume emblazoned with the letter 'S', when he wasn't given the name Superman until after he was seen in the costume. Said Mankiewicz, 'So we decided to give everyone [on Krypton] a family crest with a different letter, which didn't really exist in the comic books.' This ingenious strategy is subsequently paid off when *Daily Planet* publisher Perry White asks his reporters to find out what the 'S' stands for, a question for which Lois Lane subsequently provides an answer.

The highly reflective costumes worn by the Kryptonians were the result of a fortuitous accident during tests for the flying unit. 'We noticed that the material lit up on its own,' Donner explained, 'so we tore the material into tiny pieces and glued it on to the costumes, and designed a front-projection box for each camera. There was a little light on each camera, and it would project into a mirror, bounce out in front of the lens, hit the costume, [and] millions of little glass beads would light up and bring the image back into the camera.'

MUSIC: *Star Wars* composer John Williams had been Donner's preferred choice to score *Superman*; but since Jerry Goldsmith had just won an Oscar® for Donner's last film, *The Omen*, he felt obligated to Goldsmith. In the event, Goldsmith was not available; thus, Williams stepped in, creating one of the most memorable themes in the history of film music.

CLASSIC QUOTES:
Lara: 'He will defy their gravity.'
Jor-El: 'He will look like one of them.'
Lara: 'He won't *be* one of them.'
Jor-El: 'No. His dense molecular structure will make him strong.'
Lara: 'He'll be odd. Different.'
Jor-El: 'He'll be fast. Virtually invulnerable.'

Lois Lane: 'Any more at home like you?'
Clark Kent: 'Uh, not really, no.'

Lex Luthor: 'It's amazing that brain can generate enough power to keep those legs moving.'

Superman: 'I'm here to fight for truth, justice and the American way.'
Lois Lane: 'You're gonna wind up fighting every elected official in the country!'

Lex Luthor: 'There's a strong streak of good in you, Superman. But then, nobody's perfect.'

Superman: 'Is that how a warped brain like yours gets kicks – by planning the death of innocent people?'
Lex Luthor: 'No. By *causing* the death of innocent people.'

Lex Luthor: 'We all have our little faults. Mine's in California.'

DELETED SCENES: In 2000, a total of nine scenes cut (and one that was shortened) from the theatrical release were restored by Donner for the DVD release. The scenes, totalling eight minutes, are as follows:

- An extended scene between Jor-El and Council members, in which his pleas to evacuate Krypton fall on deaf ears.

- A scene in which the Council members report on Jor-El's unauthorised use of energy.
- A scene in which a young Lois Lane witnesses the teenage Clark Kent running faster than the speeding train on which she is travelling. Her parents in the scene are played by Kirk Alyn and Noel Neill, who played Superman and Lois Lane in the first live-action *Superman* serial.
- A scene in which Martha Kent opens up the house in the morning, calling Clark down for breakfast, unaware that he is in the garage conversing with Jor-El.
- A brief scene in which Jimmy Olsen meets Clark in the offices of the *Daily Planet*.
- A longer version of the scene in which Kal-El interacts with his father at the Fortress of Solitude.
- A brief scene in which Clark watches footage of Superman's rescue of Lois Lane on storefront TV sets, and a passer-by remarks, 'That'll be the day when a guy could fly, uh?' 'Oh, I don't know,' Clark responds. 'You'd be surprised.'
- A long scene in which Luthor tries to shoot, burn and freeze Superman as he enters Luthor's lair, in order to test his invulnerability.
- A brief scene in which the Hollywood sign falls down, almost crushing a group of schoolgirls.

Two further scenes were not reinstated for the 2000 restoration:

- A scene in which Luthor asks Otis to 'feed the babies' – ravenous unidentified wild animals he keeps in a pit hidden behind a metal grating. A reluctant Otis lowers a huge slab of meat into the pit while Luthor (in yet another of his unconvincing hairpieces) plays the piano.
- A subsequent scene in which Luthor plays and sings 'Baby Look At You Now' at the piano while Otis reluctantly lowers Eve into the pit of wild animals, presumably for betraying him. At the last second, Superman flies in and saves her, bringing her back to confront Luthor. 'By the way, Miss Teschmacher,' he tells her, 'your mother sends her love.' Luthor sighs.

TRAILERS: The 'teaser' trailer, which contains neither footage nor music from the film, appeared in cinemas a full year before the film opened. As the teaser begins, the camera flies through a sky at sunset – presumably designed to represent the point of view of Superman in flight – as the names of the principal cast members fly out into the distance. Finally, the traditional red and yellow 'S' symbol – subtitled 'THE MOVIE' – follows the names into the distance, and then returns, this time as a comic book-style red and blue 'SUPERMAN' logo, followed by credits.

Although the regular trailer utilised John Williams' music and a great deal of footage, it kept Superman himself out of the picture until the climax. Instead, it opened with a zoom into the surface of the planet Krypton, where Jor-El warns his fellow Council members of the planet's imminent destruction. Meanwhile, a voice-over intones the following: 'Once, there was a civilisation, much like ours, but with a greater intelligence, greater powers, and a greater capacity for good.' We see the infant Kal-El launched into space, as Krypton begins to explode. 'In one tragic moment, that world was destroyed. But there was one survivor.' Ma and Pa Kent witness the arrival of the spaceship, and the little boy within it, as the voiceover continues: 'Because of the wisdom and compassion of Jor-El, because he knew the human race had the capacity for goodness, he sent us his only son. His name is Kal-El.' Superman stands in the Fortress of Solitude, and finally takes flight. 'He will call himself Clark Kent. But the world will know him . . . as Superman. This year, Superman brings you the gift of flight.' A title ('SUPERMAN: THE MOVIE') is followed by an extensive credit list.

POSTERS: The main US 'one-sheet' featured the Superman 'S' symbol in chrome against a vivid blue-grey sky, with a streak of red, yellow and blue piercing it like an arrow through a heart.

TAG-LINE: 'You'll believe a man can fly'.

WHAT THE PAPERS SAID: Despite the hype which had overshadowed its release, the overall critical response to *Superman* was favourable, with *Variety* describing the film as 'a wonderful, chuckling, preposterously exciting fantasy', praising Christopher Reeve and Margot Kidder, but dismissing Brando as 'good but unremarkable'. In the UK, *Time Out*'s Martyn Auty noted that, 'by keeping the spectacular possibilities open . . . the film allows naivety and knowingness to coexist. Only when it goes all out for cold Batmanesque villainy in the second half does it narrow its focus and lose its way.'

BOX OFFICE: Released in the US on 15 December 1978, *Superman* became one of the first multi-million dollar film franchises, grossing $134 million in unadjusted US dollars – the equivalent of around half a billion today – and a total of $300 million worldwide, making *Superman* the first *bona fide* blockbuster based on a comic strip.

AWARDS: *Superman* failed to convert any of its three Academy Award® nominations – for Best Film Editing, Best Music (Original Score) and Best Sound – into statuettes, and although the film was given a Special Achievement Award for Visual Effects, Donner was disgusted that John Barry's art direction and Geoffrey Unsworth's cinematography were not recognised. 'If you look at the pictures that were nominated for best cinematography, it's a fucking sin that his name wasn't up there,' he said bitterly. As for art direction, he added, 'They put up pictures like *California Suite* – duplications of the Beverly Hills Hotel. *Big deal!* Just *look* at what John Barry did for *Superman*, and he wasn't nominated either.' Although it received nominations, *Superman* fared little better at the BAFTA awards, the British equivalent of the Oscars®: nominated for Best Cinematography, Production Design/Art Direction, Sound and Supporting Actor (Gene Hackman), only Christopher Reeve (Best Newcomer) took home an award. Science fiction fans were kinder: not only did *Superman* win a Hugo Award for Best Dramatic Presentation, the Academy of Science Fiction, Fantasy & Horror Films received nominations in the categories of Best Actor (Christopher Reeve) Costumes, Director, Supporting Actress (Valerie Perrine), and won awards for Best Science Fiction Film, Best Actress (Margot Kidder), Music, Production Design and Special Effects.

CONTROVERSY: When Siegel and Shuster had sold the first Superman strip for a mere $130 back in 1938, they had inadvertantly signed away all rights to exploit the character, which went on to make millions for its publisher through comics, radio broadcasts, television and film serials and all manner of ancilliary products, while its creators received only their salaries for as long as they continued to write and draw the syndicated strip. Siegel set out to partially rectify this when, in 1947, he returned from army service to discover that DC Comics had been publishing a successful strand, 'Superboy', based on the exploits of Superman as a boy. Siegel and Shuster sued the publisher, but although they were awarded $100,000 in compensation for unfair exploitation of Superboy, the courts denied their claim to ownership of Superman. In the 1960s, Siegel and Shuster returned to DC Comics at salaries of $20,000 and $7,500 respectively, but after another falling out, Siegel was forced to find work in a mailroom for $7,000 per annum. It was not until the announcement of the *Superman* movie in 1975 that the pair felt it was payback time: and if the courts wouldn't support them, perhaps the court of public opinion would. Siegel sent a nine-page press release to a thousand newsrooms calling upon the public to boycott the film; Warner Bros, which by now owned both the film rights and DC Comics, were wary of the potentially damaging effects of negative publicity, offering Siegel and Shuster a yearly stipend ($20,000) for life, and restoring the 'Created by Jerry Siegel and Joe Shuster' credit – dropped by DC in 1948 in protest at their first lawsuit – on all future Superman properties. Siegel died in January 1996, a few years after Shuster; but in December 1997, Siegel's widow – Joanna Carter, the original model for Lois Lane – filed a 500-page lawsuit under the US copyright office's new terms, which allow the creators and heirs of a property to receive fifty per cent of all future earnings from all media, commencing two years after the expiration of the previous sixty-year copyright term. Put simply, this meant that, from 16 April 1999, Siegel's heirs may be entitled to half the revenues from all Superman comic books, novels, video games, clothing, merchandise, and all other licensed products.

TRIVIA: Jeff East, who played the teenage Clark Kent, had his voice overdubbed by Christopher Reeve.

Despite his exorbitant salary, Marlon Brando did not memorise any of his lines. Instead, he had them pasted around the set and read them.

Donner, furious that Tom Mankiewicz had not received accreditation for the script following arbitration by the Writers Guild of America, gave Mankiewicz a special 'creative consultant' credit placed *above* those of the credited writers, infuriating the Guild but delighting Mankiewicz.

APOCRYPHA: One of the best-known stories surrounding Superman is the so-called 'Curse of Superman', which began with the suicide of 1950s Superman George Reeves. Following the deaths of several *Superman* crew members after the film wrapped (including production designer John Barry), the curse was blamed for the paralysis of Christopher Reeve following a 1995 horseriding accident, and a mental breakdown suffered by Margot Kidder the following year. Kidder has since made a full recovery, whilst Reeve, despite his paralysis, has continued to produce, direct and appear in films and television shows, written two bestsellers, *Still Me* and *Nothing Is Impossible*, and done more charity work than Superman himself.

SEQUELS & SPIN-OFFS: The closing credits of *Superman*, released in December 1978, contained the legend 'Coming Next Summer: *Superman II*', apparently giving the producers only six months to make the film. In fact, the Salkinds' original plan had been to film *Superman* and *Superman II* back to back – indeed, at one point the intention was to leave the first film on a serial-style cliffhanger. 'Superman was going to leave Hackman and Beatty in the prison, fly up past the camera just as he does, and then I was going to pan back into the sky and pick up the [nuclear] rocket that he had left tumbling,' Donner explained to *Cinefantastique*. 'You see it shut off, and you see the Zone of Silence with the three villains in it; then, all of a sudden, the rocket goes past them and there's an atomic explosion, and it blows up the Zone of Silence, freeing Terence Stamp, Jack O'Halloran and Sarah Douglas. But then,' he added, 'I finally decided, "Hey, if *Superman* is a success, they're going to do a sequel. If it ain't a success, a cliffhanger ending ain't going to bring them to see *Superman II*." ' Nevertheless, Donner claimed to have completed around eighty per cent of the sequel before being fired and replaced – by Guy Hamilton, whose departure had given Donner the *Superman* job in the first place. 'The Salkinds and [co-producer Pierre] Spengler have now seen fit to replace me with the original director,' Donner commented bitterly in 1980, 'whose material I had to radically change to make the picture you have seen.'

As it transpired, however, Hamilton was replaced again, by Richard Lester (*The Three Musketeers*), by which time the summers of 1979 and 1980 had both passed, and cinematographer Geoffrey Unsworth and production designer John Barry had passed away. *Superman II* was finally released in the US on 19 June 1981, incorporating footage shot by Donner and Lester, and although Marlon Brando refused to allow his *Superman* footage to be included, Jor-El's absence was more than made up for by the other returning cast members, including Christopher Reeve, Gene Hackman, Ned Beatty, Margot Kidder, Mark McClure, Valerie Perrine, Terence Stamp, Sarah Douglas, Jack O'Halloran, Jackie Cooper and even Susannah York. The film's box office performance – $108 million in the US alone – paved the way for two further sequels: Richard Lester's *Superman III* (1983), which grossed $60 million; and Sidney J Furie's ill-starred *Superman IV: The Quest for Peace* (1987), which sounded the death knell for the series by grossing just $15 million.

In the meantime, Superman's adventures continued in animated form, with the Hanna–Barbera series *SuperFriends: The Legendary Super Powers Show*, which debuted in September 1984, two months before the theatrical release of Jannot Szwarc's *Supergirl*, an ambitious feature film starring Helen Slater as the eponymous heroine, and an impressive supporting cast, including Faye Dunaway, Peter O'Toole, Mia Farrow, Peter Cook, Simon Ward and Mark McClure, reprising his role as Jimmy Olsen. The film failed to take off at the box office, however, and despite the poster's optimistic tag-line, 'Her first great adventure' was also her last. The animated adventures continued with *The Super Powers Team: Galactic Guardians* (1985–1986), followed by an intriguing fiftieth anniversary series entitled simply *Superman*, which combined eighteen minutes of Superman stories with a four-minute 'Superman Family Album' segment detailing Clark Kent's boyhood. In October of the same year, *Superboy* made his live-action debut in a syndicated series produced by Alexander and Ilya Salkind, which ran until 1990, when it was retitled *The Adventures of Superboy*, amassing one hundred episodes by the time it was cancelled in 1992.

Superman regained a measure of popularity in 1993, thanks to a strand of the comic book series entitled *The Death of Superman*, in which the supposedly indestructible Man of Steel meets his doom at the hands of Doomsday, a monstrous supervillain contrived by writer Dan Jurgens for the sole purpose of killing Superman. As a result, Warner Bros announced its plans to make a new Superman film, and launched a brand new ABC television series, *Lois and Clark: The New Adventures of Superman*, starring Dean Cain and Teri Hatcher, which debuted on 12 September 1993. Meanwhile, DC took the bold step of running its four *Superman* titles for six months with their hero *in absentia*, publishing the intriguing cross-over series *World Without a Superman*, followed by *Superman Reborn*, an inevitable but effective revival of both the character, and the fortunes of DC's monthly titles. Warner Bros wasted no time in capitalising on Superman's new-found comic book success, putting *Batman* producer Jon Peters in charge of the project, and hiring screenwriter Jonathan Lemkin (*Lethal Weapon 4*) to simply 'write a great film'.

Taking the comic books *The Death of Superman*, *World Without a Superman* and *Superman Reborn* as a 'stepping-off point', Lemkin opened his script with a defeated Superman in his death throes, but went on to tell the story not of his rebirth, but of the birth of his successor, who is born after Superman impregnates Lois Lane with his spirit, matures faster than a speeding bullet, and saves the universe before he is out of short tights. 'He literally dies as he professes his love to her,' Lemkin told *Cinescape*, 'and his life force jumps between them. Superman dies and Lois later finds out that she's pregnant – immaculately. She gives birth to a child who grows twenty-one years in three weeks, and is, essentially, the resurrected Superman.'

Peters subsequently hired Gregory Poirier (*Rosewood*) to rewrite Lemkin's script, adding Kal-El's existential woes about being an outsider alienated on Earth, and a popular comic book villain – the mad alien, Brainiac. Although Poirier's rewrite reportedly received a warm welcome at Warner Bros, the studio subsequently asked writer–director and comic book aficionado Kevin Smith (*Clerks*, *Chasing Amy*) to take a look at it. 'I thought it was terrible,' Smith said of Poirier's draft. Fearing, probably with some justification, that Smith – who co-owns a New Jersey comic book store – spoke for millions of Superman fans, Warner Bros and Jon Peters encouraged him to start over, albeit with certain caveats. 'The death of Superman was a major parameter – they wanted me to use that storyline; Brainiac as the villain was something they were intent on. When I had to work closer with Jon Peters on the project, he had all sorts of weird parameters. Like, "I don't wanna see him in the suit and I don't want to see him fly and I want him to fight a giant spider in the third act," ' Smith revealed. 'Shit where I'm like, "What?! A giant spider? Are you crazy?!" '

Nevertheless, Smith pitched his outline to Peters in August 1996, and immediately got the go-ahead to turn in his first draft, which he did the following month. In Smith's story, the energy-sucking extraterrestrial Brainiac is in space with his faithful robot L-Ron (a typically sly reference to Scientology founder and sci-fi author L Ron Hubbard) when he is contacted by Lex Luthor, who summons them to Earth to rid the world of the superhero formerly known as Kal-El. Discovering that Superman's superpowers are derived from the sun, Luthor and Brainiac block the sun's rays, thus diminishing his powers and allowing Doomsday to defeat the suddenly vulnerable Man of Steel. Littering the script with playful or ironic references to Superman's past, and assuming that his lover Lois Lane has already figured out that Superman's secret identity is her *Daily Planet* colleague Clark Kent, Smith further displays his fandom by incorporating fellow DC Comics characters Deadshot and Batman in cameo roles, as well as such Superman staples as *Planet* photographer Jimmy Olsen and his venerable boss, Perry White. Although details of Superman's new look are sketchy – the script introduces him simply by saying 'Superman (uh, '90s style)' – Smith accounted for audiences *not* believing a man can fly by depicting Superman in flight as a red-and-blue blur accompanied by a sonic boom, thus neatly avoiding the wire-and-blue-screen effects of the Salkinds' *Superman* series.

Warner Bros loved Smith's upbeat take on the material – as did director Robert Rodriguez (*From Dusk Till Dawn*), who almost signed to direct it. 'I really, really liked Kevin Smith's script,' he told *Cinescape*. 'I knew it would be a big movie and have big [McDonald's] Happy Meals and stuff,' he said of *Superman Lives*, 'but I also knew it would be like that no matter who made it.' By the time Rodriguez passed, Tim Burton's *Mars Attacks!* had flopped, and the director who had given Warner Bros a billion dollar *Batman* expressed interest in reviving another long-dead superhero franchise, while Oscar® winning actor Nicolas Cage (*The Rock*) signalled his willingness to don the red cape. 'With Tim Burton,' the actor said at the time, 'hopefully we're going to bring a lot to it and totally reconceive the character. The death of Superman and his resurrection will be a part of the story, but I have other points that I want to address that haven't really been examined before.'

With Cage on board, another recent Oscar® winner, Kevin Spacey (*The Usual Suspects*), reportedly expressed an interest in playing Lex Luthor, while comic actors Jim Carrey (*Batman Forever*) and Chris Rock (*Lethal Weapon 4*) were reportedly eyeing the Brainiac and Jimmy Olsen roles respectively. Jack Nicholson, who had played the Joker in Burton's *Batman*, was also mentioned in connection with the Brainiac role, while Sandra Bullock was widely reported to be the studio's first choice to play Lois Lane. Burton and Cage both signed lucrative pay-or-play deals – meaning that they got paid whether the film was made or not – worth $5 million and a staggering *$20 million* respectively, offices on the Warner lot were set up, and *Superman Lives* officially entered pre-production in the summer of 1997, by which time a new star-studded animated

Superman series was flying high on Warner Bros' own network, The WB, although the live-action *Lois and Clark* had been cancelled after four seasons.

Burton's first move was to throw out Smith's script, and bring one of *Batman Returns*' screenwriters, Wesley Strick, to reimagine the film in the director's own trademark style. Strick was given the Kevin Smith draft, which he read 'with eager anticipation, and a rising sense of bafflement. First, everywhere Superman went, he was accompanied or shadowed by someone or something called The Eradicator, who seemed to have more lines, and more things to do than Superman,' he says. 'The villain, Brainiac, had a comic sidekick called El Ron, who similarly took up as much script space as Brainiac, and wasn't all that funny. Brainiac's evil plot was to launch a disk into space that would blot out the sun, necessitating the use of his own energy production – a plot device I'd seen not long before on *The Simpsons*, [with] Mr Burns doing the Brainiac role. Lastly, the script was crammed with so much techno-jargon, there were whole pages that were – to me – nearly impenetrable.

'After going down to the comic book store and purchasing *World Without a Superman*, a collection that comprised the "death" and its traumatic and ultimately triumphant aftermath, I started, belatedly, to make sense of some of Kevin Smith's constructs – particularly the bothersome and boring Eradicator. Still determined that our Superman not play like a buddy movie, but seeing the need for the felled Superman to return to life through the ministrations of some sympathetic, off-planet intelligence, I created an entity I called "K", a sort of sprite who would flit around as a digital light-effect, representing the spirit and heritage of Krypton. Tim liked the concept, but was concerned that "K" might be a bit too "Tinkerbell" . . . and, ultimately, the clock ran it out before we were able to solve this.' Nevertheless, the screenwriter adds, 'We did take pains to characterise Clark/Superman as an alien, painfully conscious of his profoundly "outsider" status and not always in control of his powers – think "extraterrestrial Scissorhands". Plus, after "K" revives Superman in the Fortress of Solitude, [Superman] returns in a peculiar Kal-El persona – freaking out Lois, Metropolis and himself before reverting to the more familiar and comfortable Clark/Superman schism. Tim and I both relished the fact that our hero wasn't merely split down the middle like most Burton heroes, but was for a time a tri-furcated personality. And we doubled the theme by having Brainiac invade the body of Lex Luthor at story's midpoint, creating an amusing schizo/scary mega-villian we dubbed Lexiac.'

Strick's storyline also revealed that Brainiac was created by Jor-El, making him the great scientist's 'first born', whose primacy and birthright was supplanted by Kal-El, thus explaining his quest for vengeance when, years later, he encounters Kal-El/Superman on Earth. '[Burton's] take on it was quite interesting,' says Sylvain Despretz, one of the film's design team. 'To Tim, it wasn't a simple heroic story, and I think the casting of Nicolas Cage was quite good, because he wasn't a square-jawed hero. He wanted to show a very vulnerable side of Superman, similar to the way Jesus was portrayed in Martin Scorsese's *The Last Temptation of Christ*, so what you saw was a reluctant Messiah. It was the story of a man struggling with the burden of extraordinary powers.' Cage evidently relished this approach, telling *Premiere* that the film's vision of the Man of Steel would be as 'a freak, but a beautiful freak in that he really cares about people. I wouldn't be afraid to talk about his loneliness and his feeling like an alien, never fitting in and so always compulsively needing to do heroic acts so people would like him and he would feel loved.'

While Strick toiled on the script, now retitled *Superman Reborn*, the art department continued to turn out drawing after drawing, based on the few elements they knew would be included in the new draft: Superman himself; the new 'S' logo; numerous versions of Brainiac's skull ship; exteriors and interiors of the planet Krypton; the Kryptonians; the Fortress of Solitude; the city of Metropolis; and the film's chief antagonist, Brainiac. Meanwhile, Burton scouted city locations which could double for Metropolis, eventually deciding that America's most famous steel town, Pittsburg, would be the ideal home for the Man of Steel. '[Burton's] Metropolis was not Gotham *redux*,' says production designer Rick Heinrichs. 'Its character was not derived from the same sort of reference used to create what that "urbanscape" became.' Says Strick, 'What excited Tim was that, in contrast to the two *Batman* films which he associated with darkness and night, *Superman* was going to be a superhero adventure set primarily in daylight – in sunlight, even. He saw it as, ideally, a more 'American' and mainstream fable – this was the challenge. And Nic Cage, whom we sat with several times, seemed to share our concept.' With each successive draft, however, the budget rocketed alarmingly – to between $140 million and $190 million, according to several reports.

Then, in 1998, the studio began to experience caped fear. Although the animated show *The New Batman/Superman Adventures* was a hit for The WB, and the animated feature film *The Batman/Superman Movie* had scored impressive sales on video, Warner Bros still did not have a script which satisfied their budgetary requirements. On 1 May 1998, they pulled the plug. Says Strick, 'Our script was strong and getting stronger when the plug was pulled. Evidently the execs had finally accommodated themselves to a Burton Superman – stages were reserved, scenery was built, locations were scouted – when Terry Semel read my draft and, so I'm told, reacted violently against it. At that point the team did an about-face and it fell to Tim to – somewhat sheepishly and sweetly – invite me to his apartment one last time, to tell me the news. The Warner Bros "team" was never completely comfortable with our script,' he adds. 'I wasn't quite sure what their specific problems were but I think the level of nervousness and second-guessing over so valuable a franchise as Superman would have made it impossible for them to feel completely comfortable with any version.' By this time, the studio had already spent a reported $30 million developing the *Superman* movie, and ultimately engaged a fifth screenwriter, Dan Gilroy (*Freejack*), in an effort to bring the spiralling budget back down to Earth.

Warner Bros continued to develop the project between 1998 and 2001, albeit with a much lower profile than previously. For a time, Oliver Stone expressed an interest in the project, before ceding the director's chair to Ralph Zondag (*Dinosaur*). William Wisher (*Judge Dredd*) was drafted in to write yet another version, which was reportedly scrapped in favour of an entirely new seventeen-page treatment by comics writer Keith Giffen, whose story included his own popular creation: Lobo, a marauding intergalactic mercenary who might be more than a match for the Man of Steel. Then, in April 2001, *Hollywood Reporter* revealed that Oscar®-nominated screenwriter Paul Attanasio (*Quiz Show*, *Donnie Brasco*) had been commissioned to write a brand new draft, receiving a staggering $1.7 million for his trouble. 'Attanasio will sift through the three or four *Superman* scripts previously written during its five-year development at the studio,' the report said, 'but he will focus on his own, original take on material based on the death and rebirth of the Man of Steel.'

In October 2001, The WB scored impressive ratings with a small-screen spin-off, *Smallville*, staring Tom Welling as a young Clark Kent, Kristen Kreuk as Lana Lang, Michael Rosenbaum as Alexander Joseph 'Lex' Luthor and Annette O'Toole – *Superman III*'s love interest, Lana Lang – as Superman's mother, Martha. While the series built an audience, Superman appeared as part of a new ensemble of animated heroes in *Justice League*, with *Smallville*'s Rosenbaum cast as the voice of 'The Flash'.

FUTURE INCARNATIONS: Although it was widely reported that *Charlie's Angels* director McG had become attached to Paul Attanasio's script, on 14 February 2002, *Variety* announced that JJ Abrams (*Joy Ride*, a.k.a. *Roadkill*) had become the latest in a long line of screenwriters invited to put his own spin on the Superman story, this time ignoring *The Death of Superman* storyline. Abrams' 130-page screenplay, in which Superman fights a fellow Kryptonian named Ty-Zor, reportedly caused such excitement that the studio abandoned its plans to unite its two biggest superheroes in *Batman vs Superman* – a script by Andrew Kevin Walker (*Se7en*) which was being developed concurrently, with Wolfgang Petersen attached to direct. On 25 September 2002, the studio confirmed that Brett Ratner (*Rush Hour*, *Red Dragon*) had replaced McG as director. 'JJ Abrams and Jon Peters were given the daunting task of re-imagining the Superman epic and JJ met the challenge, delivering a terrific script with emotion, depth and scale that brings new dimension to this legendary character,' said Jeff Robinov, president of domestic production. 'We couldn't be more pleased to entrust the next chapter in the Superman mythology to Brett Ratner, a dynamic director whose skilful blend of action, comedy and drama has captured the imaginations of audiences worldwide.' Casting proved difficult, however, with Josh Hartnett and Paul Walker both declining the role. By March 2003, Ratner had also quit the project, blaming casting difficulties.

DVD AVAILABILITY: In the UK (Region 2), the extended and restored version of *Superman* is available as a 2.35:1 ratio double-sided disc featuring a plethora of extras, including isolated versions of the ten scenes restored for the 2000 director's cut; the two further deleted scenes not included in the restored version; feature-length commentary from Richard Donner and Tom Mankiewicz; screen tests featuring Reeve and several would-be Lois Lanes, with commentary by casting director Lynn Stalmaster; a DVD-ROM storyboard-to-screen comparison; trailers and TV spot; additional music cues; and three documentaries: *The Magic Behind the Cape* (23 mins), *Making* Superman: *Filming the Legend* and *Taking Flight: The Development of* Superman (30 mins), featuring interviews with Donner, Reeve, Kidder, Hackman and Brando. These additional features also appear on the US (Region 1) equivalent.

FINAL ANALYSIS: The opening lines of the film say it all: 'This is no fantasy, no careless product of a wild imagination.' Indeed, from the outset Richard Donner's *Superman* sets out to contextualise Siegel and Shuster's most famous creation in the real world, despite the fantastical trappings of the story, the comedic machinations of Gene Hackman's excellent Luthor and Ned Beatty's equally wonderful Otis, and Donner's inability to resist pointing up the parallels between Kal-El and Jesus ('For their capacity for good, I gave them you, my only son,' Jor-El tells his son, before his image morphs into an even more God-like countenance).

Every decision Donner made – most of them, presumably, under unimaginable pressure, given the production's rocky road – seems, with hindsight, to be the right one, from the grand set-pieces to the tiniest details. For all the ground-breaking special effects and elaborate sets, the film is scattered with unforgettable moments too numerous to list, each illustrating Donner's fondness for the source material, which remains one of the greatest American myths. In his first major film role, Christopher Reeve established a screen presence, both as Superman and a Cary Grant-like Clark Kent, which made it virtually impossible to imagine anyone else in the role. The chemistry between him and Margot Kidder is as potent as Kryptonite, and when a devastated Kal-El breaks his father's non-interference programming in order to save her life, we understand perfectly. If he was put here for a reason, it might as well be love.

Although *Superman* was the first of the comic book blockbusters, it became, over the next quarter century, far more: a benchmark by which others continue to be judged. It is no coincidence that one of the most recent such comic-to-film adaptations, *Spider-Man*, closely follows the *Superman* model. Long before the computer-generated pizzazz of *Spider-Man*, Donner truly made us believe that a man could fly.

EXPERT WITNESS: 'It was a trip I'll never forget. Every moment, every heartache, every happiness. It was one of the great experiences I've ever had in film-making, and will probably be for the rest of my life.' – **Richard Donner, Director**

Akira (1988)

(124 mins)

Directed by Katsuhiro Otomo
Written by Katsuhiro Otomo and Izo Hashimoto
Produced by Ryohei Suzuki and Shunzo Kato
Executive Producer Sawako Noma
Co-Producer Yoshimasa Mizuo
Animation Director Takashi Nakamura
Art Director Toshihiro Mizutani
Editor Takashi Seyama
Music by Shoji Yamashiro

CAST (VOICES): Mitsuo Iwata (*Shotaro Kaneda*), Nozomu Sasaki (*Tetsuo*), Mami Koyama (*Kei*), Tessho Genda (*Ryu*), Hiroshi Otake (*Nezu*), Koichi Kitamura (*Miyako/Council A*), Michihiro Ikemizu (*inspector/Council I*), Yuriko Fuchizaki (*Kaori*), Masaaki Okura (*Yamagata*), Taro Arakawa (*Eiichi Watanabe/Council G/army*), Takeshi Kusao (*Kai*), Kazumi Tanaka (*army*), Masayuki Kato (*Engineer Sakayama/Council D*), Yosuke Akimoto (*Harukiya bartender*), Masato

Hirano (*Yuji Takeyama/spy/Council F*), Yukimasa Kishino (*Mitsuru Kuwata/terrorist/assistant*), Kazuhiro Kando a.k.a. Kazuhiro Kamifuji (*Masaru*), Tatsuhiko Nakamura (*Takashi*), Sachie Ito a.k.a. Fukue Ito (*Kiyoko*), Taro Ishida (*The Colonel*), Mizuho Suzuki (*Doctor Ohnishi*), Issei Futamata, Kozo Shioya, Michitaka Kobayashi, Hideyuki Umezu, Satoru Inagaki, Kayoko Fujii, Masami Toyoshima, Yuka Ohno

TITLE SEQUENCE: The film opens on a view of Tokyo as seen from the eastern high ground. An on-screen credit announces the date as 16 July 1988, as a white ball of destruction suddenly engulfs everything to the west and rushes towards the camera. Cut to a satellite view of Tokyo, familiar to all Japanese viewers, except now Tokyo Bay has been filled in with a huge artificial island, and the Western part of the old city is still recognisable from orbit as a discoloured area of desolation. An on-screen title announces that it is '31 Years After World War III. 2019 AD Neo-Tokyo'. The screen goes black, though we pull out of the darkness to reveal that it is in fact the shadows of the Tokyo crater. As the crater fills the screen, it is masked in turn by the stark red Roman letters of the film's title.

SYNOPSIS: It is 2019 AD: Neo-Tokyo is a sprawling city plagued by overcrowding, civil unrest, student demonstrations and juvenile delinquents. At its heart lies the epicentre of the 1988 explosion, a deserted ruin scheduled for urban renewal as the site of the forthcoming Olympics. While fighting with the rival 'Clown' gang on the streets, biker-boy Tetsuo is injured in a motorcycle accident, crashing into Takashi, a psychic who has escaped from a secret government laboratory. The telekinetic Takashi is reclaimed by military forces, who also drag Tetsuo away. Discovering that Tetsuo has dormant psychic powers, the military take him back in for further tests. Tetsuo's longtime associate Kaneda joins forces with a terrorist cell to spring him, but the team arrive just as Tetsuo breaks out alone – the experimental process has awakened super-powers in him. Tetsuo goes in search of Akira, a creature rumoured to have powers even greater than his, who caused the 1988 explosion. The Colonel, leader of the military faction responsible for the secret psychic project, is threatened with the loss of his command, and orders a military coup. Meanwhile, protestors and cultists incorrectly assume that Tetsuo is Akira, the spirit of the 1988 explosion reborn, and fighting to save the city from the military. Amid the chaos, Nezu, a corrupt politician who has been secretly funding the terrorists, dies trying to escape. Tetsuo locates Akira's capsule beneath the Olympic stadium, but finds nothing but fragments inside. After a prolonged fight with Kaneda and the military, Tetsuo begins to regress into a formless protoplasm – his powers are running out of control. Takashi, Masaru and Kiyoko, the three surviving children from the original Akira experiment, summon forth Akira, in the hope that his power, combined with theirs, will somehow prevent Tetsuo's from destroying everything in the universe. Tokyo is once more engulfed in what appears to be a white explosion (in fact, a dimensional singularity as Tetsuo/Akira becomes omnipotent). The power of the Akira/Tetsuo union is contained in a tiny ball of energy – at least that's how it looks from the outside. Later, Kaneda heads for home with his surviving companions, while far, far away, Tetsuo is the creator of a new universe.

ORIGINS: Katsuhiro Otomo was born in Japan's northern prefecture of Miyagi in 1954, and grew up on American counter-culture movies such as *Easy Rider*, *Bonnie and Clyde* and *Butch Cassidy and the Sundance Kid*. 'All the movies were about leaving home,' he has said, 'about people with boring lives who wanted to go somewhere else. Everybody wanted to hitchhike their way to Woodstock.' The young Otomo eventually left town himself, and headed for the big city: Tokyo. He arrived during turbulent times. Intent on keeping bases in Japan to supply forces in Vietnam, the United States had just signed a controversial treaty with Japan. Students were rioting in the streets, colleges were deserted, and the streets of Tokyo were dark with riot gas and smoke bombs. When the riots died down, a group of diehards formed the terrorist Red Army group, which was eventually wiped out in a violent gun battle with police at the Karuizawa holiday resort in 1972.

While the older generation shook their heads and lamented the motorcycle-riding, pill-popping youth of today, others talked of the *shinjinrui*, a genuine 'new breed' who were taller, smarter, and tougher than their forebears. Science fiction writers in novels and TV were already toying with the idea that Japan's baby-boomers weren't just attitudinally different, but had different *minds*. In search of a way to make ends meet in Tokyo, the dropout Otomo began working in comics, drawing humour, fantasy and modern drama, but steering clear of science fiction. He only moved into SF at the urging of his editor at *Young Magazine*, when he wrote the 1979 epic *Fireball*. Depicting a conflict between scientists and terrorists over the mastery of a supreme energy source, *Fireball* was left unfinished – had Otomo completed it, he might never have returned to the same material in *Akira*. It also featured a supercomputer named Atom, in homage to Osamu Tezuka's *Mighty Atom*, better known in the West as *Astro Boy*.

Otomo's next work was another *homage* to a comic he read as a child, this time to Shotaro Ishinomori's *Soratobu Etchan*. However, Otomo's 'Flying Etchan' was not a kindly superheroine, but instead a psychic loner, who fights for control of an apartment block with an old man, who also has secret paranormal powers. The resultant comic, *Domu*, won a literary award normally reserved for prose, and has itself been the subject of constant rumour regarding a live-action remake. For *Akira*, his third nod to the comic heroes of his youth, Otomo chose *Ironman 28* (a.k.a. *Gigantor*) by Mitsuteru Yokoyama, the tale of a secret WW2 robot-warrior project thought to have been destroyed, only to be resurrected in the 1960s by a master-criminal. The only thing that can stop it is the son of the original inventor, who has an even more powerful weapon at his disposal. Little of *Ironman 28* remains in the final story of *Akira*, though sharp-eyed viewers might notice a weapon that survives the *Third* World War, that the Colonel is the son of one of the original Akira Project scientists, that Akira's code number is 28, and that Kaneda's full name is Shotaro Kaneda, suspiciously similar to *Ironman 28*'s boy-hero Shotaro *Haneda*.

Otomo's story debuted in *Young Magazine* on 6 December 1982, but there was no guarantee it was going to be a success. In fact, its author was already working on another job at the time, designing characters for the anime movie *Harmagedon*. It was there that he discovered how annoying anime work could be: 'I met a lot of animators who were always complaining about the working environment,' he said. 'The crucial problem was the lack of good producers, and I decided there and then that if I made an anime I'd produce it myself and give them a chance.'

DEVELOPMENT: When *Akira*'s success in the pages of *Young Magazine* seemed assured, Otomo was offered the chance to turn it into a movie – as often happens in Japanese science fiction, budgetary restrictions necessitated animation over live action. He jumped at the chance, though his desire to give his animators the chance to show their artistic abilities would cause the project to almost run out of control. Otomo planned on writing and storyboarding the film himself, though the script credit on the final print is shared with veteran scriptwriter Izo Hashimoto, whose TV credits include *Geisha Detective* and the sleuth show *Gentleman Mugen*. Otomo claimed to have filled 2,000 pages of notebooks with ideas and designs for the movie, though he was eventually persuaded to reduce his vision to a mere 738 pages of storyboards.

CASTING: Kaneda's voice was provided by Mitsuo Iwata, an actor in his early twenties who can also be heard in *Urusei Yatsura 3*, *Time Stranger* and *Initial D*. The role of Tetsuo was performed by Nozomu Sasaki, another actor whose anime performances continue to this day, in modern fan-favourites such as *Card Captors* and *Bubblegum Crisis*. The bulk of these actors' resumés remain in the world of TV animation – like most other cast members, the bulk of their film work is restricted to the relatively small number of animated movies spun off from TV shows in which they were already appearing. For the most recent

English-language dub of the movie, Kaneda was played by former Power Ranger Johnny Yong Bosch, and Tetsuo by Joshua Seth.

PRODUCTION: Though Otomo remains friends with the *Harmagedon* director Rintaro (their most recent collaboration was *Metropolis*, in 2001), his bitter experiences on the *Harmagedon* animation project would cause him to run *Akira* as a radically different production. An artist and writer given full control of a story he had created himself, Otomo pushed his production team to the limit. Over 150,000 separate animation cels were created for the production, pushing the budget far above that of the average Japanese animated movie. Otomo also broke several cardinal rules of animation, particularly the maxim that night scenes should be avoided wherever possible. Instead, large parts of *Akira* occur at night, causing immense difficulty for the crew in lighting, shadow and simple colouring. Instead of the bright, primary colours found in children's cartoons, the quest for adult, photographic realism in *Akira* led to the use of 327 different colours, causing further production nightmares in tracking which paint was supposed to go where.

Japanese animators had used computer graphics to add flash and gloss to anime since they first appeared in *Golgo 13* in 1983, but Otomo's use of them in *Akira* broke new ground. They are most conspicuous in the Professor's pattern indicator, a small scanner whose 3D read-out chimes and changes colour in accordance with the mental powers of his patient. However, the most cunning uses of computer graphics in *Akira* are not visible to the naked eye. Instead, Otomo used computers behind the scenes, to plot the paths of falling blocks, model parallax effects on backgrounds, and tweak lighting and lens flares. Otomo's interest in computers has contributed to his long absence from the anime scene after *Akira*. Intermittent reports in the Japanese press refer to his ongoing work on *Steam Boy*, a computer-animated movie set in Victorian England, that has been officially underway since 1995. After the relatively small number of colours in use in *Akira*, Otomo has reported that the potential of digital film-making has proved irresistibly tempting to his perfectionist streak: 'Until now there was always a limit to the available colour palette, now with a computer we can use 16.7 million.'

COSTUME FITTING: Though *Akira* was not intended as a superhero story, part of its appeal to foreign audiences rested on the way it played with the genre. Archie Goodwin, the editor who championed the *Akira* comic abroad, notes that Otomo 'was also dealing with beings with paranormal powers, which is a very common theme in American comics and American science fiction'. Rearrange the scenes from Tetsuo's life in chronological order, and you see a weakling who is bullied as a child, who grows up in the shadow of a local hero, and eventually receives great power through an accident – had he not hit Takashi in the road, the military scientists would never have recognised his potential and fed him the powerful Level Seven drugs. In other words, a career path not unlike a number of superhero nemeses, from the Joker to the Green Goblin.

Otomo intended that 'any of the characters could be the lead of the story' – *Akira* is designed to work as an action movie starring Kaneda, a disaster movie starring the population of Neo-Tokyo, a tragic buddy movie starring Kaneda and Tetsuo, or even an espionage thriller starring Kei. But if watched as an anti-heroic tale starring Tetsuo, we see his clothes first ripped and torn in the style of *The Hulk*. As he finally realises his true power, as he fights with tanks in the streets of Tokyo, he tears a red curtain from a destroyed store-front window and drapes it over his shoulders in a parody of *Superman*'s cape.

MUSIC: For the music of *Akira*, Otomo chose composer Shoji Yamashiro. The leader of an avant-garde choir called the Geino Yamashiro-gumi (The Yamashiro Arts Group), Yamashiro had come to prominence over the previous two decades with such world music releases as *Reincarnated Orchestra*. In search of a unique sound to represent his future Tokyo, Otomo heard something suitable in the Yamashiro-gumi's use of Bulgarian vocal styles and *kecak* (ritual choral patterns of Bali). He offered Yamashiro the chance to work on the score of *Akira*, and offered little other guidance. Yamashiro returned after six months with a symphony. Instead of the isolated pockets of incidental music common to movies, he worked out a series of interlocking themes, using voices, drums, and Balinese instruments. Yamashiro's score was recorded digitally in separate 'modules' of sound, so that the pieces could be run through a sequencer to hit the correct run-time of the animated scenes when they were eventually complete. This is somewhat different from the norm in animation, when composers are usually given precise timings to the nearest second, and told to come up with music to fit.

Two versions of the soundtrack were subsequently released: the *Akira Original Motion Picture Soundtrack* (VICL-1538), which contained soundbites from the film, and the *Akira Symphonic Suite* (VICL-23092), which returned the music to its original, pre-production symphonic whole.

CLASSIC QUOTES:

Kaneda: 'Tetsuo's our friend. If anyone's gonna kill him, it should be *us*!'

Tetsuo: 'Twin ceramic rotor drives on each wheel, and these are computer-controlled anti-lock brakes. Two hundred horsepower at twelve thousand rpm –'

Kaneda: 'You wanna ride it, Tetsuo? That bike's been customised just for me. It's too wild. You couldn't handle it.'

Kaneda: 'I was just wondering if you wanted to grab some tea or something over there. I figured we could have a nice long chat about that "revolution" deal.'
Kei: 'Skirt-chasers will do anything these days. You'll help anyone as long as it's a girl, won't you?'

DELETED SCENES: The nature of animation forces the production team to extensively plan every scene before it is made, leading to very little wastage after the storyboarding stage. Otomo himself mourned the trimming of a number of scenes featuring the Lady Miyako, a cult priestess who features heavily in the manga, but is only glimpsed for a couple of moments in the movie. If the creator had his way, another character would have been completely deleted – Otomo argued that the film would be more interesting if the figure of Akira *never* appeared, but was overruled by his producers.

TRAILERS: The original teaser for the movie, clearly made before much had been committed to film, capitalised on the distinctive lettering of the comic's logo. We see a collage of images from the comic, visible through the transparent roman letters of the word 'Akira'. Soundbites from the movie rise to a crescendo, and suddenly the letters become opaque. Just as in the original comic, the roman 'Akira' logo is then defaced with a hand-sprayed graffito in Japan's *katakana* syllabary – the letters 'A', 'KI' and 'RA.' Later teasers and theatrical trailers used footage chiefly from the opening motorcyle chase and the riots on the streets, along with the distinctive '*Rassera! Rassera! Rassera!*' chant of the Yamashiro-gumi. A legend then reads, 'What is the ultra top-secret project slumbering underground? The year's most controversial movie has arrived.'

POSTERS: The poster plumped for the iconic image of Kaneda astride his bike just after he has skidded to a halt in a game of chicken with the leader of the Clown gang. A one-sheet used outside Japan showed an image of Kaneda from later in the film, brandishing a laser rifle from the final showdown in the Olympic stadium. Still another focused on Kaneda, his back to the camera, as he steps up to his trademark bike. None of the posters featured a picture of Akira himself, leading many casual observers to assume that *Kaneda* was Akira.

TAG-LINE: The Japanese poster went for the vague 'Signal Traced to Tokyo!' Foreign tag-lines preferred the blunter 'Neo-Tokyo is about to E.X.P.L.O.D.E.'

WHAT THE PAPERS SAID: *Variety* described *Akira* as 'a lavish animation extravaganza produced at a cost of $8 million . . . a remarkable technical achievement in every respect, from the imaginative and detailed design of tomorrow to the booming Dolby effects on the soundtrack. The *Washington Post*'s Richard Harrington mentioned the fact that, at 'over one billion yen', *Akira* was the most expensive animated feature ever made in Japan, but added 'it's easily the most impressive, as well . . . super-colourful, explicitly violent, intellectually provocative and emotionally engaging with its Perils-of-Pauline pace. Otomo has condensed the narrative sprawl of the comics to provide coherence . . . the film moves with such kinetic energy that you'll be hanging on for dear life.'

'*Akira* is very probably the first animated film with a genuinely novelistic density of incident and character,' said the UK's *Monthly Film Bulletin*, only to add that its storyline was '. . . not particularly ground-breaking as science fiction'. *Time Out* similarly both praised the film's originality: 'Otomo's first excursion into movies features some of the most mind-blowing animation ever seen', but managed to find several precursors – 'An impressive achievement, often suggesting a weird expressionist blend of *2001*, *The Warriors*, *Blade Runner* and *Forbidden Planet*.'

BOX OFFICE: Though *Akira* received a limited US theatrical release, it was only intended as a loss-leader for the forthcoming video release. Consequently, the movie has only taken a paltry $553,171 at the US box office – still enough to make it the eighth most successful anime movie ever released in the States. The fact that the top three are Pokémon films suggests that *Akira* has an even bigger audience waiting in the wings. *Akira*'s real success has been on video and DVD, where it remains one of the consistent best-sellers of the anime business, selling in six-figure quantities even in the anime-shy UK – even, incredibly, to non-anime fans.

AWARDS: Magazines and polls regularly vote *Akira* as one of the top sci-fi movies of all time, and one of the most influential anime ever. The most recent was the Discovery Channel's *Top Ten Comic Heroes* (2002), in which *Akira* was the only Japanese representative.

CONTROVERSY: What controversy there was around *Akira* was deliberately engineered. Western distributors, particularly Manga Entertainment in the UK, used the movie as the vanguard of their new anime lists, breaking open an entire new market in animation for adults. Emphasis was often placed on *Akira*'s violence and nudity (a tame '15' certificate when compared to other, more notorious anime), in the deliberate hope that it would shock the establishment and encourage teenage rebels to buy the movie to spite their parents. Luckily, *Akira*'s technical quality is enough to win over most viewers, though the same cannot be said for many of the anime that followed.

TRIVIA: In order to chill the readers into thinking that the events of the story could start for real *at any moment*, the original comic of *Akira* started World War III on 6 December 1982, the date it was originally published. In the movie version, WWIII commenced on 16 July 1988, the date of the film's Japanese release. When published in the US, the war's start-date was moved a decade later to 6 December 1992, but the movie kept the Japanese opening, and the date was not altered for subsequent territories. The central action, of course, always takes place in 2019, the same year as *Blade Runner*.

In the riot scene, Kei pushes past a man who is wearing a T-shirt with the logo of *Young Magazine*, the original home of the *Akira* comic.

A two second clip from the film was featured in the promo clip/music video for Michael Jackson's 'Scream'.

The Yamashiro-gumi went on to make several other CDs, and would later reclaim the *Akira Symphonic Suite* the centrepiece of a trilogy of works, beginning with *Reincarnated Orchestra* (VICL-23091), and ending with *Ecophony Gaia* (VICL-23093).

APOCRYPHA: Thanks to a breathless 'making of' documentary, desperate to claim that every aspect of the movie was unprecedented, fans were led to believe that the movie broke new ground in recording the characters' dialogue, Disney-style, before the animation was actually shot. In fact, as the production report shows, the actors voiced their lines to animatics (semi-animated storyboards), which is costly but not particularly unusual in Japan or elsewhere.

Many critics described the blue-skinned mutants in the film as 'prematurely aged children' or 'children with the face of old men'. In fact, they are adults with the bodies of children – born at the end of the 1970s, and roughly the same age as the Colonel.

SEQUELS & SPIN-OFFS: As the events in the movie *Akira* only occupy the first couple of volumes of the comic, the print version of *Akira* is its own sequel. In fact, Otomo suspended work on the comic while he made the movie, only returning to complete the final volume after the movie was released. Thanks to this chaotic genesis, the movie received the ending Otomo had originally planned for the comic. 'I'd always felt that [the comic] would end with Tetsuo and Kaneda somehow sharing their memories of the orphanage,' he told *Monthly Film Bulletin*. 'Using that ending in the film meant I had to come up with something else for the manga; the ending there is a bit different.' In fact, the comic ends when Kaneda faces down a group of UN Peacekeepers who have arrived in the ruined city, and announces that they are trespassing on the territory of the Great Akira Empire. After making it abundantly clear that Neo-Tokyo is forever the property of the New Breed, he rides into the distance with Kei, surrounded by the ghostly figures of characters who have died or otherwise 'crossed over'.

FUTURE INCARNATIONS: After prolonged speculation that Columbia–Tristar planned to make a movie of *Akira*, the *Hollywood Reporter* announced in April 2002 that a live-action version was finally on the cards, but from Warner Bros. Acquired by Lionel Wigram, the *Akira* remake is scheduled as the next production for Stephen Norrington, director of earlier comic book adaptations such as *Blade* and *The League of Extraordinary Gentlemen. League* scriptwriter James Robinson is tagged to be on the project, though Warners' initial announcement already created controversy in US anime fandom. Why? Because their breakdown of the story already claimed that the live-action movie would feature a biker rescuing 'his younger brother' from a secret government project – already a seemingly unnecessary step away from the original plot and character relationships.

DVD AVAILABILITY: *Akira* was originally released in the US on VHS by Streamline Pictures, in both subtitled and dubbed forms – it is the Streamline version that made it to the UK as a release from ICA Projects. When broadcast on the BBC in 1995, the film appeared with new 'letterbox' subtitles, in what appeared to be a new translation, though this was never made available on video. Ten years after its original release, it was extensively remastered by Pioneer for the superb US (Region 1) DVD release, which features a beautiful digitally restored print, remastered sound, a superior new translation and a new dub. With a new generation of former Pokémon fans now old enough to appreciate it, the movie became a best-seller once more, in a print that genuinely looks as good as new. The UK (Region 2) DVD from Manga Entertainment retains the Pioneer print, but dumps most of the US edition's copious extras. Nevertheless, both editions include the Akira *Production Report* documentary.

FINAL ANALYSIS: Though press releases suggest *Steam Boy* may break his long absence soon, *Akira*'s creator has not directed a full-length animated movie since, and the movie's costs spiralled so far out of control that it could have been a disaster of *Heaven's Gate* proportions without foreign acclaim. However, Otomo's tendency to over-engineer every last detail has created a movie that stands the test of time. Watch

Akira twenty times, and there will always be something you haven't spotted before in the background of a scene or in a snippet of dialogue. Thanks also to the wonderful Pioneer restoration, *Akira* is still fresh a full generation after its initial release – indeed, it has teenage fans today who were not even born at the time of its premiere. The film remains a classic of the anime medium, and powerful enough in its own right to impress mainstream viewers.

Many of the anime released abroad in the wake of *Akira* were inferior, earlier products, some made for TV or direct-to-video like *Appleseed*, causing some new-found fans to losc interest after repeated disappointments. The controversy in Akira's earlier days was that the sheer expense of the movie, which threatened to bankrupt its original backers, had created a film of such high quality that it was impossible to match with Japanese capital alone. Not only did *Akira* create the 1990s Western anime business pre-Pokémon, but it also set a standard so high that the Japanese were unable to compete with it themselves without foreign investment. In this regard, *Akira* is the father of *Ghost in the Shell* as well as other modern co-productions like *Blood: The Last Vampire* and the new *Astro Boy*.

EXPERT WITNESS: 'It was the worst possible thing for me to make the film version of *Akira* before I finished the manga version. As I worked on the film, I came to like the idea of having two different but similar versions of the same story, but part of me still thinks that part of the original was sacrificed.' **– Katsuhiro Otomo, Writer–Director**

Batman (1989)

(126 mins)

Directed by Tim Burton
Produced by Jon Peters and Peter Guber
Screenplay by Sam Hamm and Warren Skaaren
Story by Sam Hamm
Co-Producer Chris Kenny
Executive Producers Benjamin Melnicker and Michael E Uslan
Based on Batman Characters Created by Bob Kane
Director of Photography Roger Pratt BSC
Production Designed by Anton Furst
Editor Ray Lovejoy
Songs Written and Performed by Prince

Music by Danny Elfman
Costume Designer Bob Ringwood
Ms Basinger's Costumes by Linda Henrikson
Casting by Marion Dougherty

CAST: Jack Nicholson (*Jack Napier/'The Joker'*), Michael Keaton (*Bruce Wayne/'Batman'*), Kim Basinger (*Vicki Vale*), Robert Wuhl (*Alexander Knox*), Pat Hingle (*Commissioner Gordon*), Billy Dee Williams (*Harvey Dent*), Michael Gough (*Alfred Pennyworth*), Jack Palance (*Carl Grissom*), Jerry Hall (*Alicia Hunt*), Tracey Walter (*Bob*), Lee Wallace (*William Borg*), William Hootkins (*Lt Max Eckhardt*), Richard Strange, Carl Chase, Mac McDonald (*goons*), George Lane Cooper (*Lawrence*), Terence Plummer, Philip Tan (*goons*), John Sterland (*Grissom's accountant*), Edwin Craig (*Antoine Rotelli*), Vincent Wong, Joel Cutrara (*crimelords*), John Dair (*Nic*), George Roth (*Eddie*), Kate Harper (*anchorwoman*), Bruce McGuire (*Peter McElroy*), Richard Durden (*TV director*), Kit Hollerback (*Becky*), Lachelle Carl (*Renée*), Del Baker, Jazzer Jeyes, Wayne Michaels, Valentino Musetti, Rocky Taylor (*Napier hoods*), Keith Edwards, Leon Herbert (*reporters*), Steve Plytas (*plastic surgeon*), Anthony Wellington (*Robert*), Amir Korangy (*wine steward*), Hugo E Blick (*young Jack Napier*), Charles Roskilly (*young Bruce Wayne*), Philip O'Brien (*museum maître d'*), Michael Balfour (*scientist*), Liza Ross (*tourist mom*), Garrick Hagon (*Harold*), Adrian Meyers (*Jimmy*), David Baxt (*Dr Thomas Wayne*), Sharon Holm (*Martha Wayne*), Clyde Gatell (*mugger*), Jon Soresi (*medic*), Sam Douglas (*gangster lawyer*), Elliott Stein (*man in crowd*), Denis Lill (*Bob*), Paul Birchard (*reporter*), Paul Michael (*young cop*), Carl Newman (*movement double*)

UNCREDITED CAST: Pat Gorman (*cop*)

TITLE SEQUENCE: The background of the Warner Bros logo darkens and dissolves through to shots panning over smoky blue images as yellow titles begin to appear in a simple serif font. The camera continues to move around the surfaces and curves of a blue-tinged shape, which reveals itself, as the titles conclude, to be the Batman logo.

SYNOPSIS: It is dusk in Gotham City as a couple and their son are accosted by muggers, who in turn are set upon by a mysterious winged assailant who calls himself 'Batman'. It is Gotham's two-hundredth anniversary; crime is rampant, corruption is rife and the city is controlled by Carl Grissom and his cohort Jack Napier – at least, until an accident at a chemical plant turns Napier into a grinning madman who calls himself 'The Joker', who kills Grissom, seizes control of his evil empire, and begins polluting Gothamites with poisoned products which turn them into grinning effigies of himself. Meanwhile, photographer Vicki Vale is dating billionaire Bruce Wayne, unaware that by night he dons a moulded batsuit and fights crime on the streets of Gotham. When Vale is kidnapped by The Joker, who wants her to witness his wicked deeds, Batman rescues her, and sets up a confrontation with his nemesis who, he later learns, killed his parents, an event which ultimately led to his becoming Batman. During a final showdown amid the gothic towers of downtown Gotham, The Joker is killed and Batman rescues Vale (again). Gotham returns to relative normality, under the protection of the mysterious vigilante known as Batman. Only Vicki knows his true identity.

ORIGINS: The creation of cartoonist Bob Kane and his (mostly uncredited) partner Bill Finger, Batman made his first appearance in *Detective Comics* #27, published in May 1939 – a year after Superman's debut, and a full fifty before Tim Burton's *Batman* reached the big screen. Lacking Superman's superpowers, Batman was forced to rely on his physical prowess, and the enormous wealth of his alter ego, millionaire Bruce Wayne, who provided his costumed counterpart with a house (the Batcave), a car (the Batmobile), an aircraft (the Batplane) and a utility belt full of gadgets. Kane credited numerous influences for his creation, including Zorro, The Shadow and a 1930 film entitled *The Bat Whispers*, which featured a caped criminal who shines his bat insignia on the wall just prior to killing his victims. 'I remember when I was twelve or thirteen . . . I came across a book about Leonardo da Vinci. This had a picture of a flying machine with huge bat wings . . . It looked like a bat man to me.'

PREVIOUS INCARNATIONS: Batman first reached the silver screen as early as the 1940s, with the first of two fifteen-chapter Columbia serials: *Batman* (1943), starring Lewis Wilson as Batman; and *The New Adventures of Batman and Robin* (1949), with Robert Lowery. Almost two decades later, on 12 January 1966, the ABC television series starring Adam West and Burt Ward brought the characters to an entirely new generation, running for 26 months and earning a big-screen spin-off within the first year of its run. Although Kane's earliest stories had a *noir*-ish sensibility, over time the characters developed the wisecracking personae which were magnificently captured by the camp capers of the TV series. 'Batman and Robin were always punning and wisecracking and so were the villains,' Kane said in 1965. 'It was camp way ahead of its time.' In the 1970s, Batman continued to appear in an animated series, *Superfriends*, but the legacy of the 1960s TV series meant that it was not until Frank Miller reinvented the character for the ground-breaking graphic novels *The Dark Knight Returns* and *Batman: Year One* that the world was ready to take Batman seriously again.

DEVELOPMENT: Just as Batman had made his first appearance in comic strips a year after Superman, the development of the *Batman* movie – the first since the camp caper TV spin-off *Batman* in 1966 – began a year after the box office success of *Superman*. Former Batman comic book writer Michael E Uslan, together with his producing partner Benjamin Melnicker, secured the film rights from DC Comics, announcing a 1981 release for the film, then budgeted at $15 million. Uslan and Melnicker hired *Superman: The Movie*'s (uncredited) screenwriter Tom Mankiewicz to script the story, which was set in the near future, and closely followed the *Superman* model: an extended origin story, followed by the genesis of his superhero alter ego, and his eventual confrontation with The Joker. It ended with the introduction of Robin. It was Uslan's wish to make 'a definitive Batman movie totally removed from the TV show, totally removed from camp; a version that went back to the original Bob Kane/Bill Finger strips'.

By 1983, the project was still languishing in 'development hell', as potential directors including Ivan Reitman (*Ghostbusters*) and Joe Dante (*Gremlins*) came and went. It was following the surprise success of Tim Burton's slapstick comedy *Pee-Wee's Big Adventure* that Warner Bros – whose stewardship of the project resulted from a deal with Peter Guber's Casablanca Film Works, with whom Melnicker had a development deal – offered the project to lifelong Bat-fan Tim Burton, who was busy making *Beetlejuice* for the studio. 'The first treatment of *Batman*, the Mankiewicz script, was basically *Superman*, only the names had been changed,' Burton told Mark Salisbury. 'It had the same jokey tone, as the story followed Bruce Wayne from childhood through to his beginnings as a crime fighter. They didn't acknowledge any of the freakish nature of it . . . The Mankiewicz script made it more obvious to me that you couldn't treat *Batman* like *Superman*, or treat it like the TV series, because it's a guy dressing up as a bat and no matter what anyone says, that's weird.' Although Burton had fond memories of the series, which he would run home from school to watch, he had no wish to duplicate its campy tone. Yet it would take the comic book boom of the late 1980s – notably the success of Frank Miller's darkly gothic graphic novel, *The Dark Knight Returns* – to convince Warner Bros that Burton's approach might connect with audiences. 'The success of the graphic novel made our ideas far more acceptable,' he observed.

With Warner Bros' blessing, Burton began spitballing a new draft with emerging screenwriting talent and fellow Bat-fan Sam Hamm, whose comedy script *Pulitzer Prize* had sparked a bidding war and landed him a two-year contract with Warner Bros. Hamm felt that the *Superman* model was wrong; that rather than dwell on Batman's origins, the character should be presented as a *fait accompli*, with his background and motivations emerging as the story progressed, so that the unlocking of the mystery becomes part of the plot. 'I tried to take the premise which had this emotionally scarred millionaire whose way of dealing with his traumas was by putting on the suit. If you look at it from this aspect that there is no world of superheroes, no DC Universe, and no real genre conventions to fall back on, you can start taking the character seriously. You can ask, "What if this guy actually does exist?" And in turn, it'll generate a lot of plot for you.' Burton liked the approach. 'I'd just meet Sam on weekends to discuss the early writing stages. We knocked it into good shape while I directed *Beetlejuice*, but as a "go" project it was only green-lighted by Warners when the opening figures for *Beetlejuice* surprised everybody – including myself!' By this time, Hamm's involvement had been sidelined by the writers' strike, so Burton brought in *Beetlejuice* writer Warren Skaaren and Charles McKeown (*The Adventures of Baron Munchausen*), principally to lighten the tone – not because of Keaton's casting, but because of studio fears that a troubled and disturbed Batman, full of self-doubt and unresolved psychological issues, might turn off audiences. 'I see what they're doing,' Hamm said at the time, 'in that they don't want to have a larger-than-life, heroic character who is plagued by doubts about the validity of what he's doing, but it's stuff that I miss.'

CASTING: Although Tim Curry and Robin Williams were allegedly considered, Jack Nicholson was the unanimous choice for The Joker, a fact which gave him unprecedented bargaining power when it came to negotiating his fee. As a result, Nicholson was granted the most lucrative contract in motion picture history, far outweighing *Superman* star Marlon Brando's $3.7 million for ten minutes of screen time; not only did Nicholson negotiate an impressive upfront fee, but his percentage both of first-dollar gross (i.e., box office revenue, not the studio's net) and of merchandise gave him a fee rumoured to be in the region of $75 million.

Mel Gibson, Alec Baldwin, Bill Murray, Charlie Sheen and Pierce Brosnan were all rumoured to be on Warner Bros' shortlist for the title role, although Nicholson's casting meant that the studio could afford to go with an unknown – after all, it had worked for *Superman*. Burton had his doubts. 'In my mind I kept reading reviews that said, "Jack's terrific, but the unknown as Batman is nothing special",' he told Mark Salisbury. Neither did he want to cast an obvious action hero. 'Why would this big, macho, Arnold Schwarzenegger-type person dress up as a bat for God's sake?' Finally, it came down to only one choice: Michael Keaton, whom he had just directed in *Beetlejuice*. '*That* guy you could see putting on a bat-suit; he does it because he *needs* to, because he's not this gigantic, strapping macho man. It's all about transformation . . . Taking Michael and making him Batman just underscored the whole split personality thing which is really what I think the movie's all about.'

Sean Young (*Blade Runner*) was originally cast as Vicki Vale, but when she broke her collarbone during a horse-riding scene, she was replaced with Kim Basinger (*9½ Weeks*); ironically, the sequence featuring Vale on horseback was subsequently cut out of the script. (Young evidently felt that Burton owed her; when he was casting *Batman Returns*, the actress turned up at his office unannounced, wearing a Catwoman outfit; Burton, who wanted Annette Bening (*The Grifters*) for the role, reputedly hid under the table until she left, eventually casting Michelle Pfeiffer after Bening fell pregnant – with the child of *Dick Tracy* director–star Warren Beatty.)

PRODUCTION: Early in pre-production, Burton had convinced Warner Bros to let him shoot the film at Britain's Pinewood Studios, traditional home of the Bond films and many other blockbusters, including *Raiders of the Lost Ark*. For Burton, it allowed him to work thousands of miles from the studio backing the film, giving him a degree of independence he would not have enjoyed shooting on the Warner backlot. For the studio, it made sound financial sense; at $35 million, *Batman* was modestly budgeted for a would-be blockbuster (*Terminator 2*, made just two years later, cost more than $100 million), and although the exchange rate was not entirely advantageous, every dollar counted. If the construction budget – $5.5 million, barely a quarter that of *Cleopatra* twenty years earlier – was going to be sufficient to create an authentic Gotham City in a hundred acres of Buckinghamshire backlot, Burton would need the best production designer on the planet – even if it meant waiting until he was available.

Burton had wanted to work with production designer Anton Furst ever since he saw his breathtaking designs for Neil Jordan's *The Company of Wolves*. Furst had declined to work on *Beetlejuice* (a choice he later regretted) because he was exhausted after two years on Stanley Kubrick's *Full Metal Jacket*; this time, Furst was busy designing another Neil Jordan film, *High Spirits*, and could not commit to *Batman*. Burton, however, would not take no for an answer, and his dogged determination to secure Furst's services paid dividends as their vision of Gotham City began to take shape. 'I don't think I've ever felt so naturally in tune with a director, conceptually, spiritually, visually or artistically,' Furst said later, further noting that 'When I came up with four ideas in four different directions, he'd always choose the one I liked most.'

In the comics, Batman's native city was closely modelled on New York – and even identified as such until December 1940; Burton and Furst, however, saw Gotham as the reverse of New York in its early days.

'Zoning and construction was thought of in terms of letting light in,' Burton explained. 'So we decided to take that in the opposite direction and darken everything by building up vertically and cramming architecture together.' Thus, he added, 'Gotham City is basically New York caricatured with a mix of styles squashed together – an island of big, tall cartoon buildings textured with extreme designs.' Other influences included Frank Miller's *The Dark Knight Returns*, Andreas Feininger's photographs of New York buildings, and the work of Japanese architect Shin Takamatsu.

Principal photography began under tight security in October 1988. Although Sean Young's riding accident threw the schedule out at an early stage, it could have spelled disaster for the production had it occurred later in the shoot; as it was, none of her scenes had to be re-shot when Kim Basinger stepped in to Vicki Vale's shoes. In spite of this early setback, the sheer scale of the production, the complexity of the special effects, the extensive night shoots, the large number of interior and exterior locations, and the restrictive nature of Jack Nicholson's contract – which, despite his enormous fee, meant that he could only be called for a specified number of hours per day, including time spent in the make-up chair – Burton delivered the film on schedule, and only a fraction over budget, and it came as no surprise when Warner Bros invited him back up to bat for the sequel. No one was more surprised than Burton, however, when he said yes.

COSTUME FITTING: If comic book fans were vocal in their protest at the casting of Michael Keaton and, to a lesser degree, in the choice of Burton as director, they were even more vociferous in their condemnation of the Bat-suit, which altered the colouring from grey and blue to black. Although Keaton had neither the stature nor the physique to fill a skintight costume, Burton had other reasons to select Bob Ringwood's moulded rubberised design, which eschewed tights and a cape in favour of fake muscles and wings. 'The idea was to humanise Batman,' Burton explained, noting that, since an element of reality was key to realising the comic book fantasy, it was necessary to find a psychological basis for his outlandish get-up, one that went beyond the comic book explanation. 'You can't just do, "Well, I'm avenging the death of my parents – oh, a bat's flown in through the window! Yes, that's it – I'll become a Batman!" That's all stupid comic book stuff. He dresses up as a bat because he wanted to have an amazing visual impact . . . He switches identities to become something else entirely, so why wouldn't he overdo it.' Ringwood's design was not merely an outfit, he observed, but a complete bodysuit. 'It isn't tights and underwear worn on the outside, but a complete operatic costume to overstate the image Batman has of himself.'

MUSIC: Danny Elfman had already scored Tim Burton's first two films, *Pee-Wee's Big Adventure* and *Beetlejuice*, and it came as no surprise that he was invited to score Burton's third. A more controversial choice were the soundtrack contributions of Warner Bros' music artist Prince, who composed an album's worth of new songs, two of which ('Partyman' and 'Trust') appear in the film, as The Joker insists on musical accompaniments for his crimes. '*Batman* doesn't have as blatant a soundtrack as, say, *Top Gun*,' a defensive Burton told *Cinefantastique*. 'The songs in the film I would call "scored source pieces". They are integrated seamlessly into the soundtrack. Prince worked with Elfman to ensure the songs didn't stand out when, for example, the radio is switched on. Our eyes are not on high volume soundtrack sales.' Nevertheless, *Batman* became one of the first films to spawn not one but *two* soundtracks: one containing Elfman's score, a second featuring Prince songs; both became huge sellers. Elfman's 'Batman' has subsequently appeared in many of the film's sequels and spin-offs, laying to rest the cartoonish quality of the TV series theme.

CLASSIC QUOTES:

Jack Napier: 'Decent people shouldn't live here. They'd be happier someplace else.'

Alicia Hunt: 'You look fine.'
Jack Napier: 'I didn't ask.'

The Joker: 'Haven't you ever heard of the healing power of laughter?'

The Joker: 'Where does he get those wonderful toys?'

The Joker: 'Winged freak terrorises . . .' Wait'll they get a load of me!'

The Joker: 'This town needs an enema!'

Bruce Wayne: 'Let me tell you about this guy I know: Jack. Bad seed. Mean. Hurt people.'
The Joker: 'I like him already.'

The Joker: 'Have you ever danced with the devil in the pale moonlight? I always ask that of all my prey . . .'

DELETED SCENES: Although Burton has claimed that everything he shot made it into the movie, one major deletion occurred between completion of the shooting script and commencement of principal photography: the introduction of Batman's sidekick – Dick Grayson, a.k.a. 'Robin', a.k.a. the Boy Wonder. 'We tried to put Robin in, to make that relationship work in a real way,' he told Mark Salisbury. 'In the TV series he's just *there*. We tried a slightly more psychological approach, but I felt unless you're going to focus on that and give it its due, it's like "Who is this guy?" Sam [Hamm] and I spent a lot of time going over it . . . and when we were getting ready to shoot the movie it was the easiest lift.' Given the character's prominence in both the comics and the 1960s TV series, it was a bold omission, yet one which Burton found easier to justify following the timely publication of a Batman comic book strand which climaxed with Robin lying badly wounded in Batman's arms, whereupon DC Comics invited readers to vote on whether he lived or died: the result put the Boy Wonder six feet under.

TRAILERS: The trailer opens with the film's biggest set piece – the Batwing swooping over Gotham City, shooting up the main street while The Joker stands defiant. With no narration, just a few scattered dialogue lines (mostly from The Joker), the trailer is almost over as soon as it has begun, with just two cast credits (Nicholson and Keaton), and a Bat symbol where the title ought to be. Its message was simple: *Batman* means business.

POSTERS: As befitted a film as shrouded in secrecy as Batman's true identity, the Batman logo – conveniently one of the most recognisable symbols in the world – and a release date were all that appeared on the 'teaser' poster. Although many variations of a 'regular' poster were proposed by Warner Bros' marketing department, in the event, the gold and black rendering of the Bat symbol on a black background was retained in most territories, although the cast names and a title were added for the purposes of the main campaign.

WHAT THE PAPERS SAID: Although many critics could not help but be impressed by 1989's biggest blockbuster, *Chicago Sun-Times* critic Roger Ebert arguably spoke for the silent majority when he opined that 'The Gotham City created in *Batman* is one of the most distinctive and atmospheric places I've seen in the movies. It's a shame something more memorable doesn't happen there. *Batman* is a triumph of design over story, style over substance – a great-looking movie with a plot you don't much care about.' Anticipation was running even higher in the UK, where audiences had been forced to wait almost two months to see the film, which could hardly help but be a disappointment. *Time Out* described it as 'plotless, unfocused, barely held together by mind-blowing sets, gadgets and costumes, and by director Burton's visual flair', adding that 'cackling, dancing, killing for sheer humour value and hogging the best one-liners, Nicholson . . . pulls off the greatest criminal coup of the decade: stealing a whole movie.'

BOX OFFICE: The anticipation for *Batman* was running at fever pitch by the time the film finally hit US cinemas on 21 June 1989, swooping to a record-breaking $42.7 million opening weekend, becoming the first film to hit $100 million after just ten days on release, and grossing $250 million overall. 'Bat-mania' swept the world, with the film becoming not only the biggest film of 1989, but the most successful in Warner Bros' history. Although *Jurassic Park* surpassed its worldwide gross ($413 million) by around half a billion dollars only four years later, *Batman* ruled in the ancilliary stakes, with around $150 million in video cassette sales, and a staggering $750 million worth of merchandise. As a result, 1989 would forever be known as the year of the Bat.

AWARDS: Anton Furst and Peter Young shared the film's only Academy Award®, for Best Art Direction – Set Decoration. At the Golden Globe awards, Jack Nicholson received a nomination for Best Performance by an Actor in a Motion Picture – Comedy/Musical, though many were given to wonder which of the two categories *Batman* fell into. In the UK, *Batman* received six BAFTA nominations, in the categories of Best Supporting Actor (Nicholson again), Costume Design, Make-Up Artist, Production Design, Sound and Special Effects, but failed to convert any of them into trophies.

CONTROVERSY: With hindsight, it is almost impossible to imagine the furore which surrounded the announcement that Tim Burton had been selected to direct *Batman*. At the time, the public was only aware of one Burton film, *Pee-Wee's Big Adventure*, and had yet to acknowledge Burton as a uniquely gifted director possessed of a vivid imagination, almost uniquely dark sensibilities, immense visual flair, and a highly personal perspective on 'the outsider'. Today, it would be like Warner Bros putting *Superman* in the hands of someone whose sole credit was an Adam Sandler comedy. If anything, Keaton's casting was even more controversial: *Beetlejuice* had yet to be released, almost nobody had seen *Clean and Sober*, and even Burton sympathised with those who decried his casting choice, launching petitions to 'Stop the Batman Movie!', picketing comic book stores and deluging the studio with an estimated 50,000 letters promising to boycott the film.

'The fan reaction is a surface response,' Burton said at the time. 'The moment you mention Keaton he immediately brings to mind *Mr Mom* and *Night Shift*, the comedy/romance sitcom-type picture.' Screenwriter Sam Hamm admitted that Keaton's casting 'came as a jolt', but suggested that the fans' reaction was 'based on misconceptions . . . because when they hear Tim Burton's name they think of *Pee-Wee's Big Adventure*, and when they hear Keaton's name they think of any number of Michael Keaton comedies.' Nevertheless, he added, 'It's kind of disorienting to walk into a comic book store and find a petition to stop something you worked on.' Warner Bros wisely responded to the backlash by inviting Batman creator Bob Kane aboard as creative consultant. 'Hiring Kane was a very intelligent move,' said production designer Anton Furst, '[because] if Kane goes on record saying that his concept has been brilliantly interpreted, the ardent fans buckle down.'

TRIVIA: Batman creator Bob Kane was asked to play a cameo role as a police sketch artist; although unable to accept, it was his sketch of Batman that was used in the same scene.

In the UK, the British Board of Film Classification felt that the film fell somewhere between the two existing ratings, PG and 15, and duly invented a new middle ground. Thus, *Batman* became the first film to receive a '12' certificate, meaning that children under 12 were prohibited from seeing it.

APOCRYPHA: The question of whether or not Adam West, who had been both immortalised and typecast by the 1960s Batman, was offered a cameo as Bruce Wayne's father, remains a grey area. Warner Bros has said that West declined to appear in Burton's film; however, in his otherwise gracious 1994 autobiography *Back to the Batcave*, West claims that neither he nor co-star Burt Ward were invited to make cameo appearances. Besides, he says, 'I didn't want to do a little cameo and indemnify the picture, lend my name to it, and then get blown away in twenty seconds on the screen,' he explains. 'These people can write a Brando-like turn in *Superman*, right, maybe involving the back story of Dr Wayne – Batman's father – but in the final cut, it could be twenty seconds. Thug pulls gun, shoots father, that's it. And then they use my name.' As it was, he adds, 'our contribution to the legend was ignored, ridiculed, and denigrated – though the series was aired and promoted and used in the marketing of the new films and in the merchandising.'

SEQUELS & SPIN-OFFS: Although Warner Bros left the Gotham City set standing at Pinewood Studios – at a cost of $20,000 per day – in the hopes that the success of *Batman* would warrant a sequel, *Batman Returns* was ultimately shot in Los Angeles, with Burton – who had since directed *Edward Scissorhands* for Twentieth Century Fox – again at the helm, and Michael Keaton back in the Bat-suit. This time, Burton's dark sensibilities were given a freer reign, with The Penguin (Danny De Vito) and Catwoman (Michelle Pfeiffer) as the villains. Sam Hamm's script (which also featured Catwoman) was rejected in favour of one by *Heathers* scribe Daniel Waters, which was subsequently doctored by Wesley Strick (*Cape Fear*). 'When I was hired to write *Batman Returns* (*Batman II* at the time), I was asked to focus on one (big) problem with the current script: Penguin's lack of a "master plan",' Strick recalls. 'To be honest, this didn't especially bother me; in fact I found it refreshing – in comic book stories, there's nothing hoarier or (usually) hokier than an arch-villain's "master plan". But the lack of one in *Batman II* was obsessing the Warner brass.' Strick says that he was presented with 'the usual boring ideas to do with warming the city, or freezing the city, that kind of stuff,' but pitched an alternative approach – inspired by the 'Moses' parallels of Strick's prologue, in which Baby Penguin is bundled in a basket and thrown in the river where he floats, helpless, till he's saved (and subsequently raised) by Gotham's sewer denizens – in which Penguin's 'master plan' is to kill the firstborn sons of Gotham City. Warner Bros loved it; so did Burton. 'It turned out to be a controversial addition. The toy manufacturers were not alone in disliking it – it also did substantially less business than the first [*Batman*].' Indeed, although *Batman Returns* scored a bigger opening weekend ($45.6 million) than its predecessor, its worldwide gross was $282.8 million, barely two thirds of *Batman*'s box office.

Joel Schumacher's *Batman Forever* (1995) – featuring Val Kilmer as Batman, Jim Carrey as 'The Riddler', Nicole Kidman as love interest Dr Chase Meridian, Chris O'Donnell (*Scent of a Woman*) as Robin, and (despite the casting of Billy Dee Williams as Harvey Dent in *Batman*) Tommy Lee Jones as Harvey Dent/'Two-Face' – bounced back, with a $52.7 million opening weekend and a worldwide gross of $333 million, but the same director's *Batman and Robin* (1997) – with George Clooney as Batman, Arnold Schwarzenegger as 'Mr Freeze', Uma Thurman as 'Poison Ivy', Chris O'Donnell returning as Robin and Alicia Silverstone as 'Batgirl' – effectively put the franchise on hiatus, its $42.87 million opening weekend and $237 million worldwide gross causing Warner Bros to go back to the drawing board, despite the fact that Clooney technically remains under contract for two further films.

In the meantime, Batman flew high in a highly stylised and equally successful TV show, *Batman: The Animated Series*, which amassed 85 half-hour episodes between 1992 and 1995, and spawned several feature-length spin-offs – *Batman: Mask of the Phantasm* (1995), *Batman & Mr Freeze: SubZero* (1998), *The Batman/Superman Movie* (1998), *Batman Beyond: The Movie* (1999), *Batman Beyond: Return of The Joker* (2000) and *Batman: The Mystery of the Batwoman* (2003) – and no fewer than four sister series, *Batman: Gotham Knights*, a.k.a. *The New Batman Adventures* (1997–1999), *The New Batman/Superman Adventures* (1997–2000), the futuristic *Batman Beyond* (1999–2001), and *Justice League* (2001). In October 2002, Batman returned to live action television for the first time since 1968 in The WB's short-lived series *Birds of Prey*.

FUTURE INCARNATIONS: Following the lukewarm public reception of *Batman and Robin*, Warner Bros licked its wounds and trod cautiously towards a fifth Batman film. It was not until the summer of 1999, in the wake of the success of Darren Aronofsky's π that the studio asked Aronofsky how he might approach the franchise. 'I told them I'd cast Clint Eastwood as Batman, and shoot it in Tokyo,' Aronofsky says with a grin, although the writer–director subsequently opted to collaborate with Frank Miller on a script adaptation of Miller's graphic novel, *Batman: Year One*. 'Which we did, and had a great time. Our take was to infuse the movie franchise with a dose of reality,' he adds. 'My pitch was "*Death Wish* meets *Batman*" or "*The French Connection* meets *Batman*." We tried to ask that eternal question: "What does it take for a real man to put on tights and fight crime?" Gordon for us was Frank Serpico; Wayne was Travis Bickle. I saw *Year One* as Serpico versus Travis Bickle.' Although the script was completed, Aronofsky says he is 'no longer developing the film'.

A similar fate befell a mooted big-screen version of the hit animated series *Batman Beyond*, which was set to be directed by Boaz Yakin, who scripted *The Punisher* movie and directed the surprise hit *Remember the Titans*. Although a script by *Batman Beyond* creators Paul Dini and Alan Burnett is widely rumoured to be in development at Warner Bros, little has been heard of the project since it was first proposed concurrently with *Batman: Year One*.

A far more likely prospect seemed to be a big-screen team-up of DC Comics' two biggest heroes in *Batman v Superman*. A script by Andrew Kevin Walker (*Se7en*), loosely based on the *World's Finest* comic strand, had Warner Bros excited enough to postpone its plan for a new stand-alone Superman film and a fifth *Batman* in order to fast-track *Batman v Superman* for a 2004 release, with Wolfgang Petersen (*The Perfect Storm*) at the helm. The project did not survive the departure of studio head Lorenzo di Bonaventura in later 2002, however, and in early 2003 it was confirmed that acclaimed British director Christopher Nolan (*Memento*, *Insomnia*) would hem the fifth *Batman* film, though no further details were announced. In the meantime, Warner Bros continued to develop its spin-off *Catwoman* film, scripted by John Rogers (*The Core*) and set to be directed by French visual effects veteran Pitof.

DVD AVAILABILITY: The only DVD edition currently available in the UK is a full-screen edition. Although the US equivalent has a larger picture format (1.85:1), neither edition preserves the 2.35:1 ratio of the original, nor contains any extra features.

FINAL ANALYSIS: Like its eponymous hero, Tim Burton's *Batman* seems to have a dual identity, an unsatisfying clash of its director's dark sensibilities and a studio's need to sell toys. The psychological make-up of the character is only explored in Keaton's pained expression, and although the film wisely steers clear of a lengthy origin story – choosing instead to cleverly challenge comic book mythology by having Bruce Wayne and Jack Napier the architects of each other's fate – some judicious editing would have served to speed the narrative pace; as it is, the story sags several times, and it is never clear quite what The Joker is up to.

Not that Nicholson is complaining. The Joker is clearly a role he was born to play, and he doesn't disappoint – though it doesn't hurt that his make-up and costume are supremely effective, and his dialogue is littered with terrific one-liners. Keaton, on the other hand, is far better as a bumbling, bashful Bruce Wayne than he is as Batman; this is arguably the fault of the restrictive Bat-suit, which gives his performance little room for movement, and of the large number of action scenes for which he is doubled by Carl Newman. Although Basinger looks good throughout, hers is a thankless role – she is there largely to be rescued by Batman, and the excellent Robert Wuhl is never given enough screen time to develop what initially promises to be an intriguing subplot: his and Vicki Vale's investigation of Batman's vigilantism.

The production itself looks like a million dollars – not a good thing, since it cost fifty times that sum. Although Anton Furst's masterful production design is one of the film's highlights, the studio's penny-pinching means that it is rarely fully exploited: the Batmobile seems unable to drive more than a few yards before it runs out of Gotham City set, and although Wayne Mansion and the Batcave are impressive, the city itself deserved to have a greater presence than it does. Overall, the film is never as good as Sam Hamm's script, and one can't escape the feeling that the film adds up to far less than the sum of its parts.

EXPERT WITNESS: 'While I was never a big comic book fan, I loved Batman: the split personality, the hidden person. It's a character I could relate to. Having those two sides, a light side and a dark one, and not being able to resolve them – that's a feeling that's not uncommon. So while I can see it's got a lot of Michael Keaton in it because he's actually doing it, I also see certain aspects of myself in the character. Otherwise, I wouldn't have been able to do it.' – **Tim Burton, Director**

Dick Tracy (1990)

(103 mins)

Produced and Directed by Warren Beatty
Written by Jim Cash and Jack Epps, Jr

Based on Characters Created by Chester Gould for the Dick Tracy® Comic Strip Distributed by Tribune Media Services, Inc.
Executive Producers Barrie M Osborne and Art Linson and Floyd Mutrux
Director of Photography Vittorio Storaro AIC, ASC
Production Designer Richard Sylbert
Editor Richard Marks
Co-Producer Jon Landau
Costume Designer Milena Canonero
Original Songs by Stephen Sondheim
Music by Danny Elfman
Casting by Jackie Burch

CAST: Warren Beatty (*Dick Tracy*), Charlie Korsmo (*Kid/'Dick Tracy Jr'*), Michael Donovan O'Donnell (*McGillicuddy*), Jim Wilkey (*'Stooge'*), Stig Eldred (*'Shoulders'*), Neil Summers (*'The Rodent'*), Chuck Hicks (*'The Brow'*), Lawrence Steven Meyers (*'Little Face'*), William Forsythe (*'Flattop'*), Ed O'Ross (*'Itchy'*), Glenn Headly (*Tess Trueheart*), Marvelee Cariago (*soprano*), Michael Gallup (*baritone*), Seymour Cassel (*Sam Catchum*), James Keane (*Pat Patton*), Charles Durning (*Chief Brandon*), Allen Garfield, John Schuck, Charles Fleischer (*reporters*), Madonna (*Breathless Mahoney*), Mandy Patinkin (*'88 Keys'*), Paul Sorvino (*'Lips' Manlis*), Robert Costanzo (*Lips' bodyguard*), Jack Kehoe (*customer at raid*), Marshall Bell (*Lips' cop*), Michael G Hagerty (*doorman*), Lew Horn (*'Lefty' Moriarty*), Arthur Malet (*diner patron*), Tom Signorelli (*Mike*), Tony Epper (*Steve the tramp*), Al Pacino (*'Big Boy' Caprice*), James Tolkan (*'Numbers'*), RG Armstrong (*'Pruneface'*), Dustin Hoffman (*'Mumbles'*), Kathy Bates (*Mrs Green*), Jack Goode Jr, Ray Stoddard (*lab technicians*), Dick van Dyke (*District Attorney Fletcher*), Hamilton Camp (*store clerk*), Ed McCready, Colm Meaney (*cops at Tess'*), Catherine O'Hara (*Texle Garcia*), Henry Silva (*'Influence'*), Robert Beecher (*'Ribs' Mocca*), James Caan (*Spaldoni*), Bert Remsen (*bartender*), Frank Campabella (*Judge Harper*), Sharmagne Leland-St John, Bing Russell (*club patrons*), Michael J Pollard (*'Bug' Bailey*), Tom Finnegan (*uniform cop at Ritz*), Billy Clevenger (*newspaper vendor*), Ned Claflin, John Moschitta Jr, Neil Ross, Walker Edmiston (*radio announcers*), Estelle Parsons (*Mrs Trueheart*), Ian Wolfe (*forger*), Mary Woronov (*welfare person*), Henry Jones (*night clerk*), Mike Mazurki (*old man at hotel*), Rita Bland, Lada Boder, Dee Hengstler, Liz Imperio, Michelle Johnston, Karyne Ortega, Karen Russell (*dancers*)

TITLE SEQUENCE: After a series of white titles on black, a radio sits at the centre of a red table, intoning a litany of recent crimes as a hand takes several items – wristwatch, badge, gun – from the table: 'Gangland enforcers broke the arms of an elderly news vendor this afternoon when he refused to share his week's receipts with them. Stacks of newspapers were tossed in the gutter as the thugs wrecked the business and made their getaway. Lunchtime crowds were paralysed by the suddenness of the crime. Not a hand was raised in protest.' The title appears in yellow comic book lettering against the red background, dissolving through to reveal a bright yellow hat, taken by the same hand. A figure is seen through a window, wearing the yellow hat and a matching trenchcoat, as cast names begin to appear on screen (in order of appearance, with each name accompanied by that of their character) and the newscaster continues: 'Organised crime is their name. What appeared to be organised hoods shattered the kneecaps of the beloved operator of a shoeshine parlour today as horrified customers looked on. The bootblack would not give up his receipts, and paid dearly for his failure to surrender to gang demands.' The camera pans up over a striking view of the city. 'A mother of four unable to pay a gambling debt lies dead tonight. Gangland thugs let her expire in a pool of blood as they helped themselves to the contents of a cash register inside the luncheonette . . .' The announcer's voice fades out as the camera finally comes to rest on a young street urchin in an alleyway, who finds half a sandwich in a litter bin, and then ducks into a building when he is spotted by a policeman. Inside the building, he watches a group of colourful characters, each with a deformed face, playing poker – until a car bursts through the door, felling several of the poker players in a hail of gunfire. As the final credit appears on screen, one of the assailants machine-guns a message on the wall.

SYNOPSIS: At an illegal card game, a street urchin witnesses the massacre of a group of mobsters by Flattop, one of the hoods on the pay roll of Big Boy Caprice, whose crime syndicate is taking over small businesses in the city – with extreme vengeance. Detective Dick Tracy later catches the urchin – who calls himself 'Kid' – in an act of petty theft, and after rescuing him from his ruthless guardian, temporarily adopts him with the help of girlfriend Tess Trueheart. Meanwhile, after coercing Lips Manlis into signing over the deed to Club Ritz, Caprice has him killed and steals his girlfriend, sultry singer Breathless Mahoney. His next move is to try to bring the local crime denizens – including Pruneface, Ribs Mocca, Mumbles, Itchy and Numbers – together under his leadership, and when one of them refuses, he meets an untimely demise. Tracy is on the case, but without Breathless' testimony, he cannot prove that Caprice was behind the crimes – even when Caprice tries to have him killed after Tracy refuses to accept a bribe. Rescued by the kid, Tracy leads a seemingly unsuccessful raid on Club Ritz, but rather than looking for evidence of gambling, he has one of his men plant a bug in a backroom, listening in on Caprice's plans. The resultant raids on his illegal enterprises all but wipe out his criminal empire, but when Caprice discovers the listening device, he uses it to lure Tracy to the warehouse where he had Lips killed; before Caprice's men can kill him, however, a faceless figure (the 'Blank') steps out of the shadows and saves Tracy. Meanwhile, Tess catches Tracy in a clinch with Breathless, and leaves town. She subsequently has a change of heart, but before she can tell Tracy, she is kidnapped by the Blank. Tracy receives a message to come to the greenhouse where she works, but it's another trap: Tracy is drugged by the Blank and framed for the murder of corrupt district attorney Fletcher. Caprice is back in business, but he too has been framed – for Tess's kidnapping, a federal offence, and one of the few crimes he didn't commit. Sprung from jail by his colleagues, Tracy sets out to rescue Tess, confronts Caprice, who shoots the Blank before falling to his death. Beneath the faceless figure's mask, Tracy is shocked to find Breathless Mahoney, who kisses him . . . and breathes her last. Later, in the middle of a marriage proposal to Tess, Tracy is interrupted by a robbery in progress, and takes off with the kid – now calling himself 'Dick Tracy Jr' – in tow.

ORIGINS: Initially billed as 'Plainclothes Tracy', the steel-eyed, hook-nosed, two-fisted 'tec who would become 'America's most famous detective' debuted in the 'funny pages' of the Sunday edition of the *Detroit Mirror* on 4 October 1931. With America in the grip of the Depression and organised crime at its peak, Gould felt that the country needed a two-fisted, incorruptible Eliot Ness-type hero to combat crime. 'I decided that if the police couldn't catch the gangsters, I'd create a fellow who could,' Gould explained. The *Chicago Tribune* picked up the strip in 1932, and continued to publish it (and syndicate it, through Tribune Media Services) through its life.

In 1977, crime writer Max Allan Collins – who would later write the graphic novel *Road to Perdition* – took over the writing of the Dick Tracy newspaper strip. 'Dick Tracy was my first enthusiasm as a kid, my first pop-culture obsession,' Collins explains. 'I read the comic book reprints starting at age seven. I was drawing Tracy and the villains, and my mom shipped off some of my stuff to Chester Gould, who sent me a lovely drawing of Tracy on my eighth birthday, saying I drew his picture better than anyone else my age.' Although Collins' enthusiasm for the two-fisted 'tec cooled as he grew older, when he sold his own first crime novel in 1972, he wrote to Gould thanking him for his inspiration and encouragement, and the pair began a correspondence and ultimately a friendship, visiting each other on many occasions. 'Strangely enough, my friendship with Chet had nothing to do with my getting the *Tracy* job.

The editors at the *Tribune* had decided Chet's increasingly idosyncratic stories were killing the strip; they made him an offer that essentially gave him more *not* to do the strip than to do it. Chet, capitalist that he was, foolishly gave up his "baby" because of those tempting terms.' Collins was among half a dozen crime and mystery writers put forward for the job. 'When I got the call from the *Trib*, I reread the last several years of *Tracy* and did the synopsis, literally overnight, sending it to the editors special delivery. They were as impressed with my speed as with my talent, I think.' Collins had the job, and his synopsis – a story involving Flattop's daughter 'Angeltop' – became his first continuity. 'I was twenty-four or twenty-five.

'My feeling was that Dick Tracy was the classic hard-boiled cop character, that everyone from *Dragnet*'s Joe Friday to Fleming's James Bond was indebted to him. Any detective that ever wore a trenchcoat and snapbrim fedora does so because Tracy did it first. Chet created the iconic American tough detective. And Chet, at his best – in the thirties, forties and early fifties – was an incredible writer, a great hard-boiled practitioner. But in the sixties and after, Chet got quirky – even for Chet – and in particular brought a wacky science-fiction approach to the strip, with the "Moon Maid" and magnetic spaceships and [other] stuff that didn't belong in *Tracy*, and which the fans hated. Over a period of about ten years, the strip lost papers, disastrously. He also had a habit of using villains only once – killing them dead, dead, dead at the end of a story – and would abandon wonderful recurring characters. My approach was to dump the science-fiction aspect (other than the gadgets like the two-way wrist radio and its descendents) and bring back great Gould villains like "Pruneface" and supporting characters like Vitamin Flintheart; my own villains were strongly in the Gould tradition, like "Torcher", "Putty Puss" and "Snake Eyes". One of the first things I did was blow Moon Maid up in a car. Fans applauded.

'[Chet] was thrilled that I would be his successor, and for several years, he consulted with me – I would call him on a weekly basis, and frequently more often than that.'

Unfortunately, Gould's acrimonious relationship with the strip's long-time artist, Rick Fletcher, led him to bad-mouth the strip to a reporter. Collins responded by having Gould's name removed. 'How ironic that I, of all people, would be the one to remove Chester Gould's name from the byline of that comic strip,' Collins says. 'Several years later, a new editor came into the *Tribune* and fired me, by the way – largely because he was a jerk and I had the bad sense to tell him so. I take perverse pride in being, to my knowledge, the only writer ever fired off a major comic strip for insubordination. I'm very proud of my fifteen years on *Tracy*,' he concludes, 'though getting fired opened the door to much better things – including *Road to Perdition*.' Following Rick Fletcher's death in 1983, Pulitzer Prize-winning editorial cartoonist Dick Locher began drawing the strip, written by Michael Kilian. Their collaboration continues to this day.

PREVIOUS INCARNATIONS: Dick Tracy made his first appearance outside of newspaper strips in an eponymous radio serial, which ran from 1935 to 1948. In 1937, Ralph Byrd portrayed the detective in a fifteen-chapter Republic serial entitled *Dick Tracy*, followed by three further serials: *Dick Tracy Returns* (1938), *Dick Tracy's G-Men* (1939), *Dick Tracy vs Crime Inc* (1941). A series of B-grade features followed, with Morgan Conway in the title role of *Dick Tracy* (1945), *Dick Tracy vs Cueball* (1946), before Ralph Byrd returned to the role for *Dick Tracy's Dilemma* (1947) and *Dick Tracy Meets Gruesome* (1947), co-starring Boris Karloff. Tracy's next screen outing was a short-lived television show (1951–1952), again starring Ralph Byrd; then, in 1960, UPA began producing a series of five-minute TV cartoons, but, like the brief 1971 cartoon revival, neither proved successful. Ray McDonnell donned the snapbrim fedora and trenchcoat for a 1967 pilot for a live-action *Dick Tracy* TV show. And somewhere along the way – specifically, in 1946 – a Looney Tunes parody entitled *Duck Twacy* pitted Daffy Duck against such Tracy-inspired villains as 'Jukebox Jaw', 'Pumpkin Head' and 'Neon Noodle'.

DEVELOPMENT: Producers Art Linson and Floyd Mutrux bought the rights to the Dick Tracy comic strip in 1980, and took the property to Paramount Pictures, where Jeffrey Katzenberg was head of production. Paramount began developing screenplays, pencilled in Steven Spielberg as a possible director, and finally brought in Universal as a production partner. Universal put John Landis forward as a candidate for director, courted Clint Eastwood for the title role, and commissioned *Top Gun* screenwriters Jim Cash and Jack Epps Jr to pen the screenplay. 'Before we were brought on, there were several failed scripts at Universal,' says Epps, 'then it went dormant, but John Landis was interested in *Dick Tracy*, and he brought us in to write it. Our orders from John were to do the movie about Big Boy Caprice and do it in a thirties atmosphere.' Epps sat down and read every comic strip from 1930 to 1957. 'There were all these great characters, and I said I'm just gonna put them all in one movie. So we wrote two drafts for John Landis.' Max Allan Collins, then writer of the *Dick Tracy* comic strip, remembers reading one of them. 'It was terrible,' he says. 'The only positive thing about it was a thirties setting and lots of great villains, but the story was paper-thin and it was uncomfortably campy. I advised the syndicate that this script would not do the strip any favours. The editor there agreed with me.' Landis left the project following an on-set accident on *Twilight Zone:*

The Movie, in which actor Vic Morrow was killed. 'John would have been a great choice for it,' says Epps, 'because he would have done it very "pop", much wilder and zany and far afield. At that point Walter Hill came on board with Joel Silver as producer, so we did a draft for them. The story was pretty much the same with Big Boy and the Blank and Breathless Mahoney, but Walter took the script and focused it and threw out a lot of extraneous things and really made it a *Tracy* draft.'

While Walter Hill was finishing *Streets of Fire*, pre-production had progressed as far as set building, and Hill had met with his ideal Dick Tracy, Warren Beatty. 'I think it came all the way down to whether Warren would get to look at dailies, which Walter didn't believe in,' says Epps. 'So I think that threw the kibosh on the deal.' Beatty also reportedly wanted $5 million plus fifteen per cent of the gross – a deal which Universal refused to accept. Hill and Beatty left the project, which Paramount then began developing as a lower budget version with actor-turned-director Richard Benjamin (*Racing with the Moon*). 'We did a couple of drafts with Dick Benjamin,' Epps adds, 'but the Walter Hill draft was still pretty much the draft . . . but the studio wasn't really enthused, and Dick went off to do a thirties movie with Clint Eastwood [*City Heat*]. I wouldn't be surprised if Dick went over to see Clint about *Dick Tracy*, and Clint said, "Hey, I've got this movie ready to go right now, why don't you do this?" It easily could have been that way.'

Then, in 1985, the rights lapsed, and Warren Beatty – whose interest in the project had not waned – swooped in to pick them up himself. In a rare interview with Barbara Walters, Beatty reasoned as follows: 'It's a naive kind of subject and as a kid I had a lot of affection for the strip, and the people are straightforward so I thought it would be fun to make a picture that . . . dealt in primary emotions and primary colours . . . There's a sweetness to Dick Tracy that I always kind of liked.' To Mike Bonifer, he added: 'There's something quaint about 1939/1940 crime fighting – the wrist radio, bugging a room with a huge microphone. I would just say that something about it moved me. I would say that pre-war, just on the brink of war, there probably was a *naiveté* about America in that period, about good and evil, law and order. It's just before America took over. The last days of innocence. Just before our loss of innocence as a country.'

When Katzenberg moved to Disney, the project resurfaced with Beatty attached as both star and director. 'It never occurred to me to direct the movie,' Beatty admitted, 'but finally, like most of the movies that I direct, when the time comes to do it, I just do it because it's easier than going through what I'd have to go through to get somebody else to do it.' Beatty's reputation for directorial profligacy – notably with the critically acclaimed *Reds*, a $40 million box office failure – did not sit well with the Disney ethos of bringing films in on time and on budget, however; as a result, a unique deal was struck whereby any budget overruns would be deducted from Beatty's fee as producer, director and star. 'I really think that he looked to us to bring our discipline, our self-imposed controls that have worked so effectively for us, to the film,' Katzenberg told *Empire* magazine. 'I think Warren wanted to prove to himself, and maybe the rest of the world, that he could take the responsibility and bring the movie in for a price.'

At this point, Max Allan Collins began lobbying to write the novelisation. 'I had never done a movie novelisation before, but this was 1990, and I'd been the writer of the strip since 1977, and my attitude was proprietary.' Besides, he adds, 'as a mystery novelist, I hated the idea that anyone else would write a *Tracy* novel.' Collins' wish was granted, and he was invited aboard as a consultant/Dick Tracy expert. Now all he had to do was wait for the new draft of the script from Bo Goldman (*Melvin and Howard*), the Academy Award®-winning scriptwriter whom Beatty had brought onto the project. 'Anyway, I'm eagerly awaiting the new script, to begin the novel – word was that a real Hollywood hotshot screenwriter had ghosted a great draft – and the script arrives in the mail . . . and it's the same lousy Cash and Epps script! Almost nothing had changed!'

CASTING: Almost every leading man of the 1980s – including Clint Eastwood, Harrison Ford, Richard Gere, Tom Selleck and Mel Gibson – had been mentioned in connection with Dick Tracy during development, but it was Warren Beatty, who first expressed interest in the role in 1983, who would ultimately win it. At the time, Warren Beatty was dating singer/actress/superstar Madonna, and it came as no surprise that, in true Hollywood tradition, the producer's girlfriend wound up in the picture, as nightclub singer Breathless Mahoney. 'I think she's terrific,' Beatty told Barbara Walters. 'I think I'm very lucky to have her in that movie. She's got energy, she has a kind of generosity of spirit and she works harder than anybody that I know, and she's gifted.' Said Madonna, 'I wanted to work with Warren and all the other actors who were doing it. I thought the script was very funny,' she added. 'Style's a big thing for me, and I just thought it was going to be a really original piece of work. Something different.'

Beatty filled out the rest of the supporting cast with an extraordinary ensemble of friends with famous faces – including Al Pacino, Dustin Hoffman, James Caan and Michael J Pollard – most of which Beatty then duly hid behind some of the most remarkable make-up ever put on film. One thing was for certain, however: there was no way Disney was going to allow Beatty to hide his own famous features behind prosthetic make-up; besides, as Beatty said, 'nobody's going to look like [the comic strip] Dick Tracy and occupy the audience in the way the character needs to in this movie. It's very hard to put those grotesque make-ups onto Dick Tracy or Tess Trueheart or The Kid – it is just too distracting. The make-up runs away with it. In the characters of Flattop, Pruneface, Big Boy – that's something else. That's where it works.'

PRODUCTION: Early in the development of *Dick Tracy*, Beatty decided to make the film using a palette limited to just seven colours – primarily red, green, blue and yellow – to evoke the film's comic book origins; furthermore each of the colours was to be exactly the same shade, so that every yellow is the same yellow, every red the same red, etc. 'To make movies is generally to create a reality, to make it look real,' Beatty explained. 'And this picture's sort of a style. The idea of having the primary colours match up, the idea of having things not look totally real, was hard for people to get. And everybody on the picture had difficulty with that. Because everybody's very good.' Two individuals would be key to realising his unique vision: production designer Richard Sylbert (*Chinatown*, *The Manchurian Candidate*), who had served as production designer on Beatty's directorial debut, *Reds*; and cinematographer Vittorio Storaro (*Apocalypse Now*), who had won his second Academy Award® for Beatty's *Reds* (though he had since photographed the disastrous Beatty–Dustin Hoffman flop *Ishtar*), and a third for his luminous photography of Bernardo Bertolucci's *The Last Emperor*. *Dick Tracy* would earn him his fourth nomination. 'He loves to get these different forces out on the table,' executive producer Barrie M Osborne said of Beatty. 'You've got very outspoken people on this film. He loves to get Dick Sylbert and Vittorio together, and they confront each other over their different ideas, and out of that he gets a consensus. He has his own ideas, too, and he'll use that debate to test those ideas, to get what he wants.'

Storaro and Sylbert provided *Dick Tracy* with one of the greatest challenges of their long careers. 'All the things that Vittorio, Milena [Canonero, costume designer] and myself had done through the years got us nowhere, except that your own instinct is still your instinct,' said Sylbert. For Storaro, the limited colour palette was the most challenging aspect of the production. 'These are not the kind of colours the audience is used to seeing,' Storaro noted. 'These are much more dramatic in strength, in saturation. [Besides,] it's not only the palette of the colour, it's the usage of the colour.' Colour was not the only area in which the film-makers tried to evoke the comic strip, however. 'Comic book art is usually done with very simple and primitive ideas and emotions,' he theorised. 'We were trying to use elements from the original Chester Gould drawings. One of the elements is that the story is usually told in vignette, so what we tried to do is never move the camera at all. *Never.* Try to make everything work into the frame.'

Principal photography began at Universal Studios in California on 2 February 1989, lasting 85 days, spanning 53 interior sets and 25 exterior backlot sets, and often encompassing dozens of takes of every scene. 'He's a perfectionist,' Madonna said of Beatty's directorial style. 'You can't get away with anything with him. In terms of acting, he's relentless, and if it takes a hundred takes to get it, then you're going to do a hundred takes. He's very generous, in that you can try whatever you want with him. But his favourite thing to do is to do so many takes that you forget everything you planned on doing, and you're completely broken down, and then you just do it without thinking, and that's usually your best stuff.'

As filming continued in Los Angeles, Collins continued to work on his novelisation, loosely based on an 'improved and corrected' script. Disney objected to Collins' changes however, and rejected the manuscript. 'I wound up doing an eleventh hour rewrite that was more faithful to the screenplay, even while I made it much more consistent with the strip and put Vitamin Flintheart in, for example, and fixed as many plot holes as I could. Disney didn't like this version, either, but we negotiated that if Beatty's people accepted it, Disney would, too – they wanted to have *some* book out there, after all.' As it turned out, Beatty's people loved it – so much so that executive producer Barrie Osborne began making regular calls to Collins, asking why he had made this or that change. 'For example, Osborne wanted to know why I had softened a scene in which Mrs Trueheart tries to convince her daughter Tess to dump Dick Tracy.' Collins explained that, as any true fan would know, Mrs Trueheart would more likely defend Tracy because, in the very first episode of the newspaper strip, Dick Tracy had avenged the death of her husband, Tess' father. 'When I told Osborne this, there was a long silence at the other end of the phone. They ended up reshooting the scene, my way.' Months later, at the world premiere, Osborne took Collins aside and told him that the novelisation had provided them with the solutions to many script problems, and that some of his dialogue had been used in 'ADR,' the post-production process during which additional dialogue lines can be recorded and added to the soundtrack. 'Sure enough,' says Collins, 'a number of my lines turned up in the movie. So *Dick Tracy* is the only movie that is based (in part, anyway) on its own novelisation!'

COSTUME FITTING: Costume designer Milena Canonero had already won two Academy Awards® (for *Barry Lyndon* and *Chariots of Fire*) and been nominated for two more (for *Out of Africa* and *Tucker: The Man and His Dream*) by the time she was hired by Beatty to create the unforgettable costumes for *Dick Tracy* – an endeavour which would earn her yet another nomination. 'Warren is very aware that sometimes a look can carry the film away from the audience, so you have to balance that,' Canonero noted. 'On the other hand, this film was also very much about a look. The characters are stereotypes, so their originality depended on how we presented them. If you look at the original colour comic strips, they're simplistic,' she added. 'The ones from 1930 to the early 1940s use four, five, sometimes six colours. I tried to make the characters a little more interesting in the hair, the make-up, the ties – however I could.' According to Madonna, getting the right look for Breathless Mahoney didn't come easily. 'It was trial and error,' she said. 'I felt like a mannequin on wheels for a while, because, first of all, I had finally grown my hair out, and it was long and dark, and they couldn't decide if they should make Breathless blonde or brunette. So I did a screen test in a blonde wig and of course Vittorio Storaro started "oohing" and "aahing", so that was really it.'

MUSIC: Danny Elfman had recently won acclaim for his *Batman* score, and seemed an obvious choice to compose the music for *Dick Tracy*. Beatty, like Breathless Mahoney, wanted 'more, more, *more!*' however, asking acclaimed songwriter Stephen Sondheim – whose credits included the stage musicals *Sweeney Todd* and *Sunday in the Park with George* – to pen several new songs for Madonna to sing. As a result, no fewer than three soundtrack albums were released to tie in with the film: one of Sondheim's songs, one of Elfman's music, and a stand-alone Madonna album called *I'm Breathless*. It is not difficult to guess which was the most popular.

CLASSIC QUOTES:
Sam Catchum: 'Calling Dick Tracy! Calling Dick Tracy!'
Dick Tracy: 'I'm on my way!'

Big Boy Caprice: 'Around me, if a woman don't wear mink, she don't wear nothin'.'
Breathless: 'Well I look good both ways.'

Dick Tracy: 'No grief for Lips?'
Breathless: 'I'm wearing black underwear.'
Dick Tracy: 'You know it's legal for me to take you down to the station and sweat it out of you under the lights.'
Breathless: 'I sweat a lot better in the dark.'

Breathless: 'I know how you feel. You don't know whether you wanna hit me or kiss me. I get a lot of that.'

Breathless: 'I was beginning to wonder what a girl had to do to get arrested.'
Dick Tracy: 'Wearing that dress is a step in the right direction.'

Big Boy Caprice: 'You big dumb Dick!'

DELETED SCENES: The bizarre relationship between the film and the novelisation (see above) led to another curious anomaly: since the novelisation was scheduled to be published before the film opened, Disney insisted that Collins leave out the identity of the faceless figure: 'Disney had this idea that the ending – Breathless (Madonna) turning out to be "the Blank" – was this huge surprise; of course, it was a painfully obvious twist, [and] most people had it figured out in the credits. Nonetheless, in the last few days before we went to press with the novelisation, I was told that the ending had to be omitted. Let me repeat that: *the ending had to be omitted*. I had to leave out of my mystery novel the identity of the Blank. I argued about this till my face turned blue – I even had a phone call with Jeffrey Katzenberg on the subject. I tried sneaky things, like having the dying character say, " 'I'm sorry,' the Blank said breathlessly", or some nonsense.' It was no use. A compromise was finally reached whereby the complete book, including the ending, would be published in any printings following the movie's opening – a plan which, for Collins, backfired somewhat as the book went through seven printings and sold almost one million copies before the film's premiere. As a result, says Collins, 'only a very small eighth printing – about thirty thousand copies – is complete, ending and all. This is another unique, ironic honour: no mystery writer ever sold more copies of a mystery that had no solution.' Even more bizarrely, the official *Dick Tracy* colouring book, also released before the film, featured a panel in which the identity of the Blank was revealed.

POSTERS: *Dick Tracy*'s poster campaign was as striking as the film itself, and employed an even more limited three-colour palette. Like *Batman* the previous year, the teaser poster had no title; instead, a red ring against a black background encircled a stylised hand-drawn image of Beatty as Tracy, sporting his obligatory yellow hat and coat and red striped necktie, and speaking into his wrist radio. The regular poster featured another hand-drawn image, this time a full-length view of Tracy (a more recognisable Warren Beatty) walking through a cityscape carrying a tommy gun, the kid hurrying to catch up.

TAG-LINE: 'I'm On My Way.'

WHAT THE PAPERS SAID: Most critics saw *Dick Tracy* as a victory of style over substance, with *Variety* opining that, 'though it looks ravishing, Warren Beatty's long-time pet project is a curiously remote, uninvolving film'. Nevertheless, it went on to say that 'Beatty and his collaborators have created a boldly stylised 1930s urban milieu that captures the comic strip's quirky, angled mood, while dazzling the eye with deep primary colours.' In the *Chicago Sun-Times*, Roger Ebert declared *Dick Tracy* 'a masterpiece of studio artificiality, of matt drawings and miniatures and optical effects. It creates a world that never could be . . . Beatty's decision to shoot *Dick Tracy* only in the seven basic colours of comic strips is a good one,' he added, 'because this is a movie about creatures of the imagination, about people who live in rooms where every table lamp looks like a Table Lamp and every picture on the wall represents only a Picture on the Wall . . . This is a movie in which every frame contains some kind of artificial effect. An entire world has been built here, away from the daylight and the realism of ordinary city streets.' Overall, he wrote, 'It is one of the most original and visionary fantasies I've seen on a screen.' In the UK, *Time Out*'s Colette Maud was equally enthusiastic, praising Beatty's 'wonderfully imaginative and carefully moderated' colour and the 'pleasing restraint' evident in Beatty's willingness to cede the spotlight to his supporting cast. 'A spectacular movie whose technical achievements – notably the sharp editing – will surely provide a gauge by which subsequent comic strip films are judged.'

BOX OFFICE: Released worldwide in the summer of 1990, *Dick Tracy* not only had a hard act to follow – 1989's record-breaking *Batman* – but a huge amount of competition, not only from blockbusters like *Total Recall*, *Arachnophobia* and *Days of Thunder* but from an unprecedented number of hotly-anticipated sequels: *Die Hard 2: Die Harder*, *Another 48 Hrs*, *Back to the Future III*, *RoboCop 2* and *Gremlins 2: The New Batch*. Nevertheless, Disney's huge marketing push – a reported $54 million, $9 million more than the declared cost of the film – and an effective publicity and promotional campaign gave *Dick Tracy* a satisfactory opening weekend ($22.5 million), and the film went on to break the $100 million mark, grossing $103 million overall.

AWARDS: At the Academy Awards®, *Dick Tracy* received seven nominations, by far the largest number for a comic book adaptation. Although beaten in four categories – Best Supporting Actor (Al Pacino), Best Cinematography, Best Costume Design, and Best Sound – the film took home three awards, for Best Make-up, Best Art Direction – Set Decoration and Best Song, for Stephen Sondheim's 'Sooner or Later (I Always Get My Man)'. *Dick Tracy* also received seven nominations for the BAFTA awards, and although Pacino, costume designer Milena Canonero and the sound team lost out again – along with the visual effects team and editor Richard Marks – production designer Richard Sylbert and make-up artists John Caglione Jr and Doug Drexler both took home awards. None of the film's four Golden Globe nominations – Best Motion Picture (Comedy/Musical), Best Supporting Actor (Pacino again) and Best Original Song ('Sooner or Later (I Always Get My Man)' and 'What Can You Lose?') – were converted into awards, a fate which also befell Storaro at the award ceremonies for both the American and British Society of Cinematographers.

CONTROVERSY: Following Beatty's acquisition of the rights to Dick Tracy, producers Art Linson and Floyd Mutrux launched a lawsuit against him, alleging that they were owed profit participation from the film.

TRIVIA: Warren Beatty was said to be so concerned about how his image would be drawn in the official comic book adaptation of the film that only two views of him (side and front) were ever approved. Thus, artist Kyle Baker had those two views of Beatty photocopied and used them repeatedly throughout.

Dick Tracy was the first film to use digital sound.

DVD AVAILABILITY: In the UK (Region 2) a widescreen (1.85:1) format, Dolby 5.1 transfer of *Dick Tracy* is available; its US (Region 1) equivalent contains a fullscreen transfer. Both discs are devoid of extras.

FINAL ANALYSIS: Rarely has the distance between visual splendour and dramatic poverty been as evident as in Warren Beatty's *Dick Tracy*, a deeply flawed masterwork of style over substance which never recovers from its clunking script and largely dismal performances (Pacino is the exception), despite the best efforts of production designer Richard Sylbert, cinematographer Vittorio Storaro and costume designer Milena Canonero. Anyone who accuses Beatty of vanity overlooks the fact that he is the most generous of performers in *Dick Tracy*, not least in his characterisation of Tracy himself as someone who, despite his supposedly heroic status, seems constantly to need rescuing by supporting characters. While many of Beatty's choices as director–producer are laudable, his decision to include Sondheim show tunes, most of which he gives to an outclassed Madonna to underperform, is a curious one, lending the already set-bound film the air of a stage musical which, perhaps, might yet be its best chance for a revival, thanks to the songs, outrageous costumes, stylised sets and even – for goodness' sake – an orphaned kid in a flat cap. If only Beatty's Tracy and the leaden dialogue were as colourful as the film they inhabit, *Dick Tracy* might live up to its considerable ambition, instead of being a magnificent failure which ultimately has little to recommend it beyond its startling visuals.

EXPERT WITNESS: 'While the basic script remains awful, the movie is, in its special way, wonderful. Beatty did a great job assembling a team that really brought comics and *Tracy* to life. Beatty's also a better Tracy than he's cracked up to be, but the important thing is the look of it and the villains. Plus the Sondheim music is fabulous. Still, as one critic said, it's like a lovely restored period automobile – [but] when you raise the hood, there's no engine.' – **Max Allan Collins, Dick Tracy Newspaper Strip Writer**

Teenage Mutant Ninja Turtles (1990)

(93 minutes)

Directed by Steve Barron
Produced by Kim Dawson, Simon Fields and David Chan
Story by Bobby Herbeck
Screenplay by Todd W Langen and Bobby Herbeck
Based on Characters Created by Kevin Eastman and Peter Laird
Co-Producer Graham Cottle
Executive Producer Raymond Chow
Executive in Charge of Production Thomas K Gray
Director of Photography John Frenner
Production Designer Roy Forge Smith
Music by John Du Prez
Edited by William Gordean ACE, Sally Menke and James Symons
Exclusively Licensed by Surge Licensing, Inc.
Casting by Lynn Kressel

CAST: Judith Hoag (*April O'Neil*), Elias Koteas (*Casey Jones*), Raymond Serra (*Chief Sterns*), Michael Turney (*Dan 'Danny' Pennington*), James Saito (*Oroko Saki/'The Shredder'*), Jay Patterson (*Charles Pennington*), Toshishiro Obata (*Master Tatsu*), David Forman (*Leonardo/gang member*), Michelan Sisti (*Michelangelo/pizza man*), Leif Tilden (*Donatello/Foot messenger*), Sam Rockwell (*head thug*), Kitty Fitzgibbon (*June*), Louis Cantarini (*cab driver*), Joseph D'Onofrio, John Ward (*movie hoodlums*), Ju Yu (*Shinsho*), Cassandra Ward-Freeman (*Charles' secretary*), Mark Jeffrey Miller (*technician*), John Rogers (*new recruit*), Tae Park (*talkative Foot #1*), Kenn Troum (*talkative Foot #2*), Robert Haskell (*tall teen*), Winston Hemingway, Joe Inscoe (*police officers*), Robbie Rist (*Michelangelo's voice*), Joshua Bo Lozoff (*beaten teen*), Brian Tochi (*Leonardo's voice*), Kevin Clash (*Splinter's voice*), David McCharen (*voice of Oroko Saki/'The Shredder'*), Michael McConnohie (*Master Tatsu's voice*), Corey Feldman (*Donatello's voice*)

UNCREDITED CAST: Josh Pais (*Raphael/Raphael's voice/man in cab*)

TITLE SEQUENCE: New York City is in the grip of a 'silent crime wave' of petty thefts, purse snatching and burglary, with no reliable witnesses. Channel 3 Eyewitness News reporter April O'Neil believes that the crimes are connected, but the police seem powerless to stop the crime wave. Leaving the studio one night, April is set upon by robbers, but before they know what's hit them, they are tied up and left for the police to find. From beneath a manhole, eyes wrapped in a red bandanna watch the police take the suspects away – while April finds a ninja weapon one of the assailants left behind. Titles begin as the assailants – Teenage Mutant Ninja Turtles – return to their sewer dwelling, where they report their success to their *sensei*, a giant rat named Splinter.

SYNOPSIS: Raphael goes out to a movie, and on the way home stops two thieves trying to steal a woman's purse – and then a masked vigilante named Casey Jones trying to beat them for it. Splinter chides him for his reckless nature. Meanwhile, against the advice of her boss, Charles Pennington, April questions the chief of police about a crime organisation known as 'The Foot Clan'. Their leader, Shredder, watches, calling on his minions to find and silence her. Raphael watches too – he thinks he's in love – and when the Foot Clan attempt to silence her, he rescues April and takes her back to the Turtles' lair. When she comes to, Splinter explains their background: fifteen years ago, Splinter was scavenging in a sewer when he found four baby turtles playing in a broken canister of green ooze. As they grew in size, Splinter taught them in the ways of ninjitsu, which he had learned from his master Yoshi. The Turtles take a shell-shocked April home, but when they return to their sewer, Splinter is gone. April takes the Turtles in while they try to figure out what happened to their friend and mentor. Meanwhile, Charles is having trouble with his son Danny, who is part of Shredder's gang of young hoodlums, responsible for the recent wave of street crime. With Danny's help, Shredder's goons crash April's pad and a ninja battle with the Turtles ensues, interrupted by Casey Jones, who helps April and the Turtles escape to safety – April's old family home, where Casey tells her that she's been fired. The Turtles fret about Splinter, who is chained in a dungeon being interrogated by Shredder. The Turtles return to their sewer home, where they find Danny hiding. He later returns to Splinter, who tells him that the symbol on his bandanna is that of the man who killed his master, Yoshi. Shredder confronts Danny, finds a drawing of one of the Turtles on him, and orders Splinter to be killed. Danny has a change of heart, and helps Casey rescue Splinter, while the Turtles take on Shredder's goons – and, in a final showdown, Shredder himself. When he is defeated, Danny is reunited with his father, the police round up Shredder's gang, Charles gives April her job back (with a promotion), and she and Casey find romance.

ORIGINS: In 1983, 21-year-old short-order cook Kevin Eastman and his 29-year-old illustrator friend Peter Laird, both amateur comic book artists, were sitting around sketching, when Eastman drew a bipedal humanoid turtle with nunchuks (chainsticks) which Laird promptly named a 'Teenage Mutant Ninja Turtle'. Parodying the Frank Miller comic books *Ronin* and *Daredevil*, Eastman and Laird created a comic book featuring four of the Ninja Turtles, naming them after Renaissance artists (although Michelangelo was misspelled 'Michaelangelo'). Eastman used a $500 tax rebate and $700 borrowed from his uncle to finance the 3,000-copy first print run of the first issue of the Turtles' own black-and-white comic, which made its debut at a comic convention in Portsmouth, New Hampshire, on 5 May 1984. Laird sent a four-page press release and a copy of the comic to a hundred and eighty radio and TV stations and press agencies. To their surprise, one of the agencies picked up on the self-publishing story, causing the comic to sell out its first, then second (15,000-copy), then third (35,000-copy) print runs. A licensed role-playing game by Palladium led to the production of lead miniatures, which in turn led to action figures – and, of course, more comics. By the time licensing agent Mark Freedman came aboard, hoping to take the Turtle phenomenon global, the comic was selling 125,000 copies per issue. Within a few years, the Teenage Mutant Ninja Turtles empire had expanded into a multi-billion dollar industry. Laird bought out Eastman's interest in 2000, and continues to steer the Turtles into new media, having so far conquered animation, action figures, video and arcade games – and, for a time, the movies. Meanwhile, Laird continues to write and (with penciller Jim Lawson) draw new *Teenage Mutant Ninja Turtles* comics under his own Mirage Studios imprint, with the latest incarnation, *TMNT*, launched in December 2001. 'When we created the Turtles, we wanted to spoof the world of superhero characters and poke good-natured fun at the heroic but not-so-funny characters that dominated the business,' Laird said later. 'The Turtles are fun heroes with an attitude. Basically, they act and think like average teenagers.' Added Eastman, 'They're always willing to lend a helping hand, but are constantly on the alert for the funny side of life.'

PREVIOUS INCARNATIONS: One of Mark Freedman's first moves as official licensing agent for the Turtles was to strike a deal with animation producers Murakami, Wolf, Swenson Inc., who produced a *Teenage Mutant Ninja Turtles* animated television series which became a staple of Saturday morning television following its 1987 debut, and continued to run for 10 years, amassing 197 episodes.

DEVELOPMENT: Golden Harvest, a Hong Kong-based production company with a background in low-budget martial arts movies, had optioned the rights to *Teenage Mutant Ninja Turtles* in the mid-80s, before either the comic or the cartoon had really taken off – indeed, Golden Harvest production chief Tom Gray was considered at the time to be taking quite a risk by backing the project, even with a relatively low budget ($5 million) and no necessity for stars. By 1988, former actor Bobby Herbeck (who once played a pizza delivery man on *Diff'rent Strokes*) had turned in a cheap-as-chips screenplay – which co-creators Kevin Eastman and Peter Laird, who had script approval, promptly rejected. When Tom Gray subsequently put producer David Chan (*The Cannonball Run*), who worked for Golden Harvest's international division, in charge of the project ('Gray mentioned Teenage Mutant Ninja Turtles, and I said "What!?" ' Chan recalled), his first task was to find a new screenwriter: *The Wonder Years*' staff writer Todd W Langen. 'Bobby's [script] needed restructuring,' Langen told *Cinefantastique*. 'I had to make the dialogue sophisticated where it was flat, and really delineate the characters. I didn't have time to read all of the issues [of the comic book], so I based my work on the first collection. I avoided the cartoon, since this had to be more than something on Saturday morning.' Langen did not find it difficult to delineate the characters. 'In a way, you have four different characters who are really one character with four distinct personalities,' he explained. 'You have the jokester, you have the wit, and the leader, and the shy gadget whiz. It's fun to use that when writing their dialogue and putting them in situations.'

Eastman and Laird loved the new script, as did Chan's chosen director: Steve Barron, who had directed the hit comedy *Electric Dreams*, award-winning music promos for Dire Straits ('Money for Nothing'), Michael Jackson ('Billie Jean') and A-Ha ('Take on Me'), and several episodes of *Jim Henson's The Storyteller* – all of which had harnessed the latest technology. 'When they approached me, it was going to be a three million pound movie shot in Hong Kong,' Barron recalled. 'I said I'd do it if we could spend double that and if I could use [Jim Henson's] Creature Shop.' Barron's idea was welcomed at the studio, which had been uncertain of how to put the Turtles on screen. Jim Henson, however, was unsure whether they were something with which his family-oriented family-run business wanted to be associated. 'Jim thought that family movies were the Henson tradition,' Barron explained, 'and suddenly you had these guys running around with swords and nunchuks. It wasn't a Henson sort of thing. I think in the end he did it as a favour to me.' Brian Henson, who succeeded his father as head of the Creature Shop, and acted as chief puppeteer on *Teenage Mutant Ninja Turtles*, agreed. '*Turtles* was pushing the edge of what my father thought we should be doing, because it was violent,' he admitted. 'He was always worried that it was glamourising violence for kids, but Steve Barron convinced him that the violence was very cartoon-like.'

Jim Henson had more than just moral misgivings, however – there was also the technological requirements to consider. 'It's an unwritten law that you don't try more than one new technology at a time in one film,' Barron explained. 'But in this picture, we attempted six!' 'Making the Turtles and Splinter was a little tricky because we had to follow the designs that were already in the comic book,' Jim Henson noted. 'It is a lot easier to put everything you need inside a creature when you are able to start from the beginning with your own designs.' Added Brian, '*Turtles* was an outrageous effects film. It was all about mobility – the characters had to do gymnastics, acrobatics and a lot of the fight choreography in the fully animatronic heads.' Led by Creature Shop creative supervisor John Stephenson and production supervisor William Plant, work on constructing the Turtles and Splinter began in February 1989. 'We first made fibreglass body casts of each creature, taking great care to give them all their own individual characteristics,' said Stephenson, a Creature Shop veteran who had previously developed characters for *The Dark Crystal* and *Return to Oz*. Next, the body casts were given to sculptors, who rebuilt them out of clay, sculpting the muscle structure in the feet, calves, thighs, chests, shoulders, necks, upper arms, hands, forearms, head and shell pieces. 'They were then produced as moulds to cast the whole body in foam rubber latex – and then painted, giving each character its own distinctive marks and coloration.'

Building the bodysuits was the easy part, however; making the mechanised heads was going to be trickier. Henson's resident electronics expert, Dave Housman, devised a new system combining radio control and computer technology which would allow the heads worn by the actors to be operated by puppeteers, allowing them to lip-sync and change expressions in live situations. After eighteen weeks of development, the prototypes were ready to begin filming in the autumn of 1989.

CASTING: Producer David Chan said of Judith Hoag's April O'Neil that it was 'a charming sight to see her and the Turtles together. She brings life to April. And Elias Koteas is perfect as our Casey Jones. He and Judith look very well together.' Rounding out the cast were the

Turtles themselves – David Forman, Michelan Sisti, Leif Tilden and Josh Pais – while a young Sam Rockwell (*Confessions of a Dangerous Mind*) makes an early appearance as a thief who comes a cropper when he gets on the wrong side of the Turtles.

PRODUCTION: Production designer Roy Forge Smith, who has designed such films as *Bill and Ted's Excellent Adventure* and *Monty Python and the Holy Grail*, says that when he first was given the *Teenage Mutant Ninja Turtles* assignment, he did just what Splinter would recommend before embarking on any endeavour: he meditated. 'To get motivation for the proper atmosphere in the designs, I started out by imagining I was a Turtle living in the sewers under Manhattan,' he said. 'Our director, Steve Barron, had storyboards drawn for all the action scenes, so that was a big help. I wanted to get the Turtles' domestic environment – their den – just right because it is important to a lot of kids out there who follow the comic book adventures to create the definitive home of the Turtles, the one the kids will recognise, rough but inviting, furnished by junk swept down the storm drain and made workable by Donatello, the fix-it genius who can repair anything.'

Extensive photographs were taken of the area around Bleecker Street in New York's SoHo area, and sets were built to match in far-off North Carolina. Although Smith and his team were not permitted to venture into real-life New York sewers to give an authentic look to the Turtles' subterranean dwelling, they were allowed to explore an abandoned section of the Brooklyn subway system, and a water tunnel used to pump water into the Central Park reservoir – both of which became inspiration for the underground home. 'Then,' said Smith, 'our set decorators dressed it with a dilapidated couch; old chairs; a cracked but working TV set; second-hand books; a weather-beaten table; a shattered mirror; a hanging tyre; an ancient stove; splintered bunks and a faded hammock to sleep in; torn pictures on the wall; and a battered old telephone in a broken-down phone booth where the Turtles phone for pizza all the time.'

MUSIC: The film's electronic score, by British composer John Du Prez (*A Fish Called Wanda*), was complemented by music from MC Hammer ('This Is What We Do'), Johnny Kemp ('Let the Walls Come Down'), Spunkadelic ('9.95'), RIFF ('Family'), St Paul ('Every Heart Needs a Home'), Hi Tek 3 ('Spin That Wheel') and Partners in Kryme ('T-u-r-t-l-e Power!').

CLASSIC QUOTES:

Michelangelo: 'Wise man say "Forgiveness is divine, but never pay full price for late pizza." '

Casey Jones: 'I hate punkers. Especially bald ones with green make-up who wear masks over ugly faces.'

Splinter: 'How can a face so young wear so many burdens.'

Casey Jones: 'Lead the way, toots.'
April: Toots?'
Casey Jones: 'Babe? Sweetcakes? Ah! Princess! Do you wanna throw me a clue here? I'm drowning.'

Michelangelo: 'Hey, Donnie, looks like this one's suffering from shell shock!'
Donatello: 'Too derivative!'
Michelangelo: 'Boy, I guess we can really shell it out!'
Donatello: 'Too cliché!'

Michelangelo: 'God, I love being a Turtle!'

Casey Jones: 'I look like I just called Mike Tyson a cissy.'

Splinter: 'I have always liked . . . Cowabunga!'

TRAILERS: The trailer opens with atmospheric images of the New York crime wave, and a chilling warning from Shredder, before the Turtles are revealed in a montage of fun-looking fight scenes, cut to an awful electronic version of Strauss' 'The Blue Danube Waltz'. After the title comes the legend 'LEAN, GREEN AND ON THE SCREEN' in the same green typeface.

POSTERS: The teaser poster image featured the four Turtles peering up through a manhole in the middle of a New York street, with the title in green above them. The regular one-sheet poster took the Turtles out of their New York context and placed them centre stage in an action pose, with the title writ large behind them.

TAG-LINE: 'Hey, dude, this ain't no cartoon!'

WHAT THE PAPERS SAID: 'While visually rough around the edges, sometimes sluggish in its plotting and marred by overtones of racism in its use of Oriental villains,' suggested *Variety*, 'the live-action screen version . . . scores with its generally engaging tongue-in-cheek humour.' Writing in the *Chicago Sun-Times*, Roger Ebert admitted that he 'did not walk into the screening with a light step and a heart that sang. For that matter, I did not walk out afterwards with my spirits renewed. But this movie is nowhere near as bad as it might have been, and probably is the best possible *Teenage Mutant Ninja Turtle* movie.' In the UK, *Time Out*'s Colette Maud praised Jim Henson's animatronic characters ('though extra distinguishing marks between the Turtles would be appreciated'). However, she went on, 'between the dubbed dialogue and the dark visuals, the cumulative effect is curiously dislocating. The big plus for fans, of course, is the boisterous interplay between the four heroes and some engaging slapstick humour; both redeem more functional elements.'

BOX OFFICE: Released on 30 March 1990, *Teenage Mutant Ninja Turtles* grossed over $135 million in the US, an astonishing *ten times* its declared budget of $13.5 million. This easily blew away the record established by the previous independent box office champ, *Dirty Dancing*, which grossed $67 million in 1987.

CONTROVERSY: At the height of *Teenage Mutant Ninja Turtles* mania, the British Board of Film Classification (BBFC), which certificates and sometimes cuts films prior to theatrical release, objected to the use of certain ninja weapons, notably nunchuks (chainsticks); as a result, the film was heavily cut to remove every trace of them. When the cartoon series was due to be broadcast in the UK, the network watchdogs were even uncertain about the inclusion of the word 'ninja' in the title, and it was thus decided to retitle the series *Teenage Mutant Hero Turtles*.

SEQUELS & SPIN-OFFS: Within a year of the summer they had all but ruled, the Turtles (and Paige Turco's April O'Neil) returned in Michael Pressman's *Teenage Mutant Ninja Turtles II: The Secret of the Ooze*, which scored a $20 million US opening weekend before going on to an overall gross of $78.6 million – a little more than half the box office performance of the first film. Nevertheless, they were back (along with Turco and the first film's Elias Koteas) in Stuart Gillard's *Teenage Mutant Ninja Turtles III*, which continued the trend of diminishing returns by grossing $19.8 million – just less than its predecessor's opening weekend figures – and signalled the end of Turtle-mania, at least for a while. There was talk of a fourth film, and Peter Laird told fan website *mikeystmnt.com* in 2001 'someday, I'd like to tell the story behind the aborted fourth movie and the blood, sweat and tears involved. On second thoughts, maybe I really don't need to revisit that period of intense aggravation!'

In September 1997, a short-lived live-action TV series, *Ninja Turtles: The Next Mutation* kicked off in the US, running for 26 episodes before being cancelled. Peter Laird made his feelings known about the demographically geared addition of a fifth female turtle in an interview with Dan Berger, webmaster of *ninjaturtles.com*: 'Rest assured, as long as I am alive and in charge of this ship of Turtles, Venus DeMilo, the female Turtle, will *never* again appear in any Mirage-approved TMNT project, unless it is a book about the history of the TMNT property and it is necessary to refer to her as an undeniable part of that history. She is *gone*.'

In January 2003, US children's channel 4Kids began showing a new Saturday morning animated series, *Teenage Mutant Ninja Turtles*. 4Kids boss Norman Grossfeld told *Cinescape*, 'When we started to hear that the original rights owners of the Turtles were interested in reintroducing that brand, we were very aggressive about going after it.' Grossfeld met with the rights holders, and convinced them that he shared Peter Laird's vision for the future of the characters. 'We're playing up the action,' he explained. 'They're still comedy-oriented, but we're going to reassert the idea that 'ninja' is a part of their name.' Twenty-six episodes had been produced by the time this book went to press, although it was too early to tell whether the series would repeat the success of the original animated series, which ran for ten years in the same time slot.

FUTURE INCARNATIONS: In June 2001, *Variety* reported that director John Woo (*Face/Off*) and producer Terence Chang's Digital Rim Entertainment had inked a deal with Mirage Studios to produce a brand new, all-CGI feature film based on the *Teenage Mutant Ninja Turtles* property. 'John and I look forward to working with Peter [Laird] to incorporate these original extreme martial arts characters into a terrific first CGI film for Digital Rim, fusing traditional Hollywood creative know-how and highly advanced computer technology,' said Chang, Woo's long-time producing partner. 'I've always loved the *Teenage Mutant Ninja Turtles*,' Woo added. 'It's one of the greatest action–adventure properties ever.' Digital Rim had already produced a five-minute CGI animated *Turtles* showreel which acted as a pilot for a new CGI animated series; however, the 'pilot' was so impressive it had led Digital Rim to establish a deal to produce a feature film within a $40–60 million budget range, scheduled for release in late 2003. By mid-2002, however, news spread that the proposed feature had failed to attract studio interest, and had been shelved along with plans to produce a new animated TV series. Nevertheless, Woo told *scifiwire.com* that the series was still being planned: 'I [will] work on this project as a producer with my partner, Terence Chang, as co-producer. The other companies wanted to start with television first and then make a movie. Now we're starting with a story.'

DVD AVAILABILITY: Although both sequels are available on a single DVD, the original *Teenage Mutant Ninja Turtles* is currently unavailable in the UK (Region 2). In the US, the film is available in widescreen (1.85:1) and fullscreen formats, along with the original theatrical trailer,

Turtle and character biographies, and an interactive game playable with a DVD remote control.

FINAL ANALYSIS: An estimated $4 billion empire founded on a single issue of a self-published comic book, the rise of the Teenage Mutant Ninja Turtles is one of the greatest success stories in history, the Pokémon phenomenon of its time, but one without corporate might behind it. Deeply despised or merely misunderstood by grown-ups who didn't want their kids practising ninja moves on their brothers and sisters, the transformation of the Turtles into a pop culture and merchandising phenomenon obscured the fact that the original comic book was awesomely entertaining, the 48-page black-and-white strips packed with action and humour and fantastic fight scenes as the skateboarding, pizza-chewing, surf-talking Turtles (for whom 'Cowabunga!' was just their best-known catchphrase) left their home in the New York sewers, traversed galaxies, travelled in time, saved the world – and still managed to get back before the pizza delivery guy. Rereading the comics while researching this chapter was a far greater pleasure than I had expected, and while I initially dreaded revisiting the film based on the Turtles' comic exploits, it holds up remarkably well. Steve Barron's direction is lively even though the settings are surprisingly gritty and dark, Elias Koteas' performance is hugely enjoyable, and the Jim Henson Creature Shop did a marvellous job in bringing the Turtles to life. Although the film has dated, the concept has not, and there is no earthly reason why the Ninja Turtles should not continue to mutate beyond its brand new Saturday morning cartoon shows into other media – including the movies.

EXPERT WITNESS: 'It was a hard project, but satisfying. The producers just wanted a Chinese stunt movie. They were amazed we didn't just build costumes for the stuntmen to wear. The film-makers wanted something of a higher standard than the producers.' – **Brian Henson, Chief Puppeteer**

The Crow (1994)

(102 minutes)

Directed by Alex Proyas
Produced by Edward R Pressman and Jeff Most
Screenplay by David J Schow and John Shirley
Based on the Comic Book Series and Comic Strip by James O'Barr

Executive Producer Robert L Rosen
Executive Producer Sherman L Baldwin
Co-Producers Caldecot Chubb and James A Janowitz
Director of Photography Dariusz Wolski
Production Designer Alex McDowell
Edited by Dov Hoenig, ACE and Scott Smith
Music Score Composed by Graeme Revell
Costume Designer Arianne Phillips
Casting by Billy Hopkins and Suzanne Smith

CAST: Brandon Lee (*Eric Draven*/'*The Crow*'), Ernie Hudson (*Sergeant Albrecht*), Michael Wincott ('*Top Dollar*'), David Patrick Kelly ('*T-Bird*'), Angel David ('*Skank*'), Rochelle Davis (*Sarah*), Bai Ling (*Myca*), Lawrence Mason ('*Tintin*'), Michael Massee ('*Funboy*'), Marco Rodriguez (*Torres*), Sofia Shinas (*Shelly Webster*), Anna Thomson (*Darla*), Tony Todd (*Grange*), Jon Polito (*Gideon*), Bill Raymond (*Mickey*), Kim Sykes (*Annabella*), Roch Trulbee (*lead cop*), Norman 'Max' Maxwell (*Roscoe*), Jeff Cadiente (*Waldo*), Henry Kingi (*MJ*), Erik Stabenau (*Speeg*), Cassandra Lawton (*newscaster*), Lou Criscuolo (*uniform cop*), Todd Brenner, Joe West (*paramedics*), Tom Rosales (*Sanchez*), Jeff Imada (*Braeden*), Tierre Turner (*Jugger*), Tim Parati (*bad ass criminal*), James Goodall, Brad Laner, James Putnam, Eddie Ruscha, Elizabeth Thomson (*Medicine bandmembers*), Marston Daley, Laura Gomel, Rachel Hollingsworth, Charles Levi, Mark McCabe, Frank Nardiello (*My Life With The Thrill Kill Kult bandmembers*)

TITLE SEQUENCE: Simple titles ('BRANDON LEE' and 'THE CROW') appear in white on black before the film opens on a view of Detroit, a legend explaining that this is '30 October – Devil's Night'. As the camera moves in slowly, giving a bird's eye view of a burning landscape as a tumult of voices and sirens are heard, the voice of a young girl cuts through: 'People once believed that when someone dies, a crow carries their soul to the land of the dead. But sometimes something so bad happens that a terrible sadness is carried with it and the soul can't rest. Then sometimes, just sometimes, the crow could bring that soul back to put the wrong things right.' The camera swoops into the upstairs window of a loft apartment, where a black uniformed policeman surveys the injured body of Shelly Webster, who has been found with her fiancé Eric Draven, attacked by person or persons unknown in a citywide night of violence. Sarah, a little girl whom Eric and Shelly took care of, watches the ambulance go. 'One year later' (as another on-screen caption informs us), a crow watches as the girl lays flowers on the graves of Eric and Shelly, as her voice-over continues: 'A building gets torched. All that is left is ashes. I used to think that was true about everything: families, friends, feelings. But now I know that sometimes if love proves real, two people are meant to be together, nothing can keep them apart.' As she walks away, the crow taps its beak against the gravestone.

SYNOPSIS: Later, the crow watches as Eric Draven climbs out of his grave and returns home, where he remembers the brutal attack by five individuals which left him and his beloved Shelly dead. Draven makes himself up to look like the theatrical mask 'Irony', dresses in black and, with the crow on his shoulder, sets out to avenge his own death. The crow leads him to the first of his intended victims, 'Tintin', whom he confronts in an alleyway and beats senseless before stabbing him to death. Next, he pays a call on pawnbroker Gideon, forcing him to give up the engagement ring stolen from him and Shelly on the night of their murders. When he has it, he torches the place, leaving Gideon alive. Sergeant Albrecht sees Draven leaving the scene and tries to stop him, but Draven escapes into the night – after reminding Albrecht of the events of a year earlier. Next, Draven pays a call on 'Funboy', finding him in bed with Sarah's drug-addict mother, Darla. Funboy mocks him, and shoots him several times – but Draven shows no ill effects, kills Funboy and tells Darla to go to her daughter. Draven visits Albrecht at home, and they discuss the murders. Meanwhile, Gideon warns 'Top Dollar' and his 'sister' Myca that a man named Draven attacked him. Draven confronts another gang member, 'T-Bird', in his car, and learns that Shelly was attacked because she made complaints about the apartment building she was living in; Eric just happened to be with her at the time. Draven kills him, leaving an image of a crow in fire. One of Top Dollar's henchmen visits Draven's grave and finds it empty. Darla makes an effort with Sarah, while Draven shoots up Top Dollar's whole gang, killing the last of the gang members, 'Skank'. Now he is ready to be reunited with Shelly in the afterlife – but Top Dollar stands in his way, kidnapping Sarah and insisting on payback for his dead friends. Top Dollar shoots Draven, and this time he goes down – he is no longer invincible. Albrecht bursts in and shoots the place up, but Top Dollar and Myca escape with the crow, Draven's familiar. The crow attacks her, however, and she falls to her death. With Albrecht wounded, Top Dollar holds Sarah off the roof of a church, as Draven offers to trade his life for hers. Top Dollar lets the girl go, but she hangs on as he and Draven fight to the death. Top Dollar is killed, Draven rescues Sarah, and she promises to stay with Albrecht until help comes. Eric goes to his beloved Shelly's grave, and Shelly comes to him, kissing him. Sarah visits the graves, where she finds the crow, which gives her the engagement ring. 'If the people we love are stolen from us,' she resolves, 'the way to have them live on is to never stop loving them. Buildings burn, people die, but real love is forever.'

ORIGINS: From the very beginning, *The Crow* had tragic associations. Artist James O'Barr was just eighteen when, in 1978, his girlfriend was killed by a drunk driver – a senseless tragedy with which he had difficulty coming to terms. Feeling the need for some strict regimentation in his life, O'Barr enlisted with the US Marines, and it was while stationed in West Germany that he wrote and drew the first forty pages of *The Crow*. 'I just wanted to stop thinking about it and have some structure in my life,' he said. 'But I was still filled with such rage and frustration that I had to get it out before it destroyed me. One day I just began drawing *The Crow*, [and] it came pouring out.' Driven by his own despair, and drawing on a wide range of influences from poets such as Rimbaud and Edgar Allen Poe, to musicians like Iggy Pop and Ian Curtis, and comic books such as Kazuo Koike's *Lone Wolf and Cub* (also, curiously, the inspiration for *Road to Perdition*), O'Barr created a gothic-romantic revenge fantasy. Exactly one year after Eric and his beautiful fiancée Shelly are murdered by a gang of hoodlums, Eric returns, apparently from beyond the grave, as a seemingly supernatural force, exacting bloody revenge on each of the killers. 'Writing *The Crow* didn't help at all,' O'Barr has said. 'I thought it would be cathartic, but as I drew each page, it made me more self-destructive, if anything . . . I was more messed up by the time I was done with the book.'

O'Barr amassed a large collection of rejection slips before the first issue was finally published by upstart small press Caliber Comics in February 1989. Three more issues appeared that year before O'Barr took *The Crow* to another independent publisher: Tundra Publishing, home of Eastman and Laird's *Teenage Mutant Ninja Turtles*, who repackaged the first four issues as the first two parts of a three-volume series, published in early 1992. A year later, a collected edition was published by Kitchen Sink Press. The series made an instant connection with an audience who, ironically, shared O'Barr's sense of disconnection. As John Bergin wrote in the introduction to the collected edition, 'James did this book because he died inside, but found he was still breathing. *The Crow* comes from some lonely void far beyond pain, sorrow, and words . . . a place for James to put all the rage and anger he felt at having someone he loved torn away.'

DEVELOPMENT: *The Crow*'s journey to the screen began when 'cyberpunk' writer John Shirley sent a crude outline for a comic book called *Angry Angel* to independent comics publisher Caliber, who rejected it on the basis that it too closely resembled a series they were publishing called *The Crow*. Shirley picked up the comic, and, immediately seeing the comic's cinematic potential, showed it to his friend, producer Jeff Most (*The Specialist*). 'He remembers that *he* told *me* about it,' says Shirley. 'Maybe we discovered it synchronistically, so to speak.' Most contacted James O'Barr who, it transpired, was a fan of Shirley's novels; a deal was struck which, although it did not guarantee any money up front, made sure that the creator would be rewarded if the project took off.

Shirley and Most collaborated on a treatment, and took it to New Line Cinema, which offered creator James O'Barr $60,000 for all rights to the character. Unwilling to surrender complete control of so personal a project, O'Barr turned the deal down, and Shirley and Most moved on to future *Judge Dredd* producer Edward R Pressman's production company. 'I think it was a fax I sent, the contents of which I don't remember, which finally convinced Pressman to take a flyer on the story,' says Shirley, 'but apart from a bit of salesmanship, like that fax and some meeting pitches, it was the comic book that sold the project, really, as it looked so cinematic.' O'Barr and Shirley hit it off immediately. 'We got on well having so much culturally in common,' says Shirley. 'We both liked Sisters of Mercy and so on. I had been lead singer of various punk bands (e.g. SadoNation). That punk thing was part of it all. Like me, O'Barr was also into proto-punk like the Stooges. Some of The Crow's physical appearance – the way his body is used – derives perhaps from photos of Iggy Pop shirtless and writhing. So all of this visual excitement and cinematic feel came across in the comic. But my treatment showed how it could be a movie in story terms.'

Pressman was impressed enough to commission a first draft from Shirley, who faced a number of challenges during the writing process. 'I wanted to use more of the samurai feel, and The Crow dancing with the sword and his strange sense of humour, his macabre mockery – like The Joker but for the good guys. I wanted it to be very goth and very romantic – and indeed goth is romantic, even at its darkest.' Another challenge, he says, was remaining true to its comic book origins without being obvious. 'It is a kind of superhero story – a kind of super anti-hero – but it should not seem cornily so. Trying to keep it serious – but also not getting so serious it was pretentious. Trying to balance the romance and the violence was tricky. Trying to make The Crow's internal logic work was tricky too . . . I think "Crow vision" was my idea – others may remember it differently – but it was a device to help people get caught up in the thing.'

Says Most, 'We had promised James we would be faithful to the comic book, and to all intents and purposes we [were]. It was just in particular areas where we felt that there could be embellishments made, either to make the characters more endearing . . . One of the biggest things that we did in trying to bring a cinematic storytelling approach to the comic book was that the panels of the comic really did not delineate how it was that Eric seemed to just appear places, and get information, and we wanted to cement the notion that The Crow came back from the afterlife with no memories, and that the only possible way he could be refined to proceed upon his mission was to have the familiar, the bird, [act] as the information-giver, [so that] he can remember who he is, and focus on the work at hand, which was to put the wrong things right and then return to the afterlife.' Says Shirley, 'Jeff had a lot of input. He has very good story sense and they should [have] let him use it more. My first draft was pretty much my take and that's the way it should've been done, in my opinion.'

Initially, O'Barr did not share Shirley's enthusiasm. 'The first script they had pretty much had nothing to do with the comic,' he said. 'I was like, "What the fuck is this?" They buy this property and then completely change it into something that's completely different. What was the point of buying it if you were going to change it?' Nevertheless, says Shirley, '. . . the original director, Julien Temple [*Absolute Beginners*], wanted to shoot my first draft of the script. He saw nothing wrong with it and wanted to *just shoot it!*' Just as Temple was about to strike a deal, however, Jeff Most received a copy of music promo director Alex Proyas' showreel, 'and immediately saw in his texturing and shading and shot design, virtually a duplication of the stylistic approach James O'Barr had taken with the comic. I knew immediately that he was the director of this film.' Temple was out; Proyas was in. 'I had problems dealing with Proyas who is very talented but was sort of, ah, very tense about everything and on some kind of precipice always,' says Shirley. 'But he's a great director.'

Shirley also had problems with co-producer Caldecot 'Cotty' Chubb, who began to exert his influence over the direction of the screenplay. 'Chubb wanted to get rid of a wicked corporate villain I brought into a later draft because, he said, he had seen enough wicked corporate villains and since he's related to The Chubb Group of companies, he resented them. So the bad guys had to be working-class street people. I resisted that and he didn't like me resisting that. Also I seem to recall they wanted it *more violent*, and I thought my script was plenty violent enough.' After several treatments and four drafts, Shirley was dropped, and 'splatterpunk' writer David J Schow – who had worked for Chubb on an unproduced project, *Deadly Metal* – was brought in instead. 'John originally attacked the project, I believe, for director Julien Temple,' says Schow. 'What he attempted was a transposition of the comic to script form. As is frequently the case, the producers decided to go in another direction – but they needed that full script in order to decide that was not what they wanted to film. This happens a lot, and is no slight on any writer involved in the chain. Producers change channels in a heartbeat.

'Cotty pointed out that in the comic, Eric kills a bunch of guys, does heroin, plays the guitar, kills a bunch more guys, does some more heroin, and kills still more guys. The comic wasn't even finished as we worked, so the first tasks were to hierarchise the antagonists (and pare down their number) and seek some sort of conclusion for the story. We spent about eight months tooling the script to incorporate a Vietnamese bad guy, which was our excuse, at the time, to exploit either Chow Yun-Fat or Simon Yam and "debut" one of them for American audiences. When Brandon [Lee] signed on to the project he strongly nixed the idea of Asian malefactors, and in retrospect his decision was the right one. A lot of biz goes by the wayside in constant revision.' Overall, says Schow, '. . . the story you see in the film is principally the result of Alex Proyas, Cotty Chubb, and me, meeting in endless recombination over a very long period of time. The aim of Pressman Films was to kick the project into green-light status. Upon the delivery of my first draft, we secured a studio (Paramount), a start date, and very quickly after that, a star – the three things necessary to get any project out of development hell.' Schow confirms that another screenwriter, Walon Green (*The Wild Bunch*, *Judge Dredd*), did an uncredited rewrite of the script. 'Walon spot-drafted a few scenes (including the opening scene) as a favour to Alex when Alex was back in Sydney prior to the "after-shoots". In Wilmington, Alex handed the scenes back to me and they were folded in or adapted to what we were shooting.' Although Schow admits that John Shirley was unhappy he had not been re-hired, '[which] was a little difficult since we had been friends prior to *The Crow*,' there are clearly no hard feelings on Shirley's part. 'Dave Schow did a great job – anything he did that I didn't like was only generated by certain producers. Dave is a very very good writer and brought wonderful elements to it.' All the same, he adds, 'James [O'Barr] then and now preferred my take to the Schow/Proyas/Chubb take.'

CASTING: James O'Barr had originally named Johnny Depp as the ideal actor to fill the shoes of his creation in *The Crow* movie; indeed, Depp was among the actors approached about the role. Then O'Barr met with 28-year-old Brandon Lee (*Rapid Fire*), American-born son of martial arts and movie star Bruce Lee. 'After I met him, I thought he was perfect,' said O'Barr. 'I couldn't picture anyone else besides him after meeting him one time. He was a huge fan of the comic,' he added. 'He knew phrases and lines of dialogue from it. He was real instrumental in keeping it faithful to the comic.' Lee, for his part, seemed to have a preternatural understanding of the character. 'He is reacting to a terrible tragedy, the death of the woman he loved. The only thing that makes this remarkable is that *his* death was involved, and he has come back. You are dealing with a man who has been pushed to the limits of his own sanity,' he said, 'and finds himself in a situation that he is not really capable of dealing with . . . [so] he creates someone who is capable of dealing with the situation: The Crow.'

'I think one of the most impressive things about the film was the tremendous cast that was assembled,' says Jeff Most. 'We certainly had a director in Alex Proyas who knew he wanted truly gifted, unique, standout characters. We had a very exhaustive casting process in which Alex and I . . . saw aeons and aeons of actors, and I think Alex knew that not only a great face was important, but that we needed people who could really derive at a very instinctual level these kind of characters that would form indelible images in the film.' Although Cameron Diaz (*The Mask*) reportedly turned down the role of Shelly, it ultimately marked the film debut of Sofia Shinas, although the tragic events of 31 March 1993 meant that the role was severely truncated.

PRODUCTION: All other aspects of *The Crow*'s production were eclipsed by one: the fatal shooting of star Brandon Lee shortly after midnight on 31 March 1993, just a few days before the film's 54-day shoot was due to wrap. The scene called for actor Michael Massee to fire a blank at Lee from a Magnum .44 revolver, at which point Lee would detonate a 'squib' (small explosive) in a grocery bag he was carrying, in order to simulate the effect of a gunshot, and collapse. Everything would then be reset in preparation for a second take. Lee, however, did not get up: he was rushed to hospital just after 1 a.m., with what was described as a penetrating wound to the abdomen. He was stabilised and taken to surgery, where surgeon Warren W McMurray reported intestinal and major vascular injuries with extensive bleeding. Lee's fiancée, Eliza Hutton, whom he was due to marry in New Mexico in a fortnight, was at his bedside shortly before Lee died from his injuries at 1.04 p.m.

The following day, an autopsy revealed that Lee had not been wounded by a fragment of the exploding squib, but by an actual .44 calibre bullet which had somehow found its way into the prop gun, which was supposed to be filled with dummy rounds. Investigators subsequently ruled that one of the dummy rounds still contained enough gunpowder to propel it along the barrel of the prop gun, where it became wedged, only to be discharged at Lee when the gun was fired again. The investigation raised other questions, however. Why was Massee pointing the gun directly at Lee? Why wasn't Lee wearing a garment to protect him from possible injury by the exploding squib? Why wasn't the weapon checked in between takes? Although no charges relating to reckless endangerment or negligent homicide were filed, the production company was fined $70,000 for allowing live ammunition on the set, $7,000 for not having the gun checked between each scene, and $7,000 for allowing the gun to be fired directly at the actor, and not providing protective shields to personnel in close proximity to a weapon being discharged. The producers subsequently reached an out-of-court settlement with Lee's mother, Linda Lee Caldwell, and fiancée, Eliza

Hutton. Lee was finally laid to rest beside his father, Bruce Lee, who also died tragically – and, at 32, tragically young – while making a film.

Following the accident, *The Crow* was put on hiatus while Lee's family, the producers, completion bond guarantor and insurance company decided how to proceed. At the time, almost the only scenes remaining to be filmed with Lee were flashbacks to happier times with Shelly – scenes that were remoulded in the wake of the tragedy. After an appeal from two actors, 'It was the encouragement of Brandon's mother Linda Lee and his fiancée Eliza Hutton that brought the production back into focus for Alex Proyas and allowed him to continue,' says producer Jeff Most. 'All the actors and everyone else wanted to share in the enthusiasm that Brandon Lee felt, and the passion he felt for the role, and the pride he had in all that he had committed to celluloid.' Thus, although the insurance company offered the film-makers the opportunity to shelve the film and make a claim, they elected to resume filming as soon as possible. Says Schow, 'When we returned to Wilmington after a six-week shutdown of production, we found that Brandon's death had galvanised and unified the entire crew. Before, we were all doing our jobs; now we were on a mission.' Most agrees: 'With all of this wonderful work committed, everyone just pulled themselves up by their bootstrings and finished this film, and I think this is a true testament to the great legend and heart and soul of Brandon Lee.'

'As a movie, I'd rate it as successfully conveying what we conceived at about eighty per cent, which is amazingly high,' says Schow, who was with the movie from first draft to final cut, 'or, to put it in calendar terms, from September 1991 through June 1993. As an experience and emotional crucible, nothing compares. Remember that we lived, ate and breathed this project nearly exclusively for over a year, and *then* we went to work building it. The completed product of that mission remains very close to my heart. A lot of fans visit Brandon's grave in Seattle, and leave cards and flowers and tokens. Many of the offerings are inscribed with lines from the movie that I wrote, and it's touching and dismaying at the same time to see that.'

MUSIC: 'The music we ultimately wanted to make as vibrant a player as possible in *The Crow* – virtually a character,' says producer Jeff Most. 'And that was an outgrowth of O'Barr's very consistent use of lyrics and reference to the underground music world at the time.' Although composer Graeme Revell (*Tank Girl*) composed the musical score, Jeff Most takes credit for the idea that the film should feature a number of unreleased songs by the kind of bands of which O'Barr would approve. Co-writer John Shirley's drafts specified songs for scenes, and co-writer David J Schow made a 'soundtrack' tape for general mood. 'It had never been done,' says Most. 'At the time [soundtrack] music was Top 40 hits compiled on a record, and I wanted all unreleased songs. I really wanted this world to stand on its own.' O'Barr says that he supplied a 'wish list' of bands he would like to have on the soundtrack. 'I gave the producer a list of bands to approach about doing new songs, and a list with previously recorded material – you know, the things I was listening to when I drew and wrote [the comic]. What made it on to the CD was actually one-third of what was submitted,' he added, noting that Smashing Pumpkins and Psychedelic Furs were among the more obvious omissions. 'Sisters of Mercy had a song titled 'Under the Gun', but after the accident [with Brandon Lee] they thought it was inappropriate and pulled it.' Nevertheless, the soundtrack features fourteen songs included in the film: 'Burn' by The Cure; 'Golgotha Tenement Blues' by Machines of Loving Grace; 'Big Empty' by Stone Temple Pilots; 'Colour Me Once' by Violent Femmes; a Nine Inch Nails cover of Joy Division's 'Dead Souls'; 'Darkness' by Rage Against the Machine; 'Snakedriver' by Jesus and Mary Chain; 'Time Baby III' by Medicine; 'After the Flesh' by My Life with the Thrill Kill Kult; 'Milktoast' by Helmet; 'Ghostrider' by Rollins Band; 'Slip Slide Melting' by For Love Not Ilsa; 'The Badge' by Pantera; and the Revell/Jane Siberry collaboration 'It Can't Rain All the Time'. Says Most, 'At the time I was repeatedly told that the soundtrack would never sell, that I was making too dark an underground and alternative a soundtrack. Ultimately it sold over four million records.' A second soundtrack is also available, featuring fifteen pieces of Graeme Revell's motion picture score.

CLASSIC QUOTES:

The Crow: 'I'm looking for something in an engagement ring.'
Gideon: 'You're looking for a coroner, shit-for-brains!'

Albrecht: 'I am the police and I say don't move. You move, you're dead.'
The Crow: 'And I say I'm dead, and I move.'

The Crow: 'He was already dead. He died a year ago, the moment he touched her. They're all dead. They just don't know it yet.'

Albrecht: 'Guy shows up looking like a mime from hell, and you lose him right out in the open. Well, at least he didn't do that walking against the wind shit, I hate that.'

Funboy: 'Don't you ever fuckin' die!?'

The Crow: 'Mother is the name for God on the lips and hearts of all children. Morphine is bad for you. Your daughter is out there on the streets waiting for you.'

Top Dollar: 'You know what they got now? Devil's Night greeting cards.'

The Crow: 'Guess it's not a good day to be a bad guy, huh Skank?'

Albrecht: 'So many cops, you'd think they were giving away donuts.'

DELETED SCENES: 'Films all have a certain allowance for truncation once they're shot,' says co-screenwriter David J Schow. 'You can whittle off bits and pieces here and there, and the art of cutting is the talent of knowing how much to cut before the film starts bleeding.' This was certainly true of *The Crow*, which suffered a number of cuts which most connected with the film feel did not harm the overall structure. 'It was sad to lose the liquor store robbery,' says Schow, noting that cutting the scene – in which two twelve-year-olds with guns rob a liquor store – became a political decision. 'Forget that similar things happen in the real world all the time – this one was so touchy that it's never been included in any out-take footage on any of the disc versions – that's how sensitised to the issue the studios are.' Schow also laments the loss of two other scenes. 'The Funboy fight, which explains why and how Eric turns up in mid-movie with electrical tape all over him, was omitted, apparently, because there was no time to shoot enough angles to make the fight editable. You can see the master footage for that fight on one of the DVDs, but not the liquor store robbery. [Another] regret we all had is that we did not have the time or resources to shoot the T-Bird car chase with Eric on top of the car, as originally planned. We shot cutaways for that but never completed it. Ditto the "Skull Cowboy",' he continues, referring to scenes featuring Michael Berryman, star of *The Hills Have Eyes*, 'which Alex decided, as we were shooting tests, was too monster-movie-ish for the story into which our film had evolved. Great make-up, great idea, and Michael Berryman gave it his all, but as we shot day-to-day we realised the Skull Cowboy seemed to have flown in from a different movie. Again, I think Alex decided rightly. It always hurts to let go of something into which a lot of work has been invested, but eventually, if the decisions were the correct ones, you see that they actually tighten and benefit the film.'

'A lot of scenes were cut from the first cut of the film to [the final] cut,' agrees co-screenwriter John Shirley, 'and for good reasons – ultimately it was the comic book story, the archetype, asserting itself as it should be. It was as if the comic book, in spirit anyway, was asserting itself, and the false versions of *The Crow* they wanted to do wouldn't be made – they ended up being cropped away. The comic book seemed so archetypal it insisted on being made. Not that it follows the comic in every respect, but I feel it came full circle, and started close to the comic, then came back, after many perambulations, close to the comics again. I'd have had more music. I had a great rooftop rock guitar scene I would've left in. I would have had more developed villains, perhaps. More mordant wit from The Crow, more dancing-gracefulness from him. But I think it works well.'

POSTERS: The earliest 'teaser' poster featured the splayed outline of a crow against a black background, with Brandon Lee's eyes looking from the wings. The regular poster kept this logo, placing it behind the red title, while the main image was a shot of Brandon Lee as Eric/The Crow walking into a white rectangle in the middle of a black poster.

TAG-LINE: 'Believe in Angels.'

WHAT THE PAPERS SAID: In *Variety*, Todd McCarthy described *The Crow* as 'one of the most effective live-actioners ever derived from a comic strip. Despite a simplistic script that unfortunately brandishes its cartoon origins rather too obviously,' he added, 'the combo of edgy excitement, stunning design, hot soundtrack and curiosity about Lee will rep an irresistible lure for young audiences in large numbers . . . certainly much of the attention here will rightly focus upon Brandon Lee. The 28-year-old son of the late Bruce Lee had not had a very distinguished career up until this, but this role would have made him a performer to reckon with, and perhaps a star. His striking looks, sinuous presence and agile moves lock one's attention, and the painful irony of his role as a dead man returning from the grave will not go unnoticed.' In the *Chicago Sun-Times*, Roger Ebert also acknowledged the irony, and agreed that the film may have made Lee a star. He went on to describe *The Crow* as 'a stunning work of visual style – the best version of a comic book universe I've seen . . . The story exists as an excuse for the production values of the film, which are superb,' he added; yet he also noted that the visual style 'owes a great deal to the study of comic books (or "graphic novels", as they like to be called)'. In the UK, *Time Out*'s Suzi Feay was keen to point out the post-production changes which had resulted from Lee's death. 'The sicko storyline has been softened, becoming an elegiac, not to say maudlin, portrait of lost love. This has, sadly, worked to the advantage of the film: what was once slick, vacuous and trashy is now shot through with a terrible post-production irony. This is a most morbid film,' she added, 'a twisted Gothic romance with shards of the original black wisecracking splintering through the portentousness. Visually, it's a treat; characterisation is sharp, particularly the nicely defined villains, and the action scenes, though soft-pedalled, still pack a satisfying crunch.'

BOX OFFICE: *The Crow* was released in May 1994 – on, appropriately enough Friday the 13th – grossing just over $50 million on its opening weekend. The film's US gross was almost matched by its performance overseas, ultimately grossing $94 million worldwide – an astonishing return on its declared budget of $15 million.

AWARDS: *The Crow* was nominated for three MTV Movie Awards: Best Male Performance, Best Movie and Best Movie Song (Stone Temple Pilots' 'Big Empty'). It won only in the latter category.

TRIVIA: In the comic book, Eric has no surname: the name 'Draven' was given to him for the film, a contraction of 'D'raven'.

O'Barr took all of the names of Eric and Shelly's killers (T-Bird, Tom-Tom, Top Dollar, etc.) from real-life Detroit gang members.

James O'Barr makes a cameo appearance as a looter who steals a television. Co-screenwriter David J Schow also appears as a hoodlum gunned down in the shoot-out with Top Dollar. 'I'm the second thug to get killed,' he says. 'I [also] stood-in or doubled almost every male character in the film, from Brandon's hand (for a knife-grab close-up) to Angel David's knees (inside the T-Bird) to David Patrick Kelly's hands (setting the bomb timer), and I played assorted corpses on the floor during other angles of that shoot-out. That's my baseball bat smashing the pinball machines at Arcade Games. I'm also one of the clubbers running away in the high shot after Brandon jumps through the window. I shot another cameo that we never used,' he adds, 'as a street guy by a trash can fire during the T-Bird chase, when Eric was originally supposed to be on top of the car.'

Draven's familiar, the crow, was played by two principal birds, Omen and Magic, and three back-ups: Baby, Jay, and Dart.

For more information, check out the websites of Alex Proyas (*mysteryclock.com*), David J Schow (*charon.gothic.net/~chromo/*) and John Shirley (*darkecho.com/JohnShirley*).

APOCRYPHA: It has been said that an unusually high number of accidents and mishaps occurred on the set of the film prior to Brandon Lee's death. According to some sources, a carpenter suffered severe burns after his crane hit live power lines during the first day of shooting in Wilmington, North Carolina. A grip truck subsequently caught fire, a stuntman broke two ribs, a disgruntled sculptor crashed his car through the studio's plaster shop, and a crew member accidentally drove a screwdriver through his hand. In addition, says co-screenwriter David J Schow, 'A hurricane blacked out Wilmington and blew one of our exterior sets (the cemetery and church) away. We suffered a hideous tragedy that nearly destroyed all of us. [But] the prevalent bullshit is the idea that the movie was "cursed", and that's just sheer nonsense.'

SEQUELS & SPIN-OFFS: Neither the death of Brandon Lee nor the closure inherent in the storyline prevented producer Jeff Most from capitalising on the success of *The Crow*. On 30 August 1996, Miramax released *The Crow: City of Angels*; more of a remake than a sequel, it was scripted by David S Goyer (*Blade*), directed by British music promo director Tim Pope (who had shot Iggy Pop's concert video *Kiss My Blood*, and cast Iggy as a villain), and starring Vincent Perez as Ashe Corven. 'I thought [it] had a lot of possibilities,' said O'Barr. 'It looked beautiful, like a Renaissance painting with the dark browns and scarlet reds. Vincent Perez is actually an excellent actor but I think he was miscast. It had a bad script. It was another first-time director and all of his flaws were evident.' Although the film grossed just $25 million, little more than a quarter of the original film's box office takings, it spawned a second, direct-to-video sequel, *The Crow: Salvation* (2000), starring Eric Mabius and future *Spider-Man* star Kirsten Dunst. 'It was pretty good, a lot better than the second one,' O'Barr commented. 'It had the potential to be really good. It was different; it wasn't a repetition of the first one.'

In the autumn of 1998, Mark Dacascos (*Crying Freeman*) starred as Eric Draven in a live-action television series, *The Crow: Stairway to Heaven*, which ran for one full season before the plug was pulled. 'I saw the possibilities,' said O'Barr, 'but I think that they didn't know where to go with it. I liked Mark Dacascos. I thought he had a lot of potential. Usually you have to wait until the second season before the cast and crew get their ledge, to know what direction to take it. They didn't get the chance to do that.' Two episodes of the TV series were subsequently edited into an eponymous feature-length film released direct to video.

FUTURE INCARNATIONS: 'They had the rights to do three Crow movies with me and then they have to renegotiate,' James O'Barr said in 2000, shortly before it was announced that a third sequel, *The Crow: Lazarus*, would star rapper/actor DMX (*Exit Wounds*) as the first black Crow, under the direction of music promo director Joseph Kahn. Written by James Gibson, with revisions by Joe Ide, the story has two rappers – one black, one white, one good, one evil – brought back from the dead, where they battle for dominance in the hip-hop world. Rumours were rife in early 2001 that rapper Eminem had been offered $4 million to star opposite DMX, but it was soon reported that *Lazarus* was no longer being produced as part of *The Crow* franchise – if it was being made at all.

Little also came of a proposed Rob Zombie project, *The Crow: 2087*, or the once-mooted idea of a female incarnation of The Crow. However, in late 2002, Pressman Films announced that the fourth film in the franchise would be *Six-String Samurai* writer–director Lance Munigia's adaptation of Norman Partridge's original Crow novel *Wicked Prayer*, in which a cowboy named Dan Cody and his Native American girlfriend are gunned down, following which Cody comes back to life seeking revenge. Principal photography began on 15 February 2003, with Edward Furlong (*Terminator 2: Judgment Day*) starring as Cody.

In the meantime, O'Barr has said that he will continue to expand upon *The Crow* mythos in an adult-oriented animated series. Kevin Eastman is reportedly helping O'Barr to develop the project, initially proposed as a series of three 45-minute 'R'-rated episodes which would eventually be edited together as one entity. 'I think the way to go, to expand it, is animation, where there are no limits to what you can do,' O'Barr commented. 'You're only restricted by your imagination.'

DVD AVAILABILITY: In both the UK (Region 2) and US (Region 1), *The Crow* is available as a two-disc collector's edition, featuring a widescreen (1.85:1) transfer, commentary from producer Jeff Most and screenwriter John Shirley, a profile of James O'Barr, a behind-the-scenes featurette, extended scenes, a montage of deleted scenes, a gallery of unused poster concepts, stills, storyboards and DVD-ROM extras. According to co-screenwriter David J Schow, however, the package was originally intended to be far more impressive. 'Alex Proyas had never gone on the record with commentary for the previous *Crow* releases on laserdisc and DVD, and Three-Legged Cat main man Mark Rance proposed that he do so, at long last, for this new release, which was hoped to encompass a definitive version of the original, fundamental movie. To secure his participation, Proyas entered into an agreement with Miramax Films that any and all supplementary material on the new disc was subject to his approval – and veto power. Otherwise, no deal. Based on his positive experience working with Mark Rance on the *Dark City* DVD, Proyas recorded a comprehensive audio commentary track, which was later expanded to include the input of cinematographer Dariusz Wolski, production designer Alex McDowell, art director Simon Murton, and yours truly. The footage shot for the EPK [electronic press kit] during principal photography in 1993 was unearthed and re-edited to include Proyas, myself, and most of the actors, including Brandon Lee. What began as the EPK was polished into a twenty-two-minute documentary charting the movie's development and filming.' On previous videotape, laserdisc and DVD releases, Schow noted, the Brandon Lee interview was appended in its entirety under the rather 'necrophiliac' banner 'Brandon Lee's Last Interview'; on the new disc, for the first time, that interview was edited, excerpted, and interpolated into the featurette, to be seen in the context originally intended in 1993. 'Then Mark Rance approached me about previously unseen photographs to spice up the still files with images apart from the same-old. I had shot several hundred stills in black and white and colour, one of which appeared in the studio-sanctioned 'Making of' book on The *Crow*, others being currently available on the new website for Proyas' production company, Mystery Clock [*www.mysteryclock.com*].

'I had also videotaped over sixteen hours of footage documenting the actual film-making, from pre-production through to the day prior to the accident that killed Brandon. Mark suggested we edit this material into some kind of behind-the-scenes tour, and the result was the ninety-minute *Crow Chronicle*.' Then, Schow says, producer Jeff Most protested his exclusion from the supplementary material on the debut film, although he was represented in the coverage for both sequels. 'Miramax representatives found themselves between two rocks, legally and ethically: they had signed an agreement giving Proyas complete approval over the supplements for *The Crow*, yet they were in mid-negotiation with Jeff Most for yet another sequel [*The Crow: Lazarus*] and did not wish to queer the deal.' Ultimately, says Schow, Miramax caved to pressure from Most, scrapped the Proyas/Wolski/McDowell/Murton/Schow audio track and replaced it with one by Most and Shirley. 'The still gallery was replaced with conventional stuff and *Crow Chronicle* was dumped on the basis of Proyas' unilateral approval, now denied . . . When Miramax was questioned by *Crow* fans as to whether Proyas would be featured on this new disc, Miramax's response was that he "declined to participate", which is legally true but spiritually evasive. Proyas did participate – at length – with the understanding that his participation was governed by the signed document he had from Miramax, guaranteeing his approval. When Miramax waffled on that agreement, Proyas maintained a firm stance . . . and so once again, *The Crow* is not illuminated on DVD by many of its most fundamental contributors, and the only people who really lose out are the fans, who have kept the franchise alive with their dedication.'

O'Barr has also lamented the film's shoddy treatment on DVD. 'There's probably another hour and a half of interviews with Brandon that haven't been seen, either,' he said. 'Brandon was in full costume and they did a full interview with him where he's talking about all the action scenes and gunplay – "I get shot fifty times in this next scene" – [and] they were like, "We don't want anyone to see that since he got shot." So they have forbidden Brandon Lee interviews that are just sitting on a shelf somewhere. They are great because he says a lot of really philosophical elements throughout this thing. It's stupid,' he added. 'They don't think, "We'll never see another film from this guy, because he's gone." It's just sitting on the shelf somewhere.'

FINAL ANALYSIS: Looking over the chapters of this book, a strangely high proportion of the stories seem concerned with revenge of one kind or another: *Batman*, *The Phantom* and *Spider-Man* all have at their heart heroes who fight crime because they were personally wronged; Blade hunts and kills not just those responsible for turning him into a half-human half-vampire hybrid, but *any* vampire; *Road to Perdition* is the story of a man avenging his family's brutal murder with disproportionate brutality; Spawn and The Crow both seek retribution for their deaths from beyond the grave. Of all these, however, *The Crow* is the purest kind of retribution story, since it is motivated by a force far greater than hatred or desire for vengeance: it is, at its heart, a love story.

For me, O'Barr's portentous, pretentious narrative style is rivalled only by its immature execution, notably in the painful posturing of the principal character, who looks like Neil Gaiman dressed as Bauhaus singer Pete Murphy for a fancy dress party at Clive Barker's house. And yet . . . and yet . . . O'Barr's *opus* has an undeniable power, a strength of will and a heart that beats – and bleeds – from every ingeniously framed panel of every perfectly designed page (O'Barr has an undeniable gift for composition). The extraordinary length of time – almost a decade – it took O'Barr to complete the story means that his artwork visibly improves over the course of the book, and the frequent switches from pen and ink to watercolour to paint – sometimes within a single panel – is dizzying, and marvellous to behold. At the end, it is hard to shake the feeling of having read someone's diary, for *The Crow* is carved into the pages with such force it is as though O'Barr has used his own blood instead of ink for this most personal work.

Although it resembles a two-hour music promo in almost every respect – there are even parts where the music is mixed louder than the dialogue – the film version has an equally undeniable potency, for reasons which are also rooted in tragedy. *The Crow* certainly succeeds as entertainment, with overpowering visuals, overwhelming sound and overwrought performances all but disguising the thinness of the story. Dialogue, lighting, camera work, production design, special effects, editing and choreography – Lee's secondary credit – are all top-notch, and Michael Wincott and David Patrick Kelly stand out among the sharply defined villains; nevertheless, it is, ultimately, appropriately, Brandon Lee's film – and it stands as a monument to both his acting prowess and physical skill, and a fitting epitaph to a tragically shortened life.

EXPERT WITNESS: 'It's impossible to separate the film from Brandon Lee's tragic death. The film was finished to honour Brandon's memory. I believe and still do that it was Brandon's best work and that it speaks for itself.' – **Alex Proyas, Director**

Ghost in the Shell (1995)

(Kokaku Kidotai)

(82 minutes)

Directed by Mamoru Oshii
Written by Kazunori Ito
Produced by Yoshimasa Mizuo, Ken Matsumoto, Ken Iyadomi and Mitsuhisa Ishikawa
Executive Producers Teruo Miyahara, Shigeru Watanabe and Andy Frain
Animation Director Toshihiko Nishikubo
Art Director Hiromasa Ogura
Editor Shuichi Kakesu
Music by Kenji Kawai

CAST (VOICES): Atsuko Tanaka (*Motoko Kusanagi*), Akio Ohtsuka (*Bateau*), Iemasa Kayumi (*The Puppet Master*), Tamio Ohki (*Aramaki*), Yutaka Nakano (*Ishikawa*), Kouichi Yamadera (*Togusa*), Tessho Genda (*Nakamura*)

TITLE SEQUENCE: Like the movie itself, the title sequence is complex and oblique. We zoom in through a computer model of a futuristic city, until we reach the rooftop where Motoko Kusanagi perches. A lithe, athletic woman, she sits in silence, buffeted by a stream of radio chatter from the surrounding buildings and vehicles, until she finds the right channel . . . a meeting going on several floors beneath her. In infrared photography, we see two men arguing about 'bugs' in the program known as Project 2501. They are hiding out from Section 6, the Ministry of Foreign Affairs, who will find them any second. On the rooftop, Kusanagi takes off her clothes. Back in the room, the arguing men are apprehended by a SWAT team. One flashes his badge and claims diplomatic immunity, but a government agent informs him that transporting an illegal program across the border contravenes local arms limitations treaties. Apparently naked (see below) but for the gun holster at the top of her hold-up stockings, Kusanagi swan dives off the roof. Her safety line snaps taut, and she swings in towards the building. In the room, there is an impasse. The agents can't arrest a diplomat, but nor can they let him go. Invisible in her thermoptic camouflage, Kusanagi swings in through the window and blows off the diplomat's head – solving their dilemma, so long as she does not implicate Section 9 by getting caught. She leaps out of the window amid answering gunfire, and drops from the building, fading out of sight as her thermoptics kick back in. As the credits proper begin to roll, we see a conspicuously showy mix of computer animation and cel animation, showing a cyborg being made. This prolonged sequence ends with Kusanagi waking up (has she been dreaming about her birth?), and opening the blinds to gaze out across the city. After a pause, she grabs a coat and heads out. As she leaves, the blinds close themselves.

SYNOPSIS: 2029 AD: a sentient computer virus is smuggled into an unspecified country. Several prominent scientists from the project also try to defect. Meanwhile, Major Motoko Kusanagi, a cyborg agent with the government's secret Internal Affairs team known as 'Section 9', is troubled by a series of crimes committed by the Puppet Master – a terrorist who hacks into the minds of innocent citizens. The Puppet Master proves difficult to track – leaping from the brain of a ministerial translator to a humble garbage man, to a small-time criminal. Though all the suspects are eventually apprehended, they are mere shells – the crucial soul, or 'ghost' of the Puppet Master has already found a new host by the time the squad arrives. In fact, the Puppet Master is not a foreign criminal at all, but a creation of 'Section 6', a rival espionage wing with the Ministry of *Foreign* Affairs. Section 6 has been using the Puppet Master to create terrorist incidents and crimes that are then used by the government to justify unwelcome new policies and laws, but the artificially created intelligence has now turned on its former masters. The Puppet Master asks for political asylum, but its latest body (a new cyborg fresh off the assembly line) is stolen by agents of Section 6. Kusanagi and Bateau track it down to a remote location, where a gravely wounded Motoko is finally able to link with the Puppet Master. She has become troubled by the false memory incidents around her, and wants to question it about what makes it 'sentient'. The Puppet Master reveals that to truly be alive, it must gain the ability to reproduce and die. It proposes that the two of them merge their souls to form a new being, and confesses that it has selected Kusanagi as its ideal 'mate' for some time. Section 6 attack and destroy the cyborg bodies of Kusanagi and the Puppet Master, but Bateau is able to salvage Kusanagi's brain. Acquiring a new body on the black market, Bateau downloads Kusanagi's mind into it (possibly with the Puppet Master's, too), and the new entity heads out into the world.

ORIGINS: First serialised in *Young Magazine* in 1989, *Ghost in the Shell* was written and drawn by the pseudonymous Masamune Shirow. A popular fan artist during his college years, Shirow juggled his comics work with his career as a schoolteacher for several years, until he became a full-time artist. He lived in Kobe until the 1995 earthquake, and now makes his home in Hyogo – neither city is close to the comics community in Tokyo, further adding to Shirow's reputation as a recluse. Shirow has two main visual interests – lovingly detailed, often insectoid, robotics or machinery, and long-limbed, boyish girls, preferably with guns. Popular and published since the age of 22, Shirow is a privileged loner who can dictate his terms to editors – where other artists are forced to do as they are told, he is able to work at his own pace, and pick his own stories, not necessarily always to the benefit of his work. Deprived of a large group of potential art assistants by his refusal to live in Tokyo, he is notoriously slow, and has spent the last ten years tinkering with computers and doing occasional illustration jobs – his recent comics publications have only appeared intermittently. Shirow's most mature and complex work, the original *Ghost in the Shell* covers an eighteen-month period between the founding of the Shell unit and the untimely demise of its commander, Motoko Kusanagi.

Shirow had tackled technology before in *Black Magic*, and his earlier *Dominion: Tank Police* was a lighter-hearted look at life in a police state, but *Ghost in the Shell*'s greatest resemblance is to his earlier *Appleseed*, which similarly featured a group of crime-fighting commandos working for an oppressive regime. *Ghost in the Shell* also has an outrageously right-wing milieu that may, or may not, be intended satirically. The comic's story structure is confusing at first, because it mixes the central tale of Kusanagi and the Puppet Master into episodic crimes-of-the-week like a regular cop show. For example, the first of these stories takes place in a government warehouse where orphans are enslaved to earn their keep, and ends with a homage to George Orwell's *Animal Farm*. Though Kusanagi's team frees the children, they find themselves working harder as 'free' citizens than they ever did as slaves.

In a world where man and machine are often indistinguishable it is possible to hack into someone's brain. When an interpreter's brain becomes infected with a computer virus, the chief suspect is a lowly garbage collector, who in turn has been 'hacked' by someone else. The real criminal has convinced the garbage collector that he is spying on his unfaithful wife, whereas he is really the unwitting pawn of an espionage operation. In the meantime, we get a look at what constitutes 'garbage' in Shirow's nightmare future – toxic waste and the corpses of the elderly, literally thrown on the scrap heap. Such vignettes set the scene for the major showdown between Kusanagi and the Puppet Master. Framed in a government inquest, Kusanagi is killed trying to escape, shifting the focus to her colleague Bateau, who has kept a copy of her brain. While he searches for a new 'shell' for her, the disembodied Kusanagi encounters the Puppet Master in cyberspace.

DEVELOPMENT: Two earlier Shirow comics had already been animated straight-to-video, with varying degrees of success. With *Akira* in production and its creator Katsuhiro Otomo famously in charge, Shirow himself was approached by producers and offered the director's post on *Black Magic M-66*. In a mirror of the perfectionism that was (unknown to the outside world) already dogging the *Akira* production behind the scenes, Shirow the directorial virgin pushed the production far over budget, and was eventually forced to relinquish control to his assistant Hiroyuki Kitakubo. Disenchanted with the film business, Shirow retreated back into seclusion. Subsequent projects, such as the dire *Landlock* and *Gundress*, have often trumpeted Shirow's 'cooperation', without mentioning that his interest in anime post-*Black Magic* has rarely extended to more than a few design sketches and ink on a few contracts.

Meanwhile, the success of *Akira* had caused Andy Frain at ICA Projects, its UK distributor, to create the brand name Manga Entertainment. Frain authorised the purchase of several other anime works from US companies, and began searching for new products he could bring in as Manga Entertainment originals – thereby allowing him to sell material *back* to the States, instead of having to buy US products as an end user. But with a clearly defined young adult male demographic, Frain found the Japanese industry lacking in works that fitted his profile. Though he had been selling *Akira* to the British as a typical example of the Japanese animation business, he soon discovered that it wasn't – 'It was quickly apparent that there were few films to match *Akira*.'

Frain had other concerns – impressed with Manga Entertainment's brilliant marketing campaign and the reception of *Akira*, other companies were trying to muscle in on Manga Entertainment's turf. Having bought and marketed the first two notorious *Overfiend* movies, Frain lost the profitable sequel to a rival UK company in 1993, and doubtless thought that upstarts were trying to reap the rewards of his own advertising and investment.

The simplest answer was to involve his company directly in Japanese production, ensuring that he not only got the titles he wanted, but also that he owned the rights to the films before his competitors could try to outbid him. 'I remember suggesting an animated version of *Ghost in the Shell* . . . I loved the comic and said in a meeting that it would be great animated as a series or a film . . . I put the co-producing idea on the table early on and actively pursued it.' *Ghost in the Shell* was likely be the next Shirow production to be animated with or without his suggestion, but Frain threw in roughly a third of the £2.5 million budget, ensuring that when released in the West, *Ghost in the Shell* would be a Manga Entertainment property. The money was put to good use creating a film deliberately intended to compete with *Akira*'s legendary production values.

Co-producers Bandai Visual chose Mamoru Oshii as director, calling to offer him the job six months after he had finished work on *Patlabor 2*. A former radio staffer who originally arrived in the anime business as an audio director (recording the actors' voices), Oshii had developed a reputation for surreal visuals, deep philosophical musings, and the creation of realistic futures. In particular, he was famous for the *Patlabor* TV series, for which he directed many episodes, and wrote an acclaimed episode that pastiched *Blade Runner*.

Oshii brought in writer Kazunori Ito, his long-time collaborator on the *Patlabor* series, to simplify Shirow's sprawling story. 'We changed a few minor things here and there,' confessed Oshii, 'but for me the main problem was the complexity of the comic. I really liked the story, but I found it to be extremely hard going. I had to think of a way of doing the film so that it appealed to a wider audience than just those people with an interest in computer networks.' In a masterstroke, Ito simplified the dialogue between Kusanagi and the Puppet Master, turning it from a prolonged philosophical debate, to a perverse love story. It allowed the subtext of *Ghost in the Shell* to become a retelling of *Beauty and the Beast*, with a cyborg-woman stalked by a bodiless ghost until the two are finally 'married'. As Oshii explains, 'Although "he" is a program without a real body to speak of, our image is of him as being male . . . It allowed us to simplify matters suitably.'

CASTING: Most Japanese voice actors do not limit their work exclusively to anime. For someone experienced in audio performance in Japan, the amount of anime work pales into insignificance when compared to the number of foreign movies and TV series that require new soundtracks. The actors cast in *Ghost in the Shell* all have track records both in and outside of the anime genre – the producers seem to have been deliberately aiming to ensure that the Japanese audience heard the 'voices' they associate with a number of big Hollywood names. Consequently, a Japanese audience doesn't merely hear Atsuko Tanaka playing Kusanagi. They also hear the Japanese voice of Madeline Stowe from *Unlawful Entry*. Akio Ohtsuka (Bateau) has an impressive track record, not only in the anime field as Captain Nemo in *Secret of Blue Water* and the lead in *Black Jack*, but also as Will Riker in *Star Trek: The Next Generation*. The cunning old man Aramaki is played by Tamio Ohki, who also provided the voice of Commandant Lassard in the Japanese dub of *Police Academy* and the curmudgeonly Wart in the anime *Record of Lodoss War*. Togusa, a relatively minor role in *Ghost in the Shell*, is played by Kouichi Yamadera, an incredibly versatile voice actor whose anime roles include Spike in *Cowboy Bebop*, as well as numerous Disney characters and the Japanese dub voices of Eddie Murphy and Michael J Fox. Some American anime dubs try to gain extra publicity by hiring famous names to provide their English voices, such as Keifer Sutherland in *Armitage III* or Claire Danes in *Princess Mononoke*. But to truly duplicate the star power of the voices in the original *Ghost in the Shell* would have taken serious money. The actors used in the American dub of *Ghost in the Shell* are well known to the anime fan community, but not of quite the same stature. They included Mimi Woods as Kusanagi, Richard George as Bateau, and Abe Lasser as the Puppet Master. Lasser also narrated the 'Making of' documentary on the DVD.

PRODUCTION: Anime company Production IG began as a spin-off from the Tatsunoko studio, known in Japan as the 'home of the heroes', originating such titles as *Battle of the Planets*. But IG's specialist area was computer graphics and digital animation, an art form which had dramatically fallen in cost since the days of *Akira*. It was now possible to combine cel and digital animation by scanning both and assembling them digitally – *Ghost in the Shell* used the Avid editing suite, now commonplace in TV and film around the world, to assemble these different elements into a seamless whole. Pure digital graphics, such as green-screened readouts, jostle for screen space with more traditional, hand-drawn cel imagery, and accomplished combinations of the two, such as the distortion caused by Kusanagi's camouflage.

Oshii was also able to experiment with techniques previously only available to live-action directors – 'Working with computer graphics isn't like everyday work with animation cels. It's an image that is literally untouched by human hands. If you're used to analogue rather than digital drawing, you have to relearn your entire working methods and worldview. On this production, we have been able to do a few things that simply have not been done before.' Special effects, usually employed to create fantastic imagery, were used in *Ghost in the Shell* to make everything appear more *everyday* – 'Because animation only exists in two dimensions, your camerawork is usually very limited. You can't do some of the most basic cinematic things, such as zooming in . . . But digital animation makes it a lot easier to create visual tricks that give the illusion of three-dimensional space, such as parallax, where objects in the foreground appear to move faster than those in the background, or artificial focus pulling.' Oshii even used computers to smudge images to make them appear out of focus, creating what appeared to be a genuine three-dimensional environment. There are moments in *Ghost in the Shell* that look almost *too* real.

COSTUME FITTING: Motoko Kusanagi is distinguished by the *absence* of a costume. Her body is a mass-produced shell (in fact, in one scene, she sees another 'version' of herself working as a secretary), but it resembles that of a strong, shapely woman. As shown by the title sequence, Kusanagi often works in the 'nude', in the sense that R2D2 and C3PO do, too. Her nudity causes Bateau to turn away at one point (a scene on a boat), although it does not seem to bother her – it's not her original body after all, just a titanium 'shell'. It is a handy device for the film-makers, showcasing an attractive girl with no clothes on, but also bypassing censorship codes in Japan – as a cyborg body, Kusanagi's has a smooth, hairless pubic region like a doll's, obviating the need for intrusive censorship. On several occasions when she appears to be nude, she is actually wearing a skin-tight body stocking as part of the thermoptic camouflage gear. Kusanagi's finest moments find her activating her camouflage – a retro-reflection device that bends light around her until she is all but invisible, discernible as only the merest ghost of movement against the cityscape.

MUSIC: The composer for *Ghost in the Shell* was a foregone conclusion, as Kenji Kawai has worked on most of Mamoru Oshii's feature films. Best known outside the anime world for his scores for the two Japanese *Ring* movies, Kawai also scored the thumping, relentless menace of Oshii's *Patlabor* films. For his *Ghost in the Shell* score, Kawai used two main kinds of music. The first is a series of scrapes and noises, which work as incidental music but do not hold up when removed from the film. When listened to in isolation, the *Ghost in the Shell* soundtrack often sounds like an ambient symphony for rusty hinges, with occasional breaks for the sound of someone chopping wood. But Kawai's main theme for the movie utilised music that includes the voices of traditional Japanese *minyo* chanters. Kawai made the singers work in a chorus, deliberately capitalising on the soloists' inexperience in singing as part of a group. Coupled with the dissonant tones of the classical Japanese musical scale, the effect is an unearthly choir, which sings three distinct pieces. The first, 'Making of Cyborg', runs over the opening credits, and fades back out of the human voice into irregular bells and drums. Its lyrics, like those of the other sequences, are those of a marriage ceremony in ancient Japanese – 'A god descends for a wedding, and dawn approaches while the night bird sings.' In the second, 'Ghost City', the chant is slightly faster, and ends with the introduction of a harp. Kawai's music is slowly transforming, becoming something more international and less Japanese. As Kusanagi comes together with the Puppet Master, the final chant, 'Reincarnation', introduces the previous chanting with strings over the top – the previous, almost formless cacophany segues into a Western concept of 'music', before both rival traditions return in a haunting duet of very different musical styles. It is a true musical 'marriage', and an ingenious encapsulation of the entire movie's theme. Sadly, however, the 'Reincarnation' sequence is missing from the English-language release. Keen on securing coverage for the movie in the Western music press, Manga Entertainment stripped out the original closing theme and replaced it with 'One Minute Warning', a dull piece from the Brian Eno/U2 CD *Passengers*. As a marketing decision, the switch worked, and *Ghost in the Shell* got coverage in magazines that would not have normally touched anime with a bargepole. But the removal of 'Reincarnation' destroyed Kawai's musical poetry. It would seem that the composer got his revenge in early, by spending a large chunk of his development money on a trip to India to 'research' traditional instruments. Realising that a relatively large amount of the money was still left, Kawai and Oshii decided, seemingly on a whim, to record a Cantonese pop song. Bringing in Hong Kong lyricist Pong Chack-Man, and fifteen-year-old singer Fang Ka-Wing, Kawai and Oshii made the incredibly cheesy 'See You Everyday', a pop ditty about a lover who apparently rocks the singer 'to the East and to the West'. It's a silly throwaway song, that can be heard for just a few seconds in the background as Bateau chases a criminal through a crowded marketplace. The song is included in its entirety on the *Ghost in the Shell* soundtrack album (BVCR-729), along with a tongue-in-cheek note by Kawai about its genesis.

CLASSIC QUOTES:
Motoko: 'I feel confined. Only free to expand myself within boundaries.'

Garbage Man: 'Will I get my old memories back?'
Togusa: 'Your original memory will never be restored.'

TRAILERS: The *Ghost in the Shell* trailer comprises a swift series of action clips and impressive animation, pausing only for a moment to show a Philip K Dick-inspired sequence from Togusa's interrogation of the ghost-hacked garbage man. It smartly suggests an action thriller with hidden depths, and hints at the film's other themes by using a moment of identity crisis likely to remind fans of *Blade Runner* or *Total Recall.* With the anime fan audience already guaranteed, the trailer aims at a mainstream crowd, squirrelling Kenji Kawai's music away in favour of something more Western, and using English dialogue from the dub. Perhaps realising that the film would be sold on its visuals anyway, the trailer narration is a ham-fisted jumble of inconsequential clichés – poor enough to be a bad translation of the original Japanese voice-over. Proclaiming that *Ghost in the Shell* is 'the next generation of animated entertainment', the trailer misleadingly claims that the Puppet Master is 'a life form that has evolved from the Internet' (a misreading of its claim to be born from 'a sea of information'). It also lamely announces that our heroes '. . . are forced to question the meaning of their own lives, while engaged in a non-stop action-packed fight against an unseen enemy'.

POSTERS: The poster featured a cityscape with the giant form of Motoko Kusanagi looming over it. Wearing stylish sunglasses, brandishing an automatic pistol, and with a collection of tentacle-like wires leading away from her naked frame, she looks quite ominous – passers-by would be forgiven for thinking *she* was the bad guy of the film. Another poster plumped for a more submissive and fetishised image – Kusanagi, naked again against a stark white background, on her knees with her back slightly arched and a complex spaghetti of wires, conduits and tubes plugged into her cybernetic back.

TAG-LINE: Though *Ghost in the Shell* has the same English title in Japan, it is also known by a Japanese name – *Kokaku Kidotai*, which could be translated as *Special Armored Machine Corps*, *Shell Robot Team* or *Cyber SWAT*. As a consequence, Japanese posters have two titles jostling for space. Nevertheless, the Japanese poster campaign chose the additional occidental exoticism of an English-language tag-line, the rather bland 'People Love Machines in 2029 AD. Who are you? Who slips into my robot body and whispers to my ghost?' Posters in the English-speaking world went for the punchier, more effective 'It Found a Voice . . . Now It Needs a Body'.

WHAT THE PAPERS SAID: '*Ghost in the Shell* is intended as a breakthrough film, aimed at theatrical release instead of a life on tape, disc and campus film societies,' Robert Ebert said in the *Chicago Sun-Times*. 'The ghost of anime can be seen here trying to dive into the shell of the movie mainstream. But this particular film is too complex and murky to reach a large audience, I suspect; it's not until the second hour that the story begins to reveal its meaning.' Nevertheless, he added, 'I enjoyed its visuals, its evocative soundtrack (including a suite for percussion and heavy breathing), and its ideas.' With a four-star review, *Empire* boldly proclaimed *Ghost in the Shell* as 'The kind of film James Cameron would make if Disney ever let him.' This wasn't quite the idle supposition it first appeared, as Cameron himself had contributed a positive soundbite to the movie's press pack – 'A stunning work of speculative fiction, the first truly adult animation film to reach a level of literary and visual excellence.' Kim Newman in *Sight and Sound* was less easily pleased: 'While slick and visually dazzling, the result is a somewhat graceless identikit of previous themes and ideas aspiring to a *Robocop*-like tragedy-and-transcendence that the thinly conceived hero Kusanagi can't sustain.' Newman also astutely noted that while *Ghost in the Shell* was a triumph of the 'cyberpunk-policier' genre, it shared video store shelves with many inferior imitators and predecessors, likely to dilute its achievements. *Time Out* was even more caustic: 'Oshii's sci-fi anime conjures up a dazzling future cityscape that, sadly, is not matched by the human landscapes at the heart of the story . . . much more attention should have been paid to the script and disastrous dubbed dialogue.'

BOX OFFICE: Premiered at the Tokyo Fantastic Film Festival in September 1995, and the London Film Festival two months later, *Ghost in the Shell* was officially released in early 1996, where it played in Tokyo cinemas for only four weeks. This is nothing unusual in Japan, where movie releases are often glorified advertisements for more lucrative video sales. *Ghost in the Shell* was put to work abroad in a similarly low-key way, with a handful of prints circulating the Western world in order to secure it official status as a *bona fide* movie, and not a mere straight-to-video project like its stablemates *Appleseed* and *Black Magic M-66*. The movie has taken $515,905 at the US box office, which although small, puts it just below *Akira* in terms of movie success. *Ghost in the Shell*'s true success has been in the video sell-through market, where it remains a consistent high-earner for Manga Entertainment (now a branch of Palm Pictures), selling in the tens of thousands.

CONTROVERSY: Andy Frain did not survive at Manga Entertainment to enjoy his film's success. He left in November 1995 amid arguments over finance and investment, later claiming 'a lot of my plans to pursue [other] co-productions were put under pressure' by a round of corporate belt-tightening. Soon after he quit, the company radically cut back on spending, dumping a UK animation studio and scrimping on expenses until *Ghost in the Shell* made back its investment. The result was a lean period of C-list releases such as *Psychic Wars* and *Vampire Wars* – a slide into mediocrity from which the company only truly recovered with the release of *Perfect Blue* in 1999. Said Frain: 'Manga [Entertainment] did everything I knew they were going to do. That's sort of the reason I left.'

Several years after the film was originally released, a new controversy blew up over the resemblance of certain scenes and images in *Ghost in the Shell* and in the later Wachowski brothers movie *The Matrix*. Once again, this was an argument over nothing, as the Wachowskis had acknowledged their inspiration in *Ghost in the Shell* from the early stages of their project, and even pitched their movie as 'a real life version of the anime style'. Some in the anime community, hyper-sensitive after Disney's flat denial that anyone who had worked on *The Lion King* had seen the famous anime *Kimba the White Lion*, tried to whip up a controversy over the resemblances, but Oshii himself said he regarded the steals as well-intentioned and well-executed. He added that he often swiped ideas from other movies himself, but that few anime fans had seen enough European art-house classics to notice.

TRIVIA: The opening credits announce that *Ghost in the Shell* is 'based on the manga by Masamune Shirow', a sure sign of the incredible rise in the medium's profile during the early 1990s. Only seven years earlier, *Akira*'s credits preferred to announce that it was '... based on the *graphic novel* by Katsuhiro Otomo'.

Since her cyborg body is not the one she was born with, and she is a secret agent anyway, the name 'Motoko Kusanagi' is itself a pseudonym. Kusanagi is a sacred sword from Japanese mythology, giving the heroine's name the same resonance to a Japanese audience as 'Jane Excalibur' would to an English one.

The green-screen digits that stream across the screen during the opening credits are not random numbers, but encoded numerical translations of the names of the cast and crew.

Kusanagi drops several literary references during the movie. One, slightly mangled in translation, is to St Paul's *First Letter to the Corinthians* – 'When I was a child, I spoke as a child ... but when I became a man, I put away childish things.' Her final line, 'The net is vast ...' (to which the dub adds extra words for lip-sync purposes) is a reference to the *Dao De Jing* by the Chinese philospher Lao Zi – 'Heaven's net is vast, and its meshes are wide, yet from it nothing escapes.'

APOCRYPHA: When Manga Entertainment was announced as co-producer of the movie, a rumour soon spread around the anime fan community that the company was trying to twist the original into something with extra sex and violence. The chief accusation (made without a shred of proof) was that Andy Frain had begun his role on the project by demanding extra shower scenes. This is highly unlikely, not only because *Ghost in the Shell* doesn't *have* any shower scenes, but because the nudity in the anime is tame in comparison to the original comic. In fact, considering the textual and visual resemblance of the movie to previous works by Mamoru Oshii and Production IG, it appears that Manga Entertainment's producers allowed the creatives to get on with their jobs unimpeded.

Many critics were confused by the setting of the movie, assuming it took place in a future Tokyo. In fact, as Oshii explains in the *Making Of* documentary, he deliberately located the movie in Hong Kong to make better use of a crowded, lived-in city, full of signs and information whose meanings are not always readily apparent to a non-Chinese speaker. To a Japanese audience, all the Chinese signs and background noise would also seem a little exotic and alien (compare to Darren Aronofsky's plans to shoot *Batman Year One* in Hong Kong for similar reasons), but to most audiences outside Asia, the distinction between Japanese and Chinese writing in the background was lost. The movie itself only ever refers to Shirow's fictional locale of Newport City – likely to be a reference to the artist's native Kobe (if anywhere), and not to either disputed location.

SEQUELS & SPIN-OFFS: Shirow's manga sequel, *Ghost in the Shell: Man-Machine Interface*, ran intermittently in *Young Magazine* for several years. For the US translation, published by Dark Horse, Shirow volunteered to do his own art re-touching and conversion for the US market. His involvement in the process delayed publication, but made *Man-Machine Interface* one title where the original creator could not complain about what was done to his work in the process of reversing the artwork and altering the images.

In October 2002, Japanese TV began showing *Ghost in the Shell: Stand Alone Complex*, a 26-episode animated series supposedly set in a universe where the Puppet Master had never appeared – in other words, concentrating on the kind of self-contained stories featured in some of the early *Ghost in the Shell* issues. But without the over-arching storyline of Kusanagi and the Puppet Master, some regarded it as just another anime cop show, not resembling *Ghost in the Shell* so much as its many imitators such as *AD Police*.

FUTURE INCARNATIONS: Perhaps realising their mistake, Production IG announced a *true* movie sequel to the film at the end of 2002. With Oshii assigned to direct, *Innocence: Ghost in the Shell* is scheduled for release in 2004.

DVD AVAILABILITY: *Ghost in the Shell* remains one of the best-selling anime DVDs in the English-language market. Initial copies were marred by a slight subtitle-timing glitch (in the US) and off-kilter English lip-sync (in the UK). More recent editions rectify these errors, such as the Australian release and later pressings in other territories. Since many of the early inferior volumes are on the second-hand market, interested viewers are advised to buy a brand-new copy instead of trying to save a few pennies.

FINAL ANALYSIS: What adverse criticism there was of *Ghost in the Shell* focused somewhat unfairly on its impenetrable plot. Director Oshii has always specialised in depicting 'little people', dwarfed by the events around them, with little hope of seeing the big picture. Not for him the explanatory voice-over or the cutaway to the baddie's hideout as he provides vital plot exposition. From *Patlabor* onwards, Oshii has forced the viewers to see his world through the eyes of his characters, and Kazunori Ito's script is a beautifully crafted adaptation and simplification of the admittedly arcane original. *Ghost in the Shell* is an exercise in making science fiction appear as real as the present day, and its naturalist approach extends to refusing to explain every last detail.

In this post-9/11 world, with a borderless society that is still bafflingly besieged by a new kind of terrorism, and terrorist acts . . . and *rumours* about terrorists, and *alleged* terrorist acts, *Ghost in the Shell* has assumed a new poignancy. It remains prophetic about the Internet and our relationship with technology, and its rivalry between factions who are supposed to be on the same side is a timeless satire of bureaucracy and *realpolitik*.

Its vision of the future, and of the impact of science on human life, has not dimmed or dated in the years since its release. Its digital production methods have kept it from decaying, and, like *Akira*, the money lavished on its creation has prevented it from showing its age. There are literally hundreds of other Japanese candidates for inclusion in a book about films adapted from comics, but *Ghost in the Shell* is undeniably a work of enduring quality, stunning visual imagination, and thought-provoking science fiction.

EXPERT WITNESS: 'For a film-maker, the most important question is how long will audiences appreciate your films? I think that's the sole criterion in judging a film's success.' – **Mamoru Oshii, Director**

Judge Dredd (1995)

(96 minutes)

Directed by Danny Cannon
Produced by Charles M Lippincott and Beau EL Marks
Screenplay by Steven E De Souza and William Wisher
Story by Michael DeLuca and William Wisher
Executive Producers Andrew G Vajna and Edward R Pressman
Associate Producers Tony Munafo and Susan Nicoletti
Director of Photography Adrian Biddle BSC
Production Designer Nigel Phelps
Edited by Alex Mackie and Harry Keramidas
Visual Effects Supervisor Joel Hynek
Visual Effects Producer Diane Pearlman
Visual Effects by Mass. Illusion, Lenox, Massachusetts
'Judge Dredd' Armour Costume Designed by Gianni Versace
Costume Designer Emma Porteus
Music Composed and Conducted by Alan Silvestri
Casting by Jackie Burch

CAST: Sylvester Stallone (*Judge Joseph Dredd*), Armand Assante (*Rico*), Diane Lane (*Judge Hershey*), Rob Schneider (*Herman 'Fergie' Ferguson*), Joan Chen (*Doctor Ilsa Hayden*), Jurgen Prochnow (*Judge Griffin*), Joanna Miles (*Judge Evelyn McGruder*), Balthazar Getty (*Nathan Olmeyer*), Max von Sydow (*Chief Justice Fargo*), Maurice Roeves (*Warden Miller*), Ian Dury (*Geiger*), Chris Adamson (*Mean Machine*), Ewen Bremner (*Junior Angel*) Peter Marinker (*Judge Carlos Esposito*), Angus MacInnes (*Judge Gerald Silver*), Louise Delamere (*locker Judge*), Phil Smeeton (*Fink Angel*), Steve Toussant (*Hunter squad leader*), Bradley Savelle (*Chief Judge Hunter*), Mark Morgan (*Judge killed by robot*), Ed Stobart (*barge crew member*), Huggy Lever (*brutal prisoner*), Alexis Daniel (*Judge Brisco*), John Blakey (*border guard*), Howard Grace (*pilot*), Dig Wayne (*Reggie*), Martin McDougall (*Twist*), Ashley Artus, Christopher Glover, Brendan Fleming, Stephen Lord, Phil Kingston (*squatters*), Ewan Bailey (*Aspen guard*), Stuart Mullen (*co-pilot*), Pat Starr (*Lily Hammond*), Adam Henderson (*Fuppie*), Mitchell Ryan (*Vardis Hammond*)

UNCREDITED CAST: Ian Mills, Dale Tanner (*clones*), Elly Fairman (*female cadet*), Charlie Condou, Akbar Kurtha, Patrick Pasi, Sam Barriscale, Amelia Curtis, Helena Hyklym (*cadets*), James Earl Jones (*narrator*), Scott Wilson (*Pa Angel*)

TITLE SEQUENCE: A montage of *Judge Dredd* comic book covers builds up to a shot flipping through the pages of one of them as the first of a series of yellow titles appear, ending on the title itself, rendered in the classic style of the comic book logo, complete with a shield in place of the 'U' of 'JUDGE'. The image then dissolves through to a view of a scorched landscape under an orange sky. A legend scrolls on screen, read aloud: 'In the third millennium, the world changed. Climate. Nations. All were in upheaval . . . the Earth transformed into a poisonous scorched desert, known as 'the Cursed Earth'. Millions of people crowded into a few Mega-Cities while roving bands of street savages created violence the justice system could not control. Law as we know it collapsed. From the decay rose a new order. A society ruled by a new elite force . . . a force with the power to dispense both justice and punishment . . . they were the police, jury and executioner all in one. . . . they were the Judges.' A prison shuttle emerges into view, docking with the fortress walls of a city, and a group of paroled prisoners disembark. One of them, Herman 'Fergie' Ferguson, has just finished serving a six-month sentence, and is assigned to new living quarters in 'Y' block, Heavenly Haven. Flying there in an airborne cab, he descends into the bowels of the city, only to learn that there is a citizen riot in progress. Sure enough, the streets outside 'Y' block are teeming with rioters in the middle of a 'block war'. Still, Fergie figures, 'It's better than prison.'

SYNOPSIS: The block war is interrupted by the arrival of Judges Hershey, Brisco and finally Dredd, who almost single-handedly 'pacifies' the block, executes seven of the miscreants and rearrests Fergie, sentencing him for five years. At the Halls of Justice, the Council of Judges debates how to deal with the chaos in Mega-City One, a city built for twenty million people now struggling to support three times that number. Chief Justice Fargo rejects Judge Griffin's plea for greater powers of summary execution, and later asks his former student, Dredd, to spend part of his duty teaching ethics at the academy. Meanwhile, a disgraced former Judge, Rico, escapes from Aspen prison colony and returns to Mega-City One, where his first move is to frame Dredd for murder – a crime punishable by death. Griffin suggests that Fargo consider retirement, which would allow him to spare Dredd's life, and ensure that something called the 'Janus Project' remains a secret. Fargo agrees, commuting the disgraced Dredd's sentence to life at Aspen, and sets out on his 'Long Walk' into the Cursed Earth, the ultimate fate of every retiring judge. Griffin, promoted to Chief Justice, meets with Rico, with whom he hopes to revive the Janus Project – a cloning system which could put hundreds more Judges on the street – by provoking further chaos in the streets. On the shuttle to Aspen, Dredd meets Fergie again – but just as they are getting reacquainted, the legendary Cursed Earth pirates and mercenaries known as the Angel Gang shoot down the shuttle, capturing Dredd and Fergie. The gang is defeated with the help of Fargo, who is mortally wounded; before he dies, he tells Dredd that he (Dredd) and Rico were 'brothers', clones created by the Janus Project – thus explaining the DNA evidence which convicted Dredd. With Fergie in tow, Dredd makes his way back through the Cursed Earth, entering Mega-City One through a heating duct. Meanwhile, Hershey has discovered that Dredd's family photographs have been faked, while Rico and Griffin unleash chaos in the city, wiping out judges, provoking riots and laying the foundation for the revival of the Janus Project. With the files unlocked, Rico murders the other members of the Council, Griffin frames Dredd for the deaths, but Rico kills Griffin and accelerates the cloning process. Meanwhile, Dredd and Fergie make their escape on a Lawmaster and return to Dredd's apartment, where he convinces Hershey that he has been framed. Together, they storm the nexus of the Janus Project, where a showdown with Rico, his cohort Ilsa and pet 'ABC Robot' leaves them all dead, and Dredd hailed as a hero. He is offered the position of Chief Justice, but declines, knowing that his true vocation is as a street Judge.

ORIGINS: Judge Joseph Dredd owes his creation to three individuals: John Wagner, Pat Mills and Carlos Sanchez Ezquerra. It was Wagner who first conceived the idea of a future cop with the powers of judge, jury and executioner; his first script was subsequently rewritten by Mills, who had thought up the name 'Judge Dredd' for an occult comic strip he was planning to use in a new British science fiction weekly called *2000 AD*, before deciding it fitted Wagner's future cop story better; and it was Spanish-born Ezquerra who gave the newly christened Judge Dredd the uniform, shoulder pads, boots, chains, badge and helmet which he would wear for the next quarter century. Dredd made his first appearance in the second issue of *2000 AD*, published in February 1977. The comic became an instant success, and Dredd its most popular hero – and Britain's best-known comic character.

DEVELOPMENT: Although Judge Dredd had made virtually no impact in the US, it had come to the attention of Charles M Lippincott, a marketing maven who had masterminded the campaign and licensing for *Star Wars* and *Alien*, and had ambitions to be a movie producer. As early as 1980, he inquired after the film rights to what he considered to be 'a colourful and exciting take on a *Dirty Harry*-style cop hero in the future . . . [and] one of the best comic book concepts I had seen outside of the United States'. At that time, the rights were held by a young British documentary maker, and it was not until they lapsed in 1983 that Lippincott was able to make his move. With the help of George Lucas' lawyers, and a great deal of money, Lippincott secured the rights, and commissioned a story treatment from underground comics writer Jon Strnad (*Den*), and began looking for a co-production partner with sufficient Hollywood clout – and cash – to develop and ultimately produce what was clearly going to be a big budget science fiction film, based on a comic book which few people outside the UK had read. Producer Edward R Pressman, who had found success with *Conan the Barbarian*, and would later produce *The Crow*, recognised Dredd's potential as a kind of futuristic Conan. 'It had a long history and there was a constituency that was very passionate about it. There was an essential strength to the property that separated it from other comic books that I saw. Like Conan, it seemed so logical and distinct, I never doubted its viability as a movie.'

Lippincott and Pressman shook hands on a deal in 1986, and began interviewing potential screenwriters. This proved to be difficult, since most would-be Dredd writers were either long-term fans uncomfortable with the idea of making the changes necessary to bring the character to the screen, or neophytes who hated the comic book's (albeit satirical) fascistic world view. One of the earliest candidates was Ed Neumeier, who had once tried to secure the Dredd movie rights for himself, and later wrote a 'spec' script in which a no-nonsense cop in a face-obscuring helmet polices a crime-riddled future city. The film was *RoboCop*, a film so heavily influenced by Judge Dredd that it almost led Lippincott and

Pressman to abandon their quest to bring Dredd to the screen. While directors such as Peter Hewitt and Joseph Ruben circled the project, Pressman hired *River's Edge* director Tim Hunter and his writing partner, hard-boiled crime writer James Crumley, to write a screenplay, which involved a mutant uprising in the Cursed Earth, and featured such key supporting characters as Judge Anderson, Judge Death and the Angel Gang. 'They spent over a year rewriting it before Hunter went off to work on *RoboCop 2*,' Lippincott told *Cinefantastique*. 'Their involvement didn't last either!'

Pressman liked the Hunter/Crumley script, but felt that it was too complex and too expensive to pursue. Instead, he hired comic writer Howard Chaykin (*American Flagg*), who reportedly turned in a screenplay which bore no resemblance to the previous draft *or* the pitch which had won him the job. Chaykin was out; Crash Leyland (*Sniper*) followed him out of the door after one draft. Then, in 1992, a young British screenwriter named Peter Briggs – whose 'spec' script adaptation of *Aliens vs Predator* had caused some excitement – was hired to write a new draft, while another writer, William Wisher (*Terminator 2: Judgment Day*), would pen a second, separate screenplay. At the time, Arnold Schwarzenegger had shown some interest in the project, and it was Briggs' feeling that the actor would be given both scripts and asked to pick the one he liked best.

For Wisher, 'The notion that in the future things are so grim that the police have become judge, jury and executioner all at the same time . . . is a great way to do a very exciting action-filled black comedy of where we might be going in the future if we aren't more careful.' Wisher utilised an idea put forward in a treatment by screenwriter (and future New Line boss) Michael De Luca, which used one of the comic book story strands, 'The Return of Rico', which set Dredd against his evil clone brother, as both a way to explore Dredd's origin and to give him an adversary of equal worth. Wisher's first draft establishes a story framework which largely survives to the finished film; perhaps more importantly, Wisher captures the essence of the film-friendly Dredd, painting him not as a fascist in the service of a police state, but as a naîve idealist with unswerving loyalty to the letter of the law. According to Pressman, Wisher's first draft 'catalysed the entire project . . . it was coherent and clear and told a story [that] was not overly absorbed with the artefacts. Suddenly there were lots of possibilities.'

Bizarrely, Wisher's script fell foul of that Hollywood tenet whereby writers are told, 'We love it, it's perfect, now change it.' In this case, executive producer Andrew G Vajna (*Total Recall*) wanted more science fiction elements, 'to create, within an imaginary world, an exciting roller-coaster ride for the audience that is unmatched by other movies. So as much as I liked the script we had, I thought we had to come up with more new things and new ideas and new sequences that you'd never seen before.' Vajna also had ideas about who he wanted to direct: 27-year-old British wunderkind Danny Cannon, whose debut film, *The Young Americans*, had brought him to the attention of Hollywood in general, and Vajna in particular, who met with him to discuss *Die Hard with a Vengeance*. Cannon couldn't get excited about the third *Die Hard* film, but he knew that Vajna was also developing a movie based on his favourite *2000 AD* character. 'I even drew a poster of Judge Dredd and sent it in to the comic,' said Cannon. 'Imagine how thrilled I was when they actually published it!' Without knowing which direction their script was taking, Cannon spent several hours describing what he thought a Judge Dredd movie should be like: not a science fiction cop movie, but something more grandiose – more akin to *Spartacus* or *Ben Hur* rather than a *Dirty Harry* or *Serpico* – with the Council of Judges as the Roman Senate, and Dredd as a public servant whose absolute belief in a flawed system leads to his downfall. Although Vajna liked Cannon's take on the material, Cannon was less than thrilled with the science fiction elements Vajna had been at great pains to include. 'What I didn't like were the mutants and aliens,' Cannon explained. 'I wanted it to be more human. I wanted to be able to shoot everything straight, without winking. I wanted to be able to say, "This is a society that isn't far off from our own." '

Cannon's enthusiasm ultimately won Vajna over; a tougher prospect would be convincing Sylvester Stallone to give the new guy a shot. As Stallone recalled, 'In came this English guy who knew everything and more about Judge Dredd, carrying these mindboggling storyboards which visualised the atmosphere superbly.' Once he had the job, Cannon worked on a new draft with Wisher, then drafted in Walon Green (*The Wild Bunch*), but it was Steven E De Souza (*Die Hard*) who arguably had the biggest impact on the story. 'The script dragged a great deal and had long sections of plodding exposition,' he says, 'so they began looking for artificial ways to pump up the volume: more gunfights, more special effects, more vehicles. As a fresh eye on the project, yet one who knew the whole Dredd universe, I was able to identify the principal problem[s] with the script as it stood . . . By arguing that everything that we *know* about Dredd should in fact be *unknown*, I was able to reinvent the script as a mystery to be solved, with revelations, surprises, shock and suspense . . . The biggest step in this direction was giving Dredd a complete trial on screen after he's accused of murder. That's where you see there's still a semblance of justice in the society; still a flicker of freedom for Dredd to defend, save and restore.' De Souza set to work on a page one rewrite, ignoring Green's draft and using only Wisher's as reference. 'Dredd at first is oblivious to the trends of the society as a whole,' De Souza explained. 'He's too much a part of the system to step back from it. He has to be betrayed and framed and forced into the position of an outsider before he can see the current set-up for what it is.'

CASTING: Although Arnold Schwarzenegger expressed interest in the Judge Dredd property as early as 1992, and Charles M Lippincott has said that William Wisher's script was written with Arnie in mind, executive producer Andrew G Vajna claims that Sylvester Stallone was their first and only choice, 'the one and only person we showed the script to. He fell in love with it and we decided to look no further.' For the supporting characters, director Danny Cannon wanted an international cast to reflect the diversity and cosmopolitanism of Mega-City One: thus, Armand Assante, Max von Sydow, Jurgen Prochnow, Joan Chen and Maurice Roeves joined the more obviously American Diane Lane and Rob Schneider.

PRODUCTION: Almost a dozen possible locations were considered to host the production before it was decided to shoot *Judge Dredd* in Britain, none of which had to do with the birthplace of director Danny Cannon or of Judge Dredd himself, and everything to do with the availability of studio space and the vast savings that could be made shooting in Britain, which had hosted the productions of such blockbusters as *Raiders of the Lost Ark*, *Batman* and the James Bond films. Whereas those films had been shot at Pinewood Studios, however, *Judge Dredd* set up shop at nearby rival Shepperton, where the street level and several stories of Mega-City One were constructed across a vast area, taking up almost the entire studio – including a gravel parking lot which had not previously been part of the studio's available shooting space. Construction of the set, encompassing three major Mega-City One locations, began on 5 January 1994 and continued well into July, when a second unit crew began shooting in Iceland, where the dark volcanic landscape provided an ideal location for scenes set in the Cursed Earth. Principal photography began at Shepperton on 3 August.

Heading up the art department would be British production designer Nigel Phelps, who had worked closely with Anton Furst on *Batman*, and whose team included conceptual illustrators Julian Caldow and Chris Halls, and *2000 AD* artist Kevin Walker. 'Julian Caldow, who drew the Batmobile on *Batman*, did all the vehicles and weapons for *Judge Dredd*, although Kevin Walker fine-tuned the Lawgiver gun design,' Phelps said of their responsibilities. Another former *2000 AD* artist, Chris Halls, designed the Mean Machine and ABC Robot based on his own illustrations for the comic. 'Both are brilliant artists, but they are also great team players, which is essential because their work has to relate to the overall design concept.' The concept was relatively simple: a much enlarged and expanded version of New York City – the comic book basis for Mega-City One – which takes to the *n*th degree the idea that only the super-rich can afford lofts and penthouse apartments, while the poor are stuck on the ground amid the choking traffic fumes and steam vents. Thus, said Phelps, 'The exclusive top level of the city was clean, metallic, reflective; then as you worked your way down the buildings to the blue collar street level, the look got progressively more aged and corroded.' Filming at Shepperton took place mostly at night, for a couple of reasons: first, it allowed director of photography Adrian Biddle (*Blade Runner*) greater scope and consistency in his lighting; second, it added to the gloomy atmosphere of the streets even during daylight, as the sprawl of buildings above the city block out sunlight. Principal photography wrapped in late 1994 – although, with 180 effects shots to be added in post-production, it was to be several months before the finished film was going to be ready.

COSTUME FITTING: Although costume designer Emma Porteus (*Supergirl*) was in charge of the costumes for the film, the look of Dredd and the other judges, inspired by the comic, was the responsibility of one of the world's most famous fashion designers, as Sylvester Stallone explained: '[The uniform] is partially designed by Gianni Versace, so it has a sense of style to it futuristic-wise. I said, "Try to put together what you think is going to happen in the future – the kind of materials, the kind of look, the militaristic and the fanciful" – and he came up with this.' Although production designer Nigel Phelps noted that the uniform was the most closely copied aspect of the comic book styling, 'at the same time it's vastly different to the comic book. Every artist draws them differently anyway,' he said of Dredd's comic adventures, '[so] there's not a characteristic style.' Besides, he added, 'when you do something like this you don't copy the comic book, you use it as a starting point'. Porteus agreed, 'because you can do anything in a drawing, but you can't actually physically do things with an eagle balanced on one shoulder – which it is in the comic – and a football pad on the other with no visible means of support'. Indeed, early designs had strayed far from the character's comic book look, and it was Stallone himself who argued that the uniform should be modelled as closely as possible on the comic. 'And this is in fact what we did, and embellished it. There's a lot of gold. He wanted everything really shiny, and lots of chains which we have in the comic, and gold plates up the front of his boots, so he was a really impressive figure . . . His doing that changed the whole tone of the film, so everything became more comic-like, cartoon-like. Everything had a bit more colour to it, a bit more life.'

MUSIC: The film-makers had originally signed composer Jerry Goldsmith, a veteran of dozens of science fiction films including *Superman* and the *Star Trek* movies; however, when delays in production led him to drop out to work on another film, Alan Silvestri (*Back to the Future*, *Forrest Gump*) was brought in as a replacement. 'We have to play totally opposite to what is on the film,' executive producer Andrew G Vajna said of the method behind the music. 'The film is based on a comic book character, and I think the key is to have fun with this character, so the music should really play into that fun . . . This is an action movie, but it's a roller-coaster ride so it needs to have a *Star Wars* score, which is basically also an imaginative kind of score, but it's got grandeur and it's large and harmonic and hummable.' Silvestri's theme has all of this in spades; although its rabble-rousing 'Judge Dredd Theme' is arguably used too early in the film to have the necessary impact in subsequent scenes.

CLASSIC QUOTES:
Dredd: 'How do you plead?'
Fergie: 'Not guilty?'
Dredd: 'I knew you'd say that.'

Dredd: 'Emotions? There ought to be a law against them.'

Dredd: 'You could've gone out the window.'
Fergie: 'Forty floors? It would've been suicide.'
Dredd: 'Maybe, but it's legal.'

Hershey: 'Haven't you ever heard of extenuating circumstances?'
Dredd: 'I've heard it all, Hershey.'

Dredd: 'For most of us, there's only death in the streets. For the few of us who survive to old age, the proud loneliness of the Long Walk. A walk that every Judge must take outside these city walls, into the unknown of the Cursed Earth. And there spend your last remaining days taking law to the lawless. This is what it means to be a Judge.'

Dredd: 'I never broke the law! *I am the law!*'

Dredd: 'There's a maniac loose in the city!'
Fergie: 'What a coincidence – there's one out here too!'

Rico: 'The only difference between us, Joseph, is you destroyed your life to embrace the law, and I destroyed the law to embrace life. And speaking of life . . . send in the clones.'

Rico: 'I'm the only one who never lied to you.'
Dredd: 'I'll be the judge of that.'

Rico: 'I hereby judge you to the charge of betraying your flesh – guilty. To the charge of being human when we could have been gods – guilty. The sentence is death.'

DELETED SCENES: In the UK, numerous minor cuts were made to the film in order to secure a '15' certificate from the British Board of Film Classification (BBFC).

TRAILERS: Director Danny Cannon storyboarded a 'teaser' trailer, which played like a reverse of familiar scenes from *Commando* in which the hero suits up for war. In the unproduced concept, Dredd appears in full uniform, before being stripped of his 'garb of justice', including, finally, his helmet – at which point the face of Sylvester Stallone is revealed at last.

Instead, the US trailer opens with a Plato quotation ('When there is crime in society, there is no justice') and a caption ('MEGA-CITY ONE – 2139 AD'), followed by a seemingly random montage of action sequences and soundbites, and a minimum of plot.

POSTERS: The US poster was a huge head shot of Stallone in his Dredd helmet, with a dramatic view of Mega-City One reflected in his visor.

TAG-LINE: 'In The Future, One Man Is The Law.'

WHAT THE PAPERS SAID: *Variety*'s Todd McCarthy suggested that *Judge Dredd* 'frankly acknowledges its source with a credits sequence comics montage and never veers far from it in terms of characterisation or dramatic complexity . . . utterly underdeveloped beyond its comic book origins, *Judge Dredd* is a thunderous, unoriginal futuristic hardware show for teenage boys.' In his *Chicago Sun-Times* review, Roger Ebert liked Stallone as Dredd. '[He] is ideal for a role like this because he's smart and funny enough to pull it off. The screenplay gives him little help, however, with a love interest (Diane Lane) who never really connects, a comic sidekick named Fergie (Rob Schneider) who seems badly out of tune, and a tag-line ("I knew you'd say that") that doesn't exactly rank with "Make my day" or even "I'll be back". The special effects are messy and cluttered, but atmospheric . . . *Judge Dredd* never slows down enough to make much sense; it's a *Blade Runner* for audiences with Attention Deficit Disorder. Stallone survives it, but his supporting cast, also including an uninvolved Joan Chen and a tremendously intense Jurgen Prochnow, isn't well used. Only Assante, as the rogue Judge who frames his brother, holds up under the material.' In the UK, where critics reared on Dredd's comic book exploits were liable to be harsher, *Time Out*'s Nigel Floyd praised Stallone who, he wrote, 'certainly has the square jawline and iconic presence to play Judge Dredd . . . Despite some fuzzy flying sequences, the precocious technical mastery displayed by 27-year-old Brit director Cannon is extraordinary; but . . . a question mark still hangs over his handling of actors and narrative fluidity. As a result, this slam-bang Stallone vehicle never quite delivers what its confident, fizzing visuals seem to promise.'

BOX OFFICE: In the US, *Judge Dredd* was going into virgin territory: although both Eagle and Quality Comics had published a regular *Judge Dredd* comic for many years, it was Stallone's name and the science fiction elements on which the US distributors were forced to rely. Released on 30 June 1995, the film grossed less than $35 million. The film did proportionately better in Dredd's native Brit-Cit, grossing £7.5 million despite fans' threatened boycotts.

CONTROVERSY: It would not be an overstatement to say there was an outcry among fans when the news leaked out that Judge Dredd would spend much of his feature film debut *sans* helmet, and it was deeply frustrating to those who had worked day and night for more than a year to ensure that the best of all possible Dredds made it to the big screen. 'The whole controversy about whether Sly should keep his helmet on throughout the entire picture is a stupid one,' production designer Nigel Phelps said irritably. 'Sylvester Stallone looks fantastic in the . . . Dredd outfit. With his helmet on, he *is* Dredd and he plays it with his chin out and everything. It's when he takes the helmet off for the more vulnerable material which makes his Dredd a brilliant portrayal.'

TRIVIA: Chris Halls, who designed the Mean Machine make-up and assisted in the creation of the ABC Robot, is now better known as Chris Cunningham, a visual artist and music promo director for such artists as Leftfield, Björk and Aphex Twin.

The ground transport vehicles such as the cabs were designed and built by Rover on Land Rover chassis. Several were sold off after production wrapped – in fact, you can still buy one of you know where to look.

Though the year in which *Judge Dredd* takes place is never mentioned in the film, the trailer suggests the setting is 2139 AD.

SEQUELS & SPIN-OFFS: 'Hopefully we'll be able to make several sequels and, I think, explore Mega-City and that sort of civilisation,' executive producer Andrew G Vajna said in 1995, shortly before *Judge Dredd* opened to a less than enthusiastic critical and – more importantly – commercial response. As the actual year 2000 AD came and went, Judge Dredd continued to be popular in his comic book incarnations, most notably in his own title, the *Judge Dredd Megazine*, launched in 1990. However, in 2000, Big Finish announced the production of the first in a series of original audio dramas based on several *2000 AD* characters, including Strontium Dog and Judge Dredd. Scriptwriter Jonathan

Clements, who wrote the fourth adventure, *Trapped on Titan*, says that one advantage of writing Dredd for an audio drama is that 'he can take off his helmet, and you have to imagine what's underneath. I deliberately chose a story that they wouldn't be able to do in the comic. My big problem was finding a [tone of] voice for Dredd, because he acts differently depending on which period of *2000 AD* you're looking at, and who's writing him. Eventually, I was told to ignore the different Dredds in the comic, and go to the original source – so I watched *Dirty Harry* again. When I was writing Dredd, if I could see Clint Eastwood saying it, it stayed in.' Toby Longworth provides the voice of Dredd and several other characters, with most of the seven-strong cast playing multiple roles. As for continuity, says Clements, 'the Dredd audios are supposed to take place in tandem with the ongoing weekly comic in *2000 AD*. That means everything has to be tied up within a couple of days in time for the next Dredd story in the weekly comic, and no using of off-limits characters like Judge Anderson. We can't send him off on a six-month quest, or kill off Max Normal, or nuke Brit-Cit or anything like that – the milieu has to be relatively intact in case it turns up in the following week's comic.' So far, ten Judge Dredd audio dramas have been released: *Dredd or Alive*, *Death Trap*, *Killing Zone*, *Big Shot*, *Trapped on Titan*, *Get Karter*, *I Love Judge Dredd*, *Dreddline*, *War Planet* and *99 Code Red*. In early 2003, Big Finish announced that a further dozen dramas were in the planning stages, 'probably all Dredds'.

FUTURE INCARNATIONS: In 2000 AD, the rights to several *2000 AD* characters, including Judge Dredd, were bought by British games company Rebellion, which teamed up with Shoreline Entertainment to begin developing two new Judge Dredd films – *Judge Dredd: Dredd Reckoning*, in which Dredd loses faith in the corrupt legal system; and *Judge Dredd: Possession*, in which Dredd's partner is possessed by Judge Death – which would not be linked to the earlier film. 'We are reinventing the franchise by taking it back to the edge and style of the original comic book,' Shoreline's Morris Ruskin told *Variety* of the two films, which would be filmed back-to-back at a cost of around $15 million each. With less fanfare, long-time Judge Dredd fan Chris Donaldson and his writing partner Michael Bafaro were hired to begin work on the screenplays for both films. Says Donaldson, 'They had got a few scripts written for them already but from what I could tell they weren't working out in the manner that the producers wanted, so they asked Michael and myself to throw something together to prove ourselves. Since the guys who own Rebellion now are crazy fans of the series I was asked to keep it in the same tone as the original comics stories and nothing like the Stallone movie.' A week later, Donaldson and Bafaro handed in their first draft which, Donaldson says, 'stands as the first movie to be filmed at this time. A month or so later we did the same with the *Possession* script. Both approaches differed from the synopses originally announced for the projects, except that Judge Death does appear in *Possession*.'

'The history of Dredd is very rich and full of many colourful characters which made it very easy to construct a strong story in a well thought out world that already exists,' he muses. 'I am still amazed at how the last movie fell away from that tone and fell into stock Hollywood mid-nineties action movie mode. Dredd is a hard-nosed bastard who has one job on his hands – upholding the law. It's simple and easy to follow. You stay with that and the story just unfolds for you. Bad things happen and Dredd has to stop it in the way only Dredd knows how to do – straight and to the point.' Donaldson says that *Reckoning* is 'definitely more of a street level movie, like a *Dirty Harry* movie set in a fantastical yet somehow real and conceivable world'.

Donaldson grew up in a rural backwater of Alberta, Canada, with one comic store which mainly catered to mainstream superhero tastes. 'One day I was able to snag a copy of the Eagle comics issues of Judge Dredd,' he recalls. 'Man, oh man, did that blow my skirt up! I was floored at how nihilistic it all was, how the bad guys were truly bad and would kill without a thought and how straight and hardcore Dredd was. He was like a father who wouldn't listen to your bullshit. He knew what was right and what wrong was and if you fell on the side of the wrong, watch out! He'd smack the law down on your ass so fast you didn't know what happened.' When the script offer came along, Donaldson brought himself up to speed by reading everything he had missed in the years since his youthful obsession. 'It all came flooding back to me,' he says. 'I felt like a kid again. Dredd was the same bitch's bastard that I read through my youth. He hadn't changed one bit and I realised how much I *had*. It was such a great motivator for me to delve back into my childhood with Dredd and make things simple. He's a great character, who hasn't been given a chance over here yet, but I know when everyone gets a whiff of Dredd's ass-stomping ways, they are going to be hooked.' Besides, he insists, 'Our producers here are fans from the old days. This is a dream for them and it is truly going to show when you see Big'ol Dredd smashing Judge Death in the face with his frozen chicken-sized fists on the big screen.'

DVD AVAILABILITY: In the UK (Region 2), *Judge Dredd* is available in an edition which preserves the 2.35:1 ratio of the film, and also includes the UK trailer and *Stallone's Law: The Making of* Judge Dredd, a twenty-minute documentary hosted by Stallone. In the US (Region 1), the widescreen film is accompanied only by the US trailer.

FINAL ANALYSIS: Maybe it's because I was never that big a fan of Judge Dredd as a kid; or maybe because I've always had a soft spot for Sly Stallone; or maybe because I was lucky enough to spend a few nights walking the streets of Mega-City One during filming at Shepperton; or maybe I just find Rob Schneider funny: whatever mitigating circumstances I might have, the fact is *I like this movie* – and that's probably enough evidence to convict me for life (or death). I liked it the first time I saw it, at an Odeon Marble Arch preview screening in the summer of '95. I liked it when I saw it again on TV a few years later. Having decided that *Judge Dredd* should be included among the twenty comic-to-film adaptations in this book, I thought my fondness for the film might fade, not only because I was going to have to watch it over and over again (something that most Judge Dredd comic fans would classify as cruel and unusual punishment), but because, for the first time in twenty years, I was going to be reading a lot of Judge Dredd strips. I figured I would probably see why *2000 AD* fans made all that ridiculous fuss when the movie Dredd first took his helmet off.

Well, I was wrong, *by Stomm*! For me, Sylvester Stallone is the *only* actor with the voice, the jawline and the physical presence to pull off a big-screen Dredd. And Stallone knew just how to play him, from the moment he appears in the middle of a Block War, seemingly oblivious and impervious to the gunfire around him, and declares that the blocks are under arrest. Dredd *has* to be slightly laughable, if only because he takes himself and The Law so seriously, so having Fergie as a comic foil was perfect – remember the bit on the prison shuttle where he recognises a helmetless Dredd only after covering up half of Dredd's face with his hand? And why shouldn't Dredd take his helmet off, for goodness' sake? Do you think he sleeps in it? It was kind of a running joke in the comic that he was seldom seen without it (even when he first takes it off, in 'The Cursed Earth' saga, his face is obscured by bandages), but you don't pay Sly Stallone $12 million and then cover up two thirds of his face for an entire film. And what's the point of keeping him covered up, if we all know what Stallone looks like? Besides, the plot – Dredd betrayed by the system to which he has devoted his life – gave the film-makers the perfect excuse to get Dredd out of uniform, since he spends much of the movie as an *ex*-Judge. Now, I'm not saying that 'The Return of Rico' story, which appeared in Prog #30 of *2000 AD* back in 1977, was the best to serve as the basis for the film, but throw in the Angel Gang from the 'Judge Child' saga, a trip into the Cursed Earth, Fergie (a.k.a. 'Fergee') from 'The Day the Law Died' and Hammerstein from another *2000 AD* strip, ABC Warriors, and you've piqued my interest.

Fans who bitched and moaned about every little alteration made to Dredd's uniform, weapons and vehicles really needed to get out more – production designer Nigel Phelps and resident genius Chris Cunningham (né Halls) were largely responsible for bringing the key elements of the comic book to life, but I would also praise the much-maligned director Danny Cannon and set-upon star Sylvester Stallone for the care they took in bringing Dredd to the screen, only to be mocked, pilloried and vilified by so-called fans acting more like a bunch of crazed muties from the Cursed Earth. There ought to be a law against it.

EXPERT WITNESS: 'There are layers in [*Judge Dredd*], because we cared to put them in. Yeah, it's a comic book, and yeah, it's got some elements you've seen in every other action–adventure film. But the truth is, when [the producers] looked at the storyboards I had a fight that they couldn't say no to. I had a robot in this that they couldn't say no to. The crash of a prison shuttle full of convicts, which they couldn't say no to. The Angel Gang fight, Mean Machine: they could not say no to them. I had motorcycles where the wheels went up and this thing took off . . . If they were gonna pay me to do that, I'll give it to them.' – **Danny Cannon, Director**

The Phantom (1996)

(100 minutes)

Directed by Simon Wincer
Produced by Robert Evans and Alan Ladd, Jr
Screenplay by Jeffrey Boam
Based on the Characters Created by Lee Falk
Executive Producers Richard Vane and Joe Dante
Co-Producer Jeffrey Boam
Executive Producers Graham Burke, Greg Coote, Peter Sjoquist, Bruce Sherlock
Director of Photography David Burr
Production Designer Paul Peters
Edited by O Nicholas Brown and Brian H Carroll
Music by David Newman

CAST: Billy Zane (*Kit Walker/'The Phantom'*), Treat Williams (*Xander Drax*), Kristy Swanson (*Diana Palmer*), Catherine Zeta Jones (*Sala*), James Remar (*Quill*), John Tenney (*Jimmy Wells*), Cary-Hiroyuki Tagawa (*Kabai Sengh*), Patrick McGoohan (*Phantom's father*), Bill Smitrovich (*Dave Palmer*), Casey Siemaszko (*Morgan*), David Proval (*Charlie Zephro*), Joseph Ragno (*Ray Zephro*), Samantha Eggar (*Lilly Palmer*), Robert Coleby (*Captain Horton*), Al Ruscio (*Commissioner Farley*), Leon Russom (*Mayor Krebs*), Bernard Kates (*Falkmoore*), John

Capodice (*Al the cabby*), Bo Kane (*mounted cop*), William Jones, John Prosky (*motorcycle cops*), Alan Zitner (*Dr Fleming*), Dane Carson (*Corporal Weeks*), Chatpong 'Jim' Petchlor (*Zak*), Dane Farwell (*Breen*), Jared Chandler (*Styles*), Radmar Agana Jao (*Guran*), William Zappa (*ugly pirate*), Agoes Widjaya Soedjarwo (*pirate #1*), Clint Lilley (*gangster #1*), Jo Phillips (*female pilot*), Austin Peters (*boy Phantom*), Victor Madrona (*shaman*), Valerie Flueger (*receptionist*), Rod Dailey (*short order cook*)

TITLE SEQUENCE: The film opens with a caption bearing the legend 'FOR THOSE WHO CAME IN LATE ...' This mutates with a ripple effect to form the web emblem of a pirate flag, while Patrick McGoohan describes The Phantom's legacy while the scenes he depicts play out before the camera. 'It all began a very long time ago, when a merchant ship was set upon by pirates of the Sengh Brotherhood. A small boy watched helplessly as his father was killed by the pirate leader, the evil Kabai Sengh. He jumped overboard and was washed ashore on a mysterious jungle island called Bengalla. It seemed like a case of "out of the frying pan and into the fire", but the Touganda tribesmen meant the boy no harm. They swooped him up and carried him to their village, and that night, in an ancient ceremony of fire and drums, the tribal shaman presented the boy with a ring of great significance. Then and there, the boy understood that he was destined to avenge his father's death, by fighting piracy, greed and cruelty in all their forms, and when he grew to be a man, he became *The Phantom*!' As McGoohan utters the name, a close-up of The Phantom's ring emits a blue-white light, which forms the title in the comic book's traditional typeface.

SYNOPSIS: Bengalla, 1938: A group of relic hunters, led by Quill and in the employ of an unscrupulous millionaire named Drax, find one of the three legendary Skulls of Touganda on the jungle island of Bengalla. Before they can escape, however, they are set upon by a masked figure in a purple suit, riding a white horse and bearing a ring which identifies him as the mythical figure known as 'The Phantom' – the ghost who walks. Although his men are subdued, Quill gets away with one of the skulls, which Drax intends to unite in order to unleash a destructive energy force. The Phantom encounters Quill again when he rescues his alter ego Kit Walker's old flame, Diana Palmer, the niece of a newspaper tycoon who intends to expose Drax's evil scheme. Despite The Phantom's best efforts, Drax is soon in possession of a second skull, and discovers the location of the third: an uncharted volcanic island bordering 'The Devil's Vortex'. With Diana in tow as 'Phantom insurance', Drax and his minions reach the island, secret hideaway of the Sengh Brotherhood – the evil pirates who killed the original Phantom's father four centuries earlier. The Phantom follows them there, defeats the Brotherhood's leader, Kabai Sengh, and as the three skulls are brought together, The Phantom discovers that the power can be controlled by a fourth skull – the one on the ring he has worn all his life. Together with Diana, he escapes the destruction of the island, takes her to his home, Skull Cave, and reveals himself to be the twenty-first Phantom. She, in turn, reveals that she knows that he is also her old friend Kit Walker – and vows to return to become his wife. The ghost of Kit's father looks on approvingly.

ORIGINS: The story of The Phantom begins in 1935, when 24-year-old comic strip writer/artist Lee Falk was asked to follow the success of his first creation, Mandrake the Magician, with a new adventure hero to run in William Randolph Hearst's syndicated newspaper strips, alongside such contemporary favourites as Tarzan, Krazy and Ignatz and Little Nemo. Inspired by heroes from Greek, Roman, Indian and Scandinavian mythology, Falk created The Phantom, a heroic figure who preceded both Batman and Superman as a comic book crimefighter with a skintight costume and a secret identity. However, what the Phantom's alter ego, Kit Walker, lacked in the personal wealth of, say, Bruce Wayne, he more than made up for with the richness of his background, which began with his forefather's murder some four hundred years previously, and had continued as The Phantom's secret legacy was passed down from generation to generation, from father to son, so that those who encountered him considered him to be immortal; thus, they dubbed him 'The Ghost Who Walks'.

Premiering in daily strip form on 17 February 1936, The Phantom was an instant hit with audiences which had suffered the worst recession in American history and were now watching the rest of the world prepare for war against Hitler, admiring both the character's no-nonsense pledge to fight 'piracy (i.e. crime), cruelty and injustice' in all its forms, *and* his efficient dispatch of all manner of pirates, evil-doers and master criminals *without* resorting to murder. Over the next six decades, The Phantom would become the most widely read comic strip in the world, printed in some five hundred periodicals in nearly fifty countries, translated into twenty-five languages and read by an estimated sixty million people every day. In the strip's early days, Falk used to draw as well as write them, but soon realised that six daily strips – and, from 1939, a Sunday special – was too much for one person; nevertheless, Falk himself turned out more than a thousand Phantom stories during his career, continuing to write them until his death on 13 March 1999, a few weeks short of his 88th birthday.

'I think I created the first self-effacing hero,' he has said of his most famous creation. 'Now it's become stock – all heroes are self-effacing – but it wasn't like that then. Tarzan wasn't like that – he was Tarzan. But my hero would put himself down occasionally, and he didn't like violence. In sixty years, The Phantom has never shot anybody – he's such a good shot, he shoots the guns out of their hands.' He was also not averse to giving bad guys a punch in the face. 'When he does that,' Falk added, 'he leaves a mark on them with his skull ring, "the skull mark", which stays for eternity. And on the left hand is The Phantom's good ring. If someone helps him, he puts the mark on *them*, gently, which means they have the protection of the Phantom for generations to come.'

PREVIOUS INCARNATIONS: Although it took sixty years for the purple paradigm to make his leap to the feature film format, there was no shortage of small screen outings for The Phantom prior to this, the first being a fifteen-chapter Columbia serial circa 1943, with actor Tom Tyler in the title role and an Alsatian dog playing his faithful pet wolf, Devil. 'Tom Tyler was a pretty good actor,' Falk said of the effort, 'but they shot the series in Los Angeles, very poorly – now and then in the middle of the Bengalla jungle you can see a street car go past . . .' Worst of all, he added, 'They didn't have stretch cloth in those days, so he looked like he was in wrinkled long underwear.' In the 1960s, a 'pilot' for a TV show was produced; it was not picked up as a series, and the pilot was never broadcast. Two decades later, The Phantom appeared alongside several other King Features Syndicate characters – including Flash Gordon and Falk's own Mandrake the Magician – in an animated TV series entitled *Defenders of the Earth*. More recently, an animated TV show re-imagined the character as a futuristic hero in *Phantom 2040*, which was broadcast between 1994 and 1996. In between, The Phantom also made guest appearances in 'Popeye Meets the Man Who Hated Laughter' (1973) and The Beatles' *Yellow Submarine*.

DEVELOPMENT: Paramount Pictures, which had hastily obtained the rights from King Features Syndicate when studios began snapping up the film rights to comic books following the success of *Batman*, originally considered *Gremlins* director Joe Dante – linked at the time with an unrealised big-screen version of another comic book character, Plastic Man – to helm their proposed *Phantom* feature. His departure led to a series of talks with other directors, before Australian Simon Wincer, a veteran of such television hits as *The Young Indiana Jones Chronicles* and *Lonesome Dove* who had scored a surprise box office smash with *Free Willy*, convinced the studio that both his experience as a director and his expert knowledge of (and lifelong passion for) The Phantom made him the obvious choice to helm the $45 million adaptation. '*The Phantom* comics always had a kind of good old-fashioned adventure about them with an exotic time and settings,' he says. 'It was action–adventure with a twinkle in the eye.' Screenwriter Jeffrey Boam's own experience with Indiana Jones – he scripted *The Last Crusade* – made him an equally natural choice, with a script that interwove two early Falk stories, 'The Sengh Brotherhood' and 'The Sky Pirates' into a seamless whole. 'Jeffrey Boam wrote the screenplay very much with humour in mind,' Wincer notes. 'While it's not a comedy, there's some quite funny situations. I think that's what makes it appealing – it doesn't take itself too seriously.'

CASTING: Actor Billy Zane had discovered the comic book in 1987 while on location in Australia filming his first hit movie, *Dead Calm*. 'For me, this guy was the end-all as far as role models and superheroes,' he recalls. 'I read my first [comics] and saved them – it was the only comic I ever collected. He was different – he had no superpowers, no super bank accounts; he's just super decent – not superhuman, but super *humane*. I thought, God, how refreshing! He didn't have to be rebellious, he didn't have to be dark, or twisted. It read like a very Zen-like being in a purple get-up on a white horse with animal friends fighting piracy, greed and cruelty, who made being good *cool*. I was like, "That's great." ' Upon hearing talk of a Phantom feature film being developed at Paramount, Zane began to lobby the studio for the lead. 'If there was one role I was ready to play, it was this one.' Falk remembers Paramount sending him a copy of *Dead Calm* when Zane was first considered for the role. 'I said, "He's a good actor, first of all, but where's the muscle? He doesn't look like he could knock out ten guys!" Then, when I got to Australia [for the filming], I saw Billy for the first time in his dressing room, and he looked wonderful. He told me that he had spent two years working with a trainer, four hours a day, muscle building.' 'Billy had built himself physically into great shape, 'cause it's a very unforgiving costume,' remarks Wincer. 'And there ain't no padding there – that's all Billy. That's how dedicated he became to the character.' 'Billy is out of this world,' Falk said after seeing the actor fill his character out in three dimensions. 'He *is* The Phantom.'

Kristy Swanson, who played Buffy the Vampire Slayer in the original movie, was cast as Diana Palmer, the feisty socialite/adventuress with whom The Phantom falls in love. For Swanson, what attracted her to the character were the same qualities which appealed to The Phantom. 'When I read the script for the first time I liked the fact that Diana was a very independent woman, could take care of herself, [was] very strong-willed, very spunky and feisty. I think that's why The Phantom was attracted to her, too.' Long before she was propelled to international fame by roles in *Entrapment* and *Traffic*, Welsh actress Catherine Zeta Jones was cast as Sala, the voluptuous and salacious leader of Drax's all-female platoon of private pilots. 'She's adventure-seeking [and] highly sexually charged,' the actress observes. 'I've played a lot of goody-goodies, so this was a nice change to be able to have some fun and play the period – 1930s New York. It's a wonderful period. I only had to put my costumes on and I was, like, "Wow!" '

Treat Williams (*Prince of the City*) was cast as Xander Drax, whom he describes as 'a very wealthy New York businessman of the thirties, very much a sportsman, elegant.' He says, 'There's a kitchen sink quality to this guy. I've got Howard Hughes and Clark Gable and Cary Grant, and everyone else who wore a moustache and had some style. It's a great thirties leading man gone mad.' Finally, distinguised actor Patrick McGoohan, the star and creative force behind the cult 1960s television series *The Prisoner*, rounded out the international cast as The Phantom's late father.

PRODUCTION: Filming began on 3 October 1995, with Los Angeles locations ranging from Greystone Park, Hugh Hefner's Playboy mansion, the Port of San Pedro and Los Angeles Zoo. Shooting continued on the permanent New York set on Universal's backlot, which production designer Paul Peters had dressed to create a stunningly authentic recreation of 1930s Manhattan, populated by nearly four hundred costumed extras and sixty vintage cars. In late October, the production moved to Thailand for seven weeks of location filming, with locales ranging from Krabi, once a safe haven for smugglers and pirates from Malaysia, to Phuket and Phang Nga Bay, famously featured in the James Bond film *The Man with the Golden Gun*. 'It was the hardest location to find because we needed to build a rickety bridge between two high cliffs across which we could drive an old truck,' says Wincer. 'It gets trapped in the middle, tangled in vines and the bridge actually tips the truck upside down. The Phantom saves a small boy before everything collapses and falls into the gorge five hundred feet below.' It was an enormous engineering and logistical endeavour, requiring eleven weeks of preparation and construction, made all the more perilous by a three-week spell of bad weather and some particularly harrowing stunt work. 'The final shot is basically The Phantom and the boy swinging to safety, the truck falling and the bridge collapsing, and multiple cameras squirting from every angle. It was most spectacular.' Finally, in mid-December, *The Phantom*'s globetrotting adventure reached its climax in Wincer's native Australia, where the Sengh Brotherhood's hidden cave, two hundred feet in length and stretching more than fifty feet above the stage floor, became the largest interior set ever constructed in the country. *The Phantom* wrapped on 13 February 1996, almost sixty years to the day since the character first appeared in print.

COSTUME FITTING: While the temptation to take the 'Bat-suit-with-nipples' approach to The Phantom's signature snug-fitting purple body stocking must have been great, costume designer Marlene Stewart, who previously created costumes for films as diverse as *Terminator 2*, *JFK* and *The Doors*, chose to design a costume which highlighted, rather than hid, actor Billy Zane's own physique. Curiously, the vivid purple of The Phantom's costume originally came about by accident. Originally envisaged as a character called 'The Gray Ghost', Falk saw his hero in grey (in black and white strips) or green (in colour strips) to blend in with the jungle. The publishers, however, had other ideas. 'They didn't get the colour specifications and he ended up in purple running around a green jungle,' Falk noted, '[and] for years The Phantom was in crimson red in Europe. They just got black and white proofs and didn't know what to do.'

MUSIC: As well as having worked with director Simon Wincer on *Operation Dumbo Drop*, composer David Newman had previously scored such films as *The Nutty Professor*, *The Flintstones*, *Boys on the Side* and *Matilda*. Newman's music for *The Phantom* was an intriguing and effective blend of adventure serial-style strings and ethnic instruments, creating a distinction between scenes set in the lush jungle of Bengalla and the concrete jungle of New York.

CLASSIC QUOTES:
Diana Palmer: 'Who are you?'
The Phantom: 'Good Samaritan.'
Sala: 'I bet you're better than good.'

The Phantom: 'There's a woman involved.'
Phantom's dad: 'Saints be praised. It's about time!'

Drax: 'History is about to be made, and you're all part of it. Not an equal part, of course, but an important part nonetheless.'

Quill: 'I've killed The Phantom.'
Kabai Sengh: 'Join the club. We've all killed him over the years. He keeps coming back.'

TRAILERS: Perhaps wisely, the trailer for *The Phantom* shows only glimpses of the eponymous hero, focusing on a speech by the megalomaniacal Drax, interspersed with voice-over narration: 'In a dangerous world . . . in a treacherous time . . . evil is a fact . . . and courage is a phantom.' Huge captions then fill the screen as scenes from the film play out – 'THIS SUMMER . . . THE ADVENTURE . . . THE ACTION . . . THE

LEGEND . . . BEGINS' – before the voice-over resumes: 'There are some who say he is only a myth. Soon they will discover The Phantom is real.'

POSTERS: An early teaser poster showed The Phantom, head bowed, sitting in his chair in Skull Cave, with the legend 'THE GHOST WHO WALKS' picked out by a shaft of light. The regular 'one-sheet' poster went for a more dynamic image: The Phantom with his clenched fist in the foreground, showing the skull ring with beams of light coming from its eyes, accompanied by the rather self-consciously hip 'SLAM EVIL!' tag-line.

TAG-LINE: 'THE GHOST WHO WALKS' (teaser posters); 'SLAM EVIL!' (main campaign).

WHAT THE PAPERS SAID: In the US, *Variety* suggested that, while it hardly stood to vanquish the celluloid incarnations of Superman and Batman, *The Phantom* had 'a pleasingly astute sense of its place in the great scheme of things pulp, [bringing] a light touch to appealingly old-fashioned action material'. *Variety* also praised the film-makers' resistance to the idea of modernising or complicating its hero, who, like much of the surrounding film, is 'unapologetically two-dimensional'. In the UK, *News of the World* critic Jonathan Ross wore his purple heart on his sleeve when he said, 'As far as straight-ahead, rip-roaring action goes, *The Phantom* is spot on.' Few of his countrymen were as generous, with *Time Out* largely blaming the film's failure on 'uncharismatic' performers: 'Leading man Billy Zane [is] plastic and soulless in Lycra . . . Treat Williams barks as bully-boy Drax to numbing effect and Catherine Zeta Jones proves remarkably boring as a dyke-vixen villainess.'

BOX OFFICE: *The Phantom* might as well have been a ghost who walked through empty cinemas when the film debuted in the US on 7 June 1996, grossing just $5 million in its opening weekend, and $17.3 million overall, thus giving it a lasting legacy as one of the weakest performers among big-screen comic book adaptations. Like the comic, the film fared rather better overseas, but failed to capitalise on the character's built-in recognition factor.

CONTROVERSY: The fact that two editors are credited on screen, but only one in the press handbook, is testament to the fact that the film was extensively re-edited once principal photography had been completed. Indeed, the entire pre-title sequence – in which the history of The Phantom is explained for the uninitiated – was added to appease audiences after test screenings proved disastrous.

TRIVIA: The name of the Palmers' butler, 'Falkmoore', is derived from The Phantom's creator Lee Falk and one of the comic's most famous artists, Ray Moore. Another character, Jimmy Wells, borrows his name from Falk's original nomenclature for The Phantom's alter ego.

FUTURE INCARNATIONS: In late 2002, Crusader Entertainment and Hyde Park announced plans to bring The Phantom back to the big screen in a 'gritty', 'high-tech' new film written by Judge Dredd scribe Steven De Souza. 'There is a great history there, the whole legend of The Phantom, how it was handed down four centuries with the vow to take on piracy and bad guys,' said Hyde Park chief Ashok Armitraj. 'The major thing is to put him in a contemporary setting with the weapons and gizmos and *Matrix*-style stuff which wasn't done in the previous film.'

DVD AVAILABILITY: Given the film's financial failure, it is perhaps forgivable that both the US and UK DVDs currently available have no additional features save for the theatrical trailer. Mercifully, both editions preserve the film's original theatrical ratio of 2.35:1, while the UK (Region 2) disc offers a great number of subtitling options, as befits such an internationally renowned character.

FINAL ANALYSIS: One only has to look at the number of producers, executive producers and co-producers on the credits of *The Phantom* to see how much of a struggle this adaptation of the world-famous comic book, sixty years old this year, endured before reaching the screen. There are nine producers in all, three of whom – Joe Dante (*Gremlins*), Robert Evans (*The Godfather*) and Alan Ladd Jr (*Braveheart*) – are virtually household names, a testament to the difficulty of adapting comic books to the screen even in the post-*Batman* age. The dilemma faced by the film-makers was clear: should they update and alter the story to suit modern audiences, or remain faithful to the spirit of a classic adventure? For better or worse, they chose the latter, with every aspect of The Phantom's personality, background and supporting characters painstakingly researched and fully realised. But for the bulk of contemporary mainstream audiences, the film was just *too* faithful to the comic book, which did not so much inspire it as *blueprint* it. In the six decades since The Phantom first appeared, audiences had become too sophisticated to be attracted to any film centred around ancient skulls, and rather better informed than to buy any legend about American heroes going about the jungle saving the natives – they know, in fact, that most of America's own natives were exterminated *by* their country's so-called heroes. Yet there is something laudable about the film's innocence, and something to be said for a film that might best be described as good old-fashioned fun.

EXPERT WITNESS: 'So many writers are disappointed with the adaptations of their work, but I think it's great. It's not dark like *Batman* – it has the lightness of *Indiana Jones*. They did a marvellous job, from Simon Wincer up and down, and in my view, it sounds like, feels like, looks like and *is* The Phantom.' – **Lee Falk, Creator of The Phantom**

Men in Black (1997)

(98 minutes)

Directed by Barry Sonnenfeld
Producers Walter F Parkes and Laurie MacDonald
Screen Story and Screenplay by Ed Solomon
Executive Producer Steven Spielberg
Co-Producer Graham Place
Based on the Marvel Comic by Lowell Cunningham
Director of Photography Don Peterson ASC
Production Designer Bo Welch
Editor Jim Miller
Costume Designer Mary E Vogt
Music by Danny Elfman
Visual Effects Supervisor Eric Brevig
Alien Make-up Effects by Rick Baker
Casting by David Rubin CSA and Debra Zane CSA

CAST: Tommy Lee Jones ('*K*'), Will Smith (*James Darrel Edwards III*/'*J*'), Linda Fiorentino (*Dr Laurel Weaver*/'*L*'), Vincent D'Onofrio (*Edgar*), Rip Torn (*Zed*), Tony Shalhoub (*Jack Jeebs*), Siobhan Fallon (*Beatrice*), Mike Nussbaum (*Gentle Rosenberg*), Jon Gries (*Nick, van driver*), Sergio Calderón (*Jose*) Carel Struycken (*Aquillian*), Frederic Lane (*INS agent Janus*), Richard Hamilton ('*D*'), Kent Faulcon (*1st lieutenant Jake Jensen*), John Alexander (*Mikey*), Keith Campbell (*perp*), Ken Thorley (*Zap-Em man*), Patrick Breen (*Mr Redgick*), Becky Ann Baker (*Mrs Redgick*), Sean Whalen (*passport officer*), Harsh Nayyar (*news vendor*), Michael Willis (*cop in morgue*), Willie C Carpenter (*police inspector*), Peter Linari (*tow truck driver*), David Cross (*Newton, morgue attendant*), Charles C Stevenson Jr ('*B*'), Boris Leskin (*cook*), Steve Rankin, Andy Prosky (*INS agents*), Michael Goldfinger (*NYPD* *sergeant*), Alpheus Merchant (*security guard*), Norma Jean Groh (*Mrs Edelson*), Bernard Gilkey (*baseball player*), Sean Plummer, Michael Kaliski (*first contact aliens*), Richard Arthur (*2nd first contact alien*), Debbie Lee Carrington (*alien father*), Verne Troyer (*alien son*), Mykel Wayne Williams (*scared guy*)

UNCREDITED CAST: John Darrah (*army officer*), Karen Lynn Gorney (*announcer*), Patricia McPherson (*Elizabeth Ann Reston*), Stephanie Palifero (*INS agent*), Joe Paparone (*police inspector*), Chloe Sonnenfeld, Sylvester Stallone, Danny De Vito, Barry Sonnenfeld, Al Roker, Newt Gingrich, Dionne Warwick, George Lucas, Anthony Robbins, Isaac Mizrahi, Steven Spielberg (*aliens on TV monitor*), Lowell Cunningham (*MiB agent*)

TITLE SEQUENCE: The opening titles, designed by Pablo Ferro (*The Addams Family* films), appear in a white hand-drawn font as a firefly flies out of a starry sky, only to be swallowed up by a dragonfly. As the opening titles continue, the camera follows the dragonfly as it hovers over a roadway, flies in front of a full moon (a Steven Spielberg trademark), narrowly avoids a tractor-trailer rig and another oncoming vehicle, flies on towards the camera, and is finally splatted on the windscreen of a truck. 'I always liked [this] because I thought it sets the tone,' says director Barry Sonnenfeld. 'You think you're looking at this beautiful dragonfly and then – *clap!* – I've just ended whatever dreams you've had about this little bug. I said to Alan Munro who did that part of the visual effects, "This is the feather in *Forrest Gump*," because I was the director of *Gump* for a while, so it's my own little *Gump* joke.'

SYNOPSIS: When agents from the Immigration and Naturalisation Service (INS) make a routine stop of a truckload of illegal immigrants, two black-suited agents claiming to be from 'INS Division 6' single out one of the immigrants, quickly revealing him to be a different kind of illegal alien: a blue extraterrestrial named 'Mikey'. When Mikey tries to escape, Agent D fumbles his weapon, but Agent K shoots it, leaving a mess that can only be cleared up by a 'neuraliser' – a device used to erase memories, which K uses not only on the other INS agents, but also his partner, agent D. Meanwhile, in New York City, detective James Edwards is chasing a suspect with superhuman powers, who, when cornered, tells Edwards the world is about to end, blinks with two sets of eyelids, and then throws himself off a building. During the subsequent interrogation, Edwards is visited by Agent K, who takes him to meet a local fence, Jack Jeebs, who turns out to be an alien. Although K neuralises Edwards, he invites him to 504 Battery Park – Division 6 headquarters – the following day, where he passes an entry exam and is invited to join the secret agency known as the 'Men in Black', monitoring extraterrestrial life on Earth. When he agrees, he is given a new identity ('J') and assigned, along with K, to investigate an unauthorised alien landing in upstate New York. It transpires that this illegal alien – a giant insect disguised in the suit of a farmer named Edgar – is on Earth to steal an entire galaxy so small it can be contained within the decorative collar of an Aquillian's pet cat. The Aquillians, meanwhile, park a battle cruiser in orbit around Earth, threatening to destroy the entire planet in order to prevent the galaxy getting into the hands of the bug. With a little help from mortician Dr Laurel Weaver, the bug is destroyed and the galaxy recovered – at which point K tells J he is retiring; he was training a replacement, not a partner. As K is neuralised and returns to his former life, J is seen with another partner – Dr Laurel Weaver, now dressed as a *Woman* in Black: Agent L.

ORIGINS: 'I first heard about the "Men in Black" when a friend of mine [Dennis Matheson] saw a large black car and said, "That looks like what the Men in Black would drive," ' Lowell Cunningham recalled. 'I was immediately fascinated and pressed him for information, and he told me these stories about how the mysterious Men in Black appear to cover up UFO sightings, and it struck me that this would be a great project.' Although Cunningham initially envisaged the project as a television series, he knew it would be hard to break into television. 'But I knew people who had gotten into the comics industry, so I showed the proposal around for a couple of years until I finally hooked up with Malibu Comics. I had a contract with them within a week.' The six-issue miniseries, published between 1990 and 1992, was successful enough to warrant a second mission for *The Men in Black*, but, ironically, 'both series were out of print when the studios expressed interest in it'.

DEVELOPMENT: Husband and wife producer team Walter F Parkes and Laurie MacDonald (*Twister*) optioned Cunningham's comic book in the summer of 1992, and commissioned Ed Solomon – co-writer of *Bill and Ted's Excellent Adventure* and *Bogus Journey* – to write the screenplay. Since Solomon's early drafts were faithful to the comic book, preserving the darkly humorous tone, the producers knew they needed a director who would be able to turn this kind of material into popcorn entertainment. Barry Sonnenfeld, who had performed a similar feat with Charles Addams' cartoons in *The Addams Family* and *Addams Family Values*, seemed like a natural choice. 'There really isn't anyone else like Barry with such keen comic sensibilities and great visual style,' noted MacDonald. 'He's a comedy director that doesn't rely on jokes, but instead relies on understanding the comic situation and playing it absolutely straight.'

Unfortunately, Sonnenfeld was busy developing an adaptation of Elmore Leonard's *Get Shorty*, and although he remained attached to *Men in Black*, when MGM gave *Get Shorty* the go-ahead, Sonnenfeld said goodbye to *Men in Black*. Instead, says Sonnenfeld, 'They hired another director, Les Mayfield, on the basis of [his] remake of *Miracle on 34th Street*. They hadn't seen it, but hired him because they heard it was good. Well, for whatever reason, they saw it and decided that Les was not the guy that they wanted to direct *Men in Black*, so they didn't have a director. Then, [while] I was on the last week of shooting *Get Shorty* in LA, my wife and I were at this trendy brunch place called 'Ivy at the Shore', and there was [Sony head of production] Barry Josephson at a table with Uma Thurman having brunch. So I went up to Barry and I said, "Look, I still love *Men in Black*, and if you're willing to wait until I've finished post-production on *Get Shorty*, I'd love to do the movie." And they waited. So I got to have my cake and eat it too – I got to direct *Get Shorty* and *Men in Black*.'

In early drafts, the script's locations ranged from Laurel, Kansas to Washington DC and Nevada, with much of the action taking place underground. Sonnenfeld's biggest influence on the script was the idea that the story should be centralised in New York City. 'We basically rewrote the script from scratch, putting it all in New York, because that's where I knew it had to take place [for] a lot of reasons. One is that I felt that if there are aliens, that they could exist in New York [and] blend in incredibly easily, because we're very used to people talking to themselves, having ears that are different sizes, being pasty and scaly and scratching in weird ways. And, secondly, New Yorkers are both blasé and tolerant: they're very tolerant of people being on the street, and totally blasé about it. And also, it was a good place to go, with lots of icons [that look] as if they're flying saucers or rocket ships.'

Pre-production, which would last more than a year, began in the spring of 1995, with four-time Academy Award®-winning special effects artist Rick Baker conceptualising alien creatures while production designer Bo Welch – a frequent Tim Burton collaborator who worked on *Edward Scissorhands*, *Beetlejuice* and *Batman Returns* – began imagining the world the Men in Black would inhabit. Welch took his initial inspiration from the conceit that the MiB organisation was formed in the early 1960s, 'a very Kennedyesque period in history when everyone was really motivated toward space travel and goals, and there was this weird optimism'. One of Welch's principal influences was Finnish architect Eero Saarinen, who designed the TWA terminal at New York's John F Kennedy airport. 'I looked at the headquarters as a sort of alien Ellis Island, where aliens come in and out to be monitored,' he explained. 'This is also where the MiB work, so I felt it should have the look of an airport terminal – very open and busy.'

CASTING: Although Clint Eastwood was the first actor to be offered the role of K, Academy Award® winner Tommy Lee Jones (*The Fugitive*, *Batman Forever*) also turned it down, feeling that the 1993 draft of the script had not captured what Jones had liked about the comic book when producers Parkes and MacDonald had first sent it to him; Jones has said that it was executive producer Steven Spielberg who persuaded him to change his mind, promising that the script would improve. Chris O'Donnell (*Batman and Robin*) and David Schwimmer (*Friends*) both turned down the role of J before it was offered to Will Smith; ironically, it was not his success in either *Bad Boys* or *Independence Day* that led Barry Sonnenfeld to sign the ascending star opposite Jones. He was cast before either film opened on the strength of his title role in the popular TV series *The Fresh Prince of Bel Air* and on the recommendation of the director's wife. 'She was a big fan of *Fresh Prince* and Will as a person,' says Sonnenfeld, 'and we both really liked *Six Degrees of Separation*. So I went to LA and met with Sony Pictures, and they said, "Will Smith? What about Chris O'Donnell? What about Keanu [Reeves]?" Whoever that week had the number one and number two [ranking] at the box office, you know? Tommy Lee Jones and Will Smith, in retrospect, seem like a really great idea,' he adds, 'but at the time you wouldn't necessarily have said, "That'll be the next comedy team." '

John Turturro (*Barton Fink*) was offered the role of Edgar before Vincent D'Onofrio (*Full Metal Jacket*) accepted it; Texan-born actor Rip Torn, a veteran of TV's *The Larry Sanders Show*, was chosen to fill the shoes of Zed, while Tony Shalhoub (*Big Night*), Mike Nussbaum and Carel Struycken (Lurch from Sonnenfeld's *Addams Family* films) were among those chosen to play aliens. 'Carel's great,' says Sonnenfeld. 'He's got such a great face. I feel terrible, because there's this line where he's in the refrigerator and Linda Fiorentino takes him out and points down to Carel – who's totally not in make-up, it's just him – and she says, "Look at this – he's got a unique cranial structure unlike anything I've ever seen on the planet" or something, and we're talking about *him*! He's not even in prosthetics!'

PRODUCTION: Principal photography began in March 1996. Will Smith's schedule on the TV series *The Fresh Prince of Bel Air* meant that the first elements to be filmed were, unusually, the first scenes of the film itself, with Sony sound stages doubling for the desert as Agent K finds a genuine alien hiding among a group of illegal aliens. When Smith arrived two weeks later, he and Jones quickly established a classic comedy partnership, with Jones acting as the 'straight man' to Smith's clown. Says Sonnenfeld, 'With *Men in Black* I said I want to remake *The French Connection* with aliens – that's gonna be funny. Because basically you've got Tommy Lee Jones playing Gene Hackman as 'Popeye' Doyle, but instead of having some drug dealer up against the wall and Gene saying, "All right, Billy, where'd you hide the drugs, I know they're somewhere," you've got Tommy with some alien taking him down, and never acknowledging that this is an unusual thing to do.'

Although filming progressed relatively smoothly, the biggest problem for the film-makers was to come up with an ending which was stronger than that of the script, which originally ended with a philosophical-cum-existential debate between Agent J and 'Edgar bug' about the nature of the universe. As Sonnenfeld explained, 'I convinced Sony that we needed some action in our action–adventure–comedy. [Then] we basically had a week to come up with the whole [new] ending.' Sonnenfeld says that there were at least five or six different endings mooted. 'At one point Linda got neuralised and [K] didn't. We had a year in pre-production, five months of shooting, and we still didn't have an ending. And the last weekend before we shot [the final scenes], we wrote this ending where [J] figures out to start killing Edgar-bug's relatives.'

Perhaps understandably, the decision led to friction between Sonnenfeld and creature effects supervisor Rick Baker, who had worked for a year on the sequence, only to have his animatronic creation replaced by CG. As Baker recalls, 'We made this giant "Edgar bug" for the end sequence that they ended up not using because of script changes, even though we put a lot more work into that than any of the other things in *Men in Black*. But they rewrote [the ending] the night before they started filming it, and what they wrote wasn't really appropriate for what we built. It was a shame,' he adds, 'because it was the coolest thing we made for the movie, and where we focused all our efforts, it being for the big climactic scene.'

As if changing the entire ending at such short notice were not enough, the film-makers decided to go a radical step further after preview audiences indicated their confusion at the film's actual *plot*: who the aliens are, and why they are after the tiny galaxy on the cat's collar. In the original script, two warring alien races, the Baltians and the Aquillians, are fighting for possession of a tiny galaxy, while a race of bugs thrives on the ensuing carnage. Now, the warring races are on the verge of signing an historic peace agreement as the Baltians have agreed to hand the galaxy over to the Aquillians. Since this will leave the bugs without sufficient food, one of them comes to Earth, kills the two ambassadors and steals the galaxy, causing hostilities to resume between the Baltians and Aquillians – with Earth caught in the crossfire. 'It's like in old westerns with cowboys shooting at each other from behind a rock,' says Agent Zed, to which J replies, 'We're the rock?'

Following the test screenings, the film-makers went back into the editing room and realised that the plot exposition came from three scenes: the scene at Laschky's diner where 'Edgar bug' kills the two aliens; one of the scenes at MiB HQ in front of the monitoring screen; and the scene in which K shakes down 'Frank the pug' for information. The first was subtitled, which could be made to *read* anything; the second involved a CG monitor screen, which could be made to *show* anything; the third featured a dog with an animated mouth, which could be made to *say* anything. Thus, the film-makers were able to simplify the plot, so that instead of there being three alien races, there were only two: the bugs, and the Aquillians, who are willing to destroy the Earth (albeit apologetically) in order to prevent the galaxy falling into the bugs' possession.

When filming was completed, the studio was so impressed with the material that they granted Sonnenfeld the opportunity to shoot the film's memorable bookends: the opening prologue, in which a bug flies through the night sky before being splatted on the windscreen of a truck; and the end coda, in which Earth and the rest of the entire solar system is revealed as being nothing more than a decoration inside an alien's marble. 'The truth is that there were several things I couldn't do for budgetary reasons until Sony saw the movie,' Sonnenfeld explains. 'The great thing about doing this kind of movie with Industrial Light + Magic is that once they saw the movie and liked it, they spent more money after the fact. For instance, something that was in the script that they wouldn't let me shoot was the opening credits, you know, following this dragonfly. And then the last shot of the movie – the one where it pulls back and back and back – was another shot they had said no to until they saw the movie. And in MiB headquarters there are some shots where we added aliens where there weren't any, walking in the foreground. Rick Baker's puppets, for instance, are very expensive, so when they were saying "You've got to cut Rick's budget by $300,000 or $400,000" we lost some aliens from MiB headquarters, and I always thought it was too bad because Will enters it for the first time, and we weren't seeing enough, and I said, "I think this is the problem, that Tommy's saying 'Ta-da!' but there's no 'Ta-da!' there," so they let me add some aliens to the "Ta-da!" shot.'

MUSIC: Danny Elfman, who had previously scored such comic book adaptations as *Batman*, *Dick Tracy* and *Batman Returns*, composed the memorable score for *Men in Black*, although it was the 'Men in Black' theme song, co-written and performed by Will Smith – based on Patricia Rushen's 1988 song 'Forget Me Nots' – which became most associated with the film, reaching No.1 in the summer of 1997.

CLASSIC QUOTES:
Agent K: 'Put up your arms and all your flippers.'

Edwards: 'NYPD. That means I will knock your punk-ass down.'

Edgar: 'You can have my gun when you pry it from my cold dead fingers.'
Alien: 'Your proposal is acceptable.'

Edwards: 'He said the world was coming to an end.'
Agent K: 'Did he say when?'

Agent K: 'All right, here's the deal. At any given time there are around fifteen hundred aliens on the planet, most of them right here in Manhattan. And most of 'em are decent enough, they're just trying to make a living.'
Edwards: 'Cab drivers.'
Agent K: 'Not as many as you'd think.'

Agent K: 'We at the FBI do not have a sense of humour we're aware of.'

Agent K: 'I don't suppose you know what kind of alien life form leaves a green spectral trail and craves sugar water, do you?'
Agent J: 'Oh wait, that was on *Final Jeopardy* last night.'

Agent J: 'We ain't got time for this cover-up bullshit! I don't know whether or not you forgot, but there's a alien battle cruiser about to –'
Agent K: 'There's always an alien battle cruiser or a Corillian death ray or an intergalactic plague that's about to wipe out life on this miserable little planet. The only way these people get on with their happy lives is *they do not know about it.*'

Edgar Bug: 'You ever pull wings off a fly? You care to see the fly get even?'

Agent J: 'This definitely rates about a 9.0 on my weird shit-o-meter.'

DELETED SCENES: 'I'd rather have a movie that's ten minutes too short than ten seconds too long,' says Sonnenfeld. 'I really like long post-production [periods], because the more time I have with a movie, the more I get bored with it, and the more I start cutting little things out – things that I thought were funny that I don't think are funny any more. And I don't even mind if a laugh makes you lose another line of dialogue. That's good; I like that. If it means you have to go back [and see it again], that's fine.' Sonnenfeld has worked with editor Jim Miller on all of his previous films, and claims to be 'the only director who's less in love with his stuff than the editor. It's usually the editor who's trying to convince the director that, you know, this scene is fine, but it's not working, and the director says, "Are you kidding? That shot took me eighteen hours!" But with me, I'm saying, "Get rid of it!" and Jim's saying, "Barry, hold on to that for a minute!" "No, no, *get rid of it*!" The joke amongst the crews that work with me is that I'll be the only director who has a special edition laserdisc that's shorter than the theatrical release.' Despite this, surprisingly few scenes were cut from *Men in Black*; most of the changes made in post-production concerned the plot.

TRAILERS: The *Men in Black* teaser trailer features shots of the MiB locker room, with a voice-over narration by Tommy Lee Jones: 'We are the best kept secret in the universe. We work for a highly funded yet unofficial government agency. Our mission is to monitor extraterrestrial activity on Earth. We are your best, last and only line of defence.' The teaser then cuts to a spectacular spacecraft crash landing. 'You're under arrest for violating sections 4153 of the Tycho treaty,' says K. 'Step away from your busted-ass space vehicle and put your hands on your head,' says J. 'You know how to use these things?' he asks K, indicating their weapons. 'No idea whatsoever,' K replies. (Both of these lines were cut from the final film.) 'Men in Black,' intones a voice-over. 'Protecting the Earth from the scum of the universe.'

The regular trailer continues the theme, but reveals more of the film: 'We work for a highly funded yet unofficial government agency,' runs Jones' narration. Caption: MORE SECRETIVE THAN THE CIA. Jones: 'Our mission is to monitor extraterrestrial activity on Earth.' Caption: MORE POWERFUL THAN THE FBI. AND THEY'RE LOOKING FOR A FEW GOOD MEN. THEY ARE THE MEN IN BLACK. 'From now on you will have no identifying marks of any kind,' Jones tells J. 'You are no longer a part of the system. We are the Men in Black.' A more traditional voice-over rounds up: 'Columbia Pictures and Amblin Entertainment present a new film from the director of *The Addams Family* and *Get Shorty*.'

POSTERS: Several iconographic posters were produced for the film, including three early teaser posters: one showing the 'MiB' logo and tag-line; and two separate 'one-sheets' showing full-face shots of Tommy Lee Jones ('MR JONES') and Will Smith ('MR SMITH') respectively, each wearing sunglasses and dressed in black. The regular poster put the two of them together, in front of the Manhattan skyline, now carrying large weapons.

TAG-LINE: 'Protecting the Earth from the scum of the universe.'

WHAT THE PAPERS SAID: 'A witty and sometimes surreal sci-fi comedy, *Men in Black* is a wild knuckleball of a movie that keeps dancing in and out of the strike zone,' remarked *Variety*. 'Diabolically funny at times and wonderfully matter-of-fact in its deadpan tone and presentation of aliens in our midst, this zippy curio . . . feels something like *Ghostbusters* as if done by the Coen brothers.' *Entertainment Weekly* was less enthusiastic, its C+ grade review describing the film as 'a comedy of facetiousness in which the facetious consumes everything in its path [and] celebrates the triumph of attitude over everything else – i.e. any sense that what we're watching actually matters'. Mainstream reviews were typically more complimentary, although the UK's *Time Out* magazine spoke for many when it suggested that the film was 'so much fun . . . that it's almost over before you realise that you've been watching a great idea for a movie in desperate search of a plot'.

BOX OFFICE: *Men in Black* opened in the US on 2 July 1997, scoring an astronomical opening weekend box office of $84 million and an overall worldwide gross of $576 million, making it the most successful film in the history of Columbia Pictures – at least, until another comic book adaptation, *Spider-Man*, stole its thunder five years later. 'Audiences somehow have this weird sense of smell,' says Sonnenfeld, 'and *Men in Black* was something that they were sniffing around four or five months [before the film opened]. Parents with seven-year-old kids started to call me and say, "You know, Barry, when are the action figures coming out? Josh really wants them." And I was, like, "How does Josh even *know* about *Men in Black*?" There's this strange sort of psychic, karmic thing that happens with movies. And even before word of mouth, there's this weird "stuff", which *Men in Black* got in spades. It's so weird how that "social phenomenon" thing happens. The whole two years I was directing the movie,' he adds, 'I was always saying to executive producer Steven Spielberg and producers Walter [Parkes] and Laurie [MacDonald] that this is a *small* movie. It's a buddy story with some aliens – it's not a blockbuster. There's no shot of some manly man on a motorcycle crashing through glass in slow motion with a big explosion behind him, so don't think of it as a big movie. And they kept saying, "Yeah, OK, fine, Barry, sure." The box office made it big, but for me it was always sort of a little movie about two guys. It had no design to be anything except a small buddy movie.'

AWARDS: *Men in Black* was nominated for three Academy Awards®, including Best Art Direction – Set Decoration, Best Music and Best Make-up; its success in the latter category marked Rick Baker's fifth Academy Award®. The film was also nominated for a Best Special Effects BAFTA and a Golden Globe award for Best Motion Picture – Comedy/Musical, while Danny Elfman's score was nominated for a Grammy. Will Smith won two of the film's five MTV Movie Award nominations: for Best Fight and Best Movie Song, while the Academy of

Science Fiction, Fantasy & Horror Films awarded the film three Saturn awards: Best Music, Best Science Fiction Film and – for Vincent D'Onofrio – Best Supporting Actor.

TRIVIA: The date Agent K says humankind was first visited by extraterrestrials is 2 March 1961.

Agent K attempts to arrest 'Edgar bug' for violation of article 4153 of the Tycho treaty. In American date format, 4/1/53 is Barry Sonnenfeld's birthday (yes, he was born on 1 April).

SEQUELS & SPIN-OFFS: Although *Men in Black* was successful in getting the original comic book back in print – albeit under the imprint of Marvel Comics, which had since taken over Malibu Comics – the first spin-off from the film was an animated series produced by Columbia TriStar for The Kids WB. First screened on 11 October 1997, the series ran for four years, with Ed O'Ross (and later Gregg Berger) as 'Kay', Keith Diamond as 'Jay', Charles Napier as 'Zed', Jennifer Lien and later Jennifer Martin as 'Elle'. Fans would have to wait a full five years for a big-screen sequel, however.

'People say that the end of *Men in Black* feels like it's set up for a sequel,' Sonnenfeld said in late 1997, 'and I don't think it is. I think that people just say that because they like the movie, and because it's so short, they want to see more, so they say, "It's set up for a sequel." But if you think about it – well, not really.' At that time, Sonnenfeld knew that the success of the film virtually demanded a follow-up, but he was not yet certain he wanted to direct it. 'Sequels tend to be boring to direct, because you're not discovering anything about the characters,' he explained. 'I'd only be interested in doing it if I could come up with a uniquely different movie, that didn't feel like you were plugging a new villain into the same story.' In early 1998, Sonnenfeld began work on *Wild Wild West*, an adaptation of the 1960s TV series pairing Will Smith and Kevin Kline, followed by the ensemble comedy *Big Trouble*, which suffered distribution problems following the events of 9/11. Neither was a hit, and Sonnenfeld was soon convinced to bet on the sure thing: a sequel to *Men in Black*, for which he managed to reunite Smith, Jones, Rip Torn and Tony Shalhoub – but not, despite the ending of the first film, Linda Fiorentino. Released in the crowded summer of 2002, ruled by *Spider-Man* and *Star Wars Episode II: Attack of the Clones*, *Men in Black II* received generally lukewarm reviews, but managed to gross $190 million in the US and $235 million worldwide, reaching a combined gross of $425 million – barely two-thirds the gross of the original.

Other spin-offs include an original Men in Black novel, *The Grazer Conspiracy*, written by Dean Wesley Smith, and several video games.

FUTURE INCARNATIONS: 'I've discovered Hollywood likes to take things one at a time, so they don't start making plans on a third film until they start seeing box office on the second,' Lowell Cunningham said in June 2002, shortly before *Men in Black II* opened at cinemas. 'I would like to see more Men in Black comics,' he added. 'I've written four issues that have never appeared as of yet from Marvel Comics, and I don't know if they've even been scheduled. I never had the opportunity to bring other agents into the comic book, but I was working towards them in my stories. In the comics it's not just UFOs – there's a supernatural element as well. One of the characters I've written stories [about] more than once, that just haven't appeared [yet] is a supernatural character who was an agent.' Although Sony had yet to commit to a third Men in Black film at press time, Will Smith has stated his willingness to 'put on the last suit you'll ever wear . . . again' for a third time: 'I'm going to be optimistic about the possibility of making *Men in Black III*,' he said at a UK press conference for the sequel. 'I think that as long as people laugh in the movie theatre there's always the possibility to do a sequel. Even more than doing well at the box office, I think the laughter in the movie theatre for [*MiB II*] leaves us room to make another one.'

DVD AVAILABILITY: In the UK and US, two distinct DVD editions are available. The first, suitably dressed in black, is the single-disc 'Collector's Edition' (US title: 'Collector's Series') which, despite being the most basic of the two versions, offers all manner of excellent features and surprises, of which even the most mundane – galleries of still photographs, storyboards and production sketches, the trailer and talent files, CD-ROM features and web links – are above average. More importantly, a brand new 23-minute documentary, *Metamorphosis of* Men in Black, was created especially for the DVD, taking a detailed look at the evolution of the film from comic book adaptation, through pre-production and principal photography, all the way through to a complete change of plot achieved, incredibly, in post-production. The original six-minute featurette is also included, along with the full-length music video of Will Smith's memorable 'Men in Black' rap. 'MiB means what you think you saw, you did not see,' he sings, and this fact is borne out by a fascinating five-angle deconstruction of the scene in which J and K drive upside down in the Jersey tunnel in an ILM-modified Ford. Probably the best feature of all is the unique audio and *visual* commentary, which basically has the silhouettes of Jones and Sonnenfeld in the bottom of the screen, *Mystery Science Theatre 3000*-style, chatting and pointing (and sometimes drawing on the screen!).

The second edition, packaged in silver in the UK and black in the US, is the two-disc 'Limited Edition' which has all of the above and more:

full- and widescreen Dolby 5.1 versions, expanded art galleries featuring over 1,000 still images, a detailed look at creature creation, a deconstruction of the climactic fight scene in the style of the tunnel scene in the 'Collectors Edition', an additional audio commentary track featuring Sonnenfeld, make-up genius Rick Baker, and the ILM visual effects crew, and an 'editing workshop' allowing would-be editors to re-edit three scenes from the film their own way. This edition was superseded by the virtually identical 'Deluxe Edition' in 2002.

FINAL ANALYSIS: When Lowell Cunningham first had the idea of turning the fabled Men in Black – every conspiracy theorist's most feared government spooks – into a story, he saw it as a television show, yet knew it would be easier to break into comics than television. Clearly even Cunningham knew that the Men in Black belonged on screen, but even he could not have imagined the success which would greet Barry Sonnenfeld's film upon its release in the summer of 1997. Nevertheless, as with Sonnenfeld's earlier adaptations of Charles Addams' cartoons, the *Men in Black* movie is clearly strong on premise, character and interpersonal relationships, but extremely weak on plot, squandering the opportunity to place the memorable characters in the midst of anything other than a confusing and slight story in which the Earth is threatened as an afterthought. (The fact that the plot was almost entirely re-envisioned in post-production is not exactly a testament to the film's narrative strength.) On first viewing, the film has more than enough to engage the eyes, with Rick Baker's creature designs, Eric Brevig's special effects, Don Peterman's cinematography and Bo Welch's awesome production design all contributing to one of the most visually stylish movies of the nineties. Unfortunately, subsequent viewings of the film leave the viewer with much the same feelings as those who have encountered the Men in Black: did I just see what I think I saw? Or have I been neuralised?

EXPERT WITNESS: 'I loved its sensibility because I've always believed deeply in my heart that we as humans really don't have a clue about what's going on. I loved the fact that I could make a movie, play it for the reality of the situation, with aliens in it, and let the world know that perhaps we truly don't have a clue.' – **Barry Sonnenfeld, Director**

Spawn (1997)

(94 minutes)

Directed by Mark AZ Dippé
Produced by Clint Goldman

Screenplay by Alan B McElroy
Screen Story by Alan B McElroy and Mark AZ Dippé
Executive Producers Todd McFarlane and Alan C Blomquist
Co-Executive Producers Brian Witten and Adrianna AJ Cohen
Based on the Comic Book by Todd McFarlane
Director of Photography Guillermo Navarro
Production Designer Philip Harrison
Edited by Michael N Knue, ACE
Costume Designer Daniel J Lester
Visual Effects Supervisor Steve 'Spaz' Williams
Visual Effects Producer Tom C Peitzman
Associate Producer Terry Fitzgerald
ILM Animation Supervisor Dennis Turner
ILM Animation and Visual Effects Producer Christian Kubsch
ILM Visual Effects Co-Supervisors Christophe Hery and Habib Zargarpour
Special Make-up and Animatronic Creature Effects by Robert Kurtzman, Gregory Nicotero and Howard Berger
Music by Graeme Revell
Casting by Mary Jo Slater CSA and Bruce H Newberg CSA

CAST: John Leguizamo ('*Clown*'), Michael Jai White (*Al Simmons*/'*Spawn*'), Martin Sheen (*Jason Wynn*), Theresa Randle (*Wanda Blake*), Nicol Williamson (*Cogliostro*), DB Sweeney (*Terrence R 'Terry' Fitzgerald*), Melinda Clarke (*Jessica Priest*), Miko Hughes (*Zack*), Sydni Beaudoin (*Cyan*), Michael Papajohn (*Glen*), Frank Welker (*voice of Malebolgia*), Robia La Morte (*XNN reporter*), John Cothran Jr, Tony Haney (*African liaisons*), Caroline Gibson (*news anchor*), Marc Robinson, Chris Coppola, Jay Caputo (*punks*), Darryl Warren (*security guard*), Mike Akrawi, Romeo Akrawi (*foreign dignitaries*), Jack Coleman (*doctor*), Laura Stepp (*Angela*), Garrison Singer (*anaesthesiologist*), Todd McFarlane (*bum*)

UNCREDITED CAST: Angelie Almendare (*diplomat's wife*), Anthony Genovese (*news anchor*)

TITLE SEQUENCE: The film opens with a pre-title montage of images of fire and brimstone, a dove in flight, the faces of those we will come to know as 'Clown', Malebolgia, Jason Wynn, Al Simmons and 'Spawn', as an ominous voice (belonging to Cogliostro) intones the following: 'The battle between Heaven and Hell has waged eternal, their armies fuelled by souls harvested on Earth. The devil Malebolgia has sent a lieutenant to Earth to recruit men who will turn the world into a place of death in exchange for wealth and power, a place that will provide enough souls to complete his army, and allow Armageddon to begin. All the Dark Lord needs now is a great soldier, someone who can lead his hordes to the gates of Heaven and burn them down.' From here we cut to a military airbase in Hong Kong, where a soldier in a control tower pieces together a projectile weapon which he uses to blow up a jet. Watched by a mysterious figure (Cogliostro), the soldier – whom we will come to know as Al Simmons – detonates a bomb inside the control tower, the flames of the explosion dissolve through to titles, set against more images of fire, notably a spiral descent into the inferno, as the voice continues: 'Like him, I killed in the name of good, but the violence in my life pulled my soul towards the darkness. But I fought and freed my soul. Now I watch for others like me. Men are the ones who create evil on Earth. It is the choices they make that enslave their souls to Hell. This is the test.'

SYNOPSIS: Following the rocket attack, in which 26 innocent civilians were killed along with Simmons' intended target, Jason Wynn meets with a clown-like figure to discuss a deal involving biological weapons. The Clown wants something else as part of the bargain: Simmons, the prized hitman of Wynn's secret agency. The following day, Simmons is collected from the home he shares with his fiancée, Wanda, and learns from his partner, Terry Fitzgerald, of the innocent deaths. Simmons confronts Wynn and a fellow operative, Priest, and tenders his resignation. Wynn accepts on the condition that Simmons takes one last assignment: to wipe out a biological weapons factory in North Korea. Simmons accepts, but during the operation he is betrayed by Priest and Wynn, who release the virus into a town of eight thousand innocent people, and burn Simmons alive. Simmons wakes up in an alleyway, his skin burned, his charred body wracked with pain, to find the clown-like figure mocking him. Fleeing, he encounters Cogliostro, who invites him to join a group of homeless people in Rat City. Not realising he has been gone for five years, Simmons has other ideas, however: he goes home, where he finds that his beloved Wanda has married Terry and spawned a little girl, Cyan. Later, with the help of the repulsive Clown, Simmons starts to piece his memory back together, and learns his true nature: murdered by Wynn and banished to Hell, Simmons was so desperate to see his beloved Wanda again, he struck a deal with the demon Malebolgia – to avenge his own death and lead an army against the kingdom of Heaven. Malebolgia twisted the deal so that Simmons has returned to Earth as 'Spawn', a being neither alive nor dead, with a body made of 'necroplasm' and certain superhuman powers. He vows vengeance on Wynn. Meanwhile, Wynn has not only liberated a deadly biological weapon known as 'HEAT-16' from the North Koreans, he is also in possession of the only vaccine. Spawn confronts Wynn and kills Priest, but is forced to flee when armed troops arrive. After the attack, Clown convinces Wynn to have himself rigged with a heart monitor, so that if he is killed, the virus will be released. Then Clown transforms himself into a creature called 'The Violator' for a showdown with Spawn in Rat City. Cogliostro teaches Spawn to harness his powers, and he sets off in search of Wynn. Meanwhile, Terry hacks into Wynn's files and discovers his plan, but as he tries to alert the media, Wynn bursts in with Clown, taking Terry, Wanda and Cyan hostage. Spawn arrives too, just in time for Wynn to kill Wanda – except that it's only Clown in disguise. Cogliostro and Spawn follow Clown into Hell, where Spawn destroys Malebolgia's evil army and returns to Earth. The Violator follows them, but Spawn's new-found control of his powers makes it easier for Spawn to defeat him. The biological weapons are disarmed, Wynn is taken away, Terry goes back to his family – and Spawn watches vigilantly over them all.

ORIGINS: Spawn began as the teenage doodling of one of comic book art's few superstars, Todd McFarlane, who began drawing the character in the late 1970s. 'Back then it was set in more of a *Star Wars* environment, 'cause that was the big deal back then,' he says. 'But the costume was probably about ninety-five per cent the same – I added some spikes and chains, but the markings on the mask, the cowl and the cape and even the logo were all there in those early sketches.' A decade later, after drawing a 1988 relaunch issue of *Spider-Man* which sold more than two million copies, but which failed to earn McFarlane any more than his standard fee, he quit Marvel and, with seven other comic creators, set up a new company, Image Comics, in 1991. Within a year, the upstart enterprise found itself with a third share of the US comics market, based on the popularity of a single character: a former government assassin known as Al Simmons, who returns from a five-year sojourn in Hell to become 'Spawn', a foot soldier in the ongoing war between Heaven and Hell. 'Earth is the battlefield, human souls the prize,' he is told, as he struggles to come to terms with his new 'life', which, since his beloved widow, Wanda, has already remarried and had a longed-for child, and his hideously disfigured features keep him out of daylight, is as much a netherworld as the inferno which spawned him. 'Spawn makes Batman look like a pussy,' McFarlane says of his creation, '[but] even though he has these incredible powers, he's still trying to figure out (a) what they are, and (b), what good they are. Am I gonna use [them] for personal gain? Am I gonna try and help people? Am I gonna become a bad guy, give in to the dark side? It's just about a man trying to deal with his life.' Or, more accurately, his life after death.

Published in February 1992, *Spawn* #1 sold a staggering 1.7 million copies. McFarlane's creation has since remained one of the consistent performers in the notoriously unstable comics market, selling over 80 million comics across 120 countries in over a dozen languages, and spawning video games, action figures, toys, merchandise, an adult-oriented animated series – and a live-action movie.

PREVIOUS INCARNATIONS: Spawn's screen debut came just three months before the film opened at cinemas. On 15 May 1997, HBO aired the first episode of an adult-oriented animated series based on the comic books. The inaugural production of HBO Animation, the series assembled an impressive voice cast, led by Keith David (*The Thing*) as Spawn/Al Simmons, and featuring Ronny Cox (*RoboCop*), and James Keane (*Dick Tracy*); and an equally impressive crew, including supervising director Eric Radomski (*The New Adventures of Batman*), writer Alan McElroy (who scripted the *Spawn* movie, then in post-production); voice director Jack Fletcher (*Aeon Flux*); and finally, creator and executive producer McFarlane, who had the final say in all creative aspects – a fact even he found a little surprising: 'It was kind of odd that they put me in charge,' he says. 'I knew nothing, really, about animation, [but] I asked the questions and learned along the way.'

Although initial ratings were uninspiring, the success of the two different video versions – one unedited and unrated, the other re-formatted with a PG-13 rating – led HBO Animation to commission a further six episodes. That, says McFarlane, was when the problems began. 'Ninety per cent of episodes seven through twelve were essentially rewritten from head to toe,' he reveals, adding that time pressures meant that this was often done *after* the animation had been completed. In other words, he says, 'We had to work with the visuals and the structure of the stories, but essentially rewrite everything.'

In fact, although he was more closely involved with Spawn's animated incarnation than he was with the live-action movie, McFarlane was one of the series' most vocal critics, and took a larger hands-on role at the beginning of the third series. With much of the original story arc having been resolved in the last episodes of the second series – as Simmons finally confronts Wanda with the terrible truth about his existence – series three provided the perfect opportunity for a grass roots rethink. Although all of the principal members of the voice cast returned for series three, HBO turned the calibre of guest performers up a few notches: Eric Roberts (*Doctor Who*), Robert Forster (*Supernova*) and Jennifer Jason Leigh (*The Hudsucker Proxy*) were just three of the well-known actors lending their voices to supporting characters for what would, nevertheless, prove to be the series' swansong.

DEVELOPMENT: When it was clear that his comic creation was an unprecedented success, Todd McFarlane immediately began pitching the film to Hollywood studios, coming close to signing with Sony-owned Columbia, until he realised that he would have to sign away all rights to the character, and even the comic books, if he agreed to let them make the film. Although the deal fell through, Sony ultimately bought the video-game rights, paying more than twice the sum it had offered for the film franchise. 'They just assume that because they're going to spend their forty million bucks that they own you lock, stock and barrel. It wasn't important enough to me to play that game.' After passing on Columbia's offer, McFarlane met with New Line boss Michael De Luca, who would later bring *Blade* to the big screen, in early 1993; a deal was signed less than a year later, and McFarlane immediately began looking for someone with whom to collaborate on the script. He found them when he met Mark AZ Dippé, Clint Goldman and Steve 'Spaz' Williams, digital effects pioneers who had worked on *The Abyss*, *Terminator 2* and *Jurassic Park*, and who were then looking to break out as film-makers. '[They] were around when we were doing the original pitches to the big studios, more as special effects guys just to show what they're able to accomplish,' McFarlane explained. 'But as time went by . . . we just became more hell-bent on doing this as a team effort.' Dippé and screenwriter Alan B McElroy (*Halloween 4: The Return of Michael Myers*, *Rapid Fire*) worked out a story outline – essentially a linear version of the comic book storyline. 'The comic book starts with him being Spawn and then you start to catch up,' McFarlane observed. 'The studio thought it would be better to not get too fancy in terms of the storytelling, so we tweaked that and rewrote that and fixed it up for what seemed like a long time. [But] what seems like a long time to me [was] actually a short period compared to a lot of other movies.'

CASTING: 'It's not like they gave us Tom Cruise,' says Todd McFarlane. 'They said, "Here's how much money you got for special effects, and here's a few dollars to hire a couple of actors." Nevertheless, the film-makers managed to attract an impressive supporting cast to bolster relative newcomer Michael Jai White: John Leguizamo (*William Shakespeare's Romeo + Juliet*), future *West Wing* star Martin Sheen (*Apocalypse Now*, *The Dead Zone*), Theresa Randle (*Bad Boys*) and DB Sweeney (TV's *Strange Luck*, *Eight Men Out*). 'We had a good story and a lot of interesting designs that attracted people,' director Mark Dippé told *Cinefantastique*. 'Some of the actors had kids who were fans, Martin Sheen in particular.' As for White and Leguizamo, who would be shooting for twelve hours a day in full-body prosthetics, 'I think that the opportunity to play Spawn and Clown were obviously very attractive to actors because they are very different but very powerful characters.

There's a lot of room there in terms of the range of the characters. That's basically what attracted them.'

PRODUCTION: *Spawn* got the green light in the spring of 1996, and New Line wasted no time in putting the film into production. As he watched his baby being filmed – literally, given that his real-life daughter appears in the birthday party scene – McFarlane was suddenly faced with the realities of film-making. 'The actual making of the show is a slow, tedious process,' he observed. 'It's not all that exciting to sit there and watch them moving lighting around and spending two and three hours putting on make-up. I was more concerned whether the script was where I wanted it. Are the costumes like I want? Have we talked about the mood of the story? Are the characters where they're sypposed to be? Have we talked about camera angles, storyboards and all the other things? Well, all the pieces are there – I don't need to stand here and watch them put it together.'

Although director Dippé had no objections to having McFarlane around, he understood why the character's creator might find the production process tedious – after all, this was a film where most of the work would be done in post-production. 'A big part of the film is visual effects,' Dippé told *Cinefantastique*, 'and we're seeing all these creatures and characters come to life in ways that you can't do in real life. You can't have Spawn doing these amazing things, and you can't have Violator beating the crap out of somebody in real life. So it requires these post-production processes.' Dippé was also grateful that McFarlane understood that certain changes would need to be made in bringing the character from the page to the screen. 'It's a film. It's not the comic book. There are differences,' he said. 'But I always wanted to stay true to the character, [which] I think is one of the more dynamic and brilliant characters in comic books, period. I wanted to maintain Todd's concept and creation from the beginning. But there are also things in the film that the Spawn neophyte will not appreciate whereas the Spawn fan will. The world of Spawn is a very complicated and large one. You can't really include it all. You can make a movie based on two issues whereas the world of Spawn has branched out into all these sub-stories and ideas.'

COSTUME FITTING: Costume designer Daniel J Lester had worked on two earlier comic book adaptations, *Timecop* and *The Rocketeer*, before landing the job of bringing Spawn's extraordinary comic book costume to the big screen – a challenge the scale of which its creator was all too aware. 'The biggest things were how to make a cape forty feet long that's believable,' he explains, 'because comic books are cool, but it's all frozen imagery. You can read a hundred *Superman* comics but as soon as you see a guy in tight spandex, it doesn't look the same – it's a guy in pyjamas, so you're always fighting how to make it not look goofy.' It was ultimately decided that elements of the costume would be computer-generated, such as the billowing cape, the chains and spikes, and the transformation from one kind of costume to another.

MUSIC: Having composed the music for some fifty films, including the comic book adaptations *The Crow* (and its sequel) and *Tank Girl*, New Zealand-born Graeme Revell was ideally suited to creating music for *Spawn*. Nevertheless, his visceral heavy rock score was complemented by a number of songs, many of which are collaborations between hard rock and dance music acts: 'Satan' by Orbital with Kirk Hammett, 'Familiar' by Incubus and DJ Greyboy, Marilyn Manson's 'Long Hard Road Out of Hell', Silverchair and Vitro's collaboration 'Spawn', a DJ Spooky remix of Metallica's 'For Whom the Bell Tolls (The Irony of it All)', Prodigy and Tom Morello's 'One Man Army', '(Can't You) Trip Like I Do' by The Crystal Method and Filter, and 'Skin Up Pin Up' by 808 State vs Mansun. The soundtrack features additional collaborations between Korn and The Dust Brothers, Butthole Surfers and Moby, Stabbing Westward and Wink, Henry Rollins and Goldie, Slayer and Atari Teenage Riot, Soul Coughing and Roni Size.

CLASSIC QUOTES:
Jason Wynn: 'You don't quit us, son. We're not the US Postal Service.'

Jason Wynn: 'Enjoy your retirement, old man. And don't worry about Wanda, I'll take good care of her.'
Al Simmons: 'You touch her and you're a dead man.'
Jason Wynn: 'You're the dead man. See you in Hell, Al!'

Clown: 'Oh, what an adorable little girl. Oh, look at her, can I keep her? No of course not, no pets allowed.'

Clown: 'I don't mind being short, fat and ugly, but the pay sucks. Hey, easy with that face, I'm eating!'

Clown: 'How do I put this to you? You're pushing up daisies. You're in permanent nap time. You're fertiliser. Is any of this sinking in? You're dead. D-E-D, dead.'

Spawn: 'Are there any normal people left on Earth? Or is everyone just back from Hell?'

Spawn: 'You sent me to Hell, Jason. I'm here to return the favour.'

Priest: 'It's a little early for Halloween, Simmons.'
Spawn: 'Where you're going, every day is Halloween.'

TRAILERS: The trailer wisely plays to the film's strengths, offering glimpses of the best special effects, as a stern voice-over attempts to make sense of the plot: 'Imagine a substance with the power to destroy humanity. Imagine a creature insane enough to use it. Imagine a hero on the verge of creation. From flesh to steel, from blood to blade, from man ... to Spawn. Evil has a new enemy, justice has a new weapon, and the world has a new hero.' Spawn speaks only one line in the entire trailer – instead, as with the film, Clown steals the show.

POSTERS: The *Spawn* posters featured an extremely iconic image in which a thin blue sliver of Spawn's face emerges from black, with one green eye and a portion of red cape also visible.

TAG-LINE: 'Born in darkness. Sworn to justice.'

WHAT THE PAPERS SAID: In the US, *Variety*'s Todd McCarthy described *Spawn* as 'narratively knuckleheaded [but] visually teeming ... a moodily malevolent, anything goes revenge fantasy that relies more upon special visual and digitally animated effects for its intended appeal than any comics-derived sci-fier to date.' Roger Ebert, writing in the *Chicago Sun-Times*, also felt that the film relied too heavily on (albeit 'impressive') special effects, but added that Michael Jai White 'makes a powerful Spawn with a presence both menacing and touching, and Clown is an inspired villain with one wicked one-liner after another ... As a visual experience,' he added, '*Spawn* is unforgettable.' In the UK, *Time Out*'s Nick Bradshaw was more dismissive: 'In future, Dippé, an old SFX hand, needs to think about how to tell a story, rather than merely throw together elements of *Batman*, *Blade Runner*, *Star Wars* and James Bond.'

BOX OFFICE: *Spawn* opened in the US on 1 August 1997, grossing an impressive $21.21 million from just over 2,500 screens. Although its earnings fell off sharply the following weekend – presumably hardcore Spawn fans wanted to see the film as soon as it opened – its overall US gross was a satisfactory $55 million. Overseas, however, *Spawn* grossed just $15 million, putting its worldwide gross at $70 million – still a healthy return on New Line's $45 million investment, particularly after ancilliaries such as video, DVD and TV sales were factored in.

AWARDS: *Spawn* was nominated for three awards at the 1998 Blockbuster Entertainment Awards: Favourite Male Newcomer (Michael Jai White), Favourite Supporting Actor – Horror (John Leguizamo) and Favourite Supporting Actress – Horror (Theresa Randle). It was also nominated as Best Film at the Catalonian International Film Festival in

Sitges, Spain, but walked away instead with a prize for Best Special Effects.

TRIVIA: Al Simmons and Terry Fitzgerald are named after college friends of Todd McFarlane, both of whom now work for him. The dog, Spaz, is named after visual effects supervisor Steve 'Spaz' Williams.

APOCRYPHA: In 1997, Todd McFarlane told *Cinefantastique* that '[movie offers] came out of the woodwork right when *Spawn* first came out'. Yet he remembers it differently in the sleeve notes for the DVD: 'The largest hurdle was attempting to convince Hollywood that they should create a movie centred around a character from the pit of Hell. However, once I bombarded them with all of the facts and figures proving *Spawn* was the bestselling comic book in the country, the doors opened a little faster.'

FUTURE INCARNATIONS: In June 1999, New Line Cinema boss Michael De Luca announced that the studio was developing a *Spawn* sequel, telling the website *Corona Coming Attractions* that McFarlane had turned in a treatment that was 'more like *Se7en* than the *Spawn* movie. We loved it and gave him the go-ahead to proceed with the first draft, which we should get in six weeks.' McFarlane was working with fellow comics creator and screenwriter Steve Niles, who told the website *Comics Continuum* in early 2002 that the script for what he described as an 'R'-rated sequel had gone through several polishes. 'I think the biggest surprise will be how different this film will be from the first,' he added. 'I think *Spawn 2* will be much more accessible to all types of movie fans because it will cross the lines between the superhero, horror and crime genres.' A few days later, John Leguizamo revealed to *Sci Fi Wire* that he would love to return for the sequel, but hoped that it would be darker than the original. 'I'd like this one to be really as 'R' [rated] as it should be, as the comic was,' he added.

By this time, producer Don Murphy (*From Hell*, *The League of Extraordinary Gentlemen*) was shepherding the project along at Columbia, which had snapped up the rights when New Line declined to pursue a sequel to its moderately successful *Spawn*. 'In some ways the first movies of a comic book are sometimes not their best, because you have to get the origin out,' says McFarlane. 'Then you do the next one, you hit the ground running. Part of the sale to Sony was that we all understood that the first movie did OK, but it wasn't a big blockbuster, so the way to entice them wasn't to go in there and say, "Hey, I need $100 million to do this grand thing." So we said, "Let me do it 'R' rated and make it more spooky and more of a suspense horror drama, and I don't need a huge special effects budget." And they were like, "Cool."

Steve and I sent them the screenplay, and as we were waiting for notes on one of the drafts, *Spider-Man*, *Men in Black II* and *XXX* came out, all of them PG-13 movies, and suddenly their note was, "Maybe we should think bigger than this low-budget scary 'R'-rated *Spawn*." As long as they can keep some of the creepy elements that sets Spawn apart from Superman and Batman, then I'm OK with it. If we can blow it up but really make him a guy that scares the crap out of you, that's OK. If you look at the *Lord of the Rings* movies, they're both PG-13 movies, but there's some scary stuff in there.'

By December, the script was being drastically re-tooled by another comics and scriptwriter, Hans Rodionoff (*Grendel*, *Tortured Souls*). 'One of the things Niles and Todd did with the last draft was have it be more of a Sam and Twitch story,' Rodionoff told the website *Comics2Film*, referring to two popular *Spawn* supporting characters who had minor roles in the first film. 'The problem is it became solely a Sam and Twitch movie and there wasn't enough Spawn.' Rodionoff was planning to take another approach. 'If you dropped Blade into *Lethal Weapon*, you've got sort of what I'm going for,' he explained.

DVD AVAILABILITY: In the UK (Region 2) and US (Region 1), *Spawn* is available in the 'director's cut' – the equivalent of an 'R'-rated version of the film, originally released in the US with a 'PG-13' rating – with a host of extras: commentary by Todd McFarlane, director Mark AZ Dippé, producer Clint Goldman and visual effects supervisor Steve 'Spaz' Williams; an interview with McFarlane entitled *Todd McFarlane: Chapter and Verse*; a 'making of' featurette; a gallery of over two hundred conceptual sketches; a storyboard-to-scene comparison; the music promos for songs by Filter/The Crystal Method and Marilyn Manson/Sneaker Pimps; and the US trailer.

All three seasons of HBO's animated series *Todd McFarlane's Spawn* are also available as separate DVDs – *Todd McFarlane's Spawn*, *Todd McFarlane's Spawn 2* and *Todd McFarlane's Spawn 3: The Ultimate Battle* – each containing six uncut episodes, and a four-disc DVD edition comprising uncut editions of all eighteen episodes and a bonus DVD-ROM with an exclusive interview, *Inside the Mind of Todd McFarlane*.

FINAL ANALYSIS: Sometimes the visual flair of a comic book simply refuses to be translated to the screen; other times, those who make the attempt are simply under-qualified for the job. Both are true in the case of *Spawn*, a film made by talented special effects wizards rather than film-makers *per se*, adapted from a comic book by an artist so gifted the dialogue in the first half-dozen issues was almost an unwelcome distraction. (Frankly, it was not until other writers took over scripting the comic book that Spawn began to get interesting.) Any film which credits more visual effects personnel than cast members has to be suspect, but in *Spawn* even the effects are anything but special – especially given the pedigree of the talent involved, mostly veterans of such ground-breaking films as *Terminator 2*, *The Abyss* and *Jurassic Park*. As Spawn, newcomer Michael Jai White looks lost (and not in a good just-back-from-the-dead kind of way) in his leading role – perhaps understandable next to such seasoned players as John Leguizamo and Martin Sheen, here chewing so much scenery they must have had the set decorator up all night. In fact, their performances are among the few things to recommend the movie, especially compared to the far superior HBO animated series, which made far more of the same source material. Perhaps pandering to the PG-13 audience wasn't the way for Spawn to go. Then again, perhaps there is no way to render Spawn in three dimensions; looking back at the early issues of the *Spawn* comic book (recently republished in a gorgeous new hardcover edition), I realised that McFarlane's art is so dynamic and kinetic, it seems more like a movie than the film it became. And while both scripts leave a lot to be desired, there is no bad acting in comic books, the budget is unlimited and the special effects are flawless every time.

EXPERT WITNESS: 'I don't think a movie's any different to a comic book – as soon as you're done you wanna redo it. It's just that in movie-land you've got to wait years before you get your crack at doing it again. It could be argued that we got so concerned about getting some of the visuals down that we got distracted from making a tighter, more concise story in terms of getting people interested. I would've liked to make it a little more spooky, a little less linear and friendly. There may have been too much of the little kid, and some of the Hell scenes didn't scare you enough.' – **Todd McFarlane, Creator/Executive Producer**

Blade (1998)

(120 minutes)

Directed by Stephen Norrington
Written by David S Goyer
Blade and Deacon Frost Characters Created for Marvel Comics by Marv Wolfman and Gene Colan
Produced by Peter Frankfurt, Wesley Snipes and Robert Engelman
Executive Producers Stan Lee, Avi Arad and Joseph Calamari

Executive Producer Lynn Harris
Director of Photography Theo van de Sande ASC
Production Designer Kirk M Petruccelli
Edited by Paul Rubell
2nd Assistant Director Rebecca Strickland
1st Assistant Director Barry M Thomas
Unit Production Manager Roee Sharon
Music by Mark Isham
Costume Designer Sanja Milkovic Hays
Co-Producers Andrew J Horne and Jon Divens
Make-up Effects by Greg Cannom
Music Supervisor Dana Sano
Casting by Rachel Abroms CSA and Jory Weitz

CAST: Wesley Snipes (*Eric Brooks*/'*Blade*'), Stephen Dorff (*Deacon Frost*), Kris Kristofferson (*Abraham Whistler*), N'Bushe Wright (*Dr Karen Jenson*), Donal Logue (*Quinn*), Udo Kier (*Dragonetti*), Traci Lords (*Racquel*), Arly Jover (*Mercury*), Kevin Patrick Walls (*Krieger*), Tim Guinee (*Dr Curtis Webb*), Sanaa Lathan (*Vanessa Brooks*), Eric Edwards (*Pearl*), Donna Wong (*nurse*), Carmen Thomas (*senior resident*), Shannon Lee (*resident*), Kenny Johnson (*Heatseeking Dennis*), Clint Curtis (*creepy morgue guy*), Judson Earney Scott (*Pallantine*), Sidney Liufau (*Japanese doorman*), Keith Leon Williams (*Kam*), Andray Johnson, Stephen R Peluso (*paramedics*), Marcus Aurelius (*pragmatic policeman*), John Enos III (*Blood Club bouncer*), Eboni Adams (*martial arts kid*), Lyle Conway (*Reichardt*), Freeman White III (*menacing stud*), DV De Vincentis (*vampire underling*), Marcus Salgado, Esau McKnight Jr (*Frost's goon*), Erl (*Von Esper*), Matt Schulze (*Crease*), Lennox Brown (*pleading goon*), Yvette Ocampo (*party girl*), Irene A Stepic (*Slavic vampire Lord*), Jenya Lano (*Russian woman*), Levani (*Russian vampire*)

UNCREDITED CAST: Stephen Norrington, Gerald Okamura (*vampires*)

TITLE SEQUENCE: A blood-red New Line Cinema logo precedes a few opening credits, followed by a stylised sequence set in 1967, as a pregnant black woman is wheeled into a hospital, bleeding from the neck. As her newborn baby is delivered, the titles continue over time-lapse footage of a city growing dark. A caption tells us that the time is 'NOW' as a red-haired woman and her blond boyfriend drive through the darkened city streets, and make their way through a giant meat locker into a large anteroom, where a private party is in progress. Hundreds of revellers pack the dance floor, where a DJ standing in front of a banner that reads 'BLOODBATH' pumps the crowd with driving techno beats. As the man pushes his way through the crowd of partygoers, he becomes separated from his girlfriend, gets punched by a pretty girl, bumps into a fierce-eyed man, and is surprised when he sees drops of red liquid land on his hand, apparently from the ceiling. He tastes it: blood. He looks around. He looks up. Suddenly, the sprinkler system is turned on, showering the room with blood. Equally suddenly, all of the partygoers, including the man's girlfriend, are transformed into vampires, who start to beat the living shit out of him – until they are interrupted by a black man dressed in a leather coat, wearing black shades and carrying a shotgun. They call him 'the daywalker'.

'The prologue is, in a sense, Blade's origin,' screenwriter David S Goyer explained. 'In the comic books, Blade first appeared on the scene in the mid-seventies, which would have meant that his mother was bitten by a vampire sometime in the early fifties or late forties. We obviously had to update it. But it was important to Stephen Norrington and myself, from the very beginning, to establish the fact that this film would be different from a lot of vampire stories that had come before it. We didn't want this film to be particularly gothic, so we wanted to open the film in a very mundane [setting], [like] an ER room, and kind of subvert expectations. This scene is supposed to represent the genesis not only of Blade but the genesis of his hatred. There was a bit of dialogue cut from the original script in which Blade actually says that he remembers being born, literally being cut from his mother's womb. So we felt it was important to show this scene.'

SYNOPSIS: At a party in an abattoir, the guests all transform into vampires, only to be attacked by a mysterious man they call 'the daywalker', who gatecrashes the party, killing many of the vampires and setting fire to one of them (Quinn). Later, at the morgue, the charred body comes back to life, biting the neck of a young haematologist, Dr Karen Jenson. The daywalker rescues her, appearing impervious to the bullets fired into him by cops, and takes her to his hideaway, where an old man named Whistler injects her with garlic in an attempt to prevent her from turning into a vampire. Meanwhile, the party's organiser, a vampire named Deacon Frost, is reprimanded by a council of 'pureblood' vampires for drawing too much attention to their existence. Frost, who thinks the vampires should be ruling humans, not hiding from them, is unrepentant. Karen wakes to find Whistler injecting the daywalker, who calls himself Blade, with a serum which, she learns, prevents his vampire side from taking over his human side, for he is the grown-up child of the pregnant woman bitten by a vampire. Together, Blade and Whistler are vampire hunters, the few fighting a secret war against an almost invincible foe – and Frost wants to spread the war above ground. Using Karen as bait to catch one of Frost's 'familiars',

Blade finds his way into the library containing The Book of Erebus, an archive of ancient scrolls, sacred to vampires, which Frost has translated: it prophesies the coming of 'La Magra', the blood god – a tide of blood which will turn all in its path into vampires. In the library, Blade and Karen are attacked by Quinn, Frost's right-hand man, but Whistler intervenes, and they escape. While Karen discovers that a blood anti-coagulant called 'EDTA' explodes when it comes into contact with vampire blood, Frost kills Dragonetti, the vampire overlord, and sets about making the prophecy come true. But first, he invades Blade's hideout, has Quinn bite Whistler, and kidnaps Karen. Blade finds his friend and mentor half-dead – or, worse, undead – and, having learned that Frost needs Blade's blood to make the prophecy come true, gives him a gun. As he walks away, Whistler shoots himself. Blade arms himself to the teeth, adding capsules of EDTA to his arsenal, and pays a visit to Frost's crib, where he is shocked to meet his mother – not dead, but a vampire. Caught off guard, Blade is subdued by Frost – whom, he discovers, was the vampire who bit her – and taken to a temple for the ritual by which Frost hopes to summon La Magra. Blade has other ideas, however: with Karen's help, he sets about dispatching as many vampires as possible before taking on Frost, now transformed into La Magra. An epic battle ensues, but Blade wins out, thanks to the explosive power of the EDTA. With Frost/La Magra defeated, Karen goes back to searching for a cure for vampirism, while Blade goes back to work – in Moscow.

ORIGINS: Marv Wolfman had been working as a freelance writer and editor for several comics publishers by the time he was invited to take over Marvel's *The Tomb of Dracula* title in 1972. Despite the Universal horror associations of his name, Wolfman had never seen a vampire movie, and was not particularly drawn to the horror genre; by way of research, he read Bram Stoker's *Dracula*, and fell in love with it. 'A couple of issues later Blade just came to me,' he told *Cinefantastique*, 'the concept of the black vampire hunter with the teak knives acting like stakes; the whole origin for the character . . . the attitude, the entire look, which was very unusual.' Also unusual was the fact that an amoral African-American vampire hunter with a range of razor-sharp weaponry and a stripper girlfriend, and who was himself half-vampire, managed not to fall foul of the Comics Code Authority, a self-censorship body, similar to that of Hollywood in the 1930s, set up to police morality, sexuality and profanity of comic books. (Although violence was endemic in the medium, blood was forbidden – a tricky prospect for a vampire title.) Despite such restrictions, 'Blade: The Vampire Hunter' made semi-regular appearances in *The Tomb of Dracula*, which ran for seventy issues, folding shortly after Wolfman moved to DC Comics.

Although Blade continued to appear intermittently throughout the 1980s, and was briefly revived in the 1990s, 'Blade: The Vampire Hunter' was arguably eclipsed by TV's *Buffy the Vampire Slayer*, and has never fully regained its initial popularity – except at the movies.

DEVELOPMENT: *Blade* had first been mooted as a potential movie property in the late 1980s, when New World Pictures – Marvel's parent company at the time – commissioned a screenplay from writer–producers William Rabkin and Lee Goldberg, who had written for the *Hunter* TV show, and later *SeaQuest DSV* and *She-Wolf of London*. Deliberately modelled on the classic western – notably Sergio Leone's *Once Upon a Time in the West* – the script was set in a small town which had reached an agreement with a tribe of vampires living in a housing development, whereby the vampires would prey on the weak and the dying so long as the rest of the townspeople didn't bother them. When Blade arrives in town and starts killing the bloodsuckers feeding on the local community, the vampires effectively declare war, and all hell breaks loose. Nothing came of the adaptation, and ironically it was not until Marvel was facing bankruptcy in the early 1990s that New Line Cinema expressed interest in Marv Wolfman's tale of a black vampire hunter.

Screenwriter David S Goyer – whose futuristic film noir *Dark City* was directed by Alex Proyas (*The Crow*), and who scripted *The Crow: City of Angels* and an unproduced adaptation of Marvel Comics' *Dr Strange* – had originally hoped for a career in comics, and since he wasn't a particularly good artist, writing seemed to be the way in. Finding no takers for his comic scripts, however, he switched to films. Goyer had been a fan of comics like *Tomb of Dracula* and *Blade* when he was young, and was intrigued to hear that New Line had acquired the rights to the *Blade* comics, with a view to making a low-budget ($6–8 million) 'blaxploitation' flick, with rapper-turned-actor LL Cool J (*Toys*) as the star, and African-American cinematographer-turned-director Ernest Dickerson (*Tales from the Crypt presents Demon Knight*) at the helm. Goyer, who wanted to offer an alternative approach, asked his agent to set up a meeting with New Line boss Michael De Luca. 'I went in and pitched a trilogy of big-budget films, $40 million-plus films,' he told the website *Comics2Film*. 'Three whole movies. I just had a different take on the direction they were going in that was much more fully conceived. It sprang out from the comics but it wasn't exactly the comics per se.'

De Luca gave Goyer the go-ahead to write the first script, at which point he and Dickerson, the film's potential director, watched every vampire film ever made – not to purloin ideas, but to subvert the trappings of the genre. 'I wanted to do a post-modernist vampire film,' he told *Cinefantastique*. 'I wanted to demystify vampires to a certain extent and approach it from a street [perspective].' Two films Goyer and Dickerson were unable to see were *From Dusk Till Dawn* and *Vampire in Brooklyn*, both of which took a similar approach – unfortunately, neither of them had yet been made. Having satiated himself on everything from *Captain Kronos Vampire Hunter* to *Interview with the Vampire*, Goyer wrote the first draft in three weeks. 'There have been something like three hundred and fifty vampire films made, and in most of those the focus is on the vampires,' says Goyer. 'You can only see so many movies where the vampire is this mysterious dark creature, and at a certain point people just get tired of that. I wanted to make the vampires of *Blade* not romantic at all. I was much more interested in 'heroin chic' vampires. They're not particularly attractive, there's nothing particularly romantic about living forever. They're all scumbags. I was conscious of wanting to go in a different direction from the Anne Rice subgenre of vampire movies that have been out there.' Dickerson ultimately left the project (he would later make the undead-themed *Bones* with rapper/actor Snoop Dogg), at which point, Goyer wrote another draft in collaboration with two potential directors, David Fincher (*Se7en*) and future *Spider-Man* director Sam Raimi. Finally, director Stephen Norrington, a former British-born special effects virtuoso (*Aliens*, *Hardware*) whose low-budget first feature, *Death Machine*, had earned his ticket to Hollywood, was agreed upon by all parties, signing to the project in early 1997.

By this time, the script had been sent to Wesley Snipes, then attached to another Marvel Comics adaptation, *Black Panther*. Snipes promptly agreed to both star in the film and produce it under his newly launched Amen Ra Films banner. 'I had played a lot of cops and the good guy stuff,' said Snipes, 'and wanted to do something more edgy, with more overtones of the whole *New Jack City* type image. This was perfect, because he's a good guy who's also a bad guy, and a bad guy who's really a good guy, and a guy who's misunderstood, with this kind of bio-chemical imbalance.'

CASTING: New Line boss Michael De Luca believed that there were only three black actors who had the right age, physique and box office draw to make *Blade* economically viable: Laurence Fishburne, Wesley Snipes and Denzel Washington. Snipes was the unanimous first choice, however, despite the fact that the vampire hunter seemed a far cry from his most recent films, intimate dramas like Spike Lee's *Jungle Fever* and Mike Figgis' *One Night Stand*. Nevertheless, said Goyer, 'From the very first draft he wanted to be Blade. That was a real treat. When I went over to Wesley's house to go over the script, he had a *Shaft* tape in the VCR. He wanted that kind of hipness to the character.'

In the comics, the character of Deacon Frost was a great deal older, and more of a classic vampire, than the version ultimately portrayed by Stephen Dorff (*Backbeat*, *Blood and Wine*). The fact that Norrington saw the film's chief villain differently was part of what appealed to Dorff, who typically avoided commercial films. 'Steve Norrington was the one that made me feel like this was one to go for,' says Dorff. 'I was excited about working with Wesley, but I didn't wanna do a silly comic book movie – I think most movies are that have been done about comic books – and this one I knew Steve Norrington was gonna come in with a bang and do something different, and I kind of just trusted him . . . I liked the idea of a present-day vampire movie with this comic book element,' he adds, 'I never really looked at it as a comic book movie because we were trying to make a real movie, and that was what I liked about Steve Norrington, he said, "We're gonna make a comic book movie but keep it grounded in reality." '

Although Goyer wrote the part of Whistler, a kind of modern-day Van Helsing, with British actor Patrick McGoohan (*The Prisoner*) in mind, Norrington's casting of singer/songwriter and actor Kris Kristofferson (*Lone Star*) perfectly captured Goyer's idea of the ageing gunfighter passing the baton to his protégé. Udo Kier, who played the title role in *Blood for Dracula* (1974), was an ideal choice for the role of Dragonetti. Former porn actress Traci Lords was an equally inspired choice to play Racquel. 'We decided on Traci pretty late in the game, but it was an epiphany to all of us,' producer Peter Frankfurt recalls. 'She was exactly right for the role. It's a small role but it's a pivotal role because it really sets up this world; arrogant and sexy and "Gee I wanna be them, but they're very dangerous," and she embodied all that.'

PRODUCTION: Filming took place in several Los Angeles locations, with production designer Kirk M Petruccelli – later to work on another comic book adaptation, *Mystery Men* – deliberately contrasting the down-and-dirty downtown which Blade inhabits with the vampires' more sterile and chic world – an imaginative inversion of the usual vampire stereotypes. 'The vampire world is angular; it's hard, very reflective, glossy and cold [whereas] the human world is chaotic and rusty; it's organic, it's in decay.' Nevertheless, much of the filming took place on sets, allowing the film-makers a greater degree of flexibility, particularly when staging the film's many fight scenes. Snipes worked closely with Norrington and stunt coordinator Jeff Ward in choreographing the film's many demanding fight and action sequences. 'You can count on the fingers of one hand the number of stunts that Wesley didn't do himself,' said Goyer. 'It made the shoot a lot easier since we didn't have to use a stunt double for many of the hand-to-hand combat scenes,' added Snipes.

One character who created unique challenges during production was Pearl, the 900-pound vampire librarian, as conceptual artist Miles Teves explains: 'Pearl started out fat, androgynous and Asian – and simply kept getting fatter with every new version,' he says. 'Finally Steve Norrington scanned one of my drawings into Photoshop and stretched it horizontally to show me what he really wanted. I then did a final rendering that was approved, and the maquette began. Once it was finished,' he adds, 'it was moulded, cast, cut up into sections and used as a template for the full size sculpture.' This then had to be brought to the set by forklift truck, with one actor (Eric Edwards) playing the head, two women on either side playing each of the hands, and a fourth individual acting as the feet.

COSTUME FITTING: Costume designer Sanja Milkovic Hays, who had worked on *Independence Day* and *Star Trek: Insurrection*, chose a classic look for the black vampire hunter: long black coat, black body armour and black shades. 'I thought Blade would have a sort of geometic neoprene-meets-SWAT-Team appearance,' Hays explained. 'The coat has a style which is uniquely Blade. It's also functional, with all these pockets and compartments where Blade stashes his weapons. Plus, it's lightweight, which is critical for Wesley, since he wears it during many of the heavy action sequences.' Hays chose a different look for Blade's nemesis. 'Frost's wardrobe is rising-executive-vampire-rebel,' she quipped.

MUSIC: 'I can describe what I want for the score in two words: I want it *evil* and *ambient*.' So said director Stephen Norrington to his chosen composer, Oscar® nominee Mark Isham, who had previously written music for some seventy feature films, ranging from the highly regarded horror film *The Hitcher* to the children's drama *Fly Away Home*, with a comic book adaptation (*Timecop*) and big-budget special effects films (*Waterworld*) in between. 'Action pictures can be a lot of fun because of the adrenaline and the largesse of the sound you develop,' he says, 'and in the case of *Blade* it's a dark, slightly futuristic, slightly fantastic world, but nonetheless [one] that has a lot of similarities to the darker side of present-day life. So you could develop a musical vocabulary that drew upon those things: some of the fantastic, some of the almost classic comic book devices, in the sense of *Superman*- or *Batman*-type heroic themes. But you can also have a lot of contemporary, dark, evil ambient, music.' For *Blade*, Isham eschewed the usual tradition of scoring to picture. 'I took a slightly different approach, just through my initial discussions with Stephen,' he explains. 'We decided – it may even have been his idea – to just write some music, and not even worry about [fitting it to] the picture.' The postponed release date gave Isham more time than usual to work on the film, and the result was a score as visceral as the images it complements. Although the film also features tracks by New Order ('Confusion (Pump Panel Recon Mix')), Creedence Clearwater Revival ('Bad Moon Rising'), Aphex Twin, Japanese pop band Shonen Knife, DJ Krush, Expansion Union, Solitaire, and others, only four songs from the film appear on Tee Vee Toons' *Blade* soundtrack, which features a great deal of 'inspired by' filler. Mark Isham's musical score is also available, however.

CLASSIC QUOTES:

Blade: 'Quinn, I'm getting a little tired of chopping you up. Thought I might try fire for a change.'

Whistler: 'You bringing home strays now?'
Blade: 'She's been bitten.'
Whistler: 'Then you should've killed her.'
Blade: 'I know. But I didn't.'

Deacon Frost: 'Maybe it's time we forgot about discretion. We should be ruling the humans, not running around making back alley treaties with them. For fuck's sake, these people are our food, not our allies!'

Deacon Frost: 'You may wake up one day and find yourselves extinct.'

Whistler: 'Vampires. We hunt 'em, you see. Moving from one city to the next, tracking their migrations. They're hard to kill. They tend to regenerate.'
Dr Karen Jenson: 'And I'm supposed to believe all this?'
Blade: 'Well you already met Mister Crispy at the hospital.'

Whistler: 'One other thing: buy yourself a gun. You start gettin' sensitive to daylight, find you're thirsty, regardless of how much you have to drink, I suggest you take that gun and use it on yourself. Better that than the alternative.'

Blade: 'There are worse things out tonight than vampires.'
Dr Karen Jenson: 'Like what?'
Blade: 'Like me.'

Blade: 'OK, vampire anatomy 101. Crosses and running water don't do dick, so forget what you've seen in the movies. You use a stake, silver or sunlight.'

Blade: 'You give Frost a message from me. You tell him it's open season on all suckerheads!'

Quinn: 'You took my arm, man! But it's cool – I got a new one. Think I'll ever play the piano again? "You can slice him, you can dice him, but the Quinn man keeps on coming!" '

Superman
Christopher Reeve proves that a man can fly in this shot from *Superman: The Movie.* (© Warner Bros.)

Akira
Akira was the film that took manga into the mainstream.
(© Akira)

Batman
Jack Nicholson is rumoured to have received $75 million after cutting a revenue deal for his appearance as The Joker in *Batman*.
(© Warner Bros.)

Teenage Mutant Ninja Turtles
Kevin Eastman and Peter Laird introduce the Teenage Mutant Ninja Turtles in their origin story from 1984. (© Mirage Studios)

Dick Tracy
Warren Beatty as Dick Tracy and Madonna as Breathless Mahoney in the 1990 adaptation of the newspaper strip. (© Touchstone)

X-Men
Cyclops (James Marsden), one of the leather-clad heroes who proved that the most successful comic book of all time could translate into a movie franchise.
(© 20th Century Fox)

The Crow
James O'Barr's sinister depiction of The Crow.
(© J. O'Barr)

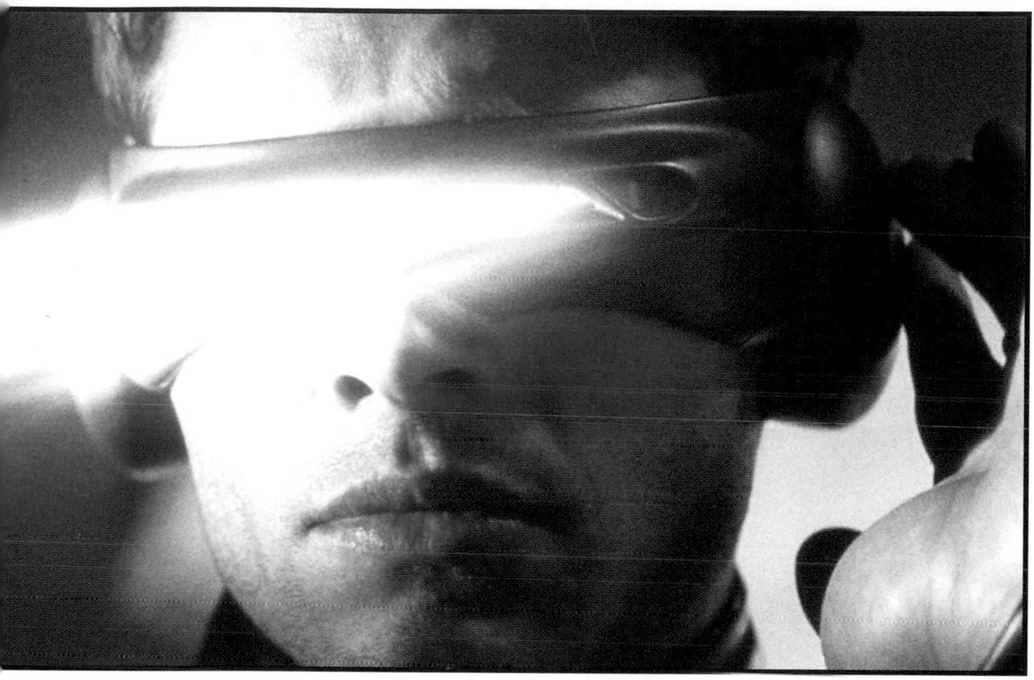

From Hell
In a scene from Moore and Campbell's original graphic novel, a victim eats laudanum-laced grapes, an historical detail that was left out of the movie. (© Alan Moore & Eddie Campbell)

Blade
Marv Wolfman, Gene Colan and Tom Palmer's original depiction of Blade, from the 1970s run of the character in Marvel's *Tomb of Dracula* series.
(© Marvel Characters, Inc.)

Ghost World
Enid and Rebecca reflect on their movie success.
(© Daniel Clowes & Terry Zwigoff)

Road to Perdition
Michael Jr finds out the hard way what his father does for a living in a panel from the *Road to Perdition* graphic novel, replicated in Sam Mendes' film. (© Max Allan Collins & Richard Piers Rayner)

Mystery Men
From zeroes to ... zeroes in superhero costumes: the Mystery Men emerge from the pages of an obscure comic book into a fully-fledged box office flop.
(© Universal Studios)

Spider-Man
Scaling new box office heights, *Spider-Man* shaped the face of comic book movies for the 21st century. (© Columbia Pictures)

Hulk
A 'Hulk Smash!' is what Universal Pictures was hoping for when they put Ang Lee's film into production in 2002. (© Universal)

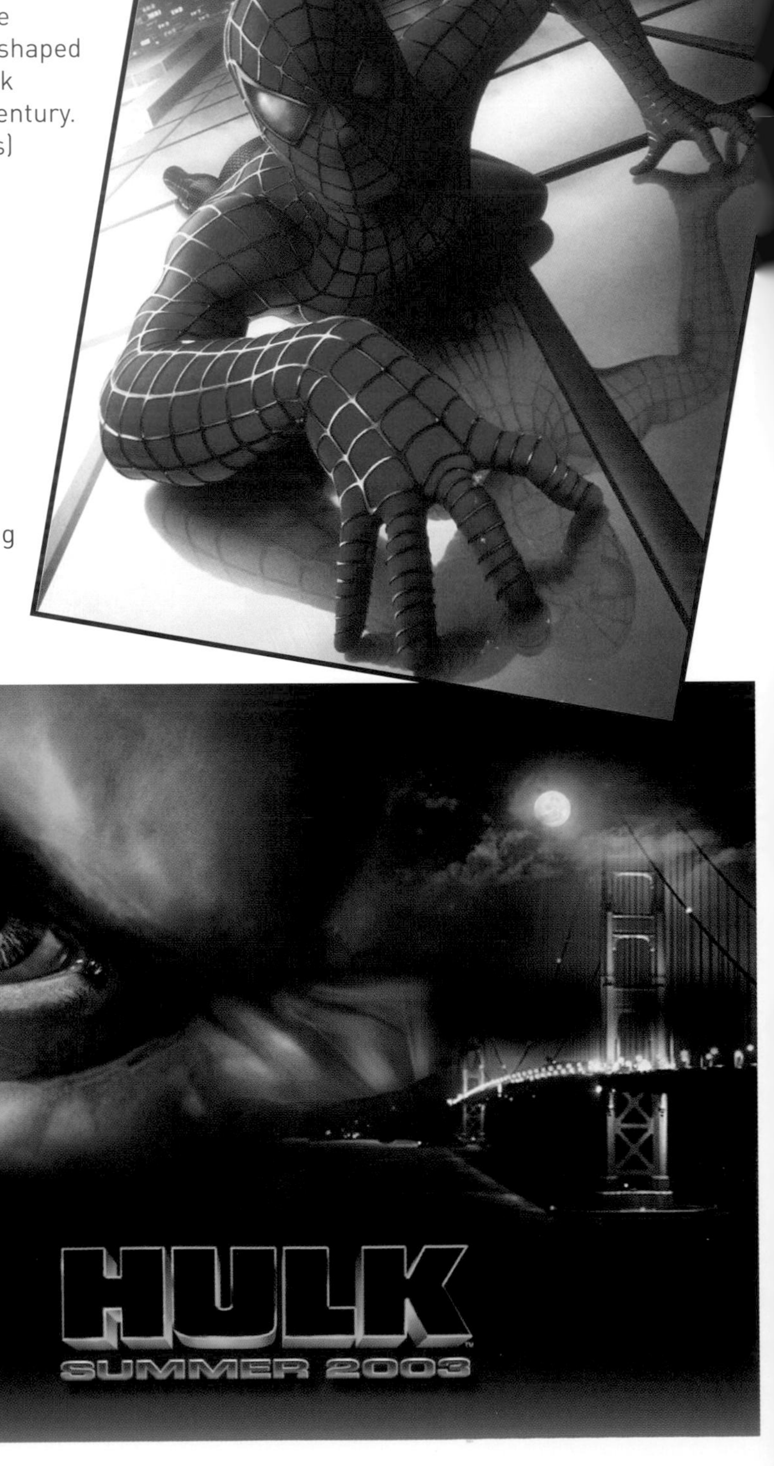

Whistler: 'Catch you fuckers at a bad time?'

Dr Karen Jenson: 'You're one of them, aren't you?'
Blade: 'No. I'm something else.'

Deacon Frost: 'When was the last time you stopped to appreciate a good sunrise?'

Quinn: 'Sorry, old dog. You just got a little long in the tooth.'

Deacon Frost: 'The goal, of course, is to be like you. A daywalker. You got the best of both worlds, don't you? All our strengths, none of our weaknesses.'

Dr Karen Jenson: 'Vampires like you aren't a species. You're just infected. A virus. A sexually transmitted disease.'
Deacon Frost: 'I'll tell you what we are, sister. We're the top of the fuckin' food chain.'

Quinn: 'I'm gonna be naughty! I'm gonna be a naughty vampire god!'

Blade: 'Some motherfucker's always trying to ice skate uphill.'

DELETED SCENES: 'After Karen tries to pick up Blade's sword and triggers the nice little booby trap in the handle, there was a sequence where she finds this muslin-covered tank,' says screenwriter David S Goyer. 'She pulls this muslin away, and there was this human child, maybe a year old, floating in this tank. She's both horrifed and fascinated by it – it looks very angelic – and as she leans in towards it, this creature suddenly jerks awake and it's alive, and it opens this horrible mouth of fangs and kind of gnashes against the side of the tank. I think it would've scared the living shit out of the audience,' he says, 'but New Line felt it was just too horrible. It's one scene I've always regretted not being in the film. The implication was that Blade and Whistler have this creature there to study it, to take genetic samples from and test their weapons on. I really think it would've freaked the audience out.'

Several other alterations were made between script and screen:

- In the original script, Blade's sword had previously belonged to Whistler, the implication being that it had been used to slay Magra a thousand years earlier, and had since been passed down from one generation of vampire hunter to another.
- 'Originally, Pearl had a number of dead children laying about him,' says Goyer, 'because I figured that Pearl was obviously too fat to get out of his bed, and that people would have to bring him bodies.'
- As scripted, it is Blade who kills Whistler, whereas in the finished film he gives Whistler a gun and allows him to take his own life. (Just as well, since Whistler returns in the sequel.)

The biggest alteration the film underwent concerned the ending, as David Goyer explains: 'We had always had trouble with the last twenty minutes of the film, ever since my first draft – how Deacon Frost gets dispatched was always something that was up in the air. There were maybe ten endings that had been written and at least two had been shot: one that involved a sort of Viking funeral for Whistler in which his body was burned in order to make sure he didn't come back. There was an extremely apocalyptic ending in which there was this sort of nuclear explosion of blood that literally decimated a number of city blocks, sort of like the atom bomb scene in *Terminator 2*, and anyone standing gets turned into a vampire, and at the end of the film, Blade and Karen pick themselves up and there are literally hundreds of vampires out on the streets, so it's become "planet of the vampires". The whole idea for the sequel was to do a *Mad Max* film in which the vampires [had] won, the "Final Solution" actually did happen, and humans were kept up in pens and concentration camps being mass-produced for food.'

The ending which was ultimately decided upon was one in which Deacon Frost turns into a CG-animated La Magra, the blood god, likened by several members of the production team to the water tentacle in *The Abyss*, but created out of blood. 'It read great on the page, and the tests seemed pretty cool,' Goyer says. 'The problem was that ultimately Blade was fighting a special effect, he wasn't fighting a person, and it just felt completely hollow.' Adds Peter Frankfurt, 'We tested the movie with that ending, and the audience was totally with it until then, and then they fell out of it. The audience wasn't interested in seeing Frost turn into this inanimate twister of blood. They were pissed off at this guy – they wanted to see *him* get the shit kicked out of him, not this vortex. You could feel the audience say, "Oh, that'll look cool – but we don't care." It just hit all of us like a ton of bricks, and we all got chastened. We had spent a lot of time and money on something the audience doesn't particularly care about.' Someone hit upon the notion of having Frost stabbed with the EDTA capsules, Blade's earlier use of which had been greeted with cheers from the preview audience.

'There was also another ending which did not get filmed, [but which] in some ways would have been the most true to the character,' says Goyer. 'This ending involved Deacon Frost turning into the blood god, and at this point Blade's mother, Vanessa, has not been killed, so Deacon Frost uses her as a shield, hoping that Blade won't attack him. And Blade stays his hand, and Frost says, "I knew it – see, you're too human, Blade." And Blade says, "It's because I'm human I can do this," and he runs his mother and Frost through with the sword, and kills them both.'

In the original version of the epilogue, set in Moscow, the vampire who attacks the girl is Whistler. 'You don't see Whistler's face until he lights a cigarette,' Goyer explains, 'and you see his face in the flame of the cigarette lighter, and then Blade makes his entrance. That was the ending that [Stephen] Norrington and I liked the most.'

TRAILERS: The US trailer opens with shots of the city as the sun goes down, before introducing Blade and the vampires, as a narrator pitches the story: 'For thousands of years, they have existed among us. A secret nation with a lust for power. Now, one will lead them to conquer mankind. And one will try to stop him dead. Half human . . . half immortal . . . he is their greatest fear, and our only hope.'

POSTERS: The poster is a ¾ length shot of Wesley Snipes as Blade, in his customary black coat and shades, looking straight ahead, holding a blade in his right hand which underscores the title (c.f. *The Matrix*). Despite the orange-red background, and the two red eyes peering out from behind him, nowhere on the poster does it suggest that *Blade* is a film about vampires.

TAG-LINE: 'The power of an immortal. The soul of a human. The heart of a hero.' 'Against an army of immortals, one warrior must draw first blood.'

WHAT THE PAPERS SAID: In the *Chicago Sun-Times*, Roger Ebert wrote that, while 'anyone patiently attending the film in the hopes of a reasoned storyline' would be disappointed, the film should be seen 'in comic book terms, as an episode in a master-myth, in which even the most cataclysmic confrontation is not quite the end of things, because there has to be another issue next month'. Over at the *Los Angeles Times*, Gene Seymour also felt that the film remained faithful to its source medium. 'The dark ooze that even tinges *Blade*'s daylight sequences is so omnipresent that, if this thing were a comic book, the black ink would come off on your fingertips. Director Stephen Norrington and his production team deserve credit for giving this story the jarring, angular design found in some of the more ambitious mainstream comic books.' In the UK, *Time Out*'s Nigel Floyd went for the jugular: 'An attempt to redefine cutting edge horror, this techno-vampire pic is spoiled by . . . weak storytelling and flashy, computer game visuals', and ultimately dismissed the film as 'a series of messily choreographed, gloatingly sadistic fights, tricked out with embarrassing one-liners and reams of exposition'.

BOX OFFICE: Postponed from January 1998 to allow additional post-production time, *Blade* finally hit US cinemas on 21 August 1998, grossing $17 million in its opening weekend, and $70 million overall. The film failed to match its US performance elsewhere, however, grossing a further $42.6 million around the world. Nevertheless, its total worldwide earnings of $112.6 million was a healthy return on its $45 million budget.

AWARDS: Stephen Dorff won two awards: Best Villain at the MTV Movie Awards, and Favourite Villain at the Blockbuster Entertainment Awards, where Wesley Snipes also won Favourite Actor (Horror). The Academy of Science Fiction, Fantasy & Horror Films also nominated the film in the categories of Best Horror Film and Best Make-up.

CONTROVERSY: In 1997, Blade creator and former Marvel Editor-in-Chief Marv Wolfman launched a lawsuit against Marvel, New Line and parent company AOL Time Warner, claiming that the then-forthcoming film infringed his copyright, since he had created the characters of Blade and Deacon Frost as a freelancer, and had never sold the rights to his creation to Marvel. Prior to the film's opening, Wolfman had successfully lobbied to receive on-screen credit for his creations; financial compensation, however, had not been forthcoming. After a two-year struggle, most of which took place in bankruptcy rather than law courts, Judge Roderick McKelvie eventually ruled in the publisher's favour, believing that freelancers like Wolfman had known that their creations would be owned by Marvel as soon as they appeared in print. Wolfman, who had spent two years and thousands of dollars contesting the case, was devastated.

TRIVIA: Stephen Norrington went on to direct the film version of another comic book, Alan Moore's *The League of Extraordinary Gentlemen*, which he intended to follow with another Goyer-scripted comic book adaptation, *Ghost Rider*.

John Eno III, who plays the Blood Club bouncer, was Traci Lords' boyfriend.

Blade's car is a modified Dodge Challenger.

SEQUELS & SPIN-OFFS: Although screenwriter David S Goyer had originally pitched *Blade* to New Line as a trilogy, and a sequel had been discussed during production of the original film, the box office performance of *Blade* made a follow-up a reality. 'On *Blade*'s opening weekend, Michael De Luca called me and said, "You'd better start thinking about *Blade II*," ' Goyer, who had since scripted *The Crow II: City of Angels*, told *Creative Screenwriting* magazine. Before he set to work on the script, Goyer and producer Peter Frankfurt watched the first film again, making a list of what worked and what didn't work. 'What worked was the attitude, and the whole new approach to vampires,' he said. 'The relationship between Blade and Whistler was an odd pairing that worked, and I wanted to bring Whistler back. I wanted to make the sequel scarier and funnier to the degree that we could.' Goyer approached the sequel the way any fan would – if he was surfing the Internet and heard about *Blade II*, what would he want it to be? 'The thing about good sequels – and James Cameron's done two of them – is that they build on what's come before, but they also subvert the paradigm or turn it on its head.'

Incoming director Guillermo del Toro (*Mimic*) was also keen to put his own mark on the series. 'I wanted to bring more of the horror element into it and make the action different from the first one,' he told *Comics2Film*. 'I made some comments about some of the parts and some of the structure of the screenplay, and the next time it came back, it came back with those changes. So when I read it the last time I found it absolutely irresistible.' *Blade* fans evidently felt the same way: opening on 22 March 2002, the film grossed $32.5 million in its opening weekend. Although it slipped 59 per cent the following weekend, *Blade II* grossed a total of $81 million in the US and a further $68.5 million elsewhere, exceeding the gross of the 1998 original by some $30 million.

FUTURE INCARNATIONS: Screenwriter David S Goyer had originally pitched a trilogy of films to New Line boss Michael De Luca, and the success of *Blade* and its sequel made a third film look feasible, despite Goyer's ambitious premise: 'What I really want to do for the third one is set it about twenty years in the future and the vampires have actually completely taken over the world, so they are the status quo,' he told the website *Comics2Film* in February 2002. 'Because Blade is actually half-vampire, he ages at a slower rate, so Wesley can still play [the part]. In all these different stories the vampires are trying to take over the world. For the third film I just want to say, "Fuck it, they've won. Now what is the world like?" ' In March, *Blade II* director Guillermo del Toro expressed his own enthusiasm for the idea. 'I would love to be involved in that one if the premise we're proposing is accepted,' he told *Comics2Film*. 'What we're proposing is to take the whole mythology of Blade one step further and make it an apocalyptic vision – what if the vampires win? That would be really attractive to me.'

By the summer, however, with news that *I Am Legend*, the long-gestating film adaptation of Richard Matheson's seminal vampire novel, was finally going into production with Will Smith – another black actor, playing a vampire hunter – Goyer evidently felt it prudent to alter his proposed storyline. 'It's been modified somewhat from the "planet of the vampires" approach,' he told *Dreamwatch* magazine. 'I'm pretty excited about it, though.' Whatever shape the sequels take, however, Goyer is determined that the tone will not be lightened for future films. 'I was very disappointed with the *Batman* films,' he says. 'I thought they got successively worse. If there's gonna be a *Blade* Happy Meal four or five years from now, I think we're in trouble.'

Goyer also revealed that he had been discussing the possibility of a *Blade* TV series with New Line's television arm. It would, he said, be 'a separate entity from the *Blade* films. I'm not sure if that means a prequel to the *Blade* movies, going with a much younger Blade, or the converse, a much older [character]. And there's another approach that we're thinking about that would be much more radical than that,' he added, before revealing to *Comics2Film* that the show might be computer-animated in the style of MTV's *Spider-Man* series. 'I would love to see it done CG and have Wesley voice himself,' he said. 'I think that would be hot, but who knows?'

DVD AVAILABILITY: The best *Blade* DVD by far is the US (Region 1) edition, presented in widescreen (2.35:1). Aside from audio commentary featuring Wesley Snipes, Stephen Dorff, screenwriter David S Goyer, producer Peter Frankfurt, production designer Kirk M Petruccelli and cinematographer Theo van de Sande, and an isolated music score featuring commentary by composer Mark Isham, there are four documentaries: *La Magra*, a look at the original ending of the film, featuring interviews with Goyer, Frankfurt and Michael De Luca; *Designing* Blade, with Petruccelli, Richard Baily, Greg Cannom and Jeff Ward; *The Origins of* Blade, exploring the difficulties of producing horror comics under the Comics Code Authority; *The Blood Tide*, a look at vampire mythology. The DVD also includes a gallery of production sketches, the US trailer, a look at the twelve tribes of the House of Erebus, and – as a DVD-ROM feature – an early draft of the screenplay accessible from any point in the film. Although the UK (Region 2) edition omits many of these features, it retains the *La Magra* and *Designing* Blade documentaries and the trailer, and includes 51 minutes of behind-the-scenes clips ('B-roll') not present on the US equivalent.

FINAL ANALYSIS: Blade creator Marv Wolfman may have been justified in his unsuccessful action against Marvel for exploiting his creation, but one look back at the comics suggests that the character's name and origin is about all *Blade* screenwriter David S Goyer lifted from the comic. In the film, as in the comics, the Blade character is filled with self-loathing and motivated by hatred for those who made him; yet, in Wolfman's tales, Blade has far more interaction with the human world, including a secret identity (Eric Brooks), romantic entanglements (effectively interracial, since Blade is only half-human), and lives more of a human life. In Goyer's version, Blade has one foot in the human world, one foot in the vampire underworld, but shuns both – he knows he is an anomaly, and feels comfortable only with fellow vampire hunter,

Whistler, Goyer's creation. Although director Stephen Norrington takes little from Wolfman's comics, he borrows heavily from the medium itself, with extreme camera angles, stylised sets, exaggerated shadows and dizzying editing – often from long shot to close up – which owes as much to Hong Kong action films as it does to comics. Few could doubt that Goyer, Norrington and Snipes reinvented the character when they came to make the movie, or that *Blade* is one of the few comic book adaptations which takes a quantum leap over its source.

Although the fact that Blade is black is irrelevant – the vampires in *Blade* come in all colours and creeds, which is the reason why 'crosses don't do dick' – the race issue permeates the subtext: Frost even calls Blade an 'Uncle Tom', implying that he denies his vampire side and kowtows to his humanity. Although his skin is black, Blade is mixed race; yet he has become a racist, killing even those vampires – purebloods – who were born that way, and therefore have no more choice in who they are than he did. Does that mean they should be killed indiscriminately? No wonder he is a troubled figure, with more depth than your average comic book hero. The fact that these issues exist in a film ostensibly designed as a visceral action film that just happens to be about vampires is testament to the talent involved. While *Blade* may be a distillation of one hundred years of vampire mythology, one only has to look at the costumes (long black coats and shades), cod philosophy (Blade telling Karen that 'The world you live in is just a sugar-coated topping. There is another world beneath it – the real world!') and even special effects (there's a prototype version of *The Matrix*'s 'bullet-time' effect as Blade squares up to Frost in the park) to see that *Blade* has outgrown its influences and become influential itself. As comic book adaptations go, *Blade* is arguably matched only by *Road to Perdition* for turning pulp into pure gold. And like the best comics, *Blade* gets better with each look.

EXPERT WITNESS: 'I loved the first *Blade* movie. It had problems at the end, but if you see the DVD, you'll know they had a different ending in mind that back then they couldn't make work in special effects. Still, that Blade is 97 per cent my Blade and I'm damn proud of it.' – **Marv Wolfman, Creator of Blade**

Mystery Men (1999)

(121 minutes)

Directed by Kinka Usher
Written by Neil Cuthbert

Produced by Lawrence Gordon, Mike Richardson, Lloyd Levin
Based on the Dark Horse Comic Book Series Created by Bob Burden
Executive Producer Robert Engelman
Director of Photography Stephen H Burum ASC
Production Designer Kirk M Petruccelli
Casting by Mindy Marin
Music by Stephen Warbeck
Music Supervisor Karyn Rachtman
Costume Designer Marilyn Vance
Co-Producer Steven Gilder

CAST: Hank Azaria (*Jeffrey, a.k.a. 'The Blue Raja'*), Claire Forlani (*Monica*), Janeane Garofalo (*Carole, a.k.a. 'The Bowler'*), Greg Kinnear (*Lance Hunt, a.k.a. 'Captain Amazing'*), William H Macy (*Eddie, a.k.a. 'The Shoveler'*), Kel Mitchell (*'Invisible Boy'*), Lena Olin (*Dr Anabel Leek*), Paul Reubens (*'The Spleen'*), Geoffrey Rush (*Casanova Frankenstein*), Ben Stiller (*Roy, a.k.a. 'Mister Furious'*), Wes Studi (*'The Sphinx'*), Tom Waits (*Dr A Heller*), Eddie Izzard (*Tony P*), Artie Lange (*'Big Red'*), Louise Lasser (*Violet*), Ricky Jay (*Victor Weens*), Jennifer Lewis (*Lucille*), Prakazrel Michel (*Tony C*), Ernie Lee Banks (*Ted*), Gerry Becker (*Banyon*), Ned Bellamy (*Funk*), Corbin Bleu (*Butch*), Philip Bolden (*Roland*), Jake Cross (*thug*), Emmy Layborne (*reporter*), Mason Lucero (*young kid*), Monet Mazur (*Becky Beaner*), Joel McCrary (*Mcguire*), Chris Mugglebee (*reporter*), Olivia Lauren Todd (*Tracy*), Frederick Usher (*thug*), Kinka Usher (*Moe*), Gayle Vance (*Sally*), Adrian Armas, Gichi Gamba, Thomas Lake, Robert Musselman, Solo Scott, Erik Michael Tristan (*Disco Boys*), James Duke (*'Big Tobacco'*), Angelica Bridges, Ungela Brockman, Kimberly James, Andreea Radutoiu (*Furriers*), Michael Bay, Noah Blake, Riki Rachtman (*Frat Boys*), Robert Barnett a.k.a. T-Mo, Thomas Burton a.k.a. Cee-Lo, Cameron Gipp a.k.a. Gipp, Willie Knighton Jr a.k.a. Khujo (*Rappers*), Michael Chieffo, Gil Christner, Carl Strand (*The Suits*), Robert Chow, John Brantley Cole, Steven Jang, Sung Kang (*Susies*), Sasha Bray, Sunny Gorg, Shane Johnson, Jennifer Lee Keyes, Marie Matiko, Jody Watley (*Disco Girls*), Margaret Wheeler (*old lady*), Billy Beck, Robert Lieb (*old men*), Florence Stone Fevergeon, Sarah Kane (*old party goers*), Ed Denette (*old veteran*), Nori T Gehr, Kiko Kiko, Kiyoko Yamaguchi (*back-up singers*), Mark Mothersbaugh (*band leader*), Nancye Ferguson (*singer*), Katie Adams, Shirley Bowden, Helen Etting, Lu Gay, Valerie Gitter, Mae Greenstein, C Elane Innes, Irene Kamsler, Miriam R Lawless, Teresa MacLean, Joanna McDermott, Crystal Gaer White (*dancers*), Joanna Richter, Stacey Travis (*Powerwomen*), Larkin Campbell (*Supervacman*),

Oliver Clark (*reverse psychologist*), Jack Plotnick (*Mr Pups*), Dane Cook (*waffler*), Robert Musselman (*Ballerinaman*), Vince Melocchi (*mailman*), Doug Jones (*Pencil Head*), Vincent Bowman (*Son of Pencilhead*), Vylette Fagerholm (*Little Miss Vengence*), Dana Gould (*Squeegeeman*), Branden Williams (*Maintainer*), The Monkey Brothers (*The Artistc, Big Billy Hill Billy*), Gabrielle Conferti (*PMS Avenger*), Jeff D Danziger (*Radio Man*), Wilbert Sampson, Kenneth W Watts (*Pigs*), Elliot Durant III (*Martial Artist*), Anthony Sebastian Marinelli (*Gorilla*), Orinda E Shaneyfelt (*Evil Devil Woman*), Felix Castro (*Globalman*), Michael Craig (*Gardener*), Ronald Lasky (*Bullfighter*), David Still (*Stilt Man*), Jonathan Khan (*Fisgernman*), Jerry Farmer (*Thirstyman*)

TITLE SEQUENCE: From the Universal logo, a nocturnal thunderstorm reveals the title crackling with energy. As it swoops towards us, the camera moves into an overhead view of Champion City, giving us a flying superhero's eye view of the metropolis, and several subliminal references to 'Captain Amazing' – including a billboard which shows his image accompanying the legend 'CRIME! Don't even THINK about it!' 'In making *Mystery Men* I really wanted to make it feel like you've entered a comic book,' director Kinka Usher explained, 'and something that was very important in the whole production aspect of this film was to really give it the feel of a comic book, and one of the ways of doing that was to get into a really interesting introduction, to sort of introduce a world, and that's what we did in these opening shots, to give you the impression that you were in a whole 'nother world, this sort of alternate reality.'

SYNOPSIS: In Champion City, crime is virtually a thing of the past thanks to the heroic deeds of local superhero Captain Amazing, a two-fisted crimefighter in the classic comic book mould – complete with bespectacled billionaire secret identity, Lance Hunt – who has locked up almost every criminal in the city. But when the notorious gang of robbers known as the 'Red-eyes' crash a party at a nursing home, wannabe superheroes 'Mister Furious', 'The Shoveler' and 'The Blue Raja' step in to save the day until – lacking actual superpowers of any kind – Captain Amazing steps in to save them. But things aren't exactly flying for Captain Amazing: with little crime left to fight, and his arch-enemy Casanova Frankenstein locked up behind padded bars, it seems he may have put himself out of a job. Thus, when Frankenstein's seventeenth parole hearing comes up, billionaire Lance Hunt/Captain Amazing – sees a way to boost his popularity ratings, and steps in to request Frankenstein's release. Mister Furious realises something is up when he sees that Frankenstein's henchmen, 'The Disco Boys', are back in town, and sets out to investigate. Sure enough, Frankenstein is soon up to his old tricks again, kidnapping Captain Amazing and plotting to destroy Champion City. Thus, with Captain Amazing out of the picture, the Blue Raja, Mister Furious and The Shoveler begin recruiting would-be crimefighters to supplement their super-squad: 'The Bowler', 'Invisible Boy', 'The Spleen' and a terribly mysterious individual known as 'The Sphinx'. Although their attempt to rescue Captain Amazing goes disastrously wrong – The Blue Raja accidentally kills him – when they come face to face with Frankenstein and his various gangs, they are forced to call upon powers they never knew they had – and some experimental weapons loaned to them by eccentric genius Doctor Heller – in order to bring Casanova Frankenstein to justice, earning themselves a place in Champion City's hall of fame as the self-styled 'Super-Squad'.

ORIGINS: The warped brainchild of Buffalo-born comic book writer and artist Bob Burden, The Mysterymen – in its comic book incarnation, the words are conjoined – first appeared in a two-part story spanning issues #16 and #17 of *Flaming Carrot Comics*, the award-winning title detailing the exploits of a teenager who, after reading five thousand comics in a single sitting, dons a flaming carrot mask and green flippers to fight crime as 'The Flaming Carrot'. The character first appeared in a 1979 issue of *Visions* magazine, reappearing in a single self-published issue two years later. Small press publishers Aardvark-Vanaheim and Renegade Press picked up the baton in 1985 and 1987 respectively, but it was Dark Horse Comics' 1988 series – which began with issue #18 – which brought the title to its biggest audience. Described by Burden as 'the world's first surrealist superhero', his sporadically published comic book is subtitled 'The further adventures of the strangest man alive', and became one of the biggest hits on the 1980s underground comics scene. 'Flaming Carrot is a second-string, mill town, blue collar superhero living in Iron City, in the rust belt of the Northeast [United States],' Burden told *westfieldcomics.com*. 'He has no superpowers and is stupid. When he gets in a spot, he just shoots his way out in a hail of gunfire. It's kind of a Monty Python version of the superhero, but it's not a satire.'

After a decade of underground success, however, Burden reached the conclusion that neither mainstream comic readers nor Hollywood executives were ever going to accept a hero with a Flaming Carrot for a head; he was, Burden explained, 'just too weird' to garner anything but 'mild and bemused interest from book publishers, movie studios and girls in bars . . . Also, in the days before CG, Flaming Carrot's big head presented some problems as to how to portray him on the big screen.' Thus, Burden decided to relaunch the character as part of a self-styled super-team known as The Mysterymen, 'a bizarre collection of oddball costumed adventurers, deemed unqualified for major-league superhero teams because of mediocre, uncontrollable, or nonexistent powers, behavioural problems, or the extreme public outrage at some of their shenanigans'. In their introductory story, 'I Cloned Hitler's Feet', the Flaming Carrot receives a phone call from his former Mysterymen partner in crime-fighting, Mister Furious, and rejoins his old comrades to battle an invasion of Nazi jackboots unleashed by 'The Vile Brotherhood'. The Mysterymen subsequently appeared in numerous issues of *Flaming Carrot Comics*, twice teamed up with the Teenage Mutant Ninja Turtles, and eventually earned their own title, *Bob Burden's Original Mysterymen*, published to coincide with the release of the film.

'The Mysterymen is a departure from the standard "morality play" inherent in comics and most everything else: TV, movies, books,' Burden has said. 'Most adventure–action TV shows these days have become nothing more than propaganda. The message is "do the right thing, and everything will turn out right". But with Mysterymen it's like a gang war between a bunch of guys with hearts and a bunch of guys without hearts. That's really what the battle between good and evil is. And it's between only the five or ten per cent of the population that cares. The rest of the world is just looking on like a bunch of rubberneckers at an accident.' Despite the comedic aspect of the stories, he added, 'The Mysterymen comic stories are, at times, a lot more serious and deep than your average comic.'

DEVELOPMENT: Dark Horse Comics publisher Mike Richardson had long been a fan of Bob Burden's surrealist strip starring The Flaming Carrot; indeed, in 1988, his company – the third largest in an industry dominated by DC and Marvel – had taken over publication of the sporadically published stories. Having brought such Dark Horse properties as *The Mask*, *Timecop*, *Barb Wire*, *Tank Girl* and *Virus* to Hollywood, however, Richardson knew that studio executives would never believe a Flaming Carrot movie would fly. Instead, he asked Burden to pen a treatment based on the supporting team of super-friends, the Mysterymen.

'I could see that *Mystery Men* had a much better shot at establishing Bob's particular universe as a film than *Flaming Carrot*,' Richardson told the *Los Angeles Times*. As Richardson willingly assumed the burden of pitching the treatment to Hollywood, producers Lloyd Levin and Lawrence Gordon – no strangers to blockbusters or comic book adaptations – immediately responded. 'What really attracted us to The Mysterymen were the characters, who were all very blue-collar, set in the margins of society,' recalled Lloyd Levin, whose credits include two *Die Hards*, two *Predators*, *Event Horizon* and an earlier comic book adaptation, *The Rocketeer*. '[There's] the guy who has a shitty job whose boss beats the crap out of him; the guy who's having problems with his wife and doesn't know how to relate to his kids; the guy who has girlfriend problems. It was a real departure from any sort of situation Bruce Wayne would find himself in.'

At least, not unless Bruce Wayne formed a super-team whose primary powers are bowling, shovelling, farting, flinging forks, getting angry and being visible. Encouraged by Gordon's interest, Burden prepared a 'bible' that outlined the characters, storylines and setting of the proposed piece which, according to Levin, 'included forty descriptions of heroes and villains – an embarrassment of riches. The challenge was actually not to come up with characters, but to edit and create a story based on the characters and villains that we chose.' 'Basically,' said Burden, 'what they did was come up with a number of characters that worked for them for the story they had, and ran with it . . . all the way down past the fifty-yard line to home plate.'

For this purpose, Levin and Gordon turned to screenwriter Neil Cuthbert, who had scripted *Hocus Pocus*, the comic book inspired *The Return of Swamp Thing* and the ill-starred sci-fi comedy, *Pluto Nash*. 'Neil wrote from the point of view of genuine heart,' Levin enthused. 'We were all sure that he was capable of writing *Mystery Men* as a comedy about wannabes and losers, without being condescending towards them. He was able to avoid parody, yet still make a comedy, and that was a fine line.' Although Cuthbert receives sole screen credit, numerous other writers contributed to the shooting script, notably Brent Forrester, then a regular writer on *The Ben Stiller Show*.

Choosing a director was the next challenge; already on board as the erstwhile leader of the Mystery Men, Ben Stiller was initially wooed by Gordon and Levin as a potential director. When Stiller passed, believing that the scale of the project may be out of his league, another actor–director, Danny De Vito (The Penguin in *Batman Returns*) was briefly considered to direct, and perhaps even play The Shoveler. In the event, however, the producers decided that it was time for award-winning commercials director Kinka Usher – whose campaigns include the popular 'Got Milk?' TV spots – to make a movie. At first, Usher didn't agree. 'I didn't really have any desire to make movies, but that all changed when I heard the concept for *Mystery Men*,' he said. 'I had seen a lot of superhero movies, but there was always something missing to me. In reading this script about superheroes who can't get themselves arrested, I found a film that I could make that would be interesting with a wonderful visual style, as well as full of humanity and great characters.'

CASTING: If ever there was a more eclectic ensemble than the Mystery Men themselves, it is the group of actors assembled to play them and the other characters in *Mystery Men*. Yet, if creator Bob Burden had had his way, the cast list might be stranger still: 'Originally, as I envisioned them, the Mysterymen were characters like Ernest Borgnine and Vic Tayback – all Mike Ditka-type guys,' he told *Comic Buyer's Guide*. 'The only current star I could've seen as a Mysteryman would've been Steve Buscemi from *Fargo*.' The fact that such a diverse group – including *Godzilla*'s Hank Azaria, comedians Ben Stiller (*There's Something About Mary*), Janeane Garofalo (*The Truth About Cats & Dogs*), Artie Lange and Eddie Izzard, William H Macy (*Fargo*), musician Tom Waits (*Bram Stoker's Dracula*) and Pras, Wes Studi (*Dances with Wolves*), Paul Reubens (a.k.a. Pee-Wee Herman), Clare Forlani (*Meet Joe Black*), Kel Mitchell (star of TV's *Kenan and Kel*) and Greg Kinnear (*As Good As It Gets*) – teamed up at all is thanks in part to Australian actor Geoffrey Rush, whose breakthrough performance as tortured pianist David Helfgot in *Shine* won him an Academy Award®, and whose enthusiasm for the project encouraged other acclaimed actors to jump aboard.

'The relationship between Geoffrey and Greg [Kinnear] actually started on an airplane between Australia and LA a few years before this movie ever even came up. The two of them sat next to each other and talked about how much they wanted to work together.' In addition, as Garofalo explained, 'I had heard about some of the other actors who were doing *Mystery Men*. I mean, oh my God – Geoffrey Rush, Bill Macy and Lena Olin? That's cool! I began to get it, so I said, "All right, I'll do it." ' Garofalo was instrumental in bringing Ben Stiller – with whom she co-authored *Feel This Book*, and co-starred in Stiller's directorial debut, *Reality Bites* – in to the fold. 'I called Ben up and said, "What else do you have to do this summer? You have to do *Mystery Men*. It'll be fun. We'll hang out." ' For producer Lloyd Levin, Stiller was a key player. 'We were after Ben for this project for quite a while . . . because his fearless comedic sensibility seemed emblematic of what we were hoping to achieve with *Mystery Men*.'

Stiller admits that he needed encouragement, but noted that 'the combination of the cast and the story and the opportunity to play something close to approximating a superhero' was what ultimately attracted him to the project. 'I knew it's the closest I would ever get to having a chance to be anything resembling a superhero.' For, just as the Mystery Men are not exactly the first on the call list when Champion City needs saving, Stiller said, 'I don't get the calls for the *Batman* movies.' Many of the minor roles were filled by actors with whom Usher had worked on commercials.

PRODUCTION: Casanova Frankenstein's parole board hearing was the first scene to be shot when filming began in Los Angeles in late 1998. A low-key, dimly lit interior scene featuring Geoffrey Rush, Greg Kinnear, Lena Olin and a few other members of the supporting cast, it could not possibly have prepared first-time feature director Kinka Usher for what the rest of the shoot would bring. 'When you have a cast this size, actors as a rule tend to be bigger pains in the ass,' Janeane Garofalo explained. 'So if you have a nice director, it can turn into too many cooks in the kitchen.' Naturally, each of the thirteen principal characters wanted their own moment to shine, but Usher was able to direct their improvisational techniques and creative energies towards – appropriately – what was best for the team, rather than the individual. 'I didn't quite realise going into this movie how absolutely fulfilling it would be to work with such strong actors and be able to connect with each actor in a unique way,' he said. 'To have these different relationships and talk with these incredibly accomplished actors in my own language, looking for the little beats and moments.' As one might expect from a production with numerous comedy writers, comic actors and stand-up comics among its cast, the screenplay continued to evolve on a daily basis, with even Mysterymen creator Bob Burden contributing at various points. 'There were times when we were kind of stumped in a scene and we asked him what he thought,' Levin told the *Los Angeles Times*. 'Ten minutes later, we'd get thirty pages in the fax machine with probably twenty-nine pages filled with the lousiest ideas that you've ever read, but that one page of pure genius.'

As with all big-screen comic book adaptations, the look of *Mystery Men* was a crucial element of the production. The film's setting, Champion City, was originally conceived as a slightly futuristic skew on contemporary Los Angeles, with its eclectic mixture of ethnic styles. 'We wanted to create a retro European or worldwide vibe for Champion City,' said production designer Kirk M Petruccelli, whose credits include another comic book adaptation, *Blade*. 'We threw in different architectural styles and colour schemes to create this wonderful multi-ethnic environment where everything is different, yet with a common thread running through it.' 'I wanted the city's exterior to feel like a Hong Kong harbour,' added Usher. 'You go visit any major city today and you will see an Asian neighbourhood, a Spanish neighbourhood, etc. We just took it a step further and created this sort of near-future reality.

'We combined a range of periods from the twenties to the seventies. Some scenes look very forties, others look very twenties, all suggested by different types of cars and wardrobe and make-up and hair. As you watch the film it's visually very interesting. It's really a blend of all these influences.' This eclecticism is present in every aspect of *Mystery Men*, as Usher observed. 'A lot of the design was actually more European than American, because I didn't want to try and reproduce films like *Dick Tracy* or *Batman*, which were wholly and completely American-type city background. I thought this one needed to be a lot more international.'

Further architectural elements were added when the studio saw some of the rushes, and agreed to increase the special effects budget to allow elaborate matte paintings to be added to sixty per cent of the city scenes.

COSTUME FITTING: Looking at the gangster era threads sported by the criminal fraternity known as 'The Suits', it is perhaps understandable that costume designer Marilyn Vance received an Academy Award® nomination for her work on *The Untouchables*. Vance, whose other credits include *The Last Boy Scout*, *Hudson Hawk*, two *Predators*, the first two *Die Hard* movies, *Pretty Woman*, *Ferris Bueller's Day Off* and another comic book adaptation, *The Rocketeer*, had her work cut out for her, designing costumes for the most rag-tag group of superheroes ever to hit the big screen. 'We talked about the background of each character,' she said of her work on the film. 'Who is this guy? How does he live? What does he do for money? What kind of car does he drive? How off-centred is he? We combined every aspect of life from the twenties through the millennium to create these costumes.'

Vance's greatest contribution to the film was arguably Greg Kinnear's costume, a flexible and inexpensive alternative to the traditional superhero outfits. '[It was] a breakthrough for us,' Vance explained, 'because to mould an outfit like a Batman [costume] is a minimum of $200,000, and the actor can barely move in it, by the way. But we needed an action character that could move and could be this Captain Amazing, so we experimented and came across this Neoprene®, the wetsuit fabric. But we quilted it and added padding to it. Everything came up, giving him this look of great strength. Basically [in] that outfit, he can do just about anything because it's so pliable. I'm really proud of that. I couldn't have imagined it worked as well as it did.'

MUSIC: Although Academy Award® nominated composer Stephen Warbeck is credited with the motion picture score, music supervisor Karyn Rachtman's contribution to the soundtrack was significant, especially given the range of musical styles featured in the film, ranging from seventies disco classics (The Trammps' 'Disco Inferno', Anita Ward's 'Ring My Bell', Chic's 'Le Freak', A Taste of Honey's 'Boogie Ooogie Oogie' and the Bee Gees' 'Night Fever') to contemporary dance music (Moloko's 'Indigo', Freak Power's 'No Way' and 'Keep, Keep Movin'' by Dub Pistols), and alt. rock (courtesy of The B-52s, Violent Femmes and Smash Mouth). In addition, former Devo frontman Mark Mothersbaugh (who appears in the film as the nursing home bandleader) wrote and performed 'The Mystery Man Mantra', while *Mystery Men* actor Kel Mitchell co-wrote and raps on 'Who Are Those Mystery Men?' by Kel and the M.A.F.T. Emcees.

CLASSIC QUOTES:

Mister Furious: 'Don't mess with the volcano, man. 'Cause I will go Pom*peii* on your butt.'

Officer McGuire: 'You keep dreaming, wannabe. Dream on, moron.'

Mister Furious: 'I will keep dreaming! I will keep dreaming, my friend! And when I wake up, you better hope you're asleep!'

Victor Weens: 'I'm a publicist, not a magician.'

Mister Furious: 'That's because Lance Hunt *is* Captain Amazing.'

The Shoveler: 'Oh, don't start that again. Lance Hunt wears glasses. Captain Amazing doesn't wear glasses.'

Mister Furious: 'He takes them off when he transforms.'

The Shoveler: 'That doesn't make any sense. He wouldn't be able to see!'

The Sphinx: 'When you can balance a tack hammer on your head, you can hammer your opponent with a balanced attack.'

Mister Furious: 'And why am I wearing watermelons on my feet?'

The Sphinx: 'I don't remember asking you to do that.'

The Sphinx: 'When you doubt your powers, you give power to your doubts!'

Mister Furious: 'I must've ripped the "Q" section out of my dictionary, 'cause I don't know the meaning of the word "quit." '

Becky: 'Whatever you call them, Champion City will forever hold a debt of gratitude to these mystery men.'

The Sphinx: 'Wait, that's it! We are . . . the Super-Squad!'

DELETED SCENES: The out-takes featured on both Region 1 (US) and Region 2 (UK) DVD editions reveal the following deletions:

- An early scene in which a bespectacled and flamboyantly dressed Dr Heller (Tom Waits) makes a pass at an elderly resident of the nursing home. 'You know I'm a doctor. I do laser hair removal, I do acupuncture, I do aromatherapy, that type of thing,' he says. 'What say we go back to your place.' 'My room-mate's there,' she replies demurely. 'Bonus!' he throws back with a grin.
- A scene in which Eddie (a.k.a. The Shoveler) disciplines his two children for leaving toys lying around, while they make fun of his so-called superpowers.
- A scene in which Jeffrey (a.k.a. The Blue Raja) locks up his Messerschmitt bubble car (glimpsed at the junkyard in the completed film) and is interrupted by his mother as he raids her silverware drawer. He claims, in his regular American accent, to be looking for a corkscrew. 'What do you need a corkscrew for? You don't drink.' He

explains, somewhat unconvincingly, that he needed the corkscrew to make a mobile as a surprise present, 'But you know what? Forget it, because the surprise is totally blown.' The scene leads into the one in which he practises witticisms while wielding his cutlery.

- A scene set at Eddie's workplace in which Eddie, learning from Roy (a.k.a. Mister Furious) of Captain Amazing's capture, tells him that he has promised his wife he will quit crime-fighting. Mister Furious reminds him of the oath they took – 'I swear that I will fight crime and oppose injustice in any form at any hour. And if I ever break this oath, a brick should fall from a building of great height, and chip a little piece off my skull, and my brain get exposed to the oxygen, and I die' – causing Eddie to pick up his shovel and rejoin his former teammate.
- A scene set at the department store where Jeffrey is busy selling silverwear to an Asian couple when Roy and Eddie turn up and try to inform him of Captain Amazing's capture. 'You know, just once I would like to yell "To the rescue!" and everyone goes running out the door,' Roy tells him, to which Jeffrey responds that it sounds hackneyed; a cliché. 'No, no, no. "Up, up and away" that's a cliché. "Shazam!" that's *way* cliché.' A short argument follows, but ultimately Roy gets his wish: 'To the rescue!' he says, and with that they place their hands on Eddie's shovel and head off . . . to the rescue.
- An extended version of the diner scene in which Roy, Eddie and Jeffrey talk about recruiting The Sphinx who, according to Jeffrey, can be summoned by ordering a certain lunchtime combination at a downtown taco stand. The following scene has the three of them visiting the taco stand, where actor Luis Guzman (*Out of Sight*) acts in a terribly mysterious way as he takes their order: a number 13 with guacamole. When this fails to produce the correct results, the three are seen dining *al fresco* among the detritus of several large orders of Mexican food, as Eddie suggests yet another combination. When Roy insists that The Sphinx is not coming, and Jeffrey claims that he couldn't eat another thing, Eddie offers another suggestion: a lead on a different guy. As they leave, however, The Sphinx – dressed as a waiter – watches them go. (When these scenes were deleted, some additional dialogue was added to the original diner scene, to smooth the passage from the diner to the home of Invisible Boy.)
- In an extension of the bar scene, in which the heroes drunkenly congratulate themselves over their attack on Casanova Frankenstein's car, Eddie takes Roy aside for a private chat, telling him he thinks Roy's showboating during the showdown is hurting the team. They argue about teamwork and leadership, and make up, but a final shot shows that Eddie has his doubts.
- A brief scene just prior to the team's break-in at Casanova Frankenstein's mansion, in which they practise bird-call signals.

- A scene in which the team takes on 'the briefcase-bearing bastards' known as The Suits, attacking them with glue bombs and forks. When The Sphinx suggests a flanking action, The Blue Raja responds, 'Yes, let's flank the flanking flankers!'
- The original ending, in which the team argues about how to destroy the psychofrakulator. 'Why don't you throw your father's head in there?' The Blue Raja says to The Bowler. 'Why don't you throw your mother's head in there?' she responds. The Sphinx suggests an alternative strategy – a group hug, followed by a canned tornado hurled into the belly of the machine. When it blows up, they run like the wind. As director Kinka Usher explained, 'Originally [Casanova] gets thrown off and he gets hung up on the disco ball. And [instead] we just threw him in the hole and let him fraculate, and sort of changed the ending so that we could really make Janeane and the bowling ball a bigger part of the story, because as we tested the film we realised that people really enjoyed Janeane and the ball and [Janeane] talking to the ball. So I went back and pitched the studio, "Look, let me re-shoot the ending, it'll be fairly simple to do, and make it more about Janeane and the ball, and less about Geoffrey hanging off the disco ball and him firing a gun." ' The revised scene, in which Janeane tells the skull of her father inside her bowling ball that 'It's time for separation,' was shot a full four months after the end of principal photography.

At least two other scenes did not make it into the final cut (or on to the DVD). 'We actually had another scene where [Casanova Frankenstein] was being released from the prison all in slow motion, and he was totally whacked out of his head, and that unfortunately got left out of the film as well, but once again [was] really really fun stuff,' Usher explained. 'There was [also] a scene I had shot with Ben and Janeane which ended up getting cut out of the movie due to time. I really wanted to find something in the movie where the two of them had their reckoning together, and it was a little unfortunate that I wasn't able to get that in the end.' Usher's editorial ruthlessness was proven by the fact that he cut his own character, Moe, from the final film.

TRAILERS: The trailer begins by setting up the superhero/nemesis relationship between Captain Amazing and Casanova Frankenstein, as Don Lafontaine voice-over intones: 'In a place called Champion City, the forces of good and evil are about to collide.' When Frankenstein kidnaps Amazing, the film's second string superheroes are introduced. 'Now, with the city's one true hero missing, who will step forward to answer the call of justice?' A giant 'MM' logo fills the screen, crackling with lightning, before the voice-over resumes: 'They've been waiting for this moment all their lives. But now that their time has come, they're gonna need all the help they can get.' A quick-fire montage of various superhero tryouts, before the heroes set out to rescue Captain Amazing. 'Universal Pictures presents a new league of heroes that step to a different beat.' Although one of the film's strengths was its ensemble cast, no actors are named in the trailer, since their contracts stipulated that if any of the thirteen principal cast were named in marketing materials, *all* of them had to be.

POSTERS: In keeping with the tradition of comic book adaptations, several 'teaser' posters were produced for *Mystery Men*, each colour-coded and depicting a single character – The Shoveler, The Blue Raja, The Bowler, Mister Furious, The Spleen, The Sphinx and Invisible Boy – in silhouette. Another teaser poster united the international men of mystery within a huge 'M', while the regular 'one-sheet' brought the characters together in more dynamic form. Although a UK equivalent of the main teaser design was also produced, a brand new 'quad' poster (landscape format) was produced making more of the cast members' faces.

TAG-LINE: 'This summer expect the unexpected', ran the US tag-line. In the UK, 'Ready to Rumble!' appeared above the title, while a second line paraphrased a line of The Shoveler's dialogue: 'Not your Classic Superheroes – They're the other guys'.

WHAT THE PAPERS SAID: 'An amiable spoof of comic book heroes,' said *Variety*, 'sharply written with a lavish look and top-drawer effects adding to the appeal of its large and talented cast, pic achieves a nice balance of fondness and satiric snap, character laughs and goofy action . . . undercut by a signal failure to follow the leave-'em-wanting-more rule so crucial to comedy. Pic is easily twenty minutes too long.' In the UK, *Time Out* also described *Mystery Men* as 'an amiable spoof of superhero movies [which] takes a brave stab at rewriting the mythology from the inside out, with lots of witty, mildly subversive stuff about working class heroes, commercial sponsorship of celebrities and casual depictions of violence'.

BOX OFFICE: When *Mystery Men* opened in the US on 6 August 1999, the film's mixture of styles arguably led to an overall lack of identity, leaving audiences unsure of what to make of it; was it supposed to be a comic book comedy, special effects extravaganza, post-modern parody, or all three? Despite studio hopes that the film would spawn a franchise, the $68 million movie's less than heroic box office performance (a shade under $30 million) made it clear that the self-styled 'super-squad' would be hanging up their capes – not to mention shovels, spoons and bowling balls – for good.

AWARDS: Marilyn Vance's costumes were nominated for a Saturn Award by the Academy of Science Fiction, Fantasy & Horror films, while Janeane Garofalo received a nomination for Funniest Actress in a Motion Picture (Leading Role) at the American Comedy Awards.

TRIVIA: Before coining the name 'Mysterymen', creator Bob Burden considered calling his not-so-super heroes 'The Danger Rangers'.

Among the comic book Mysterymen not appearing in the film are Captain Attack, Bondo-Man, Screwball, Jackpot, Red Rover and Jumpin' Jehosaphat.

Janeane Garofalo had a unique qualification for playing The Bowler: her parents met in a bowling alley. Her father's real name is Carmine.

Ricky Jay, whose character tells Captain Amazing, 'I'm a publicist, not a magician,' is a well-known magician.

The Herkimer Battle Jitney, described by Dr Heller as the greatest non-lethal vehicle the military ever built, is a composite of tank, truck and airstream trailer, designed by Kirk M Pettruccelli to look like a B-17 bomber on the outside and a submarine on the inside. Casanova Frankenstein's preferred mode of transport – a two-tone, 22-foot stretch Chevrolet Corvette limousine – was a fully functional vehicle created by welding two different Corvettes together on a stock car frame. All of the police cruisers, meanwhile, are 1970s Dodge Chargers.

Tom Waits' bizarre hand gestures while explaining the psychofrakulator are the result of his writing his dialogue on his fingers.

DVD AVAILABILITY: In the UK, *Mystery Men* is available from Universal/Columbia TriStar Home Video as a Region 2 DVD, featuring a widescreen (1.85:1) Dolby 5.1 version of the film, a seventeen-minute *Spotlight on Location* featurette, commentary by director Kinka Usher, an essay on the origin of the comic book, production notes, cast and crew information, trailer, DVD-ROM extras, a special music selection feature, and nineteen minutes of deleted and/or extended scenes. The US (Region 1) DVD is identical in all but region encoding.

FINAL ANALYSIS: In the comic series which inspired *Mystery Men*, the super-team's literally flame-haired (and carrot-topped) leader, Flaming Carrot, learned how to be a superhero by reading every comic book ever published. Watching its big-screen spin-off, it feels as though scriptwriter Neil Cuthbert might have done the same thing, since his jokes – such as The Shoveler arguing that Captain Amazing and his billionaire benefactor Lance Hunt cannot possibly be one and the same person, since Lance wears glasses and Captain Amazing has perfect eyesight – are bang on target. No doubt the likes of Azaria, Stiller, Garofalo and Kinnear – all accomplished comedy performers in their own right – contributed to the script's zingy one-liners, which deserve to be quoted long after the film is forgotten.

Mystery Men is directed with inventive camera work and impressive comic timing by commercials king Kinka Usher, who takes Cuthbert's knowing and knowledgable script and Kirk M Petruccelli's post-modern production design and fashions a fast, furious and above all fun film which, like *Buckaroo Banzai* before it, might have spawned a series of superpowered sequels, if only the rest of America had been in on the joke. Like the would-be superheroes it portrays, *Mystery Men* may be a little lacking in experience, a little rough around the edges, and require some effort to truly believe in, but somehow it has enough ambition, enthusiasm and attitude to win the day.

EXPERT WITNESS: 'We were hoping maybe we could do what *Scream* did to horror movies, to approach our story with a certain amount of self-awareness while still being sincere. We weren't making a spoof. As wild as *Mystery Men* is, there is real sincerity to it.' – **Lloyd Levin, Producer**

X-Men (2000)

(104 minutes)

Directed by Bryan Singer
Screenplay by David Hayter
Story by Tom DeSanto and Bryan Singer
Produced by Lauren Shuler Donner and Ralph Winter
Executive Producers Avi Arad, Stan Lee, Richard Donner and Tom DeSanto
Director of Photography Newton Thomas Sigel ASC
Production Designer John Myhre
Edited by Steven Rosenblum, Kevin Stitt and John Wright ACE
Co-Producers Joel Simon and William S Todman Jr
Visual Effects Supervisor Michael Fink
Special Make-up Design Gordon Smith
Music by Michael Kamen
Costume Designer Louise Mingenbach
Casting by Roger Mussenden CSA

CAST: Patrick Stewart (*Professor Charles Xavier*/'*Professor X*'), Hugh Jackman (*Logan*/'*Wolverine*'), Ian McKellen (*Erik Magnus Lehnsherr*/'*Magneto*'), Halle Berry (*Ororo Monroe*/'*Storm*'), Famke Janssen (*Dr Jean Grey*), James Marsden (*Scott Summers*/'*Cyclops*'), Bruce Davison (*Senator Robert Kelly*), Rebecca Romijn-Stamos (*Raven Darkholme*/'*Mystique*'), Ray Park ('*Toad*'), Tyler Mane ('*Sabretooth*'), Anna Paquin (*Marie D'Ancanto*/'*Rogue*'), Matthew Sharp (*Henry Gurich*), Brett Morris (*young Erik Lehnsherr*), Rhona Shekter (*Mrs Lehnsherr*), Kenneth McGregor (*Mr Lehnsherr*), Shawn Roberts (*Rogue's boyfriend*), Donna Goodhand (*Rogue's mother*), John E Nelles (*Rogue's father*), George Buza (*trucker*), Darren McGuire (*contender*), Carson Manning, Scott Leva (*waterboys*), Aron Tager (*MC*), Kevin Rushton (*Stu*), Doug Lennon (*bartender*), David Nichols (*newscaster #1*), Malcolm Nefsky (*Stu's buddy*), Sumela Kay (*Kitty*), Shawn Ashmore (*Bobby*), Katrina Florece (*Jubilee*), Alexander Burton (*John*), Quinn Wright (*lily pond kid*), Daniel Magder (*boy on raft*), Matt Weinberg (*Tommy*), Madison Lane (*Tommy's sister*), Stan Lee (*hot dog vendor*), Marsha Graham (*newscaster #2*), Amy Leland (*Cerebro*), Adam Robitel (*guy on line*), Dave Brown (*lead cop*), Ben P Jensen (*Sabretooth cop*), Tom DeSanto (*Toad cop*), Todd Dulmage (*coastguard*), Dan Duran (*newscaster #3*), Elias Zardu (*UN Secretary-General*), David Black (*President*), Robert P Snow (*Secret Service*), David Hayter (*museum cop*), Cecil Phillips (*security guard*), Dave Allen Clark (*newscaster #4*), Deryck Blake (*plastic prison guard*), Ilke Hincer, Ron Sham, Jay Yod, Gregori Miakouchkine, Eleanor Comes, Guiseppe Gallaccio, Rupinder Brar, Abi Ganem (*translators*), Joey Purpura, Manuel Verge, Wolfgang Muller, Ralph Zuljan, Andy Grote (*German soldiers*)

UNCREDITED CAST: DB Sweeney (*Statue of Liberty cop*), Eric Bryson (*cop*), Jon Davey, Donald Mackinnen, Gorav Seth (*students*), Kyler Fisher (*additional voices*), Matthew Granger (*surgeon*), Glenn Gutjahr (*motorcycle cop*), Andre Myers (*Norman Turnblad*)

TITLE SEQUENCE: Over black, a voice (belonging to Professor Charles Xavier) is heard: 'Mutation. It is the key to our evolution.' As a stylised animated sequence begins, showing DNA strands infused with electrical energy, the voice continues: 'It has enabled us to evolve from a single-celled organism into the dominant species on the planet. This process is slow and normally takes thousands and thousands of years. But every few hundred millennia, evolution leaps forward.' The first few credits end with an animated title, which dissolves as the animation runs in reverse at high speed, before being shut in behind locked steel doors with an 'X' in a circle. The camera zooms in to a circle at its centre, through which the opening scene is playing.

SYNOPSIS: Poland, 1944: a young boy is separated from his parents as he arrives at a concentration camp. As he is shut in behind enormous steel gates, the boy bends them with telekinetic powers until they are twisted out of shape. In Meridian, Mississippi, in 'the not too distant future', a young girl named Marie almost kills her boyfriend with a kiss. Evidently she is one of the new 'mutants' referred to by Senator Kelly in a Senate hearing in which he calls for regulations requiring mutants to register their powers at Ellis Island. From the public gallery, wheelchair-bound mind-reader Professor Charles Xavier (a.k.a. 'Professor X') and his old friend Erik Lensherr watch developments with interest. Meanwhile, having run away from home, Marie – now calling herself 'Rogue' – meets a fellow mutant, 'Wolverine', who can grow metal claws out of his knuckles. She stows away in his truck, and when it crashes and starts to burn, she is trapped inside while Wolverine is attacked and knocked unconscious by a beastlike assailant with incredible strength. A bolt of light fired from the eyes of another stranger defeats the attacker, and Marie is saved. The beast-man ('Sabretooth') reports the bad news to Lensherr ('Magneto'), a telekinetic who bears the mark of a concentration camp survivor. When Dr Jean Grey, a fellow telekinetic, attempts to examine Wolverine, he escapes, only to have Professor X invade his mind and lure him to the inner sanctum of his 'school for the gifted' in Westchester, New York, a sanctuary for mutants who call themselves 'X-Men'. Professor X tells him of their mutual enemy, Magneto, a very powerful mutant with the power to manipulate metal and create magnetic fields, who predicts a coming war between mutants and humanity. Professor X offers Wolverine the chance to uncover the mystery not of his mutation, extraordinary regenerative powers, but of his virtually indestructible adamantium endoskeleton. Meanwhile, Senator Kelly is attacked by a blue female shape-shifter ('Mystique') and brought before Magneto, who forces him to undergo a process which turns him into the very thing he most despises: a mutant. Now able to liquefy himself, he escapes. The same night, Rogue and Wolverine almost kill each other, and when Rogue returns to classes a fellow student, Bobby, tells her she should run away. She agrees, not realising that 'Bobby' is actually the shape-shifting Mystique, who sabotages Cerebro, Professor X's mental focusing chamber, incapacitating him when he next tries to use it. Wolverine, Storm and Cyclops track Rogue to the train station, only to be attacked by Sabretooth and 'Toad', who kidnap Rogue and take her to Magneto, who plans to use her to unleash his mutant-making device on two hundred world leaders gathering for a UN summit, unaware that the process has killed Senator Kelly. As the device gears up, the X-Men and Magneto's mutant 'Brotherhood' battle it out using all the powers at their disposal, until the X-Men succeed in shutting off the device.

Mystique escapes, Magneto is jailed, Rogue and Professor X recover, and Wolverine leaves the X-Men to go in search of answers. Meanwhile, Senator Kelly appears to have an about-face – unsurprising, since he is Mystique in disguise. The next time Professor X and Magneto meet it is for a chess game in a huge plastic prison from which he vows to escape.

ORIGINS: The X-Men, billed as 'the strangest superheroes of all', made their first appearance in their own title in September 1963, the brainchild of Spider-Man, Hulk and Fantastic Four creator Stan Lee, and his artist collaborator Jack Kirby. Lee has said that the characters, who he originally wanted to call 'The Mutants', grew out of a perennial problem for comic book creators: how did the superheroes get their superpowers? 'With every superhero story you have to mention how the hero or heroine got that way', he said. 'Well, I couldn't have everybody bitten by radioactive spiders or hit by gamma rays. It suddenly occurred to me that if I could say that people were mutants, I need no further explanation.' In the first issue, the earliest X-Men – Professor X, Scott Summers ('Cyclops'), Jean Grey ('Marvel Girl'), Hank McCoy (a.k.a. 'Beast'), Bobby Drake ('Iceman'), Warren Worthington III ('The Angel') – battled Magneto, billed as 'Earth's most powerful super-villain', and leader of 'The Brotherhood of Evil Mutants'. Although the title was not initially successful, it lasted 66 issues before declining sales forced Marvel to cease publishing new adventures, turning the title over to reprints of early issues. *Giant-Size X-Men* #1 appeared in the summer of 1975, with writers Len Wein and Chris Claremont and artist Dave Cockrum reviving the fortunes of the ailing title, with Cyclops, Jean Grey (now called 'Phoenix') and Professor X training a new group of X-Men, including Storm, Colossus, Nightcrawler, Banshee and Thunderbird. After a five-year hiatus, the X-Men began publishing new stories with issue #94. Since then, the title has enjoyed an uninterrupted run. Some 400 million comics have been sold in 75 countries, making the various X-Men titles the most popular in contemporary comics.

PREVIOUS INCARNATIONS: Although it took nearly three decades for the X-Men to graduate to the screen, their first appearance, in the 1989 animation special *Pryde of The X-Men*, was something of a curate's egg: although the animation was good, the lack of an introduction to any of the characters left the uninitiated bemused, while the lack of a cohesive storyline left fans disappointed. A more successful animated outing came in 1992, as Saban and Graz Entertainment's *X-Men* animated series made its small-screen debut. The show, closely modelled on the comic book stories and highly regarded by fans, ran for five successful seasons, amassing 76 episodes in all. The series is still repeated on the Fox Kids network.

DEVELOPMENT: Given its popularity, few could have doubted the potential of *X-Men* as a movie, but it was producer Lauren Shuler Donner, wife of *Superman* director Richard Donner, who began actively to develop the property as early as 1990. Even before a script existed, Donner began courting director Bryan Singer, who had won widespread critical acclaim for his debut feature, *The Usual Suspects*, a tale which, like the mooted *X-Men* movie, had an ensemble cast and a story which kept track of a larger than usual number of characters. Singer had never read an *X-Men* comic, and it fell to his producer partner, Tom DeSanto, to convince him. 'At first, Bryan said, "Oh, leave me alone, I'm never going to do a comic book movie!" and I'm like, "No, this one's different," ' DeSanto told *Empire* magazine. Singer began reading old *X-Men* comics, 'watching all seventy episodes of the animated series, reading the books, character bios and character encyclopaedias', and soon became hooked on 'the idea of reluctant superheroes born the way they are; outcasts, trying to find a place to belong, to be accepted. It was like finding the essence and magic of the early comics, and the darkness and the reality of the later ones, and merging the two'. Singer was particularly taken with Chris Claremont's 1982 graphic novel *God Loves, Man Kills*, a chilling allegory of religious, political and social intolerance towards mutants. He and DeSanto drafted a treatment which dealt with a clash of Professor X's and Magneto's political beliefs. Now all they needed was a script.

Although future Pulitzer Prize winner and *Spider-Man* sequel scriptwriter Michael Chabon had pitched an *X-Men* treatment as early as 1996, and *Men in Black* scribe Ed Solomon had written the first of several scripts, DeSanto, for one, was not satisfied with any of them. 'The first two scripts I read were not taking it seriously,' he told *Cinefantastique*. 'They weren't getting it. It's about Xavier and Magneto. It's Martin Luther King and Malcolm X and the next wave of human evolution. The themes of prejudice and the outcast really resonated with Bryan.' When Singer signed on, however, he and DeSanto began working on a treatment of their own, and all but jettisoned the previous drafts, and invited *The Usual Suspects*' Oscar® winning screenwriter Christopher McQuarrie to have a crack at turning the Singer/DeSanto version into a script. Joss Whedon (*Buffy the Vampire Slayer*, *Waterworld*), John Logan (*Gladiator*, *The Time Machine*) and James Schamus (*The Hulk*) would subsequently all take a turn at writing, rewriting or 'doctoring' the script; however, it was David Hayter – who voiced Captain America in the *Spider-Man* animated series, and scripted *The Scorpion King* – who finally nailed it. Now Singer's only concern was that the X-Men mythology would need to undergo an evolution of its own in order to set up almost four decades of comic book lore in two hours. 'I always try and remain respectful to the essence of the characters,' Singer said, 'and since the characters, over thirty-eight years, have gone through so many different transformations, it's an awful lot to choose from. But at the same time I try to tell an original story.'

Singer knew that he needed at least one character who would enter the story with the audience, so that everything the audience needed to learn about the world of the X-Men could be seen through a character's eyes. Although he chose two such characters – Rogue, a teenage girl with lifeforce-draining powers which means she cannot touch or be touched without deadly consequences; and Wolverine, who is aware of his steel claws and preternatural regenerative powers, but has no idea how he came by them – the fact that Rogue is an ordinary teenager with a boyfriend and plans to drive across America when she graduates, makes her easier for the intended audience, particularly those *not* reared on X-Men comics, to identify with. 'She's not the Rogue most of [the fans] know,' he explained. 'She's young, innocent, with almost no life experience. I wanted to take some of the attiributes of Kitty Pryde, Jubilee and Rogue and sort of merge them into Rogue. She is kind of a merger of these younger X-characters.' Another reason Singer chose to focus on Rogue as much as the ever-popular Wolverine was that her mutation was the most indicative of the curse of being a mutant. 'To have this amazing power, but at the same time, the inability to touch or be touched.' Singer felt that his commitment to the seriousness of the themes would compensate for any liberties he had found it necessary to take in bringing the story to a wider audience. '[I was] worried about the fans to some degree,' he told Charlie Rose. 'But my approach to that was always, "How would I want a director to treat my favourite universe, something I've loved for decades?" And I would simply want he or she to take it seriously – as seriously as you take any science fiction film.'

CASTING: Bald British actor Patrick Stewart, best known as Jean-Luc Picard in the most recent *Star Trek* movies, had been mentioned in connection with the role of Professor Xavier ever since Richard Donner first discussed it with him during the making of *Conspiracy Theory*, and Stewart had no hesitation in taking the role – not least because he was looking forward to an on-screen battle of wits with countryman Sir Ian McKellen, who had signed to the project soon after wrapping *Apt Pupil*, Singer's 1998 adaptation of the Stephen King novella. As a result, Professor X was the only *X-Men* character to avoid being the subject of furious speculation among X-fans, with almost every eligible actor (and some extremely unlikely ones) mentioned in connection with every role. Nevertheless, other cast members soon fell into place: Oscar® winner Anna Paquin (*The Piano*) as Rogue; Halle Berry, a future Oscar® winner and Bond girl, then best known for roles in *Boomerang* and *Bulworth*, as the perfect Storm; former Bond girl Famke Janssen (*Goldeneye*, *The Faculty*) as Jean Grey; James Marsden from TV's *Ally McBeal* as Cyclops; 6′10″ tall wrestler Tyler Mane (a.k.a. 'Big Sky') as Sabretooth; former model and host of MTV's *House of Style* Rebecca Romijn-Stamos (*Austin Powers: The Spy Who Shagged Me*) as Mystique; and actor Ray Park, who had recently played Darth Maul in *Star Wars Episode I: The Phantom Menace*, as Toad. Although Singer had publicly courted future *Gladiator* star and *A Beautiful Mind* Oscar® winner Russell Crowe for the role of fan favourite Wolverine, Fox was unwilling to meet his salary demands, and it was Scottish actor Dougray Scott who eventually won the most coveted part of all. Scott's involvement self-destructed when *Mission: Impossible 2* overran its shooting schedule, and Singer settled on one of Crowe's countrymen: newcomer Hugh Jackman.

PRODUCTION: Singer knew going in that both the schedule and the budget was going to be tight for a film of this scale – $75 million and 91 days respectively. 'The budget of the film, comparative to most big event kind of films, was fairly conservative, and the timing and the schedule were real challenges for us,' Singer told Charlie Rose. After numerous delays, shooting began on 27 September 1999, and immediately hit a crisis: Dougray Scott was unable to report to the set due to overruns on *Mission: Impossible* 2; his replacement, Hugh Jackman, was unavailable until November, which left only a small crossover period before Ian McKellen was due to fly to New Zealand to begin shooting *The Lord of the Rings*. As if things were not difficult enough, Fox dropped a bombshell on Singer midway through production, bringing the projected release date forward from X-mas 2000 to the summer of the same year, thus reducing the schedule by five months, without a concomitant budget increase. The post-production schedule – which includes editing, visual effects work, composition and recording of the musical score, sound recording and editing, and many other elements – was cut by eight weeks, in order to ready the film for the new release date, 14 July 2000. Singer made it, although at times, he may have felt that the movie tag-line – 'Trust a few, fear the rest' – might just as easily apply to Hollywood executives.

COSTUME FITTING: Recalling the furore that changing Batman's traditional costume had caused among Bat fans a decade earlier, the film-makers were keen to appease the legions of X-men aficionados by faithfully representing their comic book costumes, usually coloured yellow and blue, in the film. Looking at the evolution of the costume designs (a helpful feature of the *X-Men* DVD) clearly shows that many of the early sketches incorporate the X-Mens' trademark yellow and blue colouring, with the letter 'X' emblazoned on shoulders, breasts or lapels – or even incorporated into the shape of the design itself. Ultimately, however, the film-makers opted to throw out the comic book designs, for reasons which Tom DeSanto explained to *Empire*. 'I was the number one champion of sticking to the real costumes, but as soon as I saw them in reality, it looked like they should be doing balloon animals at a child's birthday party.'

'Imagine them wearing suits of any other colour in a live-action movie,' Singer suggested. 'Just picture that in your head. You can't go there. It had to be black leather. And the reason it was leather was leather is sexy, it's durable, it's the kind of thing that if they got hit with it on, it would bounce off.' Added make-up designer Gordon Smith, 'We used the comic books as much as we possibly could, but Bryan wanted to lift it out of the two-dimensional realm and make it a real-world situation, that these characters may indeed actually exist. I went through each of the characters and designed all the elements that each of the characters needed, whether it be wigs, prosthetics, eyes, hands, claws, knives.' As a humorous way of acknowledging the costume changes, Singer added a line to the script in which Wolverine dresses for the first time in X-Men 'team colours' – padded black leather jumpsuits with two silver 'X' brooches on the lapels and a third on the belt – and says, 'You actually go outside in these things?' To which Cyclops replies sardonically, 'What would you prefer? Yellow Spandex?'

Although Mystique is depicted in the comic as pale blue with long flowing red hair and a white dress, changing the curvy chameleon's look gave the film-makers fewer concerns about upsetting X-Men fans than it did about offending the US ratings board, since Rebecca Romijn-Stamos plays Mystique without a shred of clothing, leaving little mystique about her physique. Despite the scaly skin and the snake-in-the-grass personality, the shapely shape-shifter manages to be sexy as hell – a fact that made Singer nervous and proud at the same time. 'My goal was, "How do I get a naked supermodel into a PG-13 certificate",' he joked. 'You've got to be clever.' With a vast number of magazine covers and modelling sessions behind her – not to mention a recurring role as Adrienne on model-agency sit-com *Just Shoot Me* – Romijn-Stamos was no stranger to the make-up chair, yet even this could not prepare her for the eight to twelve hours a day it took for a small army of make-up artists – and possibly painters and decorators – to cover sixty per cent of her body in prosthetic patches, and the remainder in blue paint, from the soles of her feet to the inside of her ears.

MUSIC: Michael Kamen had previously scored such blockbusters as *Die Hard*, the *Lethal Weapon* series, *Last Action Hero* and *Robin Hood: Prince of Thieves* – as well as more erudite films such as *Brazil*, *Mr*

Holland's Opus and *The Winter Guest* – prior to his work on *X-Men*. Also featured in the film were Lucinda Williams' 'Still I Long for Your Kiss', and 'Atom Bomb' by Fluke.

CLASSIC QUOTES:

Senator Kelly: 'I think the American people have a right to decide whether they want their children to be at school with mutants, to be taught by mutants. Ladies and gentlemen, the truth is that mutants are very real, and they are among us. We must know who they are, and above all we must know what they can do.'

Erik Lehnsherr: 'I will bring you hope, old friend. And I ask only one thing in return: don't get in my way. We are the future, Charles, not them! They no longer matter.'

Rogue: 'Where am I supposed to go?'
Wolverine: 'I don't know.'
Rogue: 'You don't know or you don't care?'
Wolverine: 'Pick one.'

Wolverine: 'Sabretooth. Storm. What do they call you? Wheels?'

Senator Kelly: 'You know this situation? These mutants? People like this Jean Grey. If it were up to me I'd lock 'em all away. It's a war. It's the reason people like me exist.'
Mystique: 'You know, people like you are the reason I was afraid to go to school as a child.'

Wolverine: 'Where's your room?'
Jean Grey: 'With Scott, down the hall.'
Wolverine: 'Is that your gift? Putting up with that guy?'

Wolverine: 'So read my mind.'
Jean Grey: 'I'd rather not.'
Wolverine: 'Come on . . . afraid you might like it?'
Jean Grey: 'I doubt it.'

Wolverine: 'You gonna tell me to stay away from your girl?'
Cyclops: 'If I had to do that, she wouldn't be my girl.'

Professor X: 'Welcome to Cerebro.'
Wolverine: 'This certainly is a big, round room.'

Magneto: 'Let them pass that law and they'll have you in chains with a number burned into your forehead.'

Wolverine: 'It's me.'
Cyclops: 'Prove it.'

Wolverine: 'You're a dick.'
Cyclops: 'OK.'

Cyclops: 'Storm, fry 'em.'
Magneto: 'Oh yes, a bolt of lightning into a huge copper conductor. I thought you lived at a school.'

Magneto: 'You know this plastic prison of theirs won't hold me forever. The war is still coming, Charles, and I intend to fight it, by any means necessary.'

DELETED SCENES: The following scenes and scene extensions were left on the cutting-room floor:

- An extended version of the classroom scene, in which Storm lectures about the Christians eventual acceptance in the Roman Empire when Emperor Constantine converted to Christianity in 325 AD – a neat foreshadowing of Magneto's plan for the world leaders at the UN summit. While Storm talks, Kitty and Jubilee ask Rogue about Wolverine. 'Does he really have steel claws that come out of his hands?' Kitty asks, while Jubilee wants to know, 'What kind of a mutation is that?'
- A scene in which Wolverine watches Cyclops and Jean holding hands as they teach auto shop.
- A further scene in Storm's classroom in which Rogue accepts Bobby's invitation to dinner. As he leaves, Rogue asks Storm how Logan is. 'He's fine. He's . . . quite resilient,' she replies, and asks how long Rogue has been on her own. 'Eight months. I didn't know there were places like this.' 'I don't know that there are many places like this.' 'And the Professor, can he cure me?' 'I don't think it really works like that,' Storm replies candidly.
- An extended version of the scene in which Jean Grey shows Wolverine his room. 'Maybe your Professor's holding you back,' he says. 'Maybe he's not alone.' 'I hope you're not suggesting that Scott's holding me back,' she shoots back. 'I don't know. He seems a little restrained for a woman like you.' 'Really?' 'Just an observation.' 'If Scott opened his eyes without that visor, he could punch a hole through a mountain. I think it's good for all of us if he has a sense of control, don't you?' The scene then continues as per the film, although there is additional dialogue in the confrontation between Cyclops and Wolverine. 'You know, I'd feel a lot better if you were taking this seriously,' Cyclops says. 'Some mutants take pride in their gifts, especially those of us who are willing to fight for what we believe in.' 'You ever see real combat, boy?' Wolverine asks him. 'Have you?' Cyclops shoots back; then, when Wolverine doesn't answer, he adds, 'Don't like to talk about your past?' 'Not to you.'

- A scene in which Bobby walks Rogue to her dorm room, presumably after their dinner date, and he invites her for lunch the following day. (This scene sets up the meeting in the school grounds at which Mystique poses as Bobby.)
- A scene in which Jean Grey enters Cerebro as Professor X abandons his latest attempt to find Magneto. 'I'm afraid, Jean. Knowing he's out there somewhere. I had hoped we'd be much more prepared before it came to this.' She offers to try. 'Not yet,' he says. 'When you're ready.' 'I am ready, I know it. I can feel my power expanding all the time.' 'Yet in the Senate hearing . . .' 'I know. I lost control.' 'I just don't want to see you get hurt. I sometimes wonder if I should have involved all of you in this, or just let you live your own lives.' 'Well, I can't speak for the others,' she says kindly, kissing his forehead, 'but it wouldn't have been much of a life without you.'
- A scene in which Professor X and Jean Grey discuss Wolverine over tea. 'I think if you're going to read minds, there are safer places to start than Logan's,' he tells her.
- A scene in the 'Ready Room' in which Cyclops warns Wolverine that he must be a team player. 'Are you gonna have a problem taking orders?' 'I don't know. Give me one,' Wolverine replies. 'Put this on,' Cyclops says, offering him a costume. 'Whose is it?' Wolverine asks. 'It's one of mine,' says Cyclops.

One entire character, present in many of the early drafts, was dropped before shooting began. Scientist Hank McCoy, a.k.a. 'The Beast,' was cut because of difficulties with his blue fur costume. Instead, his scientific knowledge was grafted on to the character of Jean Grey, who was given an honorary doctorate. Singer had also hoped to include one of his favourite X-Men, 'Nightcrawler', and 'The Danger Room' in which the X-Men train. 'That's an example of something we toyed with early on, and when we looked at the price tag, in the end I didn't think it was necessary,' he told *Cinefantastique*. 'I could've had a Danger Room, and then that sequence would've taken a certain amount of time and money from other sequences that I like better.'

TRAILERS: Three trailers were produced for *X-Men*. Trailer A begins with Storm saying 'Hold on to something,' before intercutting quick-fire clips and graphic captions ('CHANGE IS COMING' and 'THE EVOLUTION BEGINS') to a punishing music track, and a tag-line: 'THE EVOLUTION BEGINS JULY 14TH'. Professor X's 'We're not what you think' is the only other dialogue line, and no title is given.

Trailer B opens with footage from the Senate hearing, intercut with captions: 'the world is changing . . . man is evolving . . . the time is coming . . . when all that we are afraid of . . . will be all that can save us'.

After Professor Xavier then introduces himself and talks of the coming war between humanity and mutants, the characters are introduced by animated name captions, in blue for the good guys ('TRUST A FEW'), red for the bad guys ('FEAR THE REST'). 'I've never seen anything like this before,' Professor X says as a spinning 'X' leads into a montage of fast-cut clips, and finally forms the title ('X-MEN') and another caption: 'PROTECTING THOSE WHO FEAR THEM'.

Trailer C has a generic voice-over reading the captions aloud: 'In every human being . . . there exists the genetic code . . . for mutation. A change is coming . . . and those we fear . . . will be all that can save us.' A fast-cut montage of footage and dialogue is followed by a title and Professor X's words: 'We're not what you think. Not all of us.'

POSTERS: The very first poster produced for *X-Men* featured only a metallic 'X' in a circle, with a hint of light breaking through at the centre. The next poster expanded on this image, adding a title and giving a glimpse of several of the characters through the expanded light source. Another version of the 'teaser' poster added a title to the original image. The main US 'one-sheet' featured put the title at the centre of the poster, and added images of the ten principal characters: Professor X, Storm, Toad, Cyclops, Magneto, Jean Grey, Mystique, Rogue, Sabretooth and Wolverine. Only their eyes are visible in the stylised shots – but for fans of the comic book, it was enough to identify each of the characters. Another 'main' poster campaign featured the encircled 'X' and a New York cityscape as a backdrop – the towers of the World Trade Center featured prominently – with full-length images of nine of the characters standing on opposite sides (Rogue is missing from the X-Men ensemble on the left of the poster).

TAG-LINE: 'Join the evolution.' 'Protecting those who fear them.' 'Trust a few. Fear the rest.' 'The evolution begins only in theatres.'

WHAT THE PAPERS SAID: 'X is for X-Men,' *Variety*'s Dennis Harvey wrote, 'Y is for "Like, why do these screen versions of graphic superhero fantasies hardly ever work?" Z is for the "Zzzzzz" soon to be heard around the world from those with little or no prior investment in the long-running print serial.' In the *Chicago Sun-Times*, Roger Ebert bemoaned the film's 'top-heavy' nature, whereby 'at the halfway mark, it has just about finished introducing the characters . . . It's understandable that the set-ups would play an important role in the first film,' he allowed. 'If only there were more to the pay-off.' Nevertheless, he welcomed the fact that it was not 'a manic editing frenzy for atrophied attention spans', being instead 'restrained and introspective'. In the UK, *Empire* magazine took a different view of the fact that the film did not overstay its welcome. 'If the climax leaves you feeling short changed, then consider this: is it better to be left wanting more, or to exit the cinema wishing you hadn't bothered in the first place? Roll on *X-Men II*.' *Time Out* praised the film's political standpoint: 'The conflict between Xavier and Magneto couches a dilemma familiar from ethnic and gay politics: assimilation or direct action. It's good to find an action movie which has at least one idea in its head, but apart from the brushed metal production design and pin-sharp camerawork, [*X-Men*] offers only moderate excitement.'

BOX OFFICE: *X-Men* was released in the US on 14 July 2000, grossing $54.47 million in its opening weekend, and $157.3 million overall. Worldwide, the film has grossed twice that, making it among the most successful comic book adaptations of all time.

AWARDS: Although *X-Men* was overlooked at the Academy Awards®, Golden Globes and BAFTAs, the Academy of Science Fiction, Fantasy & Horror Films made up for the oversight, awarding the film six Saturn awards – Best Actor (Hugh Jackman), Best Costume, Best Director, Best Science Fiction Film, Best Supporting Actress (Rebecca Romijn-Stamos) and Best Writing – and four further nominations: Best Make-up, Best Performance by a Younger Actor (Anna Paquin), Best Special Effects and Best Supporting Actor (Patrick Stewart). The film also converted two of its Blockbuster Entertainment Awards into prizes: James Marsden for Favourite Supporting Actor (Science Fiction), and Rebecca Romijn-Stamos for Favourite Supporting Actress (Science Fiction). Bryan Singer ultimately won the Best Director prize awarded by the readers of *Empire* magazine.

TRIVIA: Watch out for cameos by screenwriter David Hayter, executive producer Tom DeSanto and X-Men creator Stan Lee.

Toad's handling of a metal bar was a deliberate reference to actor Ray Park's previous appearance as Darth Maul in *Star Wars Episode I*.

In addition to Bobby Drake ('Iceman'), several other X-Men make cameo appearances in Professor Xavier's school: Jubilation Lee ('Jubilee') is the Asian-American girl wearing a yellow jacket; Kitty Pryde ('Shadowcat') is the girl who walks though the door of Professor X's office; and 'Colossus'.

George Buza, who plays the trucker who drops Rogue off in Northern Alberta, played the voice of 'Beast' in the animated *X-Men* series.

In 'The Perfect Mate' episode of *Star Trek: The Next Generation*, starring Patrick Stewart, Famke Janssen (Jean Grey) played a telepathic mutant.

Bryan Singer once challenged audiences to count the number of times the letter 'X' appears in the film. The first is as the 'x' in the Twentieth Century Fox logo remains on screen after the rest of the logo has faded out.

Senator Kelly's claim that he possesses 'a list of names of identified mutants living right here in the United States' is based on Senator Joseph McCarthy's almost identical claim with regard to communists working at the US State Department. It was subsequently proven to be rhetoric – McCarthy was in possession of no such list.

SEQUELS & SPIN-OFFS: Twentieth Century Fox put an *X-Men* sequel into production as soon as the opening weekend figures came in; once again, Bryan Singer was back in the director's chair, all of the cast back in place, and newcomers Brian Cox (*Manhunter*) as Stryker, Kelly Hu (*The Transporter*) as Yuriko Oyama, and Alan Cumming (*Goldeneye*) as Nightcrawler. 'If people want to see a sequel, they want to see an evolution,' Singer said of his thinking behind the second film. 'You wanna improve upon it, make it better. The intention here is not to be saddled with introducing a new universe, so it's a great opportunity to now have fun with them. And the few new characters who are going to be introduced in this film, one can do with less exposition. Fortunately, we have a little more time and a couple more dollars,' he added, 'and everyone knows what they're doing a little better – especially me.'

Meanwhile, November 2000 saw the debut of a brand new animated series, *X-Men: Evolution*, produced by Marvel Entertainment and Film Roman Productions for the Kids WB network. Although fans' opinion was divided, the series drew a sufficiently large audience to warrant a second and third season.

FUTURE INCARNATIONS: Although Singer and the principal cast members initially committed only for one sequel, if *X-Men 2* is a success, there are likely to be more. 'We very much see it as a franchise,' Lauren Shuler Donner told *Empire* prior to the first film's opening, 'and because of that there's certain characters or certain elements that we're saving for movie number two and movie number three and movie number four, because there's a million stories in the X-Men world.'

DVD AVAILABILITY: Although packaged differently, the UK (Region 2) and US (Region 1) DVDs both feature a widescreen (2.35:1) Dolby 5.1 transfer of the film, eight deleted scenes, extracts from Bryan Singer's interview on *The Charlie Rose Show*, footage from Hugh Jackman's screen test, animatics, a promo for the *X-Men* soundtrack, three trailers and three TV spots, an all-too-brief featurette; and a vast gallery of conceptual art containing hundreds of pre-production sketches of characters, costumes, props, sets and storyboards. There are also two documentaries: a short behind-the-scenes featurette featuring interviews with cast and crew, and a cleverly conceived fifty-minute 'mockumentary', *X-Men: The Mutant Watch*, which traces the characters, the history and the making of *X-Men* with the help of specially filmed links in which Bruce Davison reprises his film role as Senator Kelly. A hidden feature ('easter egg') on both versions includes 'bloopers' and out-takes – one of which shows the cast cracking up as an extra dressed as Spider-Man shows up on set, looks around, and says, 'Oops, wrong movie!'

In the lead-up to the cinema release of *X-Men 2*, a new 'definitive' two-disc DVD entitled *X-Men 1.5* was released, featuring over five hours of extras, including audio commentary by director Brian Singer and friend/prompter Brian Peck; an 'enhanced viewing mode' allowing access to seventeen featurettes and six deleted scenes (with optional commentary) in the context of the film itself; several additional featurettes, covering special effects, pre-production, production design, and more; multi-angle scene studies; animatic-to-film comparisons; three trailers, nine TV spots and a dozen web interstitials; *X-Men 2* previews; *X-Men* premiere footage; and more.

FINAL ANALYSIS: One only has to picture Gary Sinise dressed in yellow spandex to imagine the number of ways an X-Men movie could have gone awry. Instead, from conceptualisation to casting, from production design to story and script, Bryan Singer seems barely to put a foot wrong in bringing the X-Men, currently the most popular comic book characters in the world, to the big screen – especially when you factor in the bottom-line-conscious budget and shortened shooting schedule he was forced to endure. Sun Tzu said that a battle is won or lost before it is even fought, and Singer's victory may well have been secured by his casting: even the most hardened X-Men fans can hardly fail to be impressed by Patrick Stewart and Ian McKellen, whose ostensible status as respective heads of the 'heroes' and 'villains' belies their deeper motivations – although Stewart's character may perhaps have been better named 'Professor X-position', given the amount of plot he is required to explain.

Fans should be similarly impressed by Hugh Jackman and Anna Paquin as the two newcomers to Professor X's mutant ghetto, and although Halle Berry is hampered by her bizarre accent, she and the other X-women exude as much sex appeal as Wolverine and Cyclops. Although the origin story, arguably by necessity, takes up an inordinate amount of screen time, it says something for the quality of a comic book adaptation when the pyrotechnic pomp and computer-generated circumstance of the climactic showdown between the superheroes and super-villains is less satisfying than the dialogue between the principal characters. As a self-contained film, *X-Men* walks a tightrope between giving the audience value for money and leaving them wanting more; where it excels is as the first episode in what promises to be an X-traordinary series of films.

EXPERT WITNESS: 'I viewed *X-Men* as an SF film, not necessarily as a comic book movie. I used the lore of the comic book and all the wonderful characters as great pieces of inspiration and ideas. *Batman* and *Superman* are the only two analogous films, and *Batman* is more retro. If I had to compare it to anything, I'd compare it to the first act of *Superman*, which I'm very inspired by and love.' – **Bryan Singer, Director**

From Hell (2001)

(122 minutes)

Directed by the Hughes Brothers
Produced by Don Murphy and Jane Hamsher
Screenplay by Terry Hayes and Rafael Yglesias
Based on the Graphic Novel by Alan Moore and Eddie Campbell
Executive Producers Amy Robinson, Thomas M Hammel, Allen Hughes and Albert Hughes
Director of Photography Peter Deming ASC
Production Designer Martin Childs
Edited by Dan Lebental and George Bowers ACE
Music by Trevor Jones
Costume Designer Kym Barrett

CAST: Johnny Depp (*Inspector Frederick Abberline*), Heather Graham (*Mary Kelly*), Ian Holm (*Sir William Withey Gull*), Robbie Coltrane (*Detective Sergeant George Godley*), Ian Richardson (*Sir Charles Warren*), Jason Flemyng (*John Netley*), Katrin Cartlidge (*'Dark' Annie Chapman*), Terence Harvey (*Benjamin Kidney*), Susan Lynch (*Elizabeth 'Liz' Stride*), Paul Rhys (*Dr Ferral*), Lesley Sharp (*Catherine 'Kate' Eddowes*), Estelle Skornik (*Ada*), Nicholas McGaughey (*Officer Bolt*), Annabelle Apsion (*Polly Nicholls*), Joanna Page (*Ann Crook*), Mark Dexter (*Albert Sickert/Prince Edward Albert Victor*), Danny Midwinter (*Constable Withers*), Samantha Spiro (*Martha Tabram*), David Schofield (*McQueen*), Bryon Fear (*Robert Best*), Peter Eyre (*Lord Hallsham*), Cliff

Parisi (*bartender*), Sophia Myles (*Victoria Abberline*), Ralph Ineson (*Gordie*), Amy Huck (*Gull's maid*), Rupert Farley (*doss landlord*), Donald Douglas (*hospital director*), John Owens (*Marylebone governor*), Liz Moscrop (*Queen Victoria*), Ian McNeice (*Robert Drudge*), Steve John Shepherd (*special branch constable*), Al Hunter Ashton (*stonecutter*), Poppy Rogers (*Alice Crook*), Bruce Byron (*Ann Crook's father*), Melanie Hill (*Ann Crook's mother*), Andy Linden (*carpenter*), David Fisher (*carpenter/letter writer*), Gary Powell, Steve Chaplin, Dominic Cooper (*constables*), Vincent Franlin (*George Lusk*), Louise Atkins (*bold hooker*), Anthony Parker (*Joseph 'John' Merrick*), James Greene (*Masonic governor*), Carey Thring (*police photographer*), Vladimir Kulhavy (*rag-and-bone man*), Graham Kent (*records clerk*), Rupert Holliday-Evans (*sailor*), Simon Harrison (*Thomas Bond*), Paul Moody (*young doctor*), Glen Barry (*young labourer*), Charlie Parish (*labourer*), Gerry Grennell (*funeral minister/letter writer*)

UNCREDITED CAST: Roger Frost (*sidewalk preacher*), Tony Tang (*opium den owner*)

TITLE SEQUENCE: A white legend on black: 'One day men will look back and say I gave birth to the Twentieth Century – Jack the Ripper, 1888.' A match lights the wick of a gas lamp, the flame used to heat opium residue which a man (Inspector Abberline) smokes through a hookah. A title appears in red letters on black.

SYNOPSIS: London, 1888: the Nichols gang is demanding protection money from Whitechapel prostitutes like Mary Kelly and her friends; Ann promises to get the money from her artist husband, Albert, father of her newborn baby. But the next time she sleeps with him, a Special Branch officer named Kidney and several of his thugs burst in, drag Albert and Ann away, leaving the baby with Mary. Kidney interrogates her, demanding to know who else knows Albert's secret. That night, prostitute Martha Tabram is murdered, an incident seen in an opium dream by Inspector Abberline, who is woken from his drug-induced haze by Sergeant Godley, who tells him of the ritual nature of the killing. Meanwhile, the Queen's physician, Sir William Gull, watches as Ann is lobotomised. That night, the girls turn extra tricks to pay off the Nichols gang, and Polly becomes the killer's next victim. Abberline and Godley find no witnesses – only grape stalks and missing organs. Absinthe fuels Abberline's next dream, this time of his dead wife. At Polly's funeral, Abberline and Godley question Mary and the other 'bang-tails', but none are willing to testify against the Nichols boys. Netley collects Dark Annie Chapman in a black coach, and she soon becomes the next victim – disembowelled, with her intestines arranged in a certain manner around her slit throat. Abberline wants to question a surgeon, and meets with the Queen's physician, Sir William Gull, who tells him the killer has a thorough knowledge of human anatomy – in other words, he's no butcher. Later, Queen Victoria tells Gull of her concern about her son Edward's worsening condition – he has syphilis. After Mary tells Abberline what happened to Ann Crook, he coerces his way into Kidney's office, where he finds files pertaining to Ann. He takes Mary to see Ann, but her mind is gone; then he takes her to see a portrait of Prince Edward, whom she recognises as Ann's husband. Abberline suspects the Prince, but Gull dismisses the theory. Beneath Whitechapel, Kidney, Lord Hallsham and Sir Charles Warren (Abberline's boss) watch as Dr Ferrel is initiated into the Freemasons. Abberline begins to formulate a theory: that someone, possibly a Freemason, is killing Ann Crook's friends to suppress a secret which could bring down the monarchy: that Prince Edward has married a Catholic and produced a child – a legitimate heir to the throne. Mary meets her remaining friends in the Ten Bells public house, and Abberline gives them money to keep them off the streets, and out of harm's way, but Liz has a fight with her girlfriend Ada, goes out for a drink, and is killed by the Ripper. Kate Eddowes goes out looking for her, and meets the same fate. Abberline is set upon, and warned off, by Kidney's men. When he comes to, he finds the two fresh murders, and a message from the killer: 'The Juwes are the men That will not be Blamed for nothing.' Sir Charles Warren has it washed off, and suspends Abberline from duty. Abberline leaves a letter and some money for Mary, whom he has come to love – but later has visions of her death. He finally fingers Gull, confronts him, and is about to shoot him when Kidney intervenes, cold-cocking him and taking him out in the 'death coach'. Abberline escapes, but is too late to save Gull's latest victim – Ada – whom Gull has killed thinking her to be Mary. Sir Charles puts Abberline back in charge of the case, though he knows there will be no more murders. Abberline receives a letter from Mary inviting him to join her in Ireland, but he dare not – he knows he is being watched. Sir William Gull is judged by his fellow Masons, and ends his days, lobotomised, in an institution. Mary lives out her days in Ireland. Abberline ends his in an opium den.

ORIGINS: As the author of such seminal 1980s comic books as *Watchmen*, *V For Vendetta* and *Miracleman*, Alan Moore was widely considered to be the father of the modern comic book by the time he began researching the endless myths, facts and fallacies surrounding the still-unsolved 'Jack the Ripper' murders of the late nineteenth century. 'The idea was to do a documentary comic about a murder,' Moore told Danny Graydon. 'I concluded that there was a way of approaching the murders in a completely different way. I changed the emphasis from "whodunnit" to "what happened".' The result was *From Hell*, a ten-episode heavily annotated partwork published in 'prestige' format between 1989 and 1994, collected in graphic novel form in 1999. Exhaustively researched, painstakingly prepared and illustrated in a dense, scratchy monochromatic style by renowned comic book artist Eddie Campbell (*Deadman*), *From Hell* is widely regarded as one of the greatest achievements in comic book history. Although *From Hell* postulated a theory as to the identity of the Ripper, as complex and conspiracy-minded as Oliver Stone's *JFK* thesis, Moore has said that he was less interested in establishing the identity of Jack the Ripper than the behaviour of the culture, and the mythology that has grown up around the murders in the hundred years since they were committed. 'Five murders is nothing – that's the thing that fascinated me. How could this crime have somehow blossomed into all these mythic dimensions, where [conspiracy theorists] have the royal family involved, the Freemasons, all these hints of dark supernatural forces? What is it about these crimes?' Part of the fascination, of course, is that the Ripper was never caught. 'It was by escaping the noose that he also escaped history.'

DEVELOPMENT: *From Hell* was optioned in 1996 by *Natural Born Killers* producers Don Murphy and Jane Hamsher, who set the project up at Disney, and commissioned Terry Hayes (*Dead Calm*, the *Mad Max* sequels) to write the screenplay. American-Armenian twin brothers Allen and Albert Hughes (*Menace II Society*, *Dead Presidents*) were offered the project the same year, turning down *Con Air* and Fox's *Planet of the Apes* remake in order to pursue it, feeling that it was time to be taken seriously as film-makers, rather than *black* film-makers. Although the subject matter fascinated them, the Hughes brothers didn't warm to the script – 'It was interesting in parts but really Hollywood-corny,' says Allen. 'There was a love triangle, and it had a Hollywood ending where [Abberline and Mary] get together.' It was only after they went back and read the graphic novel that they saw what needed to be done in order to make it work. They brought in novelist and screenwriter Rafael Yglesias (*Fearless*, *Death and the Maiden*) who, according to Allen, 'read all the graphic novels, and I'd say in about three and a half weeks did a page one rewrite, which is incredible for something this size'.

Although the Hughes brothers liked the new script, Disney did not, putting the project in turnaround, uncertain at the new direction it was taking under their guidance, at which point New Line Cinema – the company behind such previous comic book adaptations as *The Mask*, *Spawn* and *Blade* – stepped in. Frustrated by failed attempts to sign a star for the project, however, New Line too put the project in turnaround six months later, and Murphy and Hamsher found a new home for the project at Twentieth Century Fox, whose plan was to make a lower budget version with no stars, an approach which suited the Hughes brothers and their favoured version of the screenplay. 'For me, as a writer, [*From Hell*] is about what that time was about, which was sexual hypocrisy,' Yglesias explains. 'This society is built around this monstrous sexual hypocrisy. These women are despised, this part of town is despised because it's open sex at a time when sex is not open, but in fact the engine for it are the rich, who are self-righteous about it. And as much as the film appears to be about Jack the Ripper, for me it's about that hypocrisy, that lie of Victorian England. For the film-makers,' he adds, 'it's about that time – what that world was like. How the whores lived, how the rich lived, what it looked like, what it smelled like, that there were Jews there that were despised, that there was an Asian underclass, that there was drug addiction. We figured all that would be news to people, although it's just history.'

Although Yglesias initially lobbied to tell the story from Gull's point of view, an aspect of the graphic novel he wanted to retain, the producers argued against it, feeling that the story should be Abberline's. 'The original graphic novel is very much "Jack the Ripper: Portrait of a Serial Killer",' Murphy explains, referring to John McNaughton's controversial 1986 film, *Henry: Portrait of a Serial Killer*. 'By page thirty, you know this guy is Jack, he's been sent onto a mission, and the graphic novel is about his journey into madness. I don't think Abberline shows up until probably page one hundred and fifty . . . and if you're gonna go make a studio film, there's no way you're going to convince a studio that Jack is the main character. It would be fascinating, but that's not a popular commercial film. So although Jack should be a major character, this is not Jack's story, it's Abberline's story.'

Taking this approach, Yglesias found the perfect way to bring Abberline into the murders. 'Basically I eliminated the character of the clairvoyant [from the graphic novel] and incorporated him into Abberline's character, and made him a real clairvoyant who dreams the murders ahead of time. I think that was the biggest change I made from the graphic novel, and it gave [the directors] a contextual way of doing the visuals of the graphic novel on film.' Better yet, it served to make Abberline one of a number of suspects – Kidney, Prince Albert/Walter Sickert, McQueen – put forward by the film, as red herrings, before its chosen suspect is revealed. 'I'm basically giving you all the possible theories of who Jack the Ripper is, one right after another,' says Yglesias. 'I'm relying on the fact that, like the conspiracy theories of JFK, it's interesting in and of itself. That's what the graphic novel had, this kind of "meta" view of the conspiracy theories. It gives you all of them.'

CASTING: The Hughes brothers had initially tried to meet with Oscar® winner Daniel Day-Lewis (*My Left Foot*), and later considered Sean

Connery, Ralph Fiennes, Gary Oldman and Tim Roth for the role of Inspector Abberline, before finding their leading man, Johnny Depp, who had just played a detective in another period film, *Sleepy Hollow*. 'He wasn't our first choice on this film because his agent had told us he was busy and we never thought about him,' Albert Hughes told *Total Film*. 'We went through all these other actors, then met with Johnny again and realised he was a total Ripper buff. He really fit the character too – it kinda worked out by accident, really.' Explaining his interest in the century-old murder mystery, Depp recalled seeing a documentary about the case when he was a child. 'I've always been fascinated by it,' he told *Empire*. 'Primarily because these heinous, hideous acts went unsolved. That brings up a lot of questions – how and why did the case remain unsolved?' Depp did more than just his homework, reading 'three-quarters of the stuff that's out there,' including the graphic novel which he described as 'like a hammer to the head – I was blown away by it'.

Heather Graham was not the Hughes brothers' first choice either, largely because they had originally wanted all of the cast to be British. 'We saw a lotta, lotta girls,' said Allen. 'A lot of *cheesy* so-called Hollywood semi-stars. Heather was the last one, and we said, 'Well, this won't work either.' But she really surprised me at the audition – some of the emotional stuff she did. And her whole vibe, her looks and her energy . . . they go well with Johnny.'

Sir Nigel Hawthorne (*The Madness of King George*) had originally been cast as Sir William Gull, but was forced to drop out due to ill health, and was replaced at short notice by Ian Holm (*Alien*).

PRODUCTION: Production began in July 2000 just outside of Prague, capital of the Czech Republic, where a 90,000 square metre recreation of Whitechapel was built, lain with cobblestones borrowed from nearby streets. Although there were a number of reasons for shooting in Prague – for instance, set construction and labour were all relatively inexpensive compared to Los Angeles or London, and a wealth of magnificent nineteenth-century buildings had been preserved – none of them had to do with the original idea, which was to find locations there which could be made to resemble Victorian London. In fact, the modernisation of the city which had occurred since the fall of communism made finding exteriors difficult, and it was therefore proposed to build sets in a small town some twenty miles from the capital. 'If you go to [Whitechapel] now,' production designer Martin Childs explains, 'a lot of buildings still exist, but you can't turn around and shoot the reverse of them, so what we did in Prague was create something where we could shoot three hundred and sixty degrees.' Although Alan Moore declined an invitation to visit the set, he was impressed by the photographs he was sent of *Shakespeare in Love* production designer Martin Childs' reconstruction of Victorian London in contemporary Prague. 'It looked spectacular,' Moore admitted. 'I do know Whitechapel very very well, and Christchurch Spitalfields . . . The photograph that they sent me, if I didn't intellectually know that this was a façade somewhere in Prague, I would have sworn that down to the last cobblestone it was an authentic reconstruction.'

Cinematographer Peter Deming, a regular David Lynch collaborator, had never worked in the Victorian setting before, and was eager to explore the period. 'A lot of the JtR story takes place at night, so we spent over six weeks shooting nights, six days a week,' says Deming, 'then you add to that the element of rain and smoke and horses and all the things that come with horses . . . it can get fairly unpleasant after a while. And towards the end of that stay of night work, it was Whitechapel by the end of it. It looked it and it certainly *smelled* it by that point. In fact, the studio told us there was too much horse refuse in the street, but we liked it – we thought it helped the look of the movie.'

Interiors were mostly filmed at Britain's Pinewood Studios, where the film's largely British cast felt more at home. Despite the fact that *From Hell* marked their first 'non-black' film, the Hughes brothers also felt that they were on home turf. 'This is a ghetto story,' Albert told *Empire*. 'It concerns poverty, violence and corruption, which are themes we deal with because they fascinate us.'

COSTUME FITTING: Costume designer Kym Barrett had previously worked on Baz Luhrmann's contemporary retelling of *William Shakespeare's Romeo + Juliet*, *The Matrix* and *Three Kings* before she was called upon to recreate Victorian era costumes for *From Hell*.

MUSIC: Although Trevor Jones (*The Last of the Mohicans*, *Dark City*) composed the music for *From Hell* in a muted, moody, darkly gothic orchestral style which perfectly complemeted the images, it was a far cry from the hardcore rap music the Hughes brothers played on the set. 'We would just listen to rap music and dance around in our period 1888 costumes,' Heather Graham told *Empire*. 'They'd actually bring their boom box onto the set and in between takes we'd be listening to Dr Dre or something.' Although the soundtrack features no hip hop, the dozen Trevor Jones themes included are complemented by the one contemporary track featured in the film (or rather, the closing credits): shock-rock star Marilyn Manson's 'The Nobodies (Wormwood Remix)'.

CLASSIC QUOTES:

Abberline: 'It's night.'

Godley: 'Well spotted, Inspector Abberline. It is indeed night. The genius has returned to us.'

Abberline: 'Are her petticoats soaked in blood?'
Godley: 'You know, they used to burn men like you alive.'

Godley: 'Before he cut her throat, he removed her *livelihood* as a keepsake.'

Abberline: 'Martha Tabram was raped, tortured and killed. That's cruel. But I've seen that sort of cruelty in the East End before. This is methodical. The butcher's irrational, yet meticulous and deliberate. Altogether a different breed of killer.'

Charles Warren: 'Well, one thing's for certain – an Englishman didn't do it. Maybe one of these Red Indians wandered into Whitechapel and indulged his natural instincts.'

Abberline: 'Unless one of you is prepared to testify against McQueen, I can't do nothing.'
Mary Kelly: 'Surely, Inspector, a strong, handsome man like you, you could do anything you put your brilliant mind to. I'm a coward and a weakling and I can't help meself. What's your excuse? Why are you so bloody useless?'

Sir William Gull: 'Netley, I shall tell you where we are. We are in the most extreme and utter region of the human mind. A radiant abyss where men meet themselves.'
Netley: 'I don't understand that. I don't understand, sir.'
Sir William Gull: 'Hell, Netley. We are in Hell.'

Godley: ' "From Hell." Well, at least they got the address right.'

Sir William Gull: 'Below the skin of history are London's veins. These symbols, the mitre, the pentacle star, even someone as ignorant and degenerate as you can sense that they course with energy and meaning. I am that meaning. I am that energy. One day men will look back and say I gave birth to the twentieth century.'

Lord Hallsham: 'Knight of the East, we are gathered here beneath the God of Love and before the sight of the Great Architect, to judge this case. You stand accused of mayhems that have placed our brotherhood in jeopardy. You stand before your peers, Masons and doctors both.'
Sir William Gull: 'I have no peers present here.'
Lord Hallsham: 'What?'
Sir William Gull: 'No man amongst you is fit to judge the mighty art that I have wrought. Your rituals are empty oaths you neither understand nor live by. The Great Architect speaks to me. He is the balance, where my deeds are weighed and judged. Not you.'

DELETED SCENES: 'A fraction of what we shot is in the movie,' says cinematographer Peter Deming. 'We shot some very very gory things, not meaning to use them in their entirety, but just little snips here and there – but even in that application they were too much. A company called Millennium Effects in London made the torsos and body parts; a couple of 'em you had to look twice to make sure they weren't the real person. Albert wanted to shoot some of it to freak the studio out, 'cause they would watch dailies and say, "Oh my God, what are they doing!?" '

There are also a number of more significant deletions, many of them available on the DVD:

- A scene in which Mary takes baby Alice to Ann's mother, who demands to know what happened to their daughter; Ann's father arrives home drunk, and Mary leaves as they quarrel over the baby.
- An additional scene of the girls working the streets, including a shot of Mary Kelly refusing to kiss one of her customers. This shot was important, says Rafael Yglesias, because of its relation to a subsequent scene. 'When Abberline and she finally kiss – when he finally is convinced that she's not just being a whore, she means it – earlier in the film I had a scene showing Mary Kelly turning a trick where she refuses to be kissed on the lips – a well-known thing of whores, that they will let you put your cock in them but they won't let you kiss them on the lips. So for me there was a payoff there, [when] she kisses Abberline, that is somewhat missing from the movie.'
- A scene in which crowds line the streets as Polly's funeral procession troops past; a street preacher talks of death; Godley is given a newspaper by a reporter. 'Oh, thanks, that'll come in handy,' he says. 'I was thinking of having a shit later.' Godley crosses the street, scanning the tabloid, and greets Abberline, whom he sarcastically congratulates for solving the case. 'Yeah? Who done it this time?' Abberline quips. 'A local slaughterman. Witnesses have been to you and said they saw him fleeing the scene of the murder. They're calling him "Leather Apron." ' They watch as the procession passes, several members of the crowd throwing cabbages at the coffin.
- Abberline has a dream in which he follows his wife into an alleyway, only to find Dark Annie cackling at him, her throat slit. He wakes to find his dog in bed with him.
- A scene in which Netley is seen masturbating. 'I felt you needed to see that in order to understand why he is doing it, why he is helping this monster,' Yglesias explains. 'The graphic novel has him going along with it because he wants to be a Mason,' says Allen Hughes, 'but in the film, he's just dumb, he's just going along with it, and he ends up cracking 'cause that's not really his forte to be killing women. We did

shoot some scenes where the Ripper made him cut the throat, and he wasn't very effective. He was just a sad soul.'

- A scene in which a trick takes Dark Annie from behind, boasting of his 'thick English oak'.
- A scene in which Dark Annie stumbles down an alleyway and collapses, drugged or drunk or both, before turning to face her killer. As she dies, a man peeing on the other side of the fence complains loudly about whores fucking in the street.
- A further scene at Buckingham Palace, where Queen Victoria berates Lord Hallsham for his sluggishness in solving the case.
- Netley writes a letter on the killer's behalf, addressing it 'From Hell'.
- A brief scene in which Abberline and Mary visit Ann's parents, finding labourers staying in the flat.
- A montage of cranks writing letters claiming to be the Ripper.
- A shot of Netley waiting outside the Ten Bells in the 'death coach'.
- Netley draws up at the Ten Bells in the 'death coach', and asks the man inside if he should go in and look for the girl he wants. 'That won't be necessary, Netley,' comes the reply. 'It's their destiny to come to us.' This was followed directly by another of Abberline's dreams, in which he clearly sees the face of the Ripper, but does not recognise him. Godley wakes him, and refuses to let him go to the opium den.
- Netley propositions Liz outside the Ten Bells.
- A brief shot of Abberline and Godley in a coach on the night Liz is murdered.
- A constable catches Netley looking suspicious while the Ripper kills Liz; the Ripper asks the constable if there is a problem, and sends him on his way. Later that night, Abberline walks down the same street, before getting dejectedly back into the coach as Godley tells him, 'They found another one in Berners Street.'
- A shot of Kate looking in the window of a public house as she searches for Liz.
- A shot of Netley watching Abberline as he goes into the Ten Bells.
- A scene in which McQueen pounces on Mary Kelly in an alleyway, taking her money.
- A scene in which Godley wakes Abberline in the library, giving him a book about the Freemasons.
- A scene in which Netley watches Ada.
- A shot of Netley driving the 'death coach' past Christchurch Spitalfields.
- A scene in which Netley is strangled while masturbating.
- An alternative ending in which Abberline, now old and grey, is found dead in a Shanghai opium den, holding two pennies. The opium den owner lays the coins on Abberline's eyes.

TRAILERS: Atmospheric images of London beneath blood-red skies and contemporary music open the effective trailer, which plays up the idea of Johnny Depp's Abberline as a clairvoyant who solves his cases through visions, and his personal connection to one of the victims, as suggested by the voice-over narration: 'He can foresee the victims . . . he could sense the suspects . . . but for an inspector in charge of the world's most infamous investigation . . . the last thing he expected . . . was to get close to someone who would be next.' It is almost a minute before Jack the Ripper is even mentioned as the subject of the film.

POSTERS: The black *From Hell* 'teaser' poster featured a silhouetted figure in a cloak and top hat, at the base of a blood splatter running from top to bottom. The main poster retained the startling image, but placed it beside head shots of Abberline (Johnny Depp) and Mary Kelly (Heather Graham).

TAG-LINE: 'Only the legend will survive.' 'Only the dead know the truth.'

WHAT THE PAPERS SAID: Describing the film as 'more amped-up Hammer Horror than genuinely *From Hell*,' *Variety*'s Derek Elley suggested that 'anyone expecting the combo of Allen and Albert Hughes (*Menace II Society*) and the famed Victorian serial killer to result in a gritty, Stygian, skin-crawling horror movie will be severely disappointed: pic is a surprisingly conventional Olde London Towne gaslight mystery, gussied up with some doctored visuals, an eccentric performance by Johnny Depp as an opium-smoking Cockney cop and Heather Graham as a remarkably clear-skinned working class hooker.' In the *Chicago Sun-Times*, Roger Ebert was more impressed: 'The movie feels dark, clammy and exhilarating – it's like belonging to a secret club where you can have a lot of fun but might get into trouble . . . The Hughes brothers plunge into this world, so far from their native Detroit, with the joy of tourists who have been reading up for years.' Citing the graphic novel ('i.e. transcendent comic book') as the source of more than just the story, Ebert went on to suggest that 'some of their compositions look influenced by comic art, with its sharp obliques and exaggerated perspectives'. Ultimately, he said, *From Hell* 'is a Guignol about a cross section of a thoroughly rotten society, corrupted from the top down'. In the UK, it was the film which *Time Out* found thoroughly rotten. 'The first twenty minutes are grim,' wrote Tom Charity. 'One prostitute after another is assaulted with gruesome relish – the Brothers' camera homing in for the kill, slicing through the Whitechapel fog. One fancies it's not just the Ripper who is getting off on this.' The uncharitable Charity lazily poked fun at the accents of Depp and Graham, and blamed

Twentieth Century Fox for insisting on 'a trite romance – the Brothers' disinterest is palpable – to weigh down what is otherwise a surprisingly compelling conspiracy yarn'.

BOX OFFICE: *From Hell* opened at the top spot in the US on 19 October 2001, grossing just over $11 million in its opening weekend – enough to edge out *Riding in Cars with Boys*, and earning Johnny Depp his first ever #1 opening. The film went on to gross $31.6 million in the US and an estimated $45 million worldwide.

AWARDS: The Academy of Science Fiction, Fantasy & Horror Films nominated *From Hell* for three awards: Best Horror Film, Best Actor (Johnny Depp) and Best Costume; Kym Barrett's costumes were also nominated for a Golden Satellite Award; Terry Hayes' and Rafael Yglesias' screenplay was nominated for a Bram Stoker Award; the International Horror Guild nominated the film Best Movie. None of the nominations became awards.

CONTROVERSY: In early 2001, so-called Jack the Ripper experts began decrying the fact that Inspector Abberline was being portrayed as an opium user and absinthe drinker, a deviation from historical fact. Defending the film's position, producer Don Murphy told *SFX* that opium had been chosen because 'it is more visual than the alcohol that he enjoyed buckets of in real life'. Besides, he added, although the film's Abberline was based on a real person, 'he is *not* a real person – this is a fictional film based on a work of fiction'. Ripper expert Paul Begg protested, stating that he knew 'of absolutely no evidence whatsoever that Inspector Abberline was an alcoholic'; however, Murphy subsequently produced correspondence from Begg showing that he supported the film. 'I thought that Abberline being portrayed as an opium abuser might cause some complaints, but that from the photographs I had seen of the set it looked a superbly realistic recreation and that I understood general historical accuracy to have been paramount,' Begg wrote. 'This, I felt sure, would far outweigh niggling criticism from a few purists.'

TRIVIA: For obscure legal reasons, the film-makers were unable to use the documented fact that the grapes given to the victims were injected with laudanum.

Estelle Skornik, who plays Ada, is best known to British audiences as Nicole from the Renault Clio commercials.

APOCRYPHA: Did *From Hell* solve the hundred-year-old mystery of Jack the Ripper's identity? Not according to Alan Moore. 'I was not at all interested in who Jack the Ripper was – that's Hardy Boys stuff,' he told *Newsweek*. 'Nobody is ever going to find out. And playing amateur detective to a case that's over a hundred years old seems very fruitless. I have no idea if it was in any way connected to a royal plot,' he added. 'The most interesting thing is that we could believe that it might be.' Moore chose Sir William Gull as the culprit because, by pointing the finger at the royal surgeon, he could tell the story against a larger canvas and encompass far greater aspects of the legend. So who does Moore think did it? 'Eddie Campbell once said, "I think Jack the Ripper was just the guy who was holding the breadknife and standing closest to the asylum door when they left it unlocked one day." That's probably the closest we'll ever get to the correct answer.'

Abberline's confusion over when exactly his wife died is not a continuity error: it is designed to represent the fact that he has yet to come to terms with her death.

DVD AVAILABILITY: In the UK (Region 2), *From Hell* is available as a 2-disc special edition which preserves the widescreen (2.35:1) ratio and includes the following additional features: an alternative ending and 29 deleted scenes (detailed above) with optional commentary by Albert Hughes; an interactive investigation entitled *Jack the Ripper: Six Degrees of Separation*; *A View from Hell*, an HBO featurette hosted by Heather Graham; a *Tour of the Murder Sites* hosted by the directors; a behind-the-scenes featurette hosted by production designer Martin Childs; *Absinthe Makes the Heart Grow Fonder* featurette; a graphic novel to film comparison with the Hughes brothers and producer Don Murphy; and the US theatrical trailer. In the US (Region 1), the sumptuous 2-disc 'Director's Limited Edition' features all of the above material, but replaces the directors-only commentary with one featuring Albert and Allen Hughes, co-screenwriter Rafael Yglesias, cinematographer Peter Deming and actor Robbie Coltrane.

FINAL ANALYSIS: Let's see how I'm doing so far: I may yet have escaped the wrath of fans of *The Crow*; it is possible that I am not being hunted down by Judge Dredd fans who still spend Saturday nights sticking pins in Sly Stallone action figures: but I must incur the wrath of yet another powerful group of comic book aficionados – the Alan Moore fan club – by admitting my respect for the Hughes brothers' (no relation) take on *From Hell*. This may be all the more surprising when you know that my adoration for Alan Moore's opus knows no bounds: I bought the very first issue, waited with uncharacteristic impatience for each new volume, scuttling home and devouring each one, appendices and all. I have never subscribed to the theory that a bad adaptation of a book somehow besmirches or befouls the sanctity of the original – as James M

Cain said, when asked if he minded what Hollywood had done to his novels, 'Hollywood hasn't done anything to them – they're all still up there on the shelf,' – and even if I did, I find little to criticise in the Hughes' brothers valiant effort to bring the spirit of the source material to the screen.

So what if they changed a few facts along the way? Moore did much the same thing, as he readily admits in his appendices, making gigantic leaps of faith and supposition in support of his story. Who cares if they cast Americans in the two leading roles? The supporting players more than make up for this necessary compromise, and I have no complaints about the accents of Mr Depp and Ms Graham. For me, the film's merits – the sense of time and place, performances, language, costume, *mise en scène*, Peter Deming's stunning cinematography, Rafael Yglesias' accomplished screenplay – far outweigh the weaknesses, notably the romantic subplot and the daft black eyes and deep voice with which Ian Holm is saddled as Gull. Viewed as an inspired companion to, rather than a straightforward adaptation of, the Moore–Campbell masterwork, *From Hell* has much to recommend it – at the very least because it has helped drive the graphic novel into five printings in two years.

EXPERT WITNESS: 'The thing we took [from the comic book] is that it drew from factual material and heightened it, basically. Spun a web. It's pretty far-fetched, but nobody can prove what's true and not true right now. I did what Alan Moore did – looked at all the books, all the facts, the way the bodies were placed, where they were found. Because when I saw the other Ripper movies they really didn't do justice to the real stuff.' – **Albert Hughes, Co-Director**

Ghost World (2001)

(111 minutes)

Directed by Terry Zwigoff
Written by Daniel Clowes and Terry Zwigoff
Based upon the Comic Book by Daniel Clowes
Produced by Lianne Halfon, John Malkovich and Russell Smith
Executive Producers Pippa Cross and Janette Day
Line Producer Barbara A Hall
Director of Photography Affonso Beato
Production Designer Edward T McAvoy
Editors Carole Kravetz-Aykanian and Michael R Miller ACE

Costume Designer Mary Zophres
Music by David Kitay
Casting by Cassandra Kulukundis

CAST: Thora Birch (*Enid Coleslaw*), Scarlett Johansson (*Rebecca 'Becky' Doppelmeyer*), Brad Renfro (*Josh*), Bob Balaban (*Enid's dad*), Illeana Douglas (*Roberta Allsworth*), Steve Buscemi (*Seymour*), Tom McGowan (*Joe*), Stacey Travis (*Dana*), David Cross (*Gerrold*), Pat Healy (*John Ellis*), Charles C Stevenson Jr (*Norman*), Dave Sheridan (*Doug*), Debra Azar (*Melorra*), Brian George (*Sidewinder boss*), Rini Bell (*graduation speaker*), TJ Thyne (*Todd*), Ezra Buzzington ('*Weird' Al*), Lindsey Girardot (*Vanilla*), Joy Bisco (*Jade*), Venus DeMilo (*Ebony*), Ashley Peldon (*Margaret*), Chachi Pittman (*Phillip*), Janece Jordan (*black girl*), Kaileigh Martin (*snotty girl*), Alexander Fors (*hippy boy*), Marc Vann (*Jerome*), James Sie (*Steven*), Paul Keith (*Paul*), JJ 'Bad Boy' Jones (*Fred Chatman*), Dylan Jones (*red-haired girl*), Martin Grey (*MC*), Steve Pierson, Jake LaBotz, Johnny Irion, Nate Wood (*Blueshammer members*), Charles Schneider (*Joey McCobb*), Sid Garza-Hillman, Joshua Wheeler (*Zine-O-Phobia creeps*), Patrick Fischler (*Masterpiece Video clerk*), Daniel Graves (*Masterpiece Video customer*), Matt Doherty (*Masterpiece Video employee*), Joel Michaely (*porno cashier*), Debi Derryberry (*rude coffee customer*), Joe Sikora (*reggae fan*), Brett Gilbert (*Alien Autopsy guy*), Alex Solowitz (*cineplex manager*), Tony Ketcham (*alcoholic customer*), Mary Bogue (*popcorn customer*), Brian Jacobs (*soda customer*), Patrick Yonally (*garage sale hipster*), Lauren Bowles (*angry garage sale woman*), Lorna Scott (*art show curator*), Jeff Murray (*Roberta's colleague*), Jerry Rector (*Dana's co-worker*), Sheriff John Bunnell (*Seymour's boss*) Diane Salinger (*psychiatrist*), Anna Berger (*Seymour's mother*), Bruce Glover (*Feldman*)

UNCREDITED CAST: Joan M Blair (*lady crossing street slowly*), Michael Chanslor, Ernie Hernandez, Felice Hernandez, Larry Klein, Larry Parker (*Orange Colored Sky band members*), Teri Garr (*Maxine*), Edward T McAvoy (*male satanist*), Margaret Kontra Palmer (*lady at garage sale*), Greg Wendell Reid (*yuppier*), Michelle Marie White (*mom in convenience store*)

TITLE SEQUENCE: A drumbeat begins over simple white credits on black, before a wide shot of a dance floor fades up, with ten male dancers in tuxedos and an equivalent number girls in lamé dresses, all of them wearing blindfolds, dancing frenetically to the music the live band (Ted Lyons and His Cubs) is playing: 'Jaan Pehechaan Ho', sung by Mohammed Rafi. White titles appear over the images, which are intercut with an extended pan across the exterior of a blue apartment building, through which the following images can be seen: an Asian woman smoking as she is looking out of the window; a shirtless heavy-set man with a mullet picks his teeth; an empty dining room; a kid hitting drums with a baseball bat while his couch potato parents watch television; finally, a young girl with black hair, black glasses and a red dress, who is watching the dance routine on her television, imitating the moves. As the dance routine ends, a close-up of the singer's legs come together like curtains.

SUMMARY: Although they graduate from high school the same day as their classmates, Los Angelenos Enid and Rebecca seem to have little else in common with them. Neither plans on going to college, although Enid is being made to attend a summer school art class. In the meantime, they have nothing better to do than hang out at the mall, bother their former classmate Josh at the local convenience store, or read the personal ads. Inspired by one, they decide to play a trick on a man who has placed an ad looking for a woman he met fleetingly on a plane. Enid leaves a message on the man's answering machine, and invites him to meet her at Wowsville, a supposedly authentic fifties diner in a local mini-mall. When the middle-aged loser (Seymour) shows up with bad hair and bad clothes, they watch him from afar, feeling ashamed. Nevertheless, they decide to follow him home, where they find him selling old records at a garage sale. Enid buys one and likes it. She likes him (Seymour), too, hanging out with him at the expense of her friend Rebecca. Instead of apartment-hunting with Rebecca, or job-hunting for herself, she spends more and more time girlfriend-hunting with Seymour. When Seymour finds one, however – ironically, the woman his personal ad was seeking – he finds it hard to explain his friendship with Enid. Like Enid and Rebecca, they begin to drift apart, further isolating Enid from her own life. Meanwhile, Enid has been attending her art class, where the teacher is a feminist fruitcake who, much to Enid's surprise, takes a liking to one of her pieces: a racially offensive advertising image she borrowed from Seymour, who 'borrowed' it from the firm his long-time employer. She displays it at an art show, where it causes a scandal which makes the papers. Enid misses the whole thing – she was busy seducing Seymour, prompting him to dump his girlfriend in the hopes of taking up with Enid – but Seymour's boss doesn't: he recognises the stolen ad and fires Seymour. When he tries to talk to Enid, Rebecca tells him about the fake blind date, and Seymour winds up in hospital when he gets into a fight at the convenience store. Enid packs a few things, gets on a bus and leaves town, heading for an uncertain future – but one which might just be an improvement.

ORIGINS: 'I was once walking around Chicago in a really bad neighbourhood and in the midst of some really illegible gang graffiti, somebody had written 'Ghost World' very clearly on a garage,' *Ghost World* writer and artist Daniel Clowes has said of the inspiration for his comic strip, which first appeared in the eleventh issue of Fantagraphics Books' anthology comic *Eightball* in 1993. 'I thought at the time that there was really something beautiful about that; it struck me as having a really evocative poetic quality. The America we live in is disappearing, bulldozed under our feet and constantly rehabbed and remodelled. [But the title] also refers more personally to the characters and their relationships, and the lost world of childhood, among other things.' Fantagraphics Books published the first *Ghost World* collection, just seventy pages long, in 1998.

DEVELOPMENT: Terry Zwigoff had won widespread critical acclaim and a mantelpiece full of international awards for his 1994 documentary feature, *Crumb*, a look at the life of comic book writer and artist Robert Crumb. He knew that whatever his next feature was going to be, it had better not be anything to do with comics. 'Films of comics are usually a bad idea,' he said later. 'I like parts of *Batman* but most of it is terrible; Altman's *Popeye* is terrible; Ralph Bakshi's *Fritz the Cat* is just embarrassing. Warren Beatty tried to do something interesting but it didn't really work.' Then, Zwigoff's wife pushed a copy of the collected *Ghost World* under his nose. 'She was a big fan of it, and she said, "You should really read this, this would make a great film." I read it and I liked it, and I appreciated it as a comic book. But what I also appreciated about it was how great [Daniel Clowes] was with dialogue and character. He had created these two memorable characters.'

Ghost World creator Daniel Clowes was as much an admirer of Zwigoff's film (*Crumb*) as the director was of *Ghost World*, and when Zwigoff first suggested they collaborate on a screenplay inspired by the comic, the two were already on the same page. Rather than a straightforward adaptation, Clowes and Zwigoff took the comic book's background – the faded Americana of an anonymous city whose character is being eroded by malls, brand-name cappuccino bars, restaurant and clothing chains – and its central relationship, the uneasy friendship between Enid and her childhood friend Rebecca, and wrote a new story based on a four-page sequence from one of the comics, in which Enid and Rebecca play a trick on a man who has placed a lonely hearts advertisement. 'It's like *Lolita* from the point of view of Lolita rather than Humbert,' Clowes would explain helpfully while he and Zwigoff traipsed the script around Hollywood. Perhaps understandably, they were turned down all over town.

'Terry and I were the two worst pitch-men in the history of Hollywood,' Clowes told *Sight and Sound*. 'We would mention Woody Allen films and get the most horrified looks.' Nevertheless, studios were keen to work with Zwigoff, whose *Crumb* was then the third highest grossing documentary in the history of cinema, and who claims to have been offered 'three hundred scripts a month – even that first Austin Powers movie came my way'. Then, in 1999, the pair found a new way to pitch the story, 'because then we could say, "It's like *American Beauty*," and they'd think, $200 million! Let's make that movie!' Having secured funding for the $5 million feature from MGM and such British companies as Granada Films (now defunct) and Capitol Films, *Ghost World* was on its way.

CASTING: For Terry Zwigoff, *American Beauty* actress Thora Birch was a natural choice for the role of Enid. 'She's a very accomplished actress,' he said, 'smart and sensitive and fearless. She somehow also got the wacky, goofy side of the character, and not with much help from me, I'm afraid.' Scarlett Johansson (*The Horse Whisperer*) was just fifteen when she was cast as Enid's best friend, eighteen-year-old Rebecca; although Leelee Sobieski (*Eyes Wide Shut*) was Zwigoff's first choice, he felt that neither Johansson's lower profile nor her age would be a problem. 'Scarlett's fifteen going on thirty-five – wise beyond her years,' he said at the time. 'She is a very natural actress and instinctively captured Rebecca's character; very cool and reserved, but also a bit of a weirdo.' According to Clowes, Birch and Johansson became firm friends almost as soon as filming began. 'They're very close,' he said, 'almost as close as the two characters.' 'We had some wacky, wacky times,' Johansson told *Index* magazine. 'We were sort of a team on that film. Because Terry Zwigoff and Dan Clowes are insane! Of course Thora is insane as well – in a good way.'

For the key role of Seymour, Zwigoff would accept no alternative to his first choice: Steve Buscemi. 'I could never picture anybody else in this [role], he was always the guy,' said Zwigoff. 'I'd always thought of him as kind of funny-looking,' he added, paraphrasing a description of Buscemi's character in *Fargo*, 'but my wife said "There's only one guy in Hollywood you have to worry about leaving me in a room alone with, and that's Steve Buscemi." She couldn't care less about Harrison Ford, Brad Pitt or any of those guys. Every woman I've ever talked to has a thing for Steve Buscemi.' Despite Zwigoff's certainty that Buscemi *was* Seymour, however, the actor took some convincing, and Zwigoff admits to having hounded the actor until he agreed to take the role. In the end, the director said, 'We got lucky with every single person we hired for [the] small parts as well. Illeanna Douglas was great as this pretentious, overly sincere, under-talented art teacher. All the kids in her class were terrific as well.'

PRODUCTION: Although theoretically set in 'Anytown, USA', Clowes has said that he wanted to shoot in California because 'it looks like any place in modern America – just one big happy corporate strip mall filled with Gaps and Starbucks and Burger Kings. This is part of Enid's dilemma,' he explained, 'to find something authentic to connect with in this modern monoculture.' Helping Zwigoff to get the look of the film exactly right was production designer Edward T McAvoy (*The Rock*, *Con Air* and earlier comic book adaptation *The Rocketeer*), who chose not to renew his artistic licence for the project, opting instead for verisimilitude. 'Directors and producers usually expect to see the same teenage room they've seen in so many other films,' he told *Sight and Sound*. 'But we've used books where photographers have gone into real teenagers' rooms, and you see how un-art directed they are.'

Daniel Clowes, who moved to Oakland, California, from his native Chicago, was with Zwigoff throughout the shoot. 'I guess most screenwriters aren't allowed anywhere near the set, so I feel fortunate to have been afforded this opportunity,' he said at the time. 'I wanted to be there to help in any way I could. I wouldn't have missed it for the world.' Although he resisted the urge to make a cameo appearance in the film, as he does in the comic book, Clowes' artwork permeates the film, from the hand-drawn 'Ghost World' logo in the opening credits, to the unicorn drawing in Roberta's art class.

Although the comic books were essentially black and white with greyish-green colouring adding to the ghostly atmosphere, Zwigoff and Zophres chose to go in the opposite direction, giving the girls often brightly coloured clothing in reds, greens, blues and purples, whilst the director's chosen cinematographer, Pedro Almodovar's regular cinematographer, Brazilian Affonso Beato, accentuated the richness of the colours. 'When I saw Affonso's work on *All About My Mother*, it just seemed right,' Zwigoff explained. 'It's very colourful, and yet it's an insulated little world, somewhat artificial.' For Beato, the colour palette was an ideal way of representing the film's comic book origins. 'The colours are enhanced and coordinated, as in comics,' he explained. 'It's not *Dick Tracy* – it's more realist – but there are lots of reds and yellows.' Added Zwigoff, 'I'm trying to make a film the way I see the modern world. It's very colourful, but also empty and grim. It's like a modern American strip-mall wasteland – they're painted bright, shiny colours but they all sell the same crap. It's cheery on the outside but if you look closely it's depressing.'

COSTUME FITTING: Costume designer Mary Zophres, who had previously worked on such off-beat indie hits as the Coen brothers' *Fargo* (with Steve Buscemi) and *The Big Lebowski*, continued the colour-saturated art direction by clothing the characters in brightly coloured outfits. In the comics, Enid's lack of identity leads her to frequently change her hair and clothing, an idiosyncrasy which, in the film, accentuates the directionless nature of her life after leaving high school. 'She knows everything about who she doesn't like and *doesn't* wanna be,' Birch observed, 'the only problem is she doesn't have a clue about what she *does* want to do and who she is, really, so she's constantly changing her appearances and trying different motifs and even testing out in a subtle way different personalities.'

MUSIC: 'Loosen up. Feel the music.' Like Seymour – and Robert Crumb, the subject of his previous film – director Terry Zwigoff is an avid collector and one-time dealer of 78 rpm records, mainly 1920s jazz and blues. But although their shared hobby gave Zwigoff the perfect excuse to introduce his record collection to a wider audience, *Ghost World* features an eclectic assortment of music in addition to David Kitay's achingly beautiful musical score, including tracks by Mohammed Rafi, Johanna Halvarsson, The Unknowns, Rachid, The Shadowmen, Tom Anderson, Mr Freddio, The Buzzcocks, Skip James, Vince Giordinio and The Nighthawks, Craig Ventresco, ADZ, Lionel Belasco, Joel Evans, Asfhord & Simpson, Gene Harris and Patience & Prudence. A more eclectic mix of film music would be as difficult to find as one of Seymour's rare 78s, so it's helpful that twenty of the best tracks – including, crucially Mohammed Rafi's 'Jaan Pehechaan Ho' and Skip James' 'Devil Got My Woman' – are featured on Shanachie's *Ghost World* soundtrack. Sadly, the Patience & Prudence song 'A Smile and a Ribbon', a favourite song from Enid's childhood which is featured in the comic and the film, is not included.

CLASSIC QUOTES:
Graduation speaker: 'High school is like the training wheels for the bicycle of real life.'

Enid: 'I liked her so much better when she was an alcoholic crack addict. She gets in one car wreck and all of a sudden she's Little Miss Perfect and everyone loves her.'

Enid: 'I didn't think that just 'cause you got an "F" you had to take the whole class over again.'

Rebecca: 'This is so bad it's almost good.'
Enid: 'This is so bad it's gone past good and gone back to bad again.'

Melorra: 'We have to get together this summer.'
Enid: 'Yeah, that'll definitely happen.'

Rebecca: 'So what do you do if you're a satanist anyway?'
Enid: 'Sacrifice virgins and stuff.'
Rebecca: 'Well that lets us off the hook.'

Rebecca: We should check out the personals. Maybe our future husbands are trying to contact us.'

Doug: 'Whassup, Josh? Hey, give me two packs of cigarettes today. Working overtime. Sixteen hours! And, uh, nature's nectar – wake-up juice. And give me six of these beef jerkys. I'm hungry enough to chew the crotch out of a ragdoll.'

Sidewinder boss: 'What do you think this is? Club Med?'
Doug: 'It's America, dude, learn the rules.'
Sidewinder boss: 'No, no, you learn the rules. We Greeks invented democracy!'
Doug: 'You also invented homos.'
Sidewinder boss: 'Fuck you!'
Doug: 'You wish! You gotta buy me dinner first!'

Enid: 'I kind of like him. He's the exact opposite of everything I hate. In a way, he's such a clueless dork, he's actually kind of cool.'
Rebecca: 'That guy is many things, but he's definitely not cool.'

Enid: 'You know, it's not like I'm some modern punk, dickhead. It's obviously a 1977 original punk rock look. I guess Johnny Fuckface over there is too stupid to realise it.'
Rebecca: 'I didn't really get it either.'

Masterpiece Video clerk: '*9½ Weeks* with Mickey Rourke. That would be in the erotic drama section.'
Masterpiece Video customer: 'No, not *9½*. *8½*, the Fellini film.'

Enid: 'I would kill to have stuff like this!'
Seymour: 'Please! Go ahead, kill me.'

Enid: 'We need to find a place where you can go to meet women who share your interests.'
Seymour: 'Maybe I don't want to meet someone who shares my interests. I hate my interests.'

Seymour: 'What, are we in slow motion here? C'mon, what are you, hypnotised? Have some more kids why don't you?'

Blueshammer fan: 'I just love blues.'
Seymour: 'Actually, technically, what he was mostly playing would more accurately be classified as the ragtime idiom, although of course not in the strictest sense of the classical ragtime piano music like that of Scott

Joplin or Joseph Lamb. Authentic blues has a more conventional 4/4 structure in the stanzas.'

Enid: 'Seymour's big date is tonight and I kind of wanna be around when he calls. You know, so I can see how badly it went.'

DELETED SCENES: Although no entire scenes were left on the cutting room floor, the improvisational nature of parts of the film means that several alternate takes exist, notably of the scenes involving Dave Sheridan as Doug. The trailer also contains a Seymour dialogue line referring to the 'type' of woman he prefers ('As long as they're breathing') which does not appear in the film. Finally, two scenes present in the final cut originally played longer:

- The scene at Seymour's party, in which a collector examines several records, continues with a brief reference to Bing Crosby records;
- The art show sequence continues as Roberta shows a visitor a piece called 'Wasteland', which is actually an anti-radiation suit stolen from a nuclear waste facility – and very probably radioactive.

TRAILERS: After an opening caption which reads 'From the acclaimed director of *Crumb*', the *Ghost World* trailer avoids traditional narrative devices such as captions or voice-over in favour of a stylised approach, intercutting clips of the opening dance number with staccato dialogue soundbites which effectively introduce the central characters and those around them. A brief caption-led cast list follows, before the trailer gives way to further trailer traditions, a voice-over reading along with a title and caption: 'GHOST WORLD – The Underground Comic Book Comes To Life.' After the credit block, the trailer closes with a clip of the alcoholic customer asking if the cinema serves beer. 'After five minutes of this movie,' Enid replies, 'you're gonna wish you had *ten* beers.'

POSTERS: Most of the posters produced for *Ghost World* picture Enid (in her blue 'Raptor' T-shirt and green plaid skirt) and Rebecca (in her green top and short black skirt) against a plain white background, with a hand-drawn logo by Daniel Clowes.

TAG-LINE: 'Accentuate the negative.'

WHAT THE PAPERS SAID: The critics were virtually unanimous in their praise of *Ghost World*. 'By sharp turns poignant, disturbing and hysterically funny,' said *Variety*'s Ken Eisner, '*Ghost World* explores girlhood and adult life with an acuity unexpected from two middle-aged guys, let alone such proud oddballs as *Crumb* director Terry Zwigoff . . . and artist–writer Daniel Clowes.' Counterculture magazine *Rolling*

Stone echoed *Variety*'s views, describing it as 'a film like no other, an artful spellbinder that cuts deep . . . Birch makes good on the promise she showed in *American Beauty* with a performance of riveting intensity, and Buscemi has never been better, which is saying something'. In the UK, *Time Out*'s Tom Charity suggested that 'what makes the film special is how it relishes adolescent rebellion (it's based on Daniel Clowes' graphic novel) but doesn't stop there . . . This sort-of love story could have been sticky,' he added, 'but in fact it's beautifully played. It isn't a perfect film, but it's never less than strikingly original.'

BOX OFFICE: In the US, *Ghost World* opened on just five screens on 20 July 2001, earning an impressive $98,791 in limited release. As it opened wider through August, the film crept to total earnings of $6.2 million, remaining on release until February 2002.

AWARDS: *Ghost World* began amassing awards and nominations as soon as it began playing film festivals. On 16 June 2001, the film received its world premiere at the Seattle International Film Festival, where Thora Birch won the Golden Space Needle award for Best Actress; the film went on to win special jury prizes at the Karlovy Vary and Deauville film festivals (where Birch also won an acting prize), and numerous awards from various film critics' societies around the US, including four awards (including Best Adapted Screenplay, Best Actress, Best Director and Best Picture) from the San Diego Film Critics Society, awards for both lead actresses from the Toronto Film Critics Association, and no fewer than *six* Best Supporting Actor prizes for Steve Buscemi, including one of the film's two Independent Spirit awards. Birch and Buscemi also received Golden Globe nominations, while Clowes and Zwigoff earned the film's sole Academy Award® nomination, in the category of Best Adapted Screenplay. In all, the film amassed a total of *eighteen* international film awards from over forty nominations, making it one of the most acclaimed films of the year.

TRIVIA: Uncredited cameo appearances include production designer Edward T McAvoy (as the male satanist) and Teri Garr, who previously appeared with Bob Balaban in *Close Encounters of the Third Kind*.

David Cross (Gerrold) played a mortuary attendant in an earlier comic book adaptation, *Men in Black*. Stacey Travis (Dana) previously appeared in *Mystery Men*.

Clowes wrote the lyrics for the rap song performed at the graduation ceremony.

After the film was released, Clowes received a series of some thirty photographs showing 'Ghost World' graffiti at various sites in Los Angeles.

When Enid asks after an album by R. Crumb and his Cheap Suit Serenaders, Seymour says, 'Hmm, that one's not so great.'

The Coon Chicken Inn, founded in 1925, actually exists. It has never changed its name to Cook's Chicken Inn or anything else.

'Enid Coleslaw' – Enid's name in the comic books – is an anagram of Daniel Clowes.

Stay tuned until after the end credits to see Seymour get even with Doug and Josh.

APOCRYPHA: The drawings in Enid's scrapbook are not by Clowes himself, but by Robert Crumb's daughter Sophie.

SEQUELS & SPIN-OFFS: The success of *Ghost World*, and the plethora of comic book stories which did not make it into the film – not to mention the ambiguous ending – seem to call for a sequel. Instead, Zwigoff and Clowes have stated their intention to collaborate on an adaptation of the latter's graphic novel *Art School Confidential.*

DVD AVAILABILITY: The UK (Region 2) DVD features a 1.85:1 ratio version of the film, a photo gallery, trailer, a selection of brilliantly post-modern British TV spots (in which the legend 'THIS IS AN AD FOR THE MOVIE *GHOST WORLD*' is emblazoned across the screen next to a short clip), a similarly twisted radio commercial, and three Daniel Clowes-hosted featurettes: *Mr Clowes' Neighbourhood*, in which a grainy camera follows him around his home town; *Dan Clowes in Hollywood*, in which the camera simply watches him draw a cartoon image of himself, signing it 'Please kill me now'; and *Dan Clowes Talks About* Ghost World, an affecting interview in which he talks about the inspiration for the comic books and his feelings about the film. The US (Region 1) DVD contains a different selection of material: four deleted/alternate scenes (brief extended versions of the art show and Seymour's party, and two hilarious alternate versions of the Sidewinder parking lot scene), a thirty-minute 'making of' documentary Ghost World: *A Comic Book Comes To Life*, theatrical trailer, short soundtrack promo, and a full version of the clip from the Indian film *Gumnaam* (1965), featured in the *Ghost World* opening titles.

FINAL ANALYSIS: Hollywood studios frequently fall into the trap of optioning books that have no business on the big screen – yet the very nature of most novels makes them inherently resistant to the transposition from page to celluloid, since the former are often based on characters' internalised thoughts and feelings, whereas films are all about externalising characterisation. An equally common story is the scale of most novels, which is why film-makers like Stanley Kubrick recognised that the short story or novella often made the best translation to film. When documentary film-maker Terry Zwigoff came to adapt Daniel Clowes' quietly brilliant comic book into film, he faced no such problems: he had two central characters who were beautifully drawn (in both senses of the word) and an urban backdrop more fully realised than the ones in most films – yet very little else, least of all, a story. Thus, rather than opt for a straightforward adaptation, Zwigoff wisely decided to create a new story, inspired by just a few panels of *Ghost World* seventy-page comic book span, which not only captured the spirit of the comic book, but also of the times, and of a feckless generation lost in a world of mini-malls, burger joints and coffee shops, with no more certain a future than the man who, in both the comic and the film, waits hopefully for the bus that will never come. Equally startling are the other elements – colour and sound – absent from the comic book, which Zwigoff uses with great skill and judgment to establish mood and setting. Thus, by extrapolations rather than adapting, Zwigoff avoids the pitfalls inherent in translations from one medium into another, creating a self-contained story which both encapsulates and enhances its source material. So successful is this unusual approach that *Ghost World* may just be the greatest comic book adaptation ever made.

EXPERT WITNESS: 'It has something to do with the decline of Western civilisation. It's very funny and very painful at the same time. The whole film has a strange tone to it. I'm not saying that in a self-serving way – "Oh, it's such a strange, cool film" – that's not what I'm saying. I have enough objectivity on it that I *know*, because it's very funny and sad at the same time.' – **Terry Zwigoff, Director**

Road to Perdition (2002)

(117 mininutes)

Directed by Sam Mendes
Screenplay by David Self
Produced by Richard D Zanuck, Dean Zanuck and Sam Mendes
Executive Producers Walter F Parkes and Joan Bradshaw
Director of Photography Conrad L Hall ASC
Production Designer Dennis Gassner
Editor Jill Bilcock
Costume Designer Albert Wolsky
Music by Thomas Newman

Based upon the Graphic Novel Written by Max Allan Collins
and Illustrated by Richard Piers Rayner
Casting by Debra Zane CSA
Associate Producers Cherylanne Martin and Tara B Cook

CAST: Tyler Hoechlin (*Michael Sullivan Jr*), Rob Maxey (*drugstore owner*), Liam Aiken (*Peter Sullivan*), Jennifer Jason Leigh (*Annie Sullivan*), Tom Hanks (*Michael Sullivan*), Paul Newman (*John Rooney*), Daniel Craig (*Connor Rooney*), Ciarán Hinds (*Finn McGovern*), Craig Spidle, Ian Barford (*Rooney's henchmen*), Stephen Dunn, Paul Turner (*Finn McGovern's henchmen*), Kathleen Keane, Brendan McKinney, Jackie Moran, Kieran O'Hare (*Irish musicians*), Nicholas Cade (*boy Michael fights*), David Darlow (*Jack Kelly*), Dylan Baker (*Alexander Rance*), John Sierros, Jon Sattler, Michael Brockman, John Judd, Christian Stolte, Jack Callahan (*Rooney's business associates*), Maureen Gallagher (*Michael's teacher*), Kevin Chamberlain (*Frank the bouncer*), Juanita Wilson (*brothel maid*), Doug Spinuzza (*Calvino*), Roderick Peeples, Keith Kupferer (*Nitti's henchmen*), Lee Roy Rogers (*secretary*), Stanley Tucci (*Frank Nitti*), Jude Law (*Harlen Maguire*), Kurt Naebig (*tenement murderer*), Lance Baker (*crime scene policeman*), Monte (*living corpse*), Duane Sharp (*Father Callaway*), Diane Doesey (*Aunt Sarah*), Michael Sassone (*motel manager*), John Sterchi (*cop at diner*), Robert Jones (*farmer at diner*), Lara Phillips (*Ruby the waitress*), Harry Groener (*Mr McDougal*), Jobe Cerny, Lawrence MacGowan, Timothy Hendrickson, Marty Higginbotham (*bankers*), Mina Badie (*Betty the waitress*), Ed Kross (*young bank manager*), Heidi Jayne Netzley (*prostitute*), Phil Ridarelli (*hotel manager*), Peggy Roeder (*farmer Virginia*), James Greene (*farmer Bill*)

TITLE SEQUENCE: Discreet white titles begin to appear on a black background, before the image fades up of young Michael Sullivan Jr standing on a beach, back to the camera, looking out to sea, as waves wash against the shore. As the camera moves in towards him, the young man speaks in voice-over: 'There are many stories about Michael Sullivan. Some say he was a decent man. Some say there was no good in him at all. But I once spent six weeks on the road with him, in the winter of 1931. This is our story.' The picture fades to white, then fades up to images of Michael Jr cycling through a snowbound town, before stopping and selling newspapers to the lines of men looking for work. He cycles on, stopping at a shop where he steals candy while waiting to be paid for his efforts. He cycles on home, throwing snowballs at his younger brother while his mother watches, smiling, from a window. His father pulls up in a car.

SYNOPSIS: It is 1931, and America is in the grip of the Great Depression. Michael Sullivan comes home from 'work' and eats a meal with his wife Annie and two young boys, Michael Jr and Peter. The following day, they attend a wake for a man named Danny McGovern, who worked for Sullivan's boss, local mob godfather John Rooney. McGovern's brother, Finn, begins to speak out against Rooney, but is silenced and taken outside by Sullivan and Rooney's son, Connor. Rooney asks them to talk to Finn, 'nothing more', but when the pair visit Finn, Connor shoots him in cold blood, apparently afraid that Finn knows something about one of Rooney's own men stealing from him. Worse still, Sullivan discovers that his son, Michael Jr, has stowed away in his car, and witnessed the whole thing. Connor claims to trust the boy to keep his silence – but later, while Sullivan is collecting on a debt (and is forced to kill the debtor in the process), Connor visits the Sullivans' home, killing Annie and Peter, mistaking him for Michael Jr. Sullivan returns to find his wife and son dead, but his eldest son hiding; knowing that the killer(s) will come for them, he and Michael Jr hit the road, hoping to track down Connor and avenge the deaths. First, the pair head for Chicago, where Sullivan asks Frank Nitti, Al Capone's right-hand man, for a job. Nitti declines, and vainly warns Sullivan against pursuing his vendetta. When Sullivan leaves, intending to take his son to his Aunt Sarah's house in Perdition, Nitti hides Connor and sets hired killer and freelance photographer Maguire after Sullivan and his son. Maguire and Sullivan meet in a roadside diner, but Sullivan grows suspicious and flees. Aware that Maguire will trace them to Perdition, Sullivan forms a new plan: to hit Capone where it hurts, by robbing the banks where he keeps his money. After a spree of robberies, Sullivan and son find evidence that Connor Rooney was stealing from his father, just as Maguire tracks them down. A gun battle ensues, in which Maguire is shot, his face scarred by flying glass, and Sullivan takes a bullet in the arm. Michael Jr drives him to a farmhouse, where Sullivan's wounds are tended, and when he has recovered, he goes to ask Rooney to give up his son. Although Rooney clearly sees Sullivan as more of a son than Connor, he refuses. Later, Sullivan guns down Rooney's associates, then Rooney, then – with Nitti's blessing – Connor. The murders of his family avenged, Sullivan and son head to Aunt Sarah's, where Maguire is waiting for them. Maguire shoots Sullivan, mortally wounding him. As he dies, Michael Jr levels a gun at Maguire – but Michael's dying father is there first, shooting Maguire dead, and thereby saving his son from having blood on his hands. Michael Jr resolves never to touch a gun again.

ORIGINS: First published in 1998, by DC-owned Paradox Press, the Richard Piers Rayner-illustrated *Road to Perdition* represented award-winning crime writer Max Allan Collins' (*Dick Tracy*) first foray into the world of graphic novels. Collins had run across the story about a real-life Irish 'godfather' named John Looney and his son 'Crazy' Conner Looney while researching a Nate Heller crime novel set in Rock Island, Illinois. 'Conner was the heir apparent, but he was flawed,' he says, 'and eventually Conner ill-advisedly killed an associate of the family. And then a few months later a disenfranchised lieutenant murdered Conner in the street in Rock Island in front of many witnesses. And that seemed to me to be the germ of something really interesting.' Looking for a formula by which to tell the story, Collins hit upon the idea of a homage to Kazuo Koike's long-running manga *Lone Wolf and Cub*, the basis for a live-action film series which began in 1972 with *Sword of Vengeance*. 'I didn't want to just want to rip off *Lone Wolf and Cub*,' says Collins, 'I wanted to be in the spirit of it and tip my hat to it. There's a major homage going on, but more towards the movies than the manga [because] I hadn't even started reading the manga until I was deep into the writing of *Road to Perdition*. But I made the boy an adolescent, a guy coming of age who has to deal with his father's feet of clay.'

PREVIOUS INCARNATIONS: Author Max Allan Collins is fond of drawing attention to the thematic similarities between *Road to Perdition* and *Mommie*, the low-budget independent feature film he wrote, produced and directed in 1995. 'I think that if people now go out and look at this movie I did for half a million dollars, they're going to be shocked by how similar it is to *Road to Perdition*,' he says. 'It's about a homicidal mother and her eleven- or twelve-year-old daughter who narrates the piece and who slowly realises her perfect mother is a killer. Does any of this sound familiar? They were designed to be companion pieces. The irony is that one of them cost $500,000 to make and the other one cost $80 million to make. Now, Mendes' movie is better than mine – but I'm not convinced that it's $79.5 million better than mine.'

DEVELOPMENT: The first step on the road was taken by Dean Zanuck, who represents the third generation of one of Hollywood's most famous families: his grandfather Darryl co-founded Twentieth Century Fox, and his father Richard was its youngest ever president, as well as being one of Hollywood's most successful producers, with *The Sting*, *Jaws* and both *Planet of the Apes* movies among his many credits. Dean Zanuck had never *seen* a graphic novel, much less read one, when he was given a copy of *Road to Perdition*, yet he devoured it in one sitting, and immediately sought to option it. 'The father and son story had a powerful emotional impact on me,' Zanuck admitted, 'and the illustrations by Richard Piers Rayner provided a great visual of the period. That, combined with the action in the piece, made it very appealing.' Says author Max Allan Collins, 'Comics and movies are sister forms, in that they are both visual storytelling, which is why a good graphic novel will be attractive to a film-maker. They think, 'Well, gee, it's like storyboards,' and they see storyboards all the time so they're comfortable with the vocabulary of comics. And if it's a graphic novel, they'll say, "Great, I'll take it home and I'll read over the weekend. Send me one of your novels, then I'll have to have somebody read it for me and provide the coverage." ' Zanuck immediately sent the book to his father, who was similarly struck by the piece. 'It had wonderful action and colourful characters, and just had all the elements of being a very entertaining, provocative picture. But it was the relationship between the father and son that develops through the course of the story that really got me.' Knowing that the period setting of the film was likely to require a co-production deal between studios, Zanuck asked his son to send a copy to Steven Spielberg at DreamWorks. 'To my amazement, two days later the phone rang . . . and it was Steven. He said, "I love this. Let's do it." And that's how it happened.'

With Spielberg behind it, things moved fast. First, the mogul gave the graphic novel to two-time Oscar® winner Tom Hanks, whom Spielberg had directed in *Saving Private Ryan* (and would again in *Catch Me If You Can*); Hanks was intrigued enough to ask to see the screenplay when it was completed. Next, Spielberg hired screenwriter David Self (*Thirteen Days*), who had scripted DreamWorks' remake of *The Haunting*, to begin adapting the graphic novel, a process which Self found relatively straightforward, particularly compared to adapting a prose novel. 'The graphic novel is one step closer to a film, on the visual level, in the way the story is told, than a literary novel,' he told *Creative Screenwriting*, recalling Spielberg's suggestion that the graphic novel's panel eschewed the need for traditional storyboards – an artist's rough rendering of the script into visual frames for the director's reference. In addition, he suggested, 'The graphic novel is a minimalist form, and it sometimes needs to be fleshed out a bit, expanded, to connect the dots a bit more.' While Self's generalisation may not hold up to close scrutiny, it was certainly true of *Road to Perdition*, which boils down to a straightforward revenge story which, over the course of its mostly four-frame pages, becomes repetitive, and reaches a conclusion not out of any narrative urgency, but because, as Collins admits, its editor asked for one.

Self claims that, while Collins and Rayner do not see his script as a faithful adaptation, he himself believes that 'as far as Hollywood goes it's fairly close'. Yet Collins takes only a few pages to establish the setting (1920s, Illinois) and gets to the killing of O'Sullivan's wife and child relatively swiftly; Self deliberately takes his time. 'The first act is an intentional lulling into an ordinary world of family, of a small, close-knit community, and the comfort zones that the characters inhabit. There's almost a brooding sense of secrets in this community that Michael Jr is about to discover.' Says Collins, '[Self] waits a while and for good reason – he wants to really create a sense of what the world is, and in a way there's a false sense of security because at the beginning of a movie, the world is usually defined, and you say, "Well, this is where we're going to live for the next couple of hours." And by waiting half an hour to pull the rug out from under you, kind of like Janet Leigh's death in *Psycho*, all of a sudden our expectations are fucked with. There's that moment, which is directly from the graphic novel, where [Michael] tells his son, "That's not our home any more. It's just an empty building and we've got to move on," and that has power, I think, because [Self] had the courage to build the house and build relationships for half an hour.' There is also power in the fact that, to Michael Jr, the word 'family' has no double meaning when applied to those around him; while the audience knows that they are mobsters, he does not. For Self, the dramatic impetus of the first act was, by design, watching how people live with their secrets; the first act ends when the secret is discovered (by Michael Jr); the rest of the film follows as a direct consequence.

Self's first significant invention was to codify the father–son theme implicit in the relationship between Michael and his son by making Michael's boss, John Rooney (the graphic novel's real-life figure, John Looney), more of a father figure to Michael, so that the film becomes about not one, but two generations of fathers. 'It's ultimately the killing of the father that will preserve the son, [which is] an atrocious situation,' said Self. 'The choices that spiral out of that make the drama, or come from that central conception.' Another of Self's ideas was to make Rooney's natural son, Connor, jealous of the bond between his father and Michael. 'Connor is the inciting character in both the graphic novel and the script, but one of the consequences of making Sullivan's relationship with Mr Rooney much more personal was a 'sibling rivalry' dynamic between Sullivan and Connor. Connor's motives have another layer to them that they didn't have previously. The consequences of that are Rooney's disapproval of him, and all those things that make the drama more emotionally grabbing.' In effect, Rooney has two sons, and while he ultimately chooses his blood son (Connor) over his adopted son (Michael), he secretly wishes he could choose the adopted son. 'The adopted son has been put in this position by horrible circumstances and is going to suffer dearly for it. The tragic situation that's been created – none of that existed in the graphic novel. We had to find it.'

Another of Self's clever creations was to give Sullivan a worthy adversary, a photographer-cum-hitman named Maguire (in early drafts, Harlen 'The Reporter' Maguire) whose pursuit of Sullivan and his son is as dogged as Sullivan's of Connor. In the graphic novel, Sullivan seems to belong in the pantheon of other comic book heroes; he survives countless gun battles without so much as a scratch, and none of those who wish him harm can hurt him. In the script, Maguire is dispatched by Capone's loyal lieutenant, Frank Nitti, to dispose of Sullivan and his son, and his cold professionalism is evident in the detachment demonstrated in his Weegee-style photographs of violent death, his cold-blooded killing of a photography subject who isn't quite dead, and the relentless efficiency with which he tracks Sullivan to his sister-in-law's house in Perdition, only to be killed by Sullivan, whom he has mortally wounded. For Collins, it was ironic that critics thought that the character of Maguire betrayed the film's comic book origins, 'when in fact, Maguire is the only one I didn't create. It is interesting that the most cartoony character in Sam's movie is not in the source material.'

Self's final alteration was the removal of the graphic novel's framing device. Collins tells the story from the perspective of an older Michael Jr, who is revealed in the final pages to be a Catholic priest, whom one can surmise has spent his life atoning not only for the sins of the father, but for his own – including, ultimately, the cold-blooded killing of the man who killed his father. Early drafts of the script preserved the device, so that the film opened with the older Michael in what looks like a prison cell or a halfway house. 'We intended to seed the audience with the idea that Michael Jr does follow his father's road and is now an old man in this minimum-security lock-up,' Self explained. 'We later learn that it's not a prison but an urban city rectory with bars on the windows – Michael has actually become a priest.' In early drafts, Michael Jr kills Maguire, but with the removal of the framing device, present in all but the latest drafts, Michael Jr could no longer redeem himself through his actions following the events of the story, and therefore his salvation needed to be immediate – he needed to lack the killer instinct required to dispose of Maguire himself. 'With the frame you could sustain the bleak moment of pathos when Michael Jr kills the reporter and Sullivan thinks he has failed his son completely,' Self suggested. 'When you lost the frame, you couldn't end the movie with that statement.' Yet Self knew the original framing device had to go, in order to give the story an immediacy it would otherwise lack; although it is still bookended by Michael Jr's narration, 'it's not the same as the full-blown frame set in the present, with a different tone and showing what's become of Michael Jr'. Ultimately, says Self, 'I think the frame tidied it up a little too much, so it's a little less safe as it exists in the current version of the story.'

Understandably, Self's script met with an extremely positive response, as Richard Zanuck observed, 'The graphic novel was told in pictures and images, but the screenplay evolved into a much deeper, more complex story. It delves more into the personal side of this father and son and has more heart . . . more human emotions.' Indeed, while Self's script was in some ways reductive – the death toll, for instance, was reduced, along with the omnipresent narration and several subplots – its moral and ethical concerns became richer, so that a story about a man's single-minded redemption became a parable about a man seeking redemption through his son. Tom Hanks, who had asked to see the script as soon as it was finished, was immediately hooked. 'I thought this would be the kind of genre movie that would be very familiar to me, but three pages into it I didn't know where I was or what was going to happen next,' he recalled. 'I remember thinking that here is this movie that should be predictable but is utterly *un*predictable. That, coupled with the realities of what it was going to take to make this period piece . . . I wondered who they could get to do it justice.'

The answer was British director Sam Mendes, fresh from the triumph of a Best Director Oscar® for his first film, *American Beauty*. 'I read the script first,' Mendes told *Empire* magazine, 'and I think probably any director will tell you that the key moment with a script is the first time you read it, and the images go popping into your head and the blood starts flowing.' While Mendes liked the graphic novel, he could see that Rayner and Collins' visual style was far from his own. 'I guess there were two ways the story could go: one was the John Woo way, with fabulous, balletic gunplay, where violence is kind of the subject of the film; or you can make violence the *theme* of the film, which is different [because] you are concentrating not on the violence, but on the effect that violence has; what emotional effect it has on people watching it and perpetrating it.' Indeed, while the graphic novel is certainly graphic, full of action-packed shoot-outs and bloodbaths – the body count is significantly higher than that of the film – Mendes would choose to show most of the violence off-screen, or find ways to treat it stylistically without lessening its impact.

CASTING: 'When they first sent it to me, they told me that Tom Hanks had read it and liked it,' Sam Mendes told *Academy* magazine. 'I read it with him in mind, and have to say he never left my mind.' Another Oscar® winner, Paul Newman, was also the film-makers' first choice, this time for the role of John Rooney. 'I turned up to his apartment and he said, "Jesus fucking Christ, you're young!" ' 37-year-old Mendes told *Empire* of his first meeting with the screen legend, forty years his senior. 'And then we went over the script, scene by scene, line by line [for] six or seven weeks, and at the end, he said, "Let's do it." I felt like he was going to do it when I first arrived,' he added. 'I just thought he had a bit of a twinkle.'

With two such heavyweights on board, it was not difficult to fill out the rest of the cast; as British actor Daniel Craig (*Lara Croft: Tomb Raider*) explained to the *Guardian Guide*, 'When Sam told me where it was set and what the cast was I just said, "Well, we don't need to go any further do we?" ' Jude Law, star of Steven Spielberg's *AI – Artificial Intelligence*, would play Maguire; Jennifer Jason Leigh (*eXistenZ*) agreed to play the small but pivotal role of Michael's wife, Annie; Stanley Tucci (*Big Night*) would play real-life mobster Frank Nitti, Al Capone's right-hand man. More difficult was the search for a young actor to play the pivotal role of Michael Jr. Casting director Debra Zane held open calls in cities across the US, auditioning more than two thousand boys before Mendes found his young man: thirteen-year-old Tyler Hoechlin. 'It's what you hope for,' Mendes said, 'that you will turn on a tape and within two seconds know this is the one. Then you just pray that when you actually meet the actor, he's everything you hoped he would be. The moment Tyler walked in the room, it was clear that he had something special . . . He's a very skilled young actor with a wisdom in his eyes that belies his years.' Said Richard Zanuck, 'We had four generations of great actors, starting with the iconic Paul Newman; then Tom Hanks, who is arguably the biggest actor of today; to Jude Law, who is a fast-rising star; and finally Tyler Hoechlin, a newcomer, who amazed us all.'

PRODUCTION: If the success of Mendes' *American Beauty* had been a major factor in attracting talent in front of the camera, it was more than matched by the award-winning creative team behind it: cinematographer Conrad L Hall, who had won his second Oscar® for *American Beauty*, and that film's composer Thomas Newman; Oscar®-winning production designer Dennis Gassner (*Bugsy*, *Miller's Crossing*); two-time Oscar®-winning costume designer Albert Wolsky (*Bugsy*, *All That Jazz*); editor Jill Bilcock (*Moulin Rouge*). 'It was like having an entire engine room of ideas and creative energy behind me,' Mendes said.

The crew went on the road in the winter of 2000–2001, filming entirely on location in and around Chicago, Illinois in the American Midwest. 'I wanted to shoot on location,' said Mendes, 'and what you see on screen is what's actually there. It still exists.' For the scenes in which Sullivan and son first enter the city of Chicago, which Mendes intended to be 'a kind of Oz in the middle of the movie', a little more trickery was required. Filming took place on La Salle street in downtown Chicago and required the digital removal of numerous modern-day buildings; with dozens of vintage cars and hundreds of extras in period costumes, however, the shots are among the most startling of the film, providing a sharp contrast to the rural scenes, in which the colour is all but drained from the film – a far cry from Warren Beatty's colour-saturated *Dick Tracy*. 'The film shouldn't be colourful,' said cinematographer Conrad Hall, 'so I tried to make it as monochromatic as I could. It's not exactly film noir, it's more of a 'soft noir' if you will –

soft shadows rather than harsh ones. I especially loved all the costumes with the hats. I could burn a light down and keep the face totally shaded.'

Although filming took place throughout the winter, with temperatures dropping as low as thirty below zero, the weather did not always cooperate with Mendes' intentions, and special effects coordinator Allen Hall was called upon to create acres of fake snow for the first act of the film. 'The reason there is snow and ice in the opening of the story is that it symbolises a frozen world . . . in the emotional sense. It's a paralysed family until the father and oldest son are thrown together by tragedy, and they begin to have the relationship they never had before. So out of the bad comes good, and everything that was intended to be set in ice at the beginning begins to thaw.'

COSTUME FITTING: In recreating the period in which the film is set, costume designer Albert Wolsky faced one of the toughest challenges of his career. The economic malaise which afflicted America at the time created two problems: the first was that few people could afford to dress with distinction, making authentic clothing difficult to define; the second was that few of the clothes from the period had been kept. Instead, Wolsky took patterns from the few clothes they could find – mainly three-piece suits, coats and hats made from heavy material, to withstand wear and tear and the bitter cold – and fashioned multiples of each costume. 'Once Michael Sullivan and his son are on the road, the [costume] changes are minimal – it's just the same suit, the same coat . . . getting more and more worn,' Wolsky explained. 'It means making more copies than you would usually need for normal wear and tear. And because we were shooting out of sequence, we couldn't use the same costume from day to day.' Wolsky finally found a weaver in upstate New York named Rabit Goody, who did 'wonderful work' weaving the heavy clothing required for the film. 'The weight dramatically affected the way the clothes moved,' he added. 'Without the right fabric, you lose the period.'

MUSIC: Composer Thomas Newman's music for Sam Mendes' *American Beauty* became one of the most imitated soundtracks of its time – not the least by Newman himself. His music for *Road to Perdition* follows his own model. Period songs featured in the film include 'There'll Be Some Changes Made', 'Queer Notions', 'Everybody Loves My Baby', 'Sidewalk Blues', 'Someday Sweetheart', 'Whose Honey Are You?' – and, of course, Thomas Newman's 'Perdition – Piano Duet' performed by Paul Newman and Tom Hanks.

CLASSIC QUOTES:

Finn McGovern: 'I've worked for you for many years now, nearly half my life, and we never had a disagreement. I've come to realise that you rule this town as God rules this Earth. You give and you take away . . .'

Peter Sullivan: 'What's his job?'

Michael Jr: 'He goes on missions for Mr Rooney. They're very dangerous, that's why he brings his gun. Sometimes, even the President sends him on missions, 'cause papa was a war hero and all.'

John Rooney: 'What men do after work is what made us rich. There's no need to screw them *at* work as well.'

Michael Sullivan: 'This house is not our home any more. It's just an empty building.'

John Rooney: 'There's only murderers in this room. *Michael.* Open your eyes. This is the life we chose, this is the life we lead. And there is only one guarantee: none of us will see heaven.'

DELETED SCENES: The fact that Australian actor Anthony LaPaglia (*Lantana*) is given special thanks in the closing credits of the film is a clue to one of the film's most intriguing deleted scenes, in which LaPaglia played real-life mobster Al Capone. As graphic novelist Max Allan Collins explains, 'There were a couple of scenes with Frank Nitti and one with Capone, and although the Capone scene may not have been the weakest, when they edited the film, it played fine without it. I really think that Mendes is a ruthless, brutal editor of his own work,' he adds, 'and I think that's great. If it doesn't work, it's gone.'

The following scenes were also deleted prior to release:

- a tender supper scene between Sullivan and his wife, Annie;
- two further scenes at the wake: one in which Sullivan offers Finn his condolences; another in which Connor asks Sullivan (in front of Mr Rooney) if he thinks his funeral will draw as big a crowd;
- a tender scene in which Annie puts Peter to bed;
- a longer version of the scene in which Sullivan visits Calvino, which plays as an extraordinary two-and-a-half minute Steadicam shot, from the door of the nightclub to the door of Calvinos inner sanctum;
- a scene in which Sullivan and son go to confession in a small rural church;
- a scene in which Sullivan explains to his son the danger they are in;
- a scene in which Maguire searches the Sullivans' bedroom during Annie Sullivan's wake;

- a scene in which Sullivan is asked to dance by a waitress, but declines;
- a scene in which Sullivan sleeps while Michael Jr practices with his father's gun.

TRAILERS: The trailer for *Road to Perdition* is a good lesson in how to fudge key issues in a marketing campaign. Almost three minutes in length, the trailer spends almost a minute setting up the mystery of Michael Sullivan's work for Mr Rooney – and then, just as it seems set to shock the audience by revealing that lovable everyman Tom Hanks is playing a ruthless mob hitman, the trailer fudges the issue by making it look as though Connor is the only one with blood on his hands, putting Sullivan into the role of protecting the boy who has witnessed Connor's misdeeds. Far from suggesting that Sullivan is seeking vengeance, the trailer puts him and his son on the run from Connor and Maguire, and the few times we see him wield a weapon it seems to be in self-defence. Three captions, which appear almost at random, are similarly oblique: 'EVERY FAMILY HAS A DESTINY,' says the first; 'EVERY SON HOLDS THE FUTURE FOR HIS FATHER,' says the clumsy second; and finally, 'EVERY FATHER IS A HERO TO HIS SON.' A pedigree credit 'FROM THE DIRECTOR OF *AMERICAN BEAUTY*' and three cast captions (Hanks, Newman, Law) follow.

POSTERS: The main poster image features Hanks as Michael Sullivan and Tyler Hoechlin as Michael Jr walking in the rain, the former carrying a Tommy Gun. Both figures appear in silhouette, and in a rare move for a poster featuring a star of his magnitude, Hanks' face is almost fully obscured by the shadow of his hat – though it is clear from the features that can be seen that the moustache he wears in the film has been all but digitally removed.

TAG-LINE: 'Every father is a hero to his son.' 'Pray for Michael Sullivan.'

WHAT THE PAPERS SAID: 'Moody, methodical and measured,' said *Variety*'s Todd McCarthy, '*Road to Perdition* takes a brooding look at the wages of sin and the heritage of violence among hoodlums during the dark days of Prohibition . . . absorbing drama sees Tom Hanks fitting comfortably into the role of a morally aware bad guy. . . playing his first outright bad man, albeit one with commendable traits of loyalty and filial responsibility, Hanks happily resists any temptation to soften his character or quietly suggest to the audience that he's really an OK guy under it all; Sullivan is tough, clammed up and not easily expressive even to his son.' In the UK, the *Guardian* was not so easily convinced: '[I]mprobably trapped inside a villainous role . . . Hanks has just taken his normal performance, subtracted a bit of the comedy and the warmth, and put nothing in its place.' Nevertheless, Bradshaw praised the film's 'unarguably beautiful look', 'wonderful images and tableaux' and 'stunningly ambitious, intriguingly experimental compositions devised by the director Sam Mendes, who imposes a steely, rigorous visual intelligence on every frame'.

BOX OFFICE: *Road to Perdition* opened in the US on 12 July 2002, slap bang in the middle of the summer, rather than the more traditional fourth quarter period usually reserved for Oscar® hopefuls; at the time, DreamWorks' decision to open the picture in the middle of summer raised a few eyebrows, not least at *Variety*, which suggested that the film's 'autumnal feel and A-plus awards-season pedigree will make it fascinating to see if DreamWorks can pull off its gamble of putting this over as a summer attraction'. As it turned out, the gamble paid dividends: the film grossed a respectable $22.5 million on its opening weekend, and trudged quietly past the $100 million mark after nine weeks. Its worldwide gross exceeded $160 million.

AWARDS: At the time of the film's release, critics were fond of saying that *Road to Perdition* was the first Oscar®-worthy film of the year. Sure enough, when the Academy of Motion Picture Arts and Sciences went to the polls some six months later, *Road to Perdition* received five nominations, in the following categories: Best Supporting Actor (Paul Newman), Best Cinematography, Best Art Direction, Best Music, Best Sound and Best Sound Editing. At the BAFTA awards, *Road to Perdition*'s three nominations were in the categories of Supporting Actor (Newman again), Cinematography and Production Design. Paul Newman received the film's sole Golden Globe nomination, in the category of Best Actor in a Supporting Role, but lost out to *Adaptation*'s Chris Cooper.

CONTROVERSY: Although the film is credited as being 'Based on the Graphic Novel by Max Allan Collins and Richard Piers Rayner', the fact that early promotional materials left out the 'graphic' part caused controversy, as Collins recalls: 'Sam Mendes and David Self and Conrad Hall had made a couple of ill-advised comments about the source material, you know, "We're going to transcend it," and "It's a comic book but don't hold that against us," and this kind of crap. And the comics fans, God bless them, went on the Internet and made a big fuss about this, and the people at DreamWorks quickly put that right. So when I saw the movie and it mentioned that it was based on a graphic novel – they hadn't said, "Based on *Road to Perdition*" or "Based on the novel by" or found some other way of fudging it – so I kind of cheered at that moment.'

TRIVIA: Steven Spielberg, who was arguably the most important factor in getting the film made – his studio DreamWorks had also financed Mendes' *American Beauty*, and he had directed Hanks in *Saving Private Ryan*, and Law in *A.I. Artificial Intelligence*– must have been amused to note that the graphic novel contained a frame copied from a still from his 1975 blockbuster *Jaws*.

Max Allan Collins and Richard Piers Rayner did not meet until the European premiere of the film.

Cinematographer Conrad L Hall died on 4 January 2002 at the age of 76. *Road to Perdition* was his last film. 'In a sense, I realise now, I chose to direct *Road to Perdition* partly for him,' Mendes told the *Guardian*. 'To see how he would light those rainy streets, those lonely interiors and lonely people, and although it was a hard shoot for an old man who didn't like the cold and didn't believe in violence, it lives as a testament to his extraordinary eye and consummate artistry.'

The photographs shown in Harlen Maguire's apartment are taken from Luc Sante's *Evidence*, a book of photographs taken by members of the New York police department between 1914 and 1918.

APOCRYPHA: 'That was the last time I ever held a gun,' Michael Jr says in the narration that closes the film. Since Michael is still only twelve years old when he tells us this, how would he know that?

SEQUELS & SPIN-OFFS: Comics fans who had gone to bat for Collins and Rayner when DreamWorks was trying to play down the fact that *Road to Perdition* was based on a graphic novel might have been disappointed to discover that, rather than letting fans of the film seek out the original source material, Collins had written a prose 'novelisation' based on the screenplay. 'I only did it, frankly, because (a) if I didn't, someone else would have, and (b) I felt there was a considerable audience that could not make that transition to pick up a comic book.' Besides, Collins chose to write a novel rather than a novelisation. 'I'd been led to believe I'd have a lot of freedom, and I wrote a hundred-thoursand-word book that fleshed out the screenplay and was the real *Road to Perdition* novel. But at the last minute they told me they wanted me to take everything out that wasn't directly referred to in the movie, and I was forced to cut forty thousand words. *Forty thousand words!*' Nevertheless, the saga had a happy ending: the graphic novel outsold the novelisation, bringing countless readers back to comics, and some to the medium for the first time.

FUTURE INCARNATIONS: Another reason Collins wanted to write the novelisation is that it would have provided the basis for two sequel novels he planned to write, *Road to Purgatory* and *Road to Paradise*. 'I had already written the proposal for the two sequels,' says Collins, 'and the day the movie opened we took it to publishers, and by the following Wednesday, I had a publishing deal – just like that.' Although fans of the graphic novel would be disappointed to discover that the sequels would be prose novels, Collins also has plans for further comic book stories. 'DC and Marvel have both been after me to do more *Road to Perdition*,' he says, 'and if you read the graphic novel, you may remember that I left a window: I said that the father and son were on the road for six months, because I always intended this to be a much longer story. So what we're talking about is a thing called *Tales from the Road to Perdition*, which will be a second graphic novel, or three graphic novellas that will together comprise a second graphic novel, that basically fills a hole in the narrative. It's what they sometimes call a "continuity implant".' Collins says 'there's no question' that artist Richard Piers Rayner will be involved in some capacity. 'He'll probably do at least one of them, and definitely all of the colours.'

DVD AVAILABILITY: *Road to Perdition* is available in the UK (Region 2) and US (Region 1) as a widescreen (2.35:1) Dolby 5.1 DVD featuring commentary by Sam Mendes, a 25-minute HBO 'making of' and the deleted scenes outlined above.

FINAL ANALYSIS: *Road to Perdition* stands apart from the other comic book adaptations covered by this book for many reasons: firstly, it is the only one adapted from a graphic novel – that is, a self-contained comic book rather than an ongoing series; secondly, it is not a tale of superheroes, heroes or even anti-heroes – on the contrary, the central character is a killer; most significantly, however, is the fact that *Road to Perdition* truly transcends its source – not comics in general (for me, the comic is as valid an artistic medium as film), but the graphic novel in particular. In narrative, stylistic and thematic terms, comparing Mendes' film with the graphic novel is like trying to equate the intricacies of Michelangelo's David with a Henry Moore sculpture.

The basic story is the same in both cases: Irish-American hitman betrayed by his boss sets out to avenge his wife and youngest son's murder, accompanied by his surviving son – this is what brings the audience to the film, or the reader to the graphic novel. What the audience or reader takes away with them, however, is the *theme*, and this is where the film takes a quantum leap over its source. Although Collins' story begins promisingly, it lacks moral substance and thematic depth, and – once Michael O'Sullivan sets out on his killing spree – quickly becomes as repetitive as the poses in Rayner's artwork, which seems lacking in imagination, undynamic and often derivative, owing as great a debt to *manga* artist Ryoichi Ikegami as Collins does to *Lone*

Wolf and Cub creator Kazuo Koike. Where the graphic novel perhaps has the edge is at the climax; while much of the middle of the graphic novel seems to be treading water, its redemption comes at the end, with Michael's: in the film, Michael Jr is unable to pull the trigger on his father's killer, thus demonstrating his unwillingness to follow his father's path to violence; in the novel, in which Michael Jr *did* kill to save his father's life, the final panels reveal that the narrator, Michael Jr, is now a middle-aged man dressed in the robes of a priest: writing his father's story is presumably a cathartic step on the road to redemption.

Mendes owes a few debts of his own – notably to *Miller's Crossing*, the Coen brothers' superlative (and arguably superior) tale of Irish-American gangsters, and a strong influence on the look of Mendes' film. An even greater influence, however, was cinematographer Conrad Hall, whose gift for lighting is as evident in every single shot as Mendes' talent for composition. Unfortunately, the sombre tone of the visuals seems to drain the colour from every other aspect of the film, so that ultimately, even the film's finest performances and most exciting sequences seem as drab, cold and colourless as the winter skies over the road to Perdition.

EXPERT WITNESS: '*Road to Perdition* was everything that *American Beauty* wasn't. It pushed me in another direction and I loved the scale and canvas of it . . . In fact, for me, it still remains an art-house movie with some film stars in it. It works on one level as a gripping narrative of revenge but on another level it's a meditation on violence, fathers and sons – and, of course, the period.' – **Sam Mendes, Director**

Spider-Man (2002)

(121 minutes)

Directed by Sam Raimi
Screenplay by David Koepp
Based on the Marvel Comic Book by Stan Lee and Steve Ditko
Produced by Laura Ziskin and Ian Bryce
Executive Producers Avi Arad and Stan Lee
Director of Photography Don Burgess ASC
Production Designer Neil Spisak
Editors Bob Murawski and Arthur Coburn ACE
Visual Effects Designed by John Dykstra ASC
Costumes Designer James Acheson
Music by Danny Elfman

Co-Producer Grant Curtis
Casting by Francine Maisler and Lynn Kressel

CAST: Tobey Maguire (*Peter Parker/'Spider-Man'*), Willem Dafoe (*Norman Osborn/'The Green Goblin'*), Kirsten Dunst (*Mary Jane Watson*), James Franco (*Harry Osborn*), Cliff Robertson (*Uncle Ben Parker*), Rosemary Harris (*Aunt May Parker*), JK Simmons (*J Jonah Jameson*), Joe Manganiello (*Flash Thompson*), Gerry Becker (*Maximilian Fargas*), Bill Nunn (*Joe 'Robbie' Robertson*), Jack Betts (*Henry Balkan*), Stanley Anderson (*General Slocum*), Ron Perkins (*Dr Mendel Stromm*), Michael Papajohn (*carjacker*), KK Goods (*Simkins*), Ted Raimi (*Hoffman*), Bruce Campbell (*ring announcer*) Elizabeth Banks (*Miss Brant*), John Paxton (*Houseman*), Tim de Zarn (*Philip Watson*), Taylor Gilbert (*Madeline Watson*), Randy Savage (*Bone Saw McGraw*), Larry Joshua (*wrestling promoter*), Timothy Patrick Quill (*wrestling arena guard*), Lisa Danuelle, Natalie T Yeo, Erica O Porter, Kristen Davidson (*Bone-ettes*), Jsaon Padgett (*Flash's crony*), Shah Omar Huey (*teacher*), Sally Livingstone (*girl on bus*), Evan Arnold (*doctor*), Jill Sayre (*nurse*), James K Ward (*project coordinator*), David Holcomb (*test pilot*), Octavia Spencer (*check-in girl*), Brad Grunberg (*heckler*), Shane Habberstad (*little Billy*), Deborah Wakeman (*Billy's mom*), Rachel Bruce, Mackenzie Bryce, Julia Barry (*Times Square children*), Macy Gray (*herself*), Myk Watford (*cop at fire*), William Calvert (*fireman*), Sylva Kelegian (*mother at fire*), Kristen Marie Holly (*young lady at fire*), Ajay Mehta, Peter Appel (*cabbies*), Scott Spiegel (*marina cop*), Matt Smith, Sara Ramirez (*cops at carjacking*), Lucy Lawless (*punk rock girl*), Jayce Bartok (*subway guitarist*), Maribel Gonzalez (*lady dogwalker*), Amy Bouril (*office lady*), Joseph D'Onofrio (*opinionated cop*), Jim Norton (*surly truck driver*), Corey Mendell Parker (*chaperone in tram*), Ashley Louise Edner (*girl in tram*), William Joseph Firth, Alex Black (*boys in tram*), Laura Gray (*tram group mother*), Joe Virzi, Michael Edward Thomas, Jeanie Fox (*New Yorkers on bridge*), Robert Kerman (*tugboat captain*)

TITLE SEQUENCE: The computer-animated title sequence, designed by Kyle Cooper at Imaginary Forces, is an imaginative combination of spider webs, New York skyscrapers, blood-red arteries, and elements of the Spider-Man and Green Goblin characters, with the main opening credits appearing trapped in the strands of the webs themselves. As the final credit appears, the image dissolves to a real spider web as Peter Parker's narration begins, initially overlapping with the images themselves. 'We really didn't want to show Spider-Man early in the story because it was his origin story,' says director Sam Raimi, 'but we wanted to give the audience a taste of him so we tried to design with Kyle and his team some sequence that would give the audience the flavour of the character without actually spoiling the big reveal of Spider-Man before it was due.' Cooper also designed the Marvel logo which precedes the title sequence.

SYNOPSIS: Peter Parker is an ordinary high school teenager with ambitions to be a photographer; an orphan, he lives in the New York borough of Queens with his Uncle Ben and Aunt May, and has long carried a torch for the girl next door, Mary Jane Watson. One fateful day, on a school trip to Columbia University science lab, Parker is bitten by a genetically enhanced spider, and soon begins to manifest spider-like superpowers: he can climb vertical surfaces, has an innate sixth sense and immense physical strength, and is able to shoot a sticky and extremely strong weblike substance from his wrists, which he can use to swing from building to building. When a robbery at an amateur wrestling competition in which Parker takes part results in the shooting death of his uncle, Parker decides to use his new-found powers to fight crime – which he does in the costumed guise of 'Spider-Man'. Initially misunderstood as a dangerous vigilante – not least by the publisher of the *Daily Bugle*, where he earns a crust as a freelance photographer – he is given an opportunity to prove his good intentions when the city comes under threat from a creature dubbed 'The Green Goblin'. Unbeknownst to Peter, the Goblin is actually his best friend's father, scientist/industralist Norman Osborn, whose injection of an experimental serum designed for military application has given him great strength and agility, but sent him insane. In a stolen suit and glider designed by his own company, Oscorp, the Goblin becomes the scourge of the city, setting off bombs in the middle of Times Square, and – when he learns the true identity of Spider-Man – attacking Aunt May, and later staging an elaborate set piece which forces Parker to choose between saving the lives of a cable car full of children, or his sweetheart Mary Jane. With a little help from a friendly neighbourhood, Spider-Man succeeds in saving both, and defeats the Goblin in a final showdown. As Osborn's son Harry vows vengeance on Spider-Man, Peter realises that his exploits as Spider-Man put the lives of those he loves at risk; thus, although Mary Jane reveals her love for Peter, he is forced to push her away. After all, as his uncle told him shortly before his death, 'with great power comes great responsibility'.

ORIGINS: Inspired by pulp favourite 'The Spider', Spider-Man was the creation of writer comic book writer Stan Lee (who also created such Marvel characters as the X-Men and Hulk) and defined by artist Steve Ditko. Although the publisher initially rejected the concept, Lee sneaked a Spider-Man story into the pages of the fifteenth and final issue of *Amazing Fantasy*, cover-dated August 1962. By the time the sales figures came in, it was clear that Marvel and Lee had a hit on their hands. What made him successful was what separated Spider-Man from other superheroes – he was teenager still in high school, not a billionaire or an alien; he lived in a real city (New York) rather than a Metropolis or Gotham; he had to juggle real-life responsibilities and problems with relationships, finance and school while tackling the various villains who crossed his path. At last, the declining comic book readership had found a hero they could identify with. In March 1963, *The Amazing Spider-Man* #1 gave the character a title of his own, and his stories have continued uninterrupted in a variety of Marvel titles ever since.

PREVIOUS INCARNATIONS: Spider-Man's first screen incarnation came just five years after the character's comic book debut, in a Saturday morning animated series by Ralph Bakshi, director of the animated *Lord of the Rings*. Although the show was cancelled in 1970, the character reappeared in live-action educational vignettes between 1974 and 1976, on the children's TV show *The Electric Company*. Then, in 1977, CBS premiered a live-action two-hour TV movie, subsequently released at UK cinemas, in which Nicholas Hammond played the title role; a CBS television series, *The Amazing Spider-Man*, followed, running until 1979. At the same time, a Japanese TV series was made, featuring Kagawa Kousuke in the title role. In the early 1980s, the character had two animated television serials – NBC's *Spider-Man and his Amazing Friends*, and *The Amazing Spider-Man* – while in 1995, Fox premiered *Spider-Man: The Animated Series*, which ran until 1998. Spidey's most recent television incarnation was also animated: *Spider-Man Unlimited*, which ran from 1999 to 2001.

DEVELOPMENT: *Spider-Man*'s long journey to the big screen began almost two decades before its eventual release, when Manachem Golan's Cannon Films – the company behind the limited theatrical release of CBS's two-hour TV pilot in 1978 – secured the rights for just $250,000. Golan commissioned a script from Ted Newsom and John A Brancato, who had teamed up to write scripts based on such other Marvel properties as *Sgt Fury* and *The Sub-Mariner*. Neil Ruttenberg was the next writer to tackle the film, to which director Tobe Hooper (*Poltergeist*) became attached, with Bob Hoskins in talks to play 'Doctor Octopus'. In order to retain the rights, however, Golan was contractually obliged to put *Spider-Man* into production by April 1989, and wasted no time in announcing the film, with Stephen Herek (*Bill and Ted's Excellent Adventure*, *101 Dalmatians*) at the helm: 'The world's best-selling comic book hero battles his multi-limbed arch-enemy, Doctor Octopus, in this fun and action-packed adventure comedy.' Desperate for money to finance the film before the deadline, 21st

Century sold the home video rights to Sony-owned Columbia TriStar, and international television rights to Paramount's parent company, Viacom; Golan even struck a new deal with Marvel Comics, extending the deadline to January 1992. But still the movie failed to materialise, and when 21st Century collapsed in 1991, cash-rich Carolco swooped in to pick up the remaining rights, paying Marvel $3 million to extend its option through May 1996, and courting a new director: James Cameron, the auteur behind *Terminator* and *Aliens*.

Like millions of Americans, Cameron had been a fan of superhero stories since his youth, preferring Marvel Comics' titles like *The Amazing Spider-Man* and *The Uncanny X-Men* to DC Comics' *Superman* and *Batman* tales. By the age of twelve, he had decided that he would grow up to be a comic book artist, and began copying his favourite characters – notably Spider-Man, a socially awkward but precociously bright teenager, much like the young Cameron himself. Thus, when the success of Tim Burton's *Batman* opened the floodgates for a new wave of films based on comic books, Cameron became the logical choice to bring his web-slinging idol to the big screen, not least for Spider-Man creator Stan Lee. 'I couldn't think of a better director for that movie in the whole world,' Lee enthused.

Although Cameron continued to pursue several other projects, including *Strange Days* and *True Lies*, he was interested enough in the *Spider-Man* project to write a 57-page 'scriptment', a combination of script and treatment, not unlike the one he had written for *The Terminator* a decade earlier. Cameron's first draft was delivered on 3 August 1993, the same day his fourth film, *True Lies*, began shooting in Santa Clara, California. Stan Lee immediately proclaimed the story treatment to be 'brilliant' – unsurprising, given that Cameron had been almost obsequiously faithful to Spider-Man's comic book origins. 'What Jim managed to do was do *Spider-Man* exactly the way *Spider-Man* should be [done],' Lee enthused to *Premiere*. 'The same personality, the same *gestalt*. And yet it all seems fresh and different, something we have never seen before.'

Opening with an image of the web-slinging crimefighter suspended upside down from the radio mast of the World Trade Center, Cameron uses first-person narration to describe how Peter Parker, an orphaned but otherwise unremarkable seventeen-year-old living with his aunt and uncle in Flushing, New York, is bitten by a spider whose genetic code has been altered by its ingestion of a mutagenically activated fruitfly. That night, Peter has a dream in which he imagines himself as a spider – and wakes to find himself eighty feet up a high tension tower dressed only his underwear! Peter soon begins to display other arachnid qualities, apparently brought on by the spider bite: he can climb vertical surfaces, land safely on his feet from virtually any height, perform incredible acrobatic feats, tune his senses to superhuman levels, and secrete a pearlescent white fluid ('Hopefully this will be seen correctly as a metaphor for puberty and its awakening of primal drives,' Cameron writes helpfully) which turns out to be his equivalent of a spider's silky thread. Peter, like Gregor Samsa in Frank Kafka's *Metamorphosis*, has awoken to find himself turned into a bug.

Peter hides his secret from his family and his classmates – even the object of his unrequited affection, pretty classmate Mary Jane Watson; instead, he dresses himself in a mask and makeshift spider costume, and – under the name 'Spider Man' (with no hyphen) – begins performing gymnastic feats for money, first in the street, and later on television variety shows – but always, somehow, retaining his anonymity. But when his elderly uncle is murdered by street thugs, Peter decides to use his powers for more than just financial gain and small-scale fame: instead, he begins a one-man manhunt for Ben's killer, and eventually becomes a kind of nocturnal vigilante, a masked 'superhero' who invokes the wrath of legitimate law enforcement *and* the enmity of the criminal underworld. Soon, these feelings are shared by the public at large, whose fear of the costumed vigilante who stalks the city at night is fuelled by a local newspaper eager to build its readership around the Spider Man phenomenon. Already unpopular at school, Peter now finds himself a despised public figure.

Soon, Spider Man's superhuman feats come to the attention of Carlton Strand, who developed the ability to control electricity after surviving a lightning strike, and used his powers to turn himself from small-time crook to billionaire supervillain, complete with beautiful but deadly consort, Cordelia, and shapeshifting sidekick, Sandman (not to be confused with the early DC Comics character successfully revived by Neil Gaiman). Strand tries to lure Spider Man into his criminal empire, but Peter rejects the offer, and continues his fight against crime, despite the fact that the line between good and evil is often as blurry as his vision used to be, before he gained his 'spider-sense'. There are other complications. A furious Strand frames Spider Man for murder, turning the crimefighter into a hunted criminal. Meanwhile, romance is blossoming with Mary Jane, but not for him: it is Spider Man who seduces her, and she has no more idea that Peter Parker is the man – or rather, *boy* – behind the mask than anyone else in the city. Eventually, in classic comic book style, Strand uses Mary Jane to lure Spider Man into his web, and when Spidey comes to her rescue, an almighty battle ensues. Strand is killed, Mary Jane discovers Peter's secret identity, they fall in love, Peter graduates . . . and the one-time hated vigilante becomes – you guessed it – your friendly neighbourhood Spider Man.

The closest Cameron came to directing the film was in 1995, as evidenced by interviews given for *True Lies* in which he regularly referred to *Spider-Man* as his next project. 'I'm doing the origin story and then going way beyond that and delving into the whole story of teenage angst,' he told *Platinum* magazine. 'What if you were seventeen years old and you could do whatever the fuck you wanted, anytime you wanted? There's going to be all the webs and stuff, but it's also going to be deeply philosophical.' Cameron had met with his future *Titanic* star Leonardo Di Caprio to discuss the central role, believing that Spider-Man himself was a big enough star to carry the movie. Besides, he said, 'I think the big star factor is obviated by the fact that the guy's supposed to be just seventeen or eighteen. He's a senior in high school, and I'm playing it the way it was originally written.'

Cameron also gave a hint as to the visual style of the proposed film. 'One of the things that really interests me, possibly in *Spider-Man*, possibly in some other later project, is going into some very bizarre and surreal imagery that can only be done using computer-generated images,' he added. 'I want to try something really wild. Before, there were limits to what you could do in special effects, but now there are no impossibilities. If you can imagine it, you can definitely put it up there on the screen.' Cameron may have been referring to a sequence in which Peter has an arachnid nightmare after being bitten by the spider, described in Cameron's scriptment as follows: 'An abyss of dark visions which yawns beneath him. He falls into the maelstrom, barraged by hallucinatory manifestations. Disturbing images of webs . . . from a POV as if crawling over them. Glistening eyes in the dark. Sudden predatory lunges. Prey struggling hopelessly to escape. A David Lynch bio-horror montage of spiderworld. Shadowy images of rooftops . . . crawling over buildings and fences. Leaping through the dark air . . .'

As fate would have it, by the time Cameron was free to make the *Spider-Man* movie, the feature film rights were caught in a web of their own, arising from the bankruptcy of Carolco in 1996, the result of such costly failures as *Cutthroat Island* and *Showgirls*. A year earlier, Twentieth Century Fox – which had struck a deal with Cameron after *True Lies* hit big at the box office – offered to buy the rights for $50 million, but Carolco, which had spent in the unfriendly neighbourhood of $11 million developing the project, stubbornly refused to sell. Now, the collapsing company was forced to hand over production and distribution rights – excluding television and video, still held by Viacom and Columbia respectively – to MGM, which acquired both Carolco's and 21st Century's rights in the bankruptcy sell-off.

Before MGM could make a move, however, Marvel Comics filed a lawsuit claiming that the rights to make a Spider-Man film had reverted to Marvel in July 1996, since Carolco had failed to put the film into production before the deadline. Marvel was understandably desperate to reacquire the rights to its tent-pole character, since by 1996 it had succumbed to the curse which seemed to afflict any company with an interest in a Spider-Man movie, and was facing bankruptcy proceedings of its own, precipitated by a slump in comic book sales and a disastrous attempt at direct-sales distribution. MGM promptly responded to Marvel's litigation with a three-pronged countersuit, claiming that if it did not own the rights under the Carolco agreement, it did so under its agreements with Twenty-first Century and Cannon, both of which it had acquired from Carolco. To further complicate matters, Sony stepped in to assert its claim to the video rights, while Viacom threw its hat into the ring with a particularly creative lawsuit – as fanciful as Sony's claim to the James Bond property – claiming that, rather than merely owning the TV rights it purchased from Twenty-first Century in 1989, it actually held the rights to produce and distribute. 'It's a tangled web,' Twenty-first Century Film Corp's attorney, Sam Perlmutter, told *Premiere*. 'More of a web than Spider-Man ever could have made in one of his stories. Almost all the studios have a seat at the table, claiming they have a piece of [the rights].'

The Spider-Man saga was briefly put on hold during Toy Biz's takeover of the Marvel Group in the summer of 1998, by which time the success of *Titanic* made the prospect of Cameron directing a Spider-Man movie look distinctly doubtful. 'Jim's a big fan and has the utmost respect for Stan Lee,' admitted Rae Sanchini, president of Cameron's production company, Lightstorm Entertainment. 'But who knows if it will ever get made? So many people want to make it, and that has been one of the greatest impediments to getting it made.' As Stan Lee told *Dreamwatch*, 'For years now, lawyers have been working on this, trying to untangle this terrible legal knot and get the rights back [for Marvel]. The minute the rights come back, I hope Jim will do the movie, and I hope by then he's not busy with another movie, or he hasn't lost interest.' Lee felt that Cameron's participation was crucial. 'He's not just a writer who's going to get the assignment and going to have to learn who Spider-Man is,' he explained. 'Jim has told me he's wanted to do a Spider-Man movie since he was about fourteen years old. So you have the desire and the ability in one guy, and the knowledge and the skill. I don't say other people couldn't do it, [and] probably do a wonderful job, but I think it would be awful if it isn't Jim Cameron, if only because we've both been waiting so long for this.'

The legal web surrounding Spider-Man finally became untangled in February 1999, as the US courts dismissed MGM's claim to the rights, leaving Marvel free to make a new deal – and thus, a new movie – with Sony Pictures Entertainment. 'This is a great day for the studio,' Sony chief John Calley declared. 'I am delighted that we will be able to bring this long sought-after comic book hero to the world of Sony film and television entertainment.' Describing the Spider-Man property as the 'jewel in the crown of Sony's franchise vision', Calley confirmed that Cameron was still the studio's first choice for director, but admitted, 'We haven't even looked at [his] treatment yet.' By this time, however, and in the wake of *Titanic*'s critical and commercial success, Cameron felt that the ship had sailed. 'Here's where I am philosophically,' he told *Premiere* in November 1998, 'I'm forty-four, I make a movie every two or three years – it should be something that I create. I've always done that, with the exception of *Aliens*. *The Terminator* was my creation, so were *Titanic* and *The Abyss*. With the amount of time and energy that I put into a film, it shouldn't be somebody else's superhero. I don't want to labour in somebody else's house.'

Understandably disappointed by Cameron's departure, Sony wasted no time in lining up other candidates, including Roland Emmerich (*Independence Day*, *Godzilla*), Christopher Columbus (*Mrs Doubtfire*), Tim Burton (*Batman*) and David Fincher (*Se7en*, *Fight Club*). 'I wanted to do the character's genesis only as an operatic sequence at the beginning,' said Fincher, who wanted to base the story on the famed 1970s story arc in which the Green Goblin kills Parker's then-girlfriend, Gwen Stacy. 'It would be, "OK, here's five minutes of how he became Spider-Man, and then you get deposited into the movie." But [the studio] wanted the origin story.' Finally, genre favourite Sam Raimi – who co-wrote and directed the superhero-style *Darkman*, produced the comic book-based *Timecop* and, had, like Cameron, been a Spider-Man fan since childhood – signed on to direct. 'The thing that sold me,' said Amy Pascal, chairperson of Sony-owned Columbia Pictures, 'was Sam said as a kid he'd had a picture of Spider-Man over his bed and he identified with Peter Parker, who is the heart of the movie.' Sony Pictures boss John Calley – who, almost 25 years earlier, had overseen the production of *Superman* at Warner Bros – knew that Pascal's instincts were right. 'It just made sense,' he said. 'He was attuned to the character; he has a breathtaking visual sense; he's not an uncontrollable psychotic, but a wonderful man who is, nonetheless, an artist. He was so right.'

In the meantime, screenwriter David Koepp (*Jurassic Park*) turned in a new script which replaced Cameron's villains, Electro and Sandman, with the Green Goblin, whose more personal relationship with Parker suited the film's character-based sensibility. 'Because the Goblin is the father of Harry Osborn, Peter's best friend, I thought there was a greater chance for a dramatic interaction on a personal level than with Electro or Sandman,' Raimi explained, 'neither of whom know Peter or ever relate to him. We also had a version of the script with the Green Goblin and Doctor Octopus – two great villains – but we felt there wouldn't be enough effects budget to do them properly. To tell three origin stories in one film would have compromised the different stories.' Although much of Cameron's 'scriptment' was jettisoned, one important element was retained: the idea that Parker could produce his own weblike substance from his wrists, a divergence from the comic book lore, which had Parker invent his own web spinners. 'Cameron must have been thinking, "Look, if we're going to mutate him into a spider, let's go [all the way]," ' Raimi told *Fangoria*. 'He sticks to walls; he can leap; why does he then have to invent a web fluid? Why not just mutate him far enough into a spider to produce webbing?' The idea fitted perfectly with the script's update of Spider-Man mythology, which eschewed a bite by a radioactive spider, in favour of one from a genetically recombined species created from the DNA of three separate spiders, each with different abilities.

CASTING: Although Heath Ledger (*A Knight's Tale*), Ewan McGregor (*Star Wars Episode I: The Phantom Menace*), Chris Klein (*American Pie*), Wes Bentley (*American Beauty*) and Freddie Prinze Jr (*Scooby Doo*) were on the studio's shortlist for the dual role of Peter Parker and Spider-Man, Raimi would hear none of it. 'Freddie Prinze Jr won't even be allowed to buy a ticket to see this film,' Raimi joked. His first and only choice was Tobey Maguire – who had won critical acclaim for roles in such films as *The Ice Storm* and *Pleasantville* – although it took two elaborate screen tests to convince the studio. The first actor to be cast, Maguire immediately began a three-month diet and exercise regime required to physically assume the Spider-Man role, only to have it unexpectedly extended by two months when principal photography was delayed.

Kirsten Dunst, who stole scenes from Tom Cruise and Brad Pitt in *Interview with the Vampire*, and went on to star in *Bring It On*, *The Virgin Suicides* and *Crazy/Beautiful*, won the role of Mary Jane just a month before principal photography was due to begin, following a Berlin audition in which she and Maguire clicked; Raimi felt that the chemistry between them was a crucial aspect of the part. Willem Dafoe beat *Shadow of the Vampire* co-star John Malkovich and Nicolas Cage to the role of the Green Goblin; Academy Award® winner Cliff Robertson (Ben Parker) previously played the villanous 'Shame' in the *Batman* TV series; Rosemary Harris (Aunt May) and JK Simmons (J Jonah Jameson) previously worked with Raimi on *The Gift*, the director's last film before *Spider-Man*. Spider-Man's wrestling opponent 'Bonesaw' McGraw is played by real-life wrestler Randy 'Macho Man' Savage; Bruce Campbell, who plays the boxing promoter, starred in *The Evil Dead* trilogy and several other Raimi films – his reward being that his character gets to rechristen Parker's wrestling alter ego 'The Human Spider' to his more familiar nomenclature.

PRODUCTION: Although pre-production began shortly after Sony secured the rights in April 1999, and Raimi was active on the picture while he continued to film *The Gift* in Savannah, Georgia, shooting of *Spider-Man*'s first scene – Peter Parker feeling unwell in his bedroom – did not take place until 8 January 2001. It was the beginning of a punishing production schedule encompassing 100 sets, 165 stunt people, 150 pre-production personnel, and 200 visual effects technicians, many of whom faced the biggest challenge since Richard Donner's team had made us believe a man could fly back in 1978: making a convincing wall-crawler. The film-makers knew that if the screen Spider-Man was to be as acrobatic as his comic book counterpart, a fully computer-generated Spider-Man would be necessary for certain shots, one that had to be entirely convincing. The man responsible would be visual effects legend John Dykstra (*Star Wars*), who had pioneered the 'synthetic stuntman' idea on another comic book-inspired movie, *Batman Forever*. So impressed was executive producer Laura Ziskin with the results, she decided to play a trick on the Sony executives. 'I called up John Calley and Amy Pascal and told them we'd put Tobey [Maguire] in the suit and had him crawling up a building, and we'd shot a test and wanted to show them,' Ziskin recalled. 'We went to the screening room and I showed the test of CGI Spider-Man – they thought it was Tobey! Then I told them that was the computer-generated Spider-Man.'

Although the film comprised a vast number of effects shots, ranging from computer-generated cityscapes through which both the CG and live-action versions of Spider-Man could swing, to the Goblin's glider, all the way through to the climactic set piece at New York's Queensboro bridge – one of the most difficult sequences to film was the one in which the Green Goblin attacks a crowded Times Square during a pop concert and parade for the 'World Unity Festival'. For producer Ian Bryce, who was in charge of preparing and overseeing the sequence, it was more challenging than the recreation of the D-Day landings he had staged for Steven Spielberg's *Saving Private Ryan*. 'The Times Square sequence was the single most complicated sequence I've ever been involved in,' he said later. 'This was a nearly eight-minute sequence that was one of the structural centrepieces of the picture in terms of story and action, and it was complicated because we had to shoot in four separate components. There was filming in the real Times Square; we built a huge outdoor set in a parking lot in Downey, California, that represented the lower two or three floors of a portion of Times Square; we had an enormous balcony set piece for green screen photography; and there were computer graphics in post production at Imageworks.' As if this sequence wasn't daunting enough, it also happened to be the one selected for a cameo by Spider-Man creator Stan Lee.

COSTUME FITTING: Perhaps even more so than most comic book adaptations, costume designs were an essential part of *Spider-Man*, since although the character has had many different designs in forty years of comics, the red-and-blue webbed design is the best known. British costume designer James Acheson, a three time Oscar® winner with credits ranging from *Doctor Who* to *The Last Emperor* and *Dangerous Liaisons*, worked for more than five months, he and his 24-strong team creating dozens of prototypes before settling on the character's final look, for which the black web design is raised in latex to give it a three-dimensional effect. 'Spider-Man started off far more experimental and creative than the rather "traditional" version of the costume that appeared in the final film,' says Miles Teves, one of the conceptual artists drafted in to work on the designs. 'Berni Wrightson and I drew versions of Spidey with such features as irregular and asymetrical webbing, different external web-launcher apparatus of his wrists, a wide and far more wicked variety of Spider motifs for his chest and back, more radical and interesting break-ups of the red and blue parts of the suit, cool boots with strange futuristic-looking "grip pads" on the feet, and colour renderings emphasising an irridescent blue-black, and dark blood-red colour palette. I also drew a version that was completely black save for a red patch on the chest, rather like a black widow, that was very "Giger-like" and covered with glistening insectoid surface details. I was all for that one but it fell upon deaf ears.' Thus, said Acheson, 'After this very elaborate journey, we came back to the idea of making the costume look as much like the comic book as possible. It looks simple, but it was the hardest costume I ever had to make.'

The design of the Green Goblin's costume was equally problematic, since the comic book idea of a man in a Halloween-style goblin suit might prove laughable in a film as grounded in reality as *Spider-Man*. Countless designs were put forward by concept artists including Teves, Wrightson, Warren Manser and James Lima, until finally it seemed to make sense that the Green Goblin's glider and suit could have come from the same source – experimental military designs at Osborn's company, OsCorp. Thus, what had began as an organic mask and costume ensemble became a high-tech super-soldier suit, which perfectly complemented the glider. 'The Green Goblin started out to be more like a guy covered in "black-ops" hardware and pockets, covered in belts and holsters of all kinds – green of course,' says Teves. 'I was pushing for a blackish-green, but alas . . .! The head had a good beginning as Berni, Jim Lima and I drew dozens of very radical possibilities involving a very multilayered, more mobile and expressive approach,' he adds. 'Sadly, it turned into a giant Kabuki mask after we left the project.' The mask, it was decided, would be part of a larger collection of masks owned by Osborn himself. The resulting suit, comprising 580 separate pieces, was uncomfortable, and took thirty minutes to get into; nevertheless, actor Willem Dafoe insisted on wearing it during many of the film's most complex and dangerous stunts, since he felt it would give greater authenticity to the character than a stuntman.

Spider-Man's red and blue threads and the Green Goblin's green suit proved problematic for traditional blue and green screen effects shots, since although both characters were required to appear in costume together in numerous scenes, only Spider-Man could be present during green-screen backgrounds, while the Green Goblin was required to be shot in front of a blue screen; having both in shot together would have obliterated one or the other of the costumes. Following completion of his costume work on *Spider-Man*, Acheson moved on to another Marvel property, the feature film adaptation of *Daredevil*.

MUSIC: For *Spider-Man*'s richly textured musical score, Raimi chose composer Danny Elfman, who scored no fewer than *four* previous comic book adaptations: *Batman*, *Batman Returns*, *Dick Tracy* and *Men in Black*. 'The core of the orchestra might be the same on almost every film scoring that I do,' said Elfman, 'and then I'll make adjustments depending on the film. On *Spider-Man* I definitely loaded it more towards the brass. I knew it was gonna be a very percussive, brassy score. Most of the percussion's coming from my own playing – everything from trash cans to pots and pans to Northern Indian drums and African drums, and everything in between.' The film's featured soundtrack artists include The Strokes ('When It Started'), Sum 41 ('What We're All About' (Original Version)), Laibach ('Panorama'), Oleander ('Jimmy Shaker Day'), and Chad Kroeger and Josey Scott, whose title song, 'Hero', became an international hit; in the film, Macy Gray appears during the Times Square 'World Unity Festival' scenes, singing her song 'My Nutmeg Phantasy'. Even Paul Francis Webster and Robert Harris' classic *Spider-Man* theme ('Spider-Man, Spider-Man, does whatever a spider can' etc.) makes an appearance during the final end credits roll – though not on the soundtrack available on Columbia/Roadrunner/Island Def Jam/Sony Music.

CLASSIC QUOTES:

Peter Parker: 'Who am I? You sure you wanna know? The story of my life is not for the faint of heart. If somebody said it was a happy little tale, if somebody told you I was just your average ordinary guy, not a care in the world – somebody lied. But let me assure you: this, like any story worth telling, is all about a girl.'

Aunt May: 'Feeling better this morning? Any change?'
Peter Parker: 'Change? Yep! *Big* change!'

Uncle Ben: 'I went through exactly the same thing at your age.'
Peter Parker: 'Not exactly . . .'

Uncle Ben: 'With great power comes great responsibility.'

J Jonah Jameson: 'If we can get a picture of Julia Roberts in a thong, we can get a picture of this weirdo!'

Norman Osborn: 'Sorry I was late. Work was murder.'

Peter Parker: 'You don't trust anyone, that's your problem.'
J Jonah Jameson: 'I trust my barber.'

Green Goblin: 'Can Spider-Man come out to play?'

Green Goblin: 'This is why only fools are heroes – because you never know when some lunatic will come along with a sadistic choice. Let die the woman you love, or suffer the little children.'

DELETED SCENES: Devoted Spider-fans will have had an early glimpse of one of the film's deleted scenes in the very first teaser trailer, in which some bad guys escaping a robbery in a helicopter become ensnared in a giant spider web suspended between the twin towers of New York's World Trade Center. A record 1.9 million web-heads downloaded the trailer within a week of its on-line debut; however, following the destruction of the towers by terrorists on 11 September 2001, the teaser was withdrawn from circulation and the scene cut from the film. 'We were really pleased with [the footage] and included it as part of a montage in the movie when Spider-Man is developing his powers,' Laura Ziskin told *Empire*. 'But post-9/11 we took it out.' As a tribute to New Yorkers' resilience, Raimi added a shot showing defiant locals pelting the Green Goblin from the Queensboro Bridge, one shouting, 'You mess with one of us, you mess with all of us!'

Several other scenes which appeared in the shooting script were storyboarded but were never actually shot. These include:

- A scene between the school cafeteria and the fight with Flash, in which Parker examines his wrists, and accidentally shoots web on to the ceiling.
- A scene after Parker's first vertical climb, in which he visits a public library to research spiders on the Internet.
- An elaborate sequence in which the Green Goblin tracks down Fargas, the wheelchair-bound OsCorp board member who survives the Times Square attack, in an attempt to finish him off.
- A scene in which the Green Goblin attacks an OsCorp 'Weapons of the Future' industry show, featuring jet-packs, remote drones and robots.
- An action set piece, designed to take place while Parker is still getting used to his powers, in which Spider-Man attempts a dramatic hostage rescue on a subway train, only to fall foul of a SWAT team's tear gas.

Raimi did not have sufficient budget to put together the sequence of shots for the nightmare Parker experiences during his transformation; instead, he purloined shots from the title sequence, throwing in one from his own earlier film, *Darkman*, and an Italian horror film.

Conceptual artist Miles Teves talks of another element which, while never officially included in the script, would have put an interesting spin on things – the 'Goblin-ettes'. 'The costume designer James Acheson saw a recent painted Spider-Man comic featuring sexy goblin girls accompanying the Green Goblin on their own little sleds,' Teves explains, 'and saw an opportunity to try to convince the director to add the characters to the film for the sake of cool costumes! Berni [Wrightson] and I did a few pencils of the girls, some fetish-like, others more Vegas showgirl-like. Acheson was keen on circuitry motifs which I incorporated into tattoos on the girl's body. Alas,' he adds, 'Raimi gave the thumbs down.'

TRAILERS: Following the withdrawal of the World Trade Center teaser described above, a second preview was prepared, in which Tobey Maguire's narration ('Not everyone is meant to make a difference, but for me, the choice to live an ordinary life is no longer an option') is heard over a sequence which intercuts between the film's final shots of Peter Parker, and Spider-Man at work. As rock music plays over a series of 'money' shots featuring Spidey, Mary Jane and the Green Goblin, mainly from the Queensboro Bridge sequence, a caption card – 'THIS SEASON' – leads into a series of shots intercutting between separate caption cards featuring the legend 'TURN YOUR WORLD UPSIDE DOWN' and the title. Finally, Mary Jane sees Spider-Man in the rain, and tells him, 'You are amazing.'

POSTERS: Like the teaser trailer, the early posters put out for *Spider-Man* – featuring Spider-Man on the World Trade Center – also fell foul of the events of 9/11, and were withdrawn by Sony. Several other posters were produced, however, featuring Spider-Man in several classic poses: swinging through New York, crawling up a building, or looking out at the city from behind a building. In each of the posters, the city has the same yellow-tinted look. Two highly effective posters were produced for France, one featuring Spidey's hand at the centre of a web, the other a close-up of his eye. In some territories, separate posters were produced featuring the Green Goblin flying his glider over the city.

TAG-LINE: 'Go for the ultimate spin!'

WHAT THE PAPERS SAID: *Variety*'s Todd McCarthy damned *Spider-Man* with feint praise, describing it as 'a perfectly serviceable early summer popcorn picture that will satisfy its core teen constituency and not displease general viewers looking for some disposable entertainment' and 'a competent film that's critically lacking in true inspiration or a poetic imagination that would take it to an exciting level'. In the UK, *Sight and Sound*'s Kim Newman praised the film's successful thematic and stylistic translation of the comic book, but noted that, 'like too many first films in superhero franchises, *Spider-Man* doesn't quite hold together: the story hits all the emotional beats, but the action too often devolves into the cartoonish contortions of a pair of high-flying opponents, with plot leaps patched over by speech balloon-style expositions'. The tabloids were more complimentary, with The *News of the World*'s Jonathan Ross stating that *Spider-Man* had 'raised the game for every single blockbuster'.

BOX OFFICE: Although *Spider-Man* opened at cinemas in Malaysia at midnight on 30 April 2002, the film officially debuted at the US box office on 3 May 2002, almost exactly forty years after the web-head made his first appearance in the pages of *Amazing Fantasy*. The film scored the biggest weekend opening in history, grossing $114,844,116 – the first film ever to gross more than $100 million on its weekend debut – and subsequently climbed to $200 million in just nine days, $300 million in 22 days, and $403.7 million overall. With record-breaking openings in almost every territory in the world, *Spider-Man*'s worldwide gross reached in excess of $800 million, placing it among the five most successful films of all time. The future of the franchise was assured.

AWARDS & NOMINATIONS: *Spider-Man* received nominations in the category of Best Visual Effects at both the Academy Awards® and BAFTA awards.

CONTROVERSY: In the fall of 2002, barely six months after *Spider-Man*'s US release, eighty-year-old Spider-Man creator Stan Lee filed a lawsuit against Marvel, claiming that he had not received due remuneration for the character's big-screen incarnation. Lee had reportedly signed a 1998 agreement with the company, his employer since 1939, entitling him to a ten per cent share of profits from TV and film exploitation of his characters – including $10 million for the *Spider-Man* movie. Marvel responded by claiming that it, too, had yet to receive any profit participation from the billion-dollar blockbuster.

TRIVIA: When Peter is attempting to spin his web for the first time, he uses two other comic book characters' catchphrases: 'Up, up and away!' (Superman) and 'Shazam!' (Captain Marvel). Superman is also referenced by Aunt May ('You're not Superman, you know') and – in a more direct reference to *Superman: The Movie* – in a shot in which Peter

Parker opens his clothing to reveal his Spider-Man outfit. Other comic book characters knowingly namechecked include Dr Conners (a.k.a. 'The Lizard'), *Daily Bugle* photographer Eddie Brock ('Venom') and Mendell Stromm ('Robot Master'). In the comics, Harry Osborn blames Spider-Man for his father's death, and later takes up the mantle of the Green Goblin.

It was Raimi's older brother Ted who introduced Sam to Spider-Man; Sam rewarded him with a cameo role in the film. Other cameos include Spider-Man co-creator Stan Lee and 1970s TV Spider-Man Nicholas Hammond, both of whom appear in the Times Square sequences; and, actress Lucy Lawless, star of the Raimi-produced TV series *Xena: Warrior Princess*. Spider-Man makes a cameo appearance of his own – in an out-take from *X-Men* (2000) featured on the *X-Men* DVD.

Uncle Ben drives a light beige 1973 Oldsmobile Delta 88. A similar car has appeared in every single one of Raimi's films – except, for obvious reasons, the period western *The Quick and the Dead*.

Although David Koepp receives sole screenplay credit, Oscar® winner Alvin Sargent (*Ordinary People*, *Unfaithful*) and Scott Rosenberg (*Things to Do in Denver When You're Dead*) contributed additional dialogue to several scenes.

In director Ang Lee's *The Ice Storm*, Tobey Maguire's character reads and discusses another Marvel comic, *The Fantastic Four*; Lee went on to direct the feature film adaptation of *The Hulk*. Rosemary Harris, who plays Aunt May, played Willem Dafoe's mother-in-law in *Tom and Viv*. Kirsten Dunst previously appeared in another comic book-inspired creation, *The Crow: Salvation*.

The Green Goblin's mask was inspired by one attached to the front of a possessed eighteen-wheeler truck in the Stephen King-directed movie *Maximum Overdive*. A similar mask appeared in Raimi's *Army of Darkness*.

SEQUELS & SPIN-OFFS: Tobey Maguire and Kirsten Dunst had already been signed up for two potential *Spider-Man* sequels when the first film began smashing box office records in May 2002, and Sony wasted no time in signing director Sam Raimi and announcing a tentative release date for *Spider-Man II*, a.k.a. *The Amazing Spider-Man*: 7 May 2004. With *Spider-Man* scribe David Koepp busy directing the Stephen King adaptation *Secret Window, Secret Garden*, *Smallville* creators Alfred Gough and Miles Millar, who also scripted *Shanghai Noon*, were commissioned to write the screenplay; before they could turn in their draft, however, *Spider-Man* scribe David Koepp swung back on to the project. 'David had an idea and agreed to take some time off from the other project to write the first draft,' Columbia Pictures chairperson Amy Pascal told *Variety*. 'Gough and Millar will then take his first draft and start working from there.' By September, however, Michael Chabon – author of such novels as *Wonder Boys* (the film version of which co-starred Tobey Maguire) and the comic book flavoured Pulitzer Prize winning-novel *The Amazing Adventures of Kavalier & Clay*, as well as an unproduced early draft of *X-Men* – had been tapped to write a new version of the script, retaining elements of the earlier drafts. 'I'm completely the man for the job,' Chabon told *Entertainment Weekly*. 'It's my destiny.'

In May 2002, MTV announced the production of *Spider-Man: The Animated Series*, a computer-animated series with Brian Michael Bendis – writer of the *Ultimate Spider-Man* comic, which put a fresh spin on Spidey's origin – as writer and executive producer, and a voice cast which included Neil Patrick Harris (*Doogie Howser, MD*), singer–actress Lisa Loeb (*The House on Haunted Hill*) as Mary Jane, with Michael Clarke Duncan (*Armageddon*) as 'The Kingpin', the character he plays in the *Daredevil* movie. 'The series is being created in a unique computer-animated style, providing a new look for the classic hero,' said Brett Gannon, president of Mainframe Entertainment, the animation company behind the show. 'Combining state of the art CG imaging (CG neon noire) processed in a classic feature animation style, the series will combine bright, lively abstract colours including a seemingly realistic neon-lit city of the immediate future.'

DVD AVAILABILITY: Virtually identical 2-disc DVD editions are available in both the UK (Region 2) and US (Region 1), each featuring a plethora of extras. As well as a widescreen (1.85:1), Dolby 5.1 transfer of the film, with two audio commentaries – one with Sam Raimi, producer Laura Ziskin and Kirsten Dunst; the other with the visual effects designer and key crew – disc one contains several multi-angle features, pop-up factoids relating to the film and the comics mythology, character files and DVD-ROM materials, two music videos ('What We're All About' and 'Hero'), trailer and TV spots. Split into two sections, covering the comic and the film, disc two comprises three documentaries, one about the comic book, two about the film; brief documentary profiles of Raimi and Danny Elfman; screen tests featuring Tobey Maguire and JK Simmons; an out-takes/gag reel; one gallery of *Spider-Man* art, and another of covers spanning four decades; a detailed look at Spidey's most famous foes and romantic relationships. The DVD also contains seven 'easter eggs' (hidden features), including a CGI 'gag reel', interviews with Spider-Man artists Todd McFarlane, John Romita and John Romita Jr.

FINAL ANALYSIS: James Cameron's unproduced version of *Spider-Man* and Sam Raimi's finished film share several elements, among them a sequence in which a post-bite Peter Parker has a nightmare. For years, fans of one of Marvel's most popular and arguably most interesting superheroes may have dreamed – or had nightmares – concerning how the long-gestating movie about their favourite web-slinger might turn out. Few could have imagined that screenwriter David Koepp and Sam Raimi, as accomplished as they are in their respective fields, would have pulled off the seemingly impossible feat of bringing Spider-Man to the big screen with such pizzazz, pleasing the fans and welcoming newcomers with equal success. While *Fight Club* director David Fincher had wanted to dismiss the origin story in an opening montage, in the manner of *Blade* (another comic book adaptation which Fincher almost directed), Koepp and Raimi took their time, introducing us to a geeky high school kid in love with the girl next door, and making us like them both long before a bite from a genetically altered spider changes Peter's destiny.

Raimi also chose wisely when it came to casting the film, eschewing stars in favour of talent, and finding the perfect Peter Parker in Tobey Maguire, and a perfect match for him in Kirsten Dunst. While the choice of the Green Goblin/Norman Osborn as Spider-Man's first foe seemed odd – Spider-Man has far more exciting foes, from Doctor Octopus to The Lizard, Electro and Sandman, all the way through to the PG-unfriendly Carnage and Venom – Parker's close relationship with Osborn, his best friend's father, made the encounter personal in a way that no other villain from the Marvel universe could, and allowed a 'love triangle' element to colour his relationship with Mary Jane. Few could doubt that Raimi made the right choice. While such choices are perhaps a testament to Raimi's own fondness for the character he superhero-worshipped as a boy, Bryan Singer's adaptation of an even more popular Marvel series had proven that objectivity is not an impediment to bringing a beloved comic book to the screen. Yet Raimi seemed to approach Spider-Man with a fan's desire to *get it right*. He did.

Although it took almost twenty years to reach the screen, Raimi's *Spider-Man* owes as much of a debt to Richard Donner's *Superman* as it does to Stan Lee, Steve Ditko, John Romita, Todd McFarlane and the other writers and artists who have shaped the Spider-Man stories over the years; Donner proved that if audiences care about the characters, and the fantastical story is grounded in the real world – elements missing from many of the comic book adaptations of the intervening years – even those who have never picked up a comic in their lives will respond. The film's record-breaking box office proves it, as surely as Sam Raimi and the rest of his team proved themselves the perfect people to bring our friendly neighbourhood Spider-Man to the big screen.

EXPERT WITNESS: 'When I came to make the film, because kids have a connection with him, I felt a responsibility. I wanted to put something on the screen that would be worthy of a kid's admiration. I knew that a lot of kids would come to this picture and, whatever we did, would point at the guy in the Spider mask and say, "I wanna be like him." So I wanted to make sure that a mother could take her kid to the movie and feel pretty good about what was up there.' – **Sam Raimi, Director**

Daredevil (2003)

(105 minutes)

Directed by Mark Steven Johnson
Produced By Arnon Milchan, Gary Foster and Avi Arad
Screenplay By Mark Steven Johnson
Executive Producers Stan Lee and Bernie Williams
Director of Photography Ericson Core
Production Designer Barry Chusid
Film Editors Dennis Virkler ACE and Armen Minasian
Costume Designer James Acheson
Co-Producers Kevin Feige and Becki Cross Trujillo
Visual Effects Supervisor Rich Thorne
Music Supervisor Dave Jordan
Music by Graeme Revell
Casting by Donna Isaacson CSA and Eyde Belasco CSA

CAST: Ben Affleck (*Matthew 'Matt' Murdock/'Daredevil'*), Jennifer Garner (*Elektra Natchios*), Colin Farrell (*'Bullseye'*), Michael Clarke Duncan (*Wilson Fisk/'Kingpin'*), Jon Favreau (*Franklin 'Foggy' Nelson*), Scott Terra (*young Matt Murdock*), Ellen Pompeo (*Karen Page*), Joe Pantoliano (*Ben Urich*), Leland Orser (*Wesley*), Lennie Loftin (*Manolis*), Erick Avari (*Nikolas Natchios*), Derrick O'Connor (*Father Everett*), Paul Ben-Victor (*José Quesada*), David Keith (*Jack 'The Devil' Murdock*), Frankie Jay Allison (*abusive father*), Joe J Garcia (*meat packer*), John Rothman (*Quesada's attorney*), Jim Fitzgerald (*ring announcer*), Casey McCarthy (*Angela Sutton*), Louis Bernstein (*judge*), Josie DiVincenzo (*Josie*), Jorge Noa (*NY cop*), Levett M Washington, Albert Gutierrez, Lakeith S Evans (*kids*), Stefanos Miltsakakis (*Stavros*), Pat Crawford Brown (*sweet old lady*), Carrie Geiben (*flight attendant*), Luke Strode (*little boy*), Bruce Mibach (*rookie cop*), David Doty (*drunken Englishman*), Ron Mathews (*sharpshooter*), Jack Kirby (*Kevin Smith*), Daniel B Wing, Jeff Padilla, Sonja Didenko (*Quesada's friends*),

Dan Brinkle, Jackie Reiss (*referees*), Stan Lee (*old man at crossing*), Greg 'Christopher' Smith (*SWAT leader*), Christopher Prescott (*policeman*), Ari Randall (*waitress*), John S Bakas (*Greek priest*), Greg Collins (*Fisk bodyguard*), Robert Iler, Chad Christopher Tucker, Jamie Mahoney (*bullies*), Jorn H Winther (*Stavros' friend*), Frank Miller (*man killed by pen*)

TITLE SEQUENCE: The camera swings around a virtual nocturnal New York cityscape, from building to building, the lights on the buildings forming what look like Braille letters, which in turn form into the principal credits. As the titles continue, sirens wail as the camera zooms into the round stained glass window of a church. Above, clinging to the steeple, is an injured man dressed in a crimson leather costume, a horned mask covering half his face: Daredevil. He drops down onto the floor of the church, where he is found by a priest who calls him 'Matthew'. As he lies injured, his life flashes before his eyes . . .

SYNOPSIS: Matthew, a twelve-year-old in the New York district known as Hell's Kitchen, is being picked on by three kids, who beat him up. He goes home to wake his father, a former prizefighter named Jack 'The Devil' Murdock, who puts him to bed, after assuring his son that he doesn't work for a criminal named Fallon. But Matt discovers his father's lie when he sees him roughing someone up in an alleyway; he runs – straight into a truck carrying biohazardous material, which spills into his eyes, blinding him. He wakes in hospital, unable to see, but with a heightened sense of hearing, touch and smell which provides a kind of 'radar sense' which allows him to 'see' in a different way. Although his new-found senses terrify him, he soon learns to control them. Matt's father hits the comeback trail, but he is killed outside a club after refusing to take a dive for Fallon; a red rose is left on his corpse. Matt trains his body and his senses, and, when he grows up, works as a lawyer by day, while prowling the rooftops at night as the costumed crime fighter known as 'Daredevil'. *New York Post* reporter Ben Urich is on his trail, however, in articles read avidly by Matt's friend and law firm partner, Franklin 'Foggy' Nelson, who has no idea that his blind colleague has a dual identity. One day, Matt meets a beautiful and athletic girl named Elektra Natchios, daughter of billionaire Nikolas Natchios, who is having problems with his business associate, the crime boss known as 'Kingpin', rumoured to control all of the crime in New York. While Matt and Elektra begin to fall in love, Kingpin hires a bald Irish hitman with perfect aim ('Bullseye') to kill Nikolas and his daughter. Bullseye kills Nikolas, injures Daredevil and makes Elektra think that Daredevil killed her father. Unaware that the objects of her love and hatred are one and the same person, Elektra retreats further into herself, obsessively training herself to kill Daredevil. Meanwhile, Urich finds a connection between Daredevil and Matt Murdock, and warns him that Elektra may be in danger. He has problems of his own, however: in a rooftop confrontation, during which he vainly protests his innocence, Elektra wounds Daredevil . . . only to discover her lover's face under the mask. Before she can react, Bullseye attacks her, stabs her in the stomach and leaves her for dead. He then pursues the wounded Daredevil into the church where we first encountered him. Another fight ensues, during which Bullseye reveals that it was Kingpin who killed Matt's father. As police surround the church, Bullseye is shot through the hands, and Daredevil throws him from the rooftop. He falls several storeys, landing on the bonnet of Ben Urich's car. Daredevil goes to face Kingpin, who is shocked to discover that Matt Murdock and Daredevil are one and the same. After another epic battle, Matt gets the drop on the much larger man, but cannot bring himself to kill the man who murdered the only three people he ever loved, because doing so will make him a bad guy. Kingpin vows vengeance even as the police arrive to arrest him for his criminal activities, and Matt returns to his rooftop vigil over the city, thanks in part to Ben Urich's decision not to reveal his identity. Meanwhile, Bullseye lies prone in a hospital bed, almost completely covered with bandages, with two policemen guarding his door. Despite his injuries, he still manages to pin a fly to a wall with a hypodermic needle.

ORIGINS: Almost a quarter century before Stan Lee and artist Bill Everett created blind superhero Daredevil, 'the man without fear', a character by the name of Daredevil appeared in Lev Gleason Publications' *Silver Steak Comics* #6. The creation of Charles Biro, this Daredevil's alter ego was a boomerang-throwing acrobat named Bart Hill, who had a handicap of his own: he was born mute. The character continued to appear in *Silver Steak Comics* until 1941, before earning his own title, *Daredevil Comics*, which ran until 1956. Eight years later, Lee and Everett's Daredevil made his first appearance in his own title during the same 'silver age' period which also saw the origins of Spider-Man, The Incredible Hulk, The Fantastic Four and The X-Men. Although Daredevil's 'origin story' – the archetypal accident with radioactive waste which imbues young Matt Murdock with superhuman powers (in this case enhanced senses of hearing, touch and smell), a parent killed by criminals (Murdock's father, prizefighter Jack 'The Devil' Murdock), a sworn dedication to justice – was hardly a major departure from other superheroes, Daredevil's powers came with a heavy price: total blindness.

As Lee wrote in his introduction to the collection of the first eleven issues of *Daredevil*, 'I had just run into the legendary Bill Everett, creator of Prince Namor the "Sub-Mariner", after having lost track of him for a number of years. Bill told me he'd like to try his hand at a new superhero. That was all I had to hear. Within minutes I had chewed Bill's ear off about our newest concept, a blind lawyer named Matt Murdock who was the world's greatest and most agile crime-fighting gymnast. I told him about Karen Page and 'Foggy' Nelson and about the weird and wild super-villains we were planning to unleash upon the happy hordes of Marveldom. Even before I stopped talking he had whipped out a pencil and was making preliminary sketches on some scrap paper. I knew he was hooked!'

His handicap aside, Daredevil was also different in other significant ways, as writer and artist Frank Miller – whose stewardship of the title during the 1980s was the foundation for its current popularity – remarked in the introduction to a collection of his best stories: 'He's got all the makings of a villain. He's a natural born rascal, a mischief-maker, and a scrapper. He's a liar, who wears a mask to betray the solemn oath he made his father a thousand times. He's a dangerous adept, gifted with a nearly superhuman talent for violence. He's a loner, a sinner, a lawyer who breaks the law. But Matt Murdock is no villain, and no victim. There's something strong inside him, passed from unknown mother and doomed father to son. Something tested by tragedy. Tempered by conscience. Honed by discipline. Something that holds back the bloodthirsty beast within and forces it to serve the cause of justice. Most of the time, anyway.' *Daredevil* ran uninterrupred for 380 issues, until 1998, when it was cancelled and immediately relaunched as a *Marvel Knights* title, with writer–director – and avowed comics fan – Kevin Smith reviving its popularity once again.

PREVIOUS INCARNATIONS: Although Daredevil made an appearance in the live-action television series *The Incredible Hulk*, and appeared with Spider-Man in his animated series, *Daredevil* marks his first cinematic appearance. It had long been rumoured, however, that Oliver Stone had been trying to make a film based on Frank Miller's Epic Comics mini-series *Elektra: Assassin*, but Stone's plans did not come to fruition before the character of Elektra was sold to Fox along with Kingpin and Bullseye, as part of the Daredevil package.

DEVELOPMENT: Initially optioned by Twentieth Century Fox, along with fellow Marvel Comics characters X-Men and the Fantastic Four, the *Daredevil* movie was being shepherded along at the studio by writer/producer/director Chris Columbus' 1492 Pictures, where Columbus and director Carlo Carlei (*The Adventures of Pinocchio*) had reportedly collaborated on a treatment. By 1998, as Marvel went into bankruptcy, Fox had let the rights lapse and put the project into turnaround. Upon learning that the rights were once again up for grabs, *Clerks* and *Chasing Amy* writer–director Kevin Smith – who was then writing a successful run of the *Daredevil* comic for Marvel – called his friends at Miramax. 'I called up Bob and Harvey [Weinstein] and said, "There's this great comic book. It'd be perfect for [Matt Damon] and he's familiar with it and he used to collect the comic and you could get Robert Rodriguez to direct it and I'll do a draft." And they said, "Great, let's do it." They started pursuing it, and Marvel's [chief executive officer] Avi Arad was asking for . . . a $60–70 million film with a $40 million marketing budget, [when] it's not really a special effects extravaganza – it's a blind guy in tights. There was just no way we were gonna pay that much for this movie and I said "Look, I'm with you – let it go." '

Meanwhile, another writer–director was circling the project. As writer of the comedy *Grumpy Old Men* and its sequel, and director of the tear-jerker *Simon Birch*, Mark Steven Johnson was not the most obvious choice to bring Daredevil to the big screen – except for the fact that he had been a fan of the character since boyhood. 'All I wanted in the third grade was to be Matt Murdock,' Johnson told *Variety*. 'I believed he was real. I'd watch the news with my parents, fully expecting to see him.' Even as a boy, Johnson knew what it was that set Daredevil apart from other comic book heroes. 'He's a real guy with real problems. He doesn't have the strength or web-spinning powers of Spider-Man, the brawn of The Hulk, or the healing powers of Wolverine. Daredevil is just a guy. If you shoot him he dies. His very humanity and flaws are the source of his moral dilemma. I'm reminded of the quote, "He who fights monsters must take care lest he become a monster." That's what is happening to Matt Murdock. He's realising that he's starting to become the thing that he's sworn himself to protect against.'

Johnson had already met with Fox to discuss the Columbus–Carlei screenplay. 'I read their draft, wrote meticulous notes, and told [Fox] what I'd do,' Johnson told *Variety*. 'They said, 'Great, when can you start writing?' I told them I couldn't. I was off to make *Simon Birch*, and just wanted to make sure [*Daredevil*] was good. They looked at me kind of funny.' By the time Fox's rights lapsed, Johnson had finished *Simon Birch* and was ready to begin pursuing the project once again – this time by having his producing partner, Gary Foster, bombard Marvel Comics CEO Avi Arad with phone calls. 'Gary truly drove me crazy,' said Arad. 'They were running from studio to studio, saying they had the rights. Finally, I met Mark. He had a love for Daredevil's universe that was unsurpassed.'

Johnson's commitment to the project was evident: he spent $7,000 of his own money on storyboards, and even camped outside one studio executive's office for two hours until he agreed to hear Johnson's pitch.

'I always believed in it,' Johnson told *SFX*, 'always loved it and always tried pitching it to people, and they would be, like, "A blind superhero?" They just couldn't get it. I'm like, "Well, that's what's so cool about him – he's handicapped." It's just unlike anything they've seen before.' It was only when Johnson turned in his own draft of the script that people started to understand where he was coming from. 'I did a bunch of drawings, just to show them what the world would look like and what radar sense would look like and everything else. Pretty soon people started to understand.' Finally, after six years of determined lobbying, Johnson got the gig. 'He was not the logical choice for this,' producer Gary Foster admitted to *Entertainment Weekly*. And yet, added Arad, 'He was decisive. He said, "This is what I want to do, and it's the *only* thing I want to do." ' The film was still a long way from being granted the 'green light' that would signal the studio was willing to go into production, however. Then, in summer 2001, Fox's *X-Men* opened to excellent business, and the studio finally overcame its doubts and put its faith in the man without fear. Although production was delayed from its original scheduled start date due to a Canadian actors' strike, the cameras finally rolled in March 2002.

CASTING: Edward Norton (*Red Dragon*), Guy Pearce (*Memento*), Vin Diesel (*The Fast and the Furious*) and Matt Damon (*The Bourne Identity*) were among the contenders for the title role, with Diesel nosing ahead as Fox's clear favourite. 'That's more of the untouchable superhero,' he remarked. 'The quips, the Schwarzenegger kinda vibe. That's not what I wanted.' The role ultimately went to Damon's friend Ben Affleck, a longtime Daredevil fan. 'Matt Murdock lost Elektra to Bullseye when I was just twelve years old,' Affleck had written in his introduction to the collection of nine issues written by Kevin Smith, in whose film *Chasing Amy* Affleck had starred. 'That saga [now known famously to those in the comics world as the 'Frank Miller Daredevils'] touched and moved me in ways I was then and still now am reluctant to admit, even to myself. I was fascinated by this man, this red-suited saint, who always seemed to end up a martyr. It was my own personal introduction into the world of personal ambiguity. It was a dark corner, a place where my sympathies were uncertain. It was a strange and wonderful place where true love was always tragic, heroes had a dark side, villains were roguishly likable and the best one could hope for was some sliver of redemption.' Smith introduced Affleck to Mark Steven Johnson at a meeting which – given that Affleck's role in *Gigli* appeared to rule him out of the lead role in *Daredevil* – was supposedly intended to discuss the possibility of Affleck playing the smaller role of Bullseye. No sooner had the meeting begun, however, than Johnson admitted he wanted Affleck for the lead. 'I said, "Look, I've got to be honest right away. I came here to talk you into playing Daredevil." ' The actor dutifully looked at Johnson's storyboards, listened to mood-setting music, listened to the pitch – and subsequently managed to move the *Gigli* schedule around to accommodate his fourteenth film in four years.

Jolene Blalock (*Star Trek Enterprise*), Mia Maestro and Rhona Mitra were among those who read for the past of Elektra, but it was Jennifer Garner, the Golden Globe winning star of TV's *Alias* (not to be confused with Marvel's *Alias* comic book), who ultimately nailed it. 'A lot of people were clamouring for the part,' noted producer Gary Foster. 'We saw people in Los Angeles, New York, Europe and Australia. We had always wanted to bring in Jennifer Garner to read, but she wasn't available because of her television series. Then schedule changes made it possible for her to meet with us. At that point we had seen hundreds of actresses, but when she came in to read we just knew: "There's Elektra." ' Said Arad, 'Jennifer has an ability to be so sweet and so pure looking, but then you dress her up, she's sexy and exotic. She's a real chameleon with her looks, acting styles and athletic ability. That was exactly what we were looking for in Elektra.'

Irish actor Colin Farrell (*Minority Report*) was not familiar with the *Daredevil* comic before the film-makers made him their target for the part of Bullseye, but quickly caught up in order to study the facial expressions and body movements of the comic book character. Farrell also practised sleight-of-hand techniques, and martial arts and fighting training.

When Academy Award® nominee Michael Clarke Duncan (*The Green Mile*) was cast, fans were curious to know why a black actor had been cast as the Caucasian crime boss Kingpin. 'The spirit of the character is much better served by going for the best person for the role instead of trying to match skin tones,' said Johnson. 'I'm confident even the most diehard comics fan will agree that Michael [Clarke Duncan] *is* Kingpin.' Indeed, although the comics' Kingpin stands 6 feet 7 inches and weighs 450 pounds, at 6 feet 5 inches and 340 lbs, Duncan was probably closer in physical stature to the character than any other actor in Hollywood.

Rounding out the cast are Jon Favreau (*Swingers*) as Murdock's friend and law firm partner Franklin 'Foggy' Nelson, Joe Pantoliano (*The Matrix*) as *New York Post* reporter Ben Urich, and David Keith (*U-571*) as Matt's father, Jack 'The Devil' Murdock. Finally, one-time *Daredevil* comic writer Kevin Smith makes a cameo appearance as a mortuary attendant, named Jack Kirby after one of the best-known Daredevil artists. 'Mark Steven Johnson was goodly enough to offer a brother a cameo in the *Daredevil* movie . . . to potentially ruin his picture with my ham-handed theatrics,' said Smith. Countered Johnson, 'Kevin is the reason I'm back into Daredevil. I'd been a fan of Daredevil my whole life, but at some point I lost interest until Kevin's "Guardian Devil" storyline came out. Then I got back into it in full force.'

PRODUCTION: When Daredevil creators Stan Lee and Bill Everett placed Matt Murdock in the Hell's Kitchen area of midtown Manhattan – situated between 34th and 59th Streets, from 8th Avenue to the bank of the Hudson River – the primarily Irish neighbourhood was a far cry from its current incarnation as a gentrified area which is home to artists, celebrities and upscale professional New Yorkers. Thus, production designer Barry Chusid chose to recall an earlier period when the neighbourhood earned its moniker. Some of Chusid's designs are closely linked to the work of visual effects supervisor Rich Thorne, whose team built a virtual area of Hell's Kitchen in the computer in order to render Murdock's extrasensory perception.

Just as Matt Murdock had begun an intense regimen of physical training in order to fight crime, actor Ben Affleck endured a similar regimen of fighting and fitness training when he was cast in the dual role. Working under stunt coordinator Jeff Imada and veteran British fight instructor Dave Lea, Affleck trained for three months in a variety of fighting styles. 'It was a new training regimen for Ben,' said Lea. 'I started with stretching and then hand-drills, stick-drills and kicking. Then we devised a combination of street fighting, jailhouse rock, hand fighting, various kung fu styles, and boxing styles. For Daredevil, every fight is different. He uses what he needs to use at the time, and he takes a hit as often as he gives one. Daredevil can be fluid and graceful, or just plain down and dirty.'

Although renowned martial arts specialist Cheung Yan Yuen (*Charlie's Angels*), who choreographed several of the film's major action set pieces, was impressed with the willingness of his stars to perform their own stunt work, Affleck and Garner did not share his confidence in their abilities. 'We have more stunt guys than actors,' Affleck remarked. 'Which is great, 'cause I'm not Jackie Chan. I didn't come into this with forty years of martial-arts training going "Stand back!" ' As for Garner, 'I feel so ignorant and behind,' she admitted. 'I'd like to just go to an island somewhere and twirl my *sais* for three straight months and *then* come back and finish the movie,' she added, referring to the twin daggers she wields as Elektra. Affleck wasn't so sure. 'She's fabulous,' he said. 'She's actually better at it than I am. She has had so much training from *Alias* and she's a dancer, so she shames me every time!'

Martial arts wasn't the only area in which Ben Affleck was required to train: he also needed lessons in how to portray a blind man convincingly. To this end, blind actor Tom Sullivan – whose life story served as the basis for the made-for-TV movie *If You Could See What I Hear* – served as a sight consultant to both Ben Affleck and Scott Terra, who plays the young Matt Murdock. 'My job was to teach Ben to be the best blind person on Earth,' said Sullivan, noting that Murdock's 'radar sense' allows him to 'see' more than the average blind person. 'We tried to set up a situation where Matt always has the capacity to be Daredevil, only he has to hide that from the world at large,' he added. In other words, 'As Matt, he has to remember to be "more blind" than he is.' Sullivan, a lifelong athlete and US Nationals wrestling champion, also worked closely with Affleck and his trainer, Dave Lea, in the techniques of close-quarter combat.

By the time production wrapped in the summer of 2002, Fox was so impressed by what it had seen – and, perhaps more significantly, by the box office takings of rival studio Sony's *Spider-Man*, which had put *X-Men* in the shade – that they agreed to increase *Daredevil*'s special effects budget. Nevertheless, Johnson knew his own superhero film was going to be very different to *Spider-Man*. 'Right now, *Spider-Man* is kind of a blessing and a curse, because if people are expecting that, they're going to be disappointed,' he said shortly before the film opened in February 2003. 'I always felt that Spider-Man is wish fulfilment and Daredevil is the repercussions of being a superhero.' Although both characters are from the Marvel Comics stable, both live in New York, and both were ordinary kids when they first began to exhibit superhuman powers, 'they're [from] very different worlds and they're very different *looking* worlds, too. We're doing a "bleach bypass" to the film which washes out a lot of the colour and gives it a grainy, gritty look. It's not the bright primary colours of something like *Spider-Man*. There is no purse-snatcher that you grab and you return the purse to the lady. It's not that kind of world. It's the kind of world where he's trying to do the right thing during the daytime and being a lawyer, but it's real life: rapists go free and killers get [away with murder]. It's not black and white. There are all these different shades of grey.'

COSTUME FITTING: Writer–director Mark Steven Johnson has always made his feelings about the Daredevil costume well known. 'You don't make a movie like *Daredevil* and change the costume,' he once said. 'You might as well be making *Random-Vigilante-in-New-York Guy*.' Yet Johnson has also admitted that the biggest battle he fought on the film related to Fox and Regency's inability to agree on the costume the crime fighter would wear. 'For a while, there was no costume at all, just a sweatshirt, hood and sunglasses; more of a hip hop, extreme-athlete type.' Added producer Gary Foster, 'We didn't want to do a spandex costume. We wanted this to be form following function, and to make sure that the suit had some protective value [since] Daredevil is mortal and he needs that protection.' According to film-maker and former *Daredevil* comic scribe Kevin Smith, the arguments resembled those which had dogged *Judge Dredd* since Sylvester Stallone had signed to play the lawman with the omnipresent helmet. 'Apparently the studio felt like, "We're paying Ben Affleck – why do we want to cover his face?" '

Thankfully, the first single image released from the film, in early 2002, told fans of the comic what they wanted to know: that *Spider-Man* costume designer James Acheson's Daredevil *looked* like Daredevil – sure, the costume was a deeper red, but the overall idea had been preserved intact, complete with red eyes and horns. But by the time shots began to emerge of Acheson's interpretations of Elektra and Bullseye – the cut of their cloth rather different from their comic book counterparts – fans were getting twitchy, putting Ben Affleck on the defensive: 'On the Internet, people hated the *X-Men* idea,' he told *Empire*, referring to the film's radical costume changes, 'and I was one of them – until it came out. It's one of those things where you just have to see it.' Added Garner, 'Jim Acheson has done an incredible job of making Elektra's costumes as cool as possible. All of our superhero looks have a real hip element to them and are not your average man – or woman – in tights. Mine is no exception to that.' While Daredevil and Elektra comics fans know the character from her signature long, red sash, the film-makers wanted a more functional, though equally sexy look. Elektra's 'assassin' costume is made of a material known as 'pleather', which is stretch vinyl embossed to have the texture of leather. She wears black to signify her state of mourning for her murdered father, while her costume carries Japanese *kanji* symbols signifying justice, victory and strength, and built-in sheaths to hold her *sais*.

MUSIC: With *Tank Girl*, *The Crow* and *Spawn* behind him, Graeme Revell was more than qualified to compose the score for *Daredevil*, his fourth comic book adaptation in less than a decade. For *Daredevil*'s guitar-heavy music, Revell was assisted by Mike Einziger, lead guitarist for the heavy rock group Incubus. The soundtrack features twenty new songs, by Fuel ('Won't Back Down'), The Calling ('For You'), Saliva ('Bleed for Me'), Seether ('Hang On'), Nickelback ('Learn the Hard Way'), The Drowning Pool featuring Rob Zombie ('The Man Without Fear'), Nappy Roots featuring Marcos Curiel of P.O.D. ('Right Now'), Moby ('Evening Rain'), Evanescence ('Bring Me to Life' and 'My Immortal'), Finger Eleven ('Sad Exchange'), Endo ('Simple Lies'), 12 Stones ('Let Go'), Chevelle ('When You're Reformed'), Hoobastank ('Right Before Your Eyes'), Paloalto ('Fade Out/In'), Revis ('Caught in the Rain'), Boysetsfire ('High Wire Escape Artist'), Autopilot Off ('Raise Your Rifles') and Graeme Revell and Mike Einziger's 'Daredevil Theme (Blind Justice Remix).'

CLASSIC QUOTES:

Matt Murdock: 'They say your whole life flashes before your eyes when you die. And it's true, even for a blind man. I grew up in Hell's Kitchen. The politicians and real estate developers call it Clinton now, but a neighbourhood, like everything else, has a soul, and souls don't change with a name.'

Matt Murdock: 'One day I took a shortcut home from school. What I saw I would never forget, because it would be the last thing I would ever see.'

Priest: 'A lawyer during the day, and then judge and jury at night. Is that what you want?'

Bullseye: 'I missed! I never miss!'

Elektra: 'I want revenge.'
Matt Murdock: 'Revenge won't make the pain go away. Trust me, I know.'

Kingpin: 'How do you kill a man without fear.'
Bullseye: 'By putting the fear in him.'

Kingpin: 'Is there anything else?'
Bullseye: 'Yeah. I want a bloody costume.'

Elektra: 'I want to look into the eyes of my father's killer as he dies.'

Bullseye: 'You're good, baby, I'll give you that. But me, I'm magic.'

Bullseye: 'He hired me to kill Natchios and gut your pretty girlfriend too. But me, I'm going for the hat-trick. I told him I'd do you for free.'

Matt Murdock: 'You killed the only three people I ever loved. Why?'
Kingpin: 'Business. That's all it ever is. Business. I was working for Fallon at the time. Your father was supposed to throw a fight. And your girl was in the wrong family at the wrong time.'

TRAILERS: The earliest 'teaser' trailer was primarily comprised of music and moody shots of Hell's Kitchen at night, seen from the point of view of the shadowy gargoyles on brownstone buildings . . . until one of the 'gargoyles' reveals itself to be a costumed hero – Daredevil. The music kicks up a gear, and there is a fast-cut montage of fighting, followed by a shot of Daredevil standing on top of another building – an image not dissimilar to the poster.

A second trailer begins in teaser mode, opening with Ben Urich showing a detective proof that Daredevil exists: by tossing a match on a 'double D' symbol left on the ground in a flammable liquid. As it catches fire, the trailer kicks in with more mystery surrounding the Daredevil, as discussed by Matt Murdock and Franklin 'Foggy' Nelson. A voice-over narrates as follows: 'He can hear it before it makes a sound . . . He can sense it before it happens . . . He can vanish before you realise he's there

. . . And he's the last person you'd ever expect.' Thus, the trailer reveals that Ben Affleck's character is blind – just as he meets Elektra. Following introductions to Kingpin and Bullseye, three captions appear – 'TAKE . . . THE . . . DARE' – followed by a montage of action sequences, a 'DD' caption, and finally a title.

A third trailer begins much like the teaser, with a pan across the rooftops of Hell's Kitchen buildings, and an introduction to Matt Murdock as he (Ben Affleck) narrates the trailer in voice-over: 'I prowl the rooftops and alleyways at night searching for justice. Blind justice. A guardian devil. When I was twelve years old, I had lost my sight. But I got something back in return. My remaining four senses function with superhuman sharpness. I can hear a whisper a block away. But the most amazing of all was a kind of "radar sense". Soon the world will know the truth. That one man can make a difference.' As a song by Evanescence kicks in, the trailer then introduces Elektra, Kingpin and Bullseye, and adds a more traditional voice-over narration: 'In a city ruled by fear . . . one man will face his greatest challenge . . . and a new hero will be born.' A few captions – 'TAKE . . . THE . . . DARE' – round off an impressive trailer, which manages to combine action, humour, romance, incredible fighting – and the best shots of Daredevil in action seen in any of the other marketing materials.

POSTERS: Although some 'teaser' posters were produced with a flaming 'DD' symbol, the main poster pictures Daredevil standing in the rain on the roof of a building with skyscrapers towering above into a fiery sky. The approach to the copy on the poster is bold: there is none (no tag-line, no 'Ben Affleck' banner), beyond the title, credit block, release date and web address. Another poster comps Elektra, Bullseye and Kingpin into an identical image, shifting Daredevil over in order to accommodate the three supporting characters. Although there is still no tag-line, Ben Affleck and Jennifer Garner's names now appear above the title – although, contractually speaking, only Affleck's was required.

WHAT THE PAPERS SAID: '*Daredevil* is a pretender in the realm of bona fide superheroes,' proclaimed *Variety*'s Todd McCarthy. 'Grimly going through the motions and resembling Marvel stablemate *Spider-Man* in too many ways, this franchise-hungry champion of the underdog brings no sense of fun to his pursuit of bad guys; it's just the fate he's stuck with. Charm- and humour-free exercise in pushing commercial buttons will ride a massive marketing push, a surfeit of Ben Affleck publicity, the current cache of Marvel, and audience hopes for Spidey-like thrills to boffo openings. But it's unlikely to be a film auds take to heart, which spells less than gangbuster biz in the long run.' 'The movie is actually pretty good,' admitted the *Chicago Sun-Times*' Roger

Ebert. 'Affleck and Garner probe for the believable corners of their characters, do not overact, are given semi-particular dialogue, and are in a very good-looking movie. Most of the tension takes place between the characters, not the props . . . [the actors] play their roles more or less as if they were real, which is a novelty in a movie like this, and Duncan in particular has a presence that makes the camera want to take a step back and protect its groin. The movie is, in short, your money's worth, better than we expect, more fun than we deserve.' In the UK, *Time Out*s Trevor Johnston noted that, 'since the storyline lays out confrontations in an unadorned straight line, the film has to make up in flashy post-*Matrix* wireworked fight choreography and slick nocturnal visuals what misses in surprise . . . Convincing in the physical demands of the role, Affleck persuades us of the pain of sightlessness and supersensitive hearing, although writer–director Johnson's scrappy construction fails him and everyone else . . . as the showdown approaches. Not unambitious, then, but most successful as a set-up for a sequel; the spadework's been done.'

BOX OFFICE: *Daredevil* opened in the US on 14 February 2003, grossing an impressive $45 million over the four-day Presidents Day weekend, more than doubling the previous record, and making *Daredevil* the second-highest February opener ever (after *Hannibal*). Overall, the film grossed $100 million in the US.

TRIVIA: Daredevil co-creator and executive producer Stan Lee makes a cameo appearance as an elderly man who is about to step into the path of oncoming traffic, only to be stopped – and thus saved – by a young Matt Murdock. Seminal Daredevil writer and artist Frank Miller also makes a cameo appearance as a man Bullseye kills with a pen.

The script namechecks several of Jack 'The Devil' Murdock's boxing opponents – Miller, Mack, Bendis – after key figures in the 29-year history of the *Daredevil* comic, while a lab assistant played by Kevin Smith is named 'Kirby'. Most charmingly of all, the rapist whom Murdock allows to be cut in half by a train is named 'José Quesada' in a tribute (of sorts) to *Daredevil* artist Joe Quesada.

SEQUELS & SPIN-OFFS: 'The good thing about a Marvel property is that they're franchise builders,' Avi Arad told *Entertainment Weekly*. 'So, yes, we're already working on *Elektra*, and you'll see a *Daredevil* 2 and possibly a third. It's a young cast and they won't be with us forever,' he added, 'but we absolutely plan for sequels. There are forty years of stories.' No wonder Fox signed up Ben Affleck, Jennifer Garner, Michael Clarke Duncan, Jon Favreau and Joe Pantoliano – in other words, every *Daredevil* star except Colin Farrell (whose character, Bullseye, survives the film) – for at least one sequel.

One storyline we won't be seeing in any future *Daredevil* sequel is one which pairs up – or squares off – Daredevil and fellow New York costumed crime fighter Spider-Man. 'In the comic books, you know, Spider-Man and Daredevil have been at it,' Michael Clarke Duncan pointed out to *Entertainment Weekly*. 'I'm telling you, Tobey Maguire and Ben Affleck in the same movie, *that* would be a big movie. And the Kingpin, he's the enemy of both.' Affleck was quick to shoot down the possibility, however. 'The thing that's fucked up, actually, is that Marvel sold the properties to different studios. Spider-Man is the property of Sony, and Daredevil is the property of Fox and Regency. They're stuck in different universes.' Besides, he added, 'At this point, I don't think the people who made *Spider-Man* feel as though they need any help.'

DVD AVAILABILITY: Although the release of *Daredevil* on DVD was not scheduled at press time, Johnson is a self-confessed DVD buff who promises that the disc will contain 'everything' – even, if the director has his way, PG-13 and unrated versions of the film. 'From the minute Ben showed up to get a plaster cast of his face to the first costume training, we have hundreds of hours of stuff,' he told *Entertainment Weekly*.

FINAL ANALYSIS: Released little more than half a year after the billion dollar *Spider-Man* movie, based on Marvel Comics' best-known superhero, *Daredevil* was always going to be an interesting prospect, based as it was on a character with virtually no recognition among non-comics readers. As Mysterio tells Daredevil in Kevin Smith's terrific nine-issue *Daredevil* series, 'Unlike Spider-Man, yours was not a reputation that was known the world over.' Yet on the surface, Spider-Man and Daredevil have much in common: both were born to Stan Lee at Marvel Comics, within a year of each other; both received their unearthly powers at tender ages; both live in boroughs of New York; the death of a parent (real or surrogate) is instrumental in both characters' decision to fight crime; both are often misunderstood by the press and the authorities; over the years, they have fought the same bad guys; both have had lady loves killed by supervillains; both are conflicted about the validity of their vigilantism; both are prone to injury; and so on.

Despite the similarities of their titular heroes, however, Sam Raimi's *Spider-Man* and Mark Steven Johnson's *Daredevil* are light and shade. Where *Spider-Man* is all daytime, sun-bleached skyscrapers of Manhattan, *Daredevil* is the rain-soaked, nocturnal New York of Hell's Kitchen. When we first encounter *Daredevil*, he is near death – and his situation gets worse as the film progresses: his mother is (presumed) dead; his father is a washed-up prizefighter/palooka; he gets the shit beaten out of him as a kid, and again as a superhero; his 'gift' is also a curse; he's been blind since the age of twelve, but can hear so much he can only find peace underwater in an isolation tank; his girlfriend leaves him because she doesn't know where he goes at night; he falls in love with a girl who winds up wanting to kill him, and later dies in his arms . . . you get the picture. In many ways, *Daredevil* is everything the first *Batman* should have been – and would have been, if Warner Bros hadn't been more interested in selling toys than tickets.

That *Daredevil* succeeds is largely thanks to Mark Steven Johnson, one of the very few comic book movie directors who filmed his own screenplay, whose pursuit of the project showed superhuman determinations, and whose knowledge of his subject matter is seemingly second to none – like Sam Raimi, he even knows which digressions he can make from the source material without betraying it. It also helps that Johnson's leading man, Ben Affleck, is also a lifelong Daredevil fan; his emotional and physical investment in his dual role is evident throughout. The film has much else to recommend it: among the actors, Jennifer Garner's Elektra is electric, Michael Clarke Duncan's casting as Kingpin is inspired, and Colin Farrell's Bullseye is right on target; behind the camera, Ericson Core's photography is moody and murky, and production designer Barry Chusid's Hell's Kitchen is suitably hellish; Johnson's direction is assured, even if his dialogue leaves something to be desired.

Where the film fails is in the climactic series of showdowns, which reek perhaps a little too much of comic book structure: Elektra vs Daredevil, Bullseye vs Elektra, Bullseye vs Daredevil, Daredevil vs Kingpin, the audience vs the sandman . . . the fight with Kingpin is particularly disappointing, perhaps because *Spider-Man* had already used the old 'I'm-not-going-to-kill you-oops-you-died-anyway' trick twice – first when a robber accidentally falls to his death, and later when the Green Goblin is killed by his own sled. When Daredevil leaves Kingpin alive – after he has discovered Daredevil's secret identity, no less – it is unsatisfying in the wake of what has gone before: it is almost as though the audience needs as much cathartic payback as Murdock himself, whereas the studio (presumably) needs Kingpin alive – indeed, Johnson adds insult to injury by fudging the deaths of Bullseye and Elektra in order to pave the way for sequels and spin-offs, an unnecessary conceit given that Elektra's death in the *Daredevil* comic was one of the character's best career moves (*Elektra: Assassin* came later). These are minor gripes, however. Like its titular hero, *Daredevil* succeeds because it believes in itself, and is determined to succeed. And although the film failed to capture *Spider-Man* or *X-Men* sized audiences, its $100 million US gross suggests that the world has not seen the last of *Daredevil*.

EXPERT WITNESS: 'The movie's heavy; the movie's dark. It's very much the real world of a superhero, what it would really do to your body and your head. It's interesting. The scene that I always think about is when he comes home at night – it's so lonely and it's so kind of heartbreaking to see this guy come home, there's no Batcave, there's no millionaire, no Alfred, no one he can talk to. You see him taking off his clothes in this shitty little brownstone in Hell's Kitchen. He's covered in scars, he's popping painkillers, there's an answering-machine message he's playing with his girlfriend breaking up with him – "Where do you go at nights? I don't even know who you are." It's so real.' – **Mark Steven Johnson, Writer/Director**

Hulk (2003)

Directed by Ang Lee
Written by James Schamus
Produced by Avi Arad, Larry J Franco, Gale Anne Hurd and James Schamus
Executive Producers Kevin Feige and Stan Lee
Associate Producers Cheryl A Tkach and David Womark
Director of Photography Fred Elmes
Edited by Tim Squyres
Production Designer Rick Heinrichs
Music by Mychael Danna
Costume Designer Marit Allen
Casting by Avy Kaufman and Franklyn Warren

PRINCIPAL CAST: Eric Bana (*Dr Robert Bruce Banner/'The Hulk'*), Jennifer Connelly (*Betty Ross*), Nick Nolte (*Dr David Banner*), Brooke Langton (*Jennifer Sussman*), Sam Elliott (*General Thunderbolt Ross*), Josh Lucas (*Major Glenn Talbot*)

ORIGIN: The creation of Stan Lee and Jack Kirby, The Incredible Hulk made his debut in his own title in 1962, which detailed his origin as a scientist named Dr Bruce Banner who is caught in the blast of a gamma radiation bomb of his own invention, and subsequently discovers that (at various times, and for various reasons) he turns into a gigantic green (originally – due to a printer's error – grey) behemoth with increased strength but diminished intellect. Originally, Banner became The Hulk only at night, giving the Jekyll and Hyde story a lycanthropic twist; this was soon dropped, however, initially by having Banner expose himself to gamma radiation for a second time, allowing him to transform into The Hulk by day, but later the transformations became triggered by stress –

typically anger. Perhaps surprisingly, *The Incredible Hulk* did not immediately catch on; indeed, the title was cancelled in 1963 after just six issues, before re-appearing in *Tales to Astonish* #60, retitled 'Incredible Hulk' from #102 (1968). *Rampaging Hulk* (retitled *Hulk* in 1978) was launched to coincide with *The Incredible Hulk* TV show, running 27 issues from 1977 to 1981. *Rampaging Hulk* was relaunched in 1998, but cancelled the following year after only six issues. *Incredible Hulk* was also cancelled in 1999, but relaunched almost immediately as *Hulk*, which became *Incredible Hulk* once again in 2000.

PREVIOUS INCARNATIONS: The first screen appearance of The Hulk came as early as 1966, just four years after his less than incredible comic book debut. *The Incredible Hulk* aired as part of Grantray–Lawrence Animation's Marvel Superhero's animated series, which ran from 1966 to 1967, with Paul Soles as Bruce Banner and Bernard Cowan as the narrator.

The Hulk's first live-action incarnation came ten years after the cancellation of the first animated series. The two-hour TV movie, *The Incredible Hulk*, was first broadcast on 4 November 1977, and was quickly followed by a second, subtitled *A Death in the Family* (a.k.a. *Return of the Incredible Hulk*), both starring Lou Ferrigno as the green Goliath and Bill Bixby as Dr Banner, who was renamed David for the show though Banner used a variety of pseudonymous surnames throughout the series which followed, beginning in the spring of 1978. Eighty-one episodes (not including the TV movies) were broadcast before the show was cancelled in 1982. Three further made-for-TV 'reunion' movies were produced – *The Incredible Hulk Returns* (1988), *Trial of The Incredible Hulk* (1989) and *The Death of The Incredible Hulk* (1990) – all of which were directed by Bixby himself. His association with the show was such that no further TV movies were produced following his death in 1993.

As far as executive producer (and Marvel executive) Kevin Feige is concerned, the television show, not the comic, is the reason that awareness of The Hulk is so high. 'My grandmother had no idea who the X-Men were, but she knows The Hulk,' he told *Cinefantastique* by way of example. 'There is name recognition with The Hulk, which is second only to Spider-Man in terms of non-comic readers.' Michael France, one of the many screenwriters who worked on the *Hulk* movie, agrees: 'I think the main reason The Hulk has survived as a character in the greater public mind is the work Bill Bixby did on that show. It was very realistically done. It primarily showed how Banner dealt with his Hulk problem, and he reacted the way you or I would – he was scared to death of the whole thing. It would have been very easy for the people who did that show to camp it up . . . but Kenneth Johnson and Bill Bixby both wanted to keep the show grounded in reality. It's funny,' he adds, 'when I was a kid and I saw it, I hated it because I wanted to see *Tales to Astonish* brought to life which is impossible on a TV budget or even a feature budget now. But I was very surprised how good it was when I watched it again before getting into the script. Just that one line "Don't make me angry. You wouldn't like me angry," the way he says it, it's both a threat and a plea at the same time. And as that bit of dialogue reverberates through every promotion for the new movie, let's not forget [that] Kenneth Johnson wrote that line.' Says Johnson, 'It is odd, isn't it, that with all the feature [script]writers and ten years of writing, the line they use in the promos is the one I wrote twenty-five years ago. Very flattering indeed.'

Before the spate of Marvel movies which appeared between 2000 and 2003 – *X-Men*, *Spider-Man*, *Daredevil* and *Hulk* – Stan Lee had often said that the pilot for *The Incredible Hulk* was his favourite screen adaptation of a Marvel Comics character. 'It was done by Kenneth Johnson, who's a brilliant writer/producer/director,' he told the website *IGN Filmforce* in 2000, 'and he made it an intelligent, adult show that kids could enjoy. He took a comic book character and made him somewhat plausible. Women liked it and men liked it and teenagers liked it. It was beautifully done. He changed it quite a bit from the comic book, but every change he made made sense. In the comics, when The Hulk talked he'd go, "Me Hulk! Me smash! Hulk kill!" That type of thing. Well, that would have been corny as hell on the screen. He left that out; he didn't have The Hulk talk at all. He made Bill Bixby, playing Bruce Banner, the star . . . You only really saw the Hulk for about five minutes in an hour show. You saw him for about two and a half minutes in the beginning and about two and a half minutes towards the end. The rest of it was Bill Bixby. It was like *The Fugitive*. It was a real, great, suspenseful, adult show with enough of the Hulk to please the young kids.' The two-hour pilot was released theatrically in some European territories.

In 1982, shortly after the cancellation of the live-action series, a new animated version of *The Incredible Hulk* appeared, starring Michael Bell as the voice of both Bruce Banner and The Hulk. It lasted thirteen episodes before it was cancelled. In 1996, a new half-hour animated series debuted on network television, with a voice cast which had Lou Ferrigno reprise his most famous role, and co-starred Neal McDonough and Luke Perry. Twenty-one episodes were produced before the series' cancellation in November 1997.

DEVELOPMENT: Universal Pictures first became interested in The Hulk around 1994, at which point screenwriter Michael France (*Cliffhanger*, *Goldeneye*) remembers meeting with Stan Lee and the producer then assigned to the project, who, France says, 'wanted a Hulk versus terrorists storyline' which he felt was 'terrible'. By late 1996, writer Jonathan Hensleigh (*Die Hard with a Vengeance*, *Armageddon*) and his wife, *Aliens*, *Terminator* and *Armageddon* producer Gale Anne Hurd, had signed on to the project, for reasons she explained to *Cinefantastique*: 'Hulk is the antithesis of a superhero, because it's Bruce Banner's inner nature; his rage that comes out. Consequently, he's very character-driven. This is a character fighting the rage inside of him; the demons all of us have . . . Hulk is not a villain either,' she added. 'He's not The Joker or The Riddler. Consequently, it's important to be able to identify with the character the way you identify with Frankenstein's monster or King Kong. Hulk isn't a character with a villainous agenda; he only attacks when attacked. And he's not really aware of his own strength.'

The plan was to feature a fully CGI rendering of The Hulk created by Industrial Light + Magic, rather than an actor playing Dr Banner's alter ego, as in the television series. For the second time, Michael France – who had since written *The Fantastic Four* for Fox – was invited to write the script. 'Marvel was happy with my stuff and they convinced Universal to hire me basically over the phone,' France recalls. 'I had about a twenty minute phone conversation with Jonathan Hensleigh, who had signed on as a producer, and we made a deal immediately. Contracts were signed, J' Johnston [*Jumanji*] was courted to direct, everyone was happy . . .' And then France was fired, before he had written a single page. 'I still have no idea why,' he says. 'Somehow, the powers that be decided that Hensleigh should write the script – J' Johnston and Hensleigh worked together before on *Jumanji*, so I suppose that was the connection.' Since he was fired without a reason, France got paid – but he still wanted to write the script. It would be several years until he had his chance.

In July 1997, Johnston quit the project, paving the way for Hensleigh to consider *The Hulk* as his directorial debut. John Turman (*The Crow: Stairway to Heaven*) wrote two drafts, the second of which was rewritten by Zak Penn (*Last Action Hero*); then Hensleigh himself started from scratch, coming up with a brand new storyline and set-up, which featured Dr Bruce Banner as a geneticist developing new forms of life that could survive long range space travel, who, prior to the accident which will turn him into The Hulk, performs some experiments with gamma-irradiated insect DNA on convicts – only to turn them into insect men who run amok. Hensleigh subsequently rewrote the script with JJ Abrams (future creator of the hit TV show *Alias* and a 2002 draft of *Superman*) and then Scott Alexander and Larry Karazewski (*Ed Wood*, *The People vs Larry Flynt*) were drafted in to rewrite Hensleigh's second draft, though Hensleigh was still attached as director.

Then, in March 1998, Universal put *Hulk* in turnaround, claiming that the $100 million budget – with $20 million already spent in development – was more green than they were willing to spend. This made Hensleigh angry – very angry. 'They knew the budget for the last six months,' he told *Premiere*. 'Now we're talking about chipping off $20 to $25 million. I have to go into a dark corner and re-dream the script to get as much entertainment value within those constraints.' Although he remained attached to the project at that point, the writing was on the wall when he said, 'If anyone in this industry thinks that I am going to work on *Hulk* indefinitely, they should seek psychiatric help.' With Hensleigh out of the picture, Michael France was invited aboard for a third time. 'This time it took a lot more than a phone call,' he says. 'I had to do about eight months of treatments and conference calls with Avi Arad, [Marvel executive] Matt Edelman, Gale Hurd, and the Universal executives Mary Parent and Stacy Snider. There seemed to be a lot of insecurity about which way to go,' he adds. 'My perspective on this is, somewhere, someone within the Universal hierarchy wasn't sure if this was a science fiction adventure, or a comedy, and I kept getting directions to write both. I think that at some points when I wasn't in the room, there may have been discussions about turning it into a Jim Carrey or Adam Sandler movie. I was asked to come up with a lot of jokes about the so-called "wish fulfilment" aspect of it – you know, the guy at the burger counter who blows your order and is rude to you when you complain . . . wouldn't you like to Hulk out and get him? Well, yeah, maybe I would – I just didn't want to write a lot of that stuff.'

France's work on the script was informed by his thorough knowledge of the various comic incarnations of The Hulk. 'I felt like something had to be done a little differently with Banner as a character,' he explains. 'All the previous scripts kind of used the 1960s version of Banner – you know, an amiable, nerdy genius. I knew too that there were a lot of Banner/Hulk gags in previous drafts that were highly predictable – that is, Banner gets shoved around, then he says, "You wouldn't like me when I'm angry," and he tosses a bully over a wall. I really wanted to do something different to humanise Banner. I was aware of some of the changes Peter David made in the 1980s comics – specifically, that Banner had an abusive father and that he carried around a lot of psychological baggage from that. I took that aspect and tried to build on it. I also wanted to take Banner all the way out of a military setting. I made him a scientist looking into peaceful uses for gamma rays – specifically, medical uses to rebuild cells from the inside out. I made Banner a guy who was aware of his horrible family history – that his father was abusive, and that he killed his mother – and his whole life, he's trying to convince himself, "That's not me – I'm not like that", and his whole life, he's failing, because he has terrible spells of anger. So he's worried about containing his anger *before* he has the gamma ray accident. Once it does happen, The Hulk is his greatest nightmare of what he could be – ten feet tall and six feet wide – and he has to confront who he really is. In fact, I made a point of playing around with the "Don't make me angry" line – because once I thought about it, it sounded like something a bully would say. I made this something Banner's father would say to him, right before beating the hell out of him. I wrote a scene that put a spin on that line: Banner is in a restaurant, and he's been ducking confrontation to avoid Hulkouts – but he starts to realise that maybe he has to avoid internalising anger. He has to confront someone when it's necessary. When he sees a family sitting at a booth, and the father is smacking his kids for no reason, and this abusive father is saying, "Don't make me angry – you wouldn't like me angry," it just brings up too many memories for Banner – he walks over and confronts the guy, who then throws a punch at Banner. Banner catches the punch, stares him down, and tells him, "*Make* me angry. I really want you to." The guy backs down, goes back to the table, and apologises to his son. Banner handled it without a Hulkout or even a near Hulkout.' France's drafts, delivered in late 2000 and early 2001, were well received by Universal and Marvel. '[They were] very, very excited,' he says. 'I remember Mary Parent telling me that I turned in the first script that gave them a Bruce Banner they could believe in as a character. That was my biggest goal, so I was happy to hear that from her. And I always enjoy working with Avi. He really does know a lot about the characters, and he wants the movies to be spectacles that are grounded in realistic characters. I don't think I've ever had a creative conversation with him that we couldn't intelligently, easily resolve within about fifteen minutes.'

Despite the producers' and executives' enthusiasm for France's script, however, it continued mutating at a gamma-irradiated pace. Michael Tolkin (*Deep Impact*) was subsequently brought in to rewrite France's script, following which David Hayter (*X-Men*) wrote yet another draft which, according to France (who read them all during the Writers Guild of America arbitration to establish which writers deserved screen credit), mostly melded his work with Tolkin's. 'David Hayter did a kick-ass job on the script,' Kevin Feige told the website *Comics2Film*, noting that Hayter had used the France and Tolkin drafts 'as a sort of guide point'. 'We love the script,' he added, 'Universal wants to make it and we want to make it. We're just trying to figure out when the best time to do that is.' Even more exciting news came in early 2001, when Academy Award®-winning director Ang Lee (*The Ice Storm*, *Crouching Tiger, Hidden Dragon*) became attached to the project, although he was reported to be less than enamoured with the latest script, and brought in his regular writing and producing partner James Schamus to pen another draft. 'David [Hayter]'s script was the inspiration that got Ang and I into the project,' Schamus admitted, but went on to say that the changes he had made at Lee's behest were significant. 'Believe me, Ang leaves no rock unturned,' he said. Although he assured fans that 'what people are gonna see onscreen is the Hulk that they recognise from the comic books', he also admitted the influence of the TV show. 'I'd have to say that particularly the tone of the series is something that has stayed with me for many, many years,' he said. 'There was something really brooding and intelligent and smart about Bill Bixby's presence and the way that the show used it and I hope that we've managed to keep a great deal of that.'

CASTING: Before aptly named Australian actor Eric Bana (*Chopper*, *Black Hawk Down*) signed to play Bruce Banner in September 2001, it was widely reported that Billy Crudup had been offered but turned down the role, which had also previously been linked to Johnny Depp and Steve Buscemi. Bana, a fan of the *Incredible Hulk* television series, rather than the comic, told *Empire*, 'I think The Hulk is the only reluctant superhero. Superman puts on the cape, Spider-Man puts on the suit, and Batman goes into the cave, but The Hulk has no control, and for me that's an awesome prospect.' As for Ang Lee, 'He's interested in making soulful pictures and I think he sees The Hulk as that in a comic style. Ang's up to a challenge and I'm really up to being on that ride with him.'

The Rocketeer and *Requiem for a Dream* actress Jennifer Connelly was still several months away from winning an Academy Award® (Best Supporting Actress, for *A Beautiful Mind*) when she signed to play Bruce Banner's girlfriend Betty Ross. 'It's really interesting and ambitious,' she said of Ang Lee's approach to the material. 'He's not talking about a guy running around in green tights and a glossy fun-filled movie for kids. He's talking along the lines of tragedy and psychodrama . . . the green monster of rage and greed, jealousy and fear in all of us.'

Sam Elliot (*We Were Soldiers*) as General Thunderbolt Ross, Betty's father and Banner's nemesis; and Nick Nolte (*48 Hrs*) as Bruce Banner's father; Josh Lucas (*Sweet Home Alabama*), who appeared with Connelly in *A Beautiful Mind*, as a childhood friend of Betty Ross; and Brooke Langton (*The Replacements*) round out the principal cast.

PRODUCTION: Principal photography began in March 2002, with California locations including San Francisco (the principal setting of the film), to Berkeley, Los Angeles, China Lake, Mountain Home State Park, Porterville, Yermo, Springville and Treasure Island, with additional filming in Arizona and on the Universal Studios lot. When filming finished in August 2002, Lee chose not to leave the special effects team to work in his absence, deciding instead to stay on and work in tandem with Industrial Light + Magic in order to direct Bruce Banner's computer-generated alter ego as if he were a live-action character. 'I'm a hands-on kind of person,' he explained to *Entertainment Weekly*. 'This way, I can never know what can't be done.' As for the look of the CG Hulk, Lee added: 'I didn't want a big, lumbering dinosaur. I wanted swiftness. I wanted Jackie Chan in Arnold Schwarzenegger's body.' Of Lee's approach to the material, producer Gale Anne Hurd told *Cinefantastique* that 'his attention to detail, his attention to the emotional element, the dramatic element of the character, is apparent in every frame of the film. Everything reinforces choices that are consistent with the dramatic choices of the film.' She added 'The layers are just unbelievable. It's not simply, "How can we make this shot cooler?" It's, "How can we make this frame, this scene, this choice of angle, reinforce the theme of the movie?" That's just unheard of in a movie that's this big.' Speaking to attendees of a comic convention shortly after principal photography wrapped, she also stated: 'I can absolutely vouch that Ang Lee has preserved The Hulk, a project I've been working on with Avi [Arad] for twelve years. I can't tell you how stunning Ang's vision [is] for this film, which is true to the comic books, true to the characters and true to everything that makes a movie great. He has been a man on a mission, and the mission is to bring you the very best *Hulk* anyone could ever imagine.'

MUSIC: Canadian composer Mychael Danna had previously worked with Ang Lee on his two previous Hollywood films, *The Ice Storm* and *Ride with the Devil*. Danna had also composed the musical scores for several films by Atom Egoyan (*Exotica*, *The Sweet Hereafter*, *Ararat*) as well as *8MM*, *Girl, Interrupted* and *Antwone Fisher*.

TRAILERS: The 'teaser' trailer opens with a view of an ordinary suburban house, in which a man (Bruce Banner) stares at himself in his bathroom mirror as he intones (in voice-over): 'Even now I can feel it. Buried somewhere deep inside me. Watching me, waiting. But you know what scares me the most? When I can't fight it any more, when it takes over, when I totally lose control . . . *I like it*!' The camera moves in on a close-up of his eye, the pupil of which dilates, then the skin surrounding the eye turns green . . . and suddenly the wall of the house explodes, sending bathroom fittings flying out towards the camera, followed by the title treatment (simply 'HULK') and captions for the principal cast.

POSTERS: The earliest 'teaser' poster for *Hulk* featured an illustrated green eye looking out from the first two letters of a black 'HULK' logo with a green drop shadow, the date ('SUMMER 2003') and website ('www.thehulk.com'). A second poster featured a more dynamic image of The Hulk lunging out of frame, with a San Francisco skyline behind him. No title appeared on the poster, just a (US) release date – '6.20.03'

CONTROVERSY: In early 2002, the Writers Guild of America began the complicated process of arbitration in order to establish which of the dozen or so screenwriters who had worked on various versions of *Hulk* would wind up with a credit on the final film. According to Michael France, the studio proposed to give James Schamus sole credit which, he says, is '. . . preposterous. He did a lot of work, primarily in bringing Banner's father into the picture as a physical presence, and I think he deserves credit – but it's really shameful to try to deny the work I did on this movie. Schamus has a great deal of power on this, as a producer and as Ang Lee's partner, and he may get away with hogging the credit. That doesn't make it right. The mechanics of the new origin, with Banner as a gamma researcher who's invented and built a "gammasphere", is from my drafts,' says France. 'The way "The Absorbing Man" is created and used in the movie came from my work. A lot of the action when The Hulk escapes from the "black ops" base, as well as the psychological material dealing with Banner's character and the way that Banner's romance with Betty is so tragically handled, that's all from my drafts. I did not have anything to do with the "Hulk dogs", though – James Schamus can have those. Both Schamus and Hayter have indulged in some boasting in the press about how they both started from scratch, particularly in making Banner a realistic character, when they did their respective drafts – and that was a little bit dishonest. Both of them used huge chunks of my drafts. I do rewrite work, too, and I make a point of never denigrating the writers I follow, or somehow pretending that they didn't exist as a way of building myself up. I wish that the writers who followed me on this project behaved that way as well.' Nevertheless, he adds, 'I know how much work I have in the movie and I do take pride in that. Getting paid twice helps too.'

TRIVIA: Lou Ferrigno, who played The Hulk in the original TV series, makes a cameo appearance as a security guard.

EXPERT WITNESS: 'I believe Hulk is the first Marvel creature, in the comic book world, that is a mixture of monster and superhero and we want to make him that way. I think it's possible to do a mixture in a very rational way. I think we all have that Hulk inside of us – our alter ego – and not only Hulk, but also Bruce Banner. And everybody [in the film] dealing with [Banner] is dealing with their own "Hulk-ness" inside of them. I hope eventually that that, in fact, will prevail to the audience.' – **Ang Lee, Director**

Index of Quotations

Introduction

2 'films were really nothing but frames on celluloid . . .' Will Eisner, quoted in 'Strip Tease' by David Chute, *Empire*, July 1990

2 'A lot of people make this parallel between comics and film . . .' Dave Gibbons, quoted in *Artists on Comic Art* edited by Mark Salisbury, Titan Books, 2000

2 'The vibe feels much the same as when George Lucas and Steven Spielberg took black-and-white adventure serials . . .' Stephen Norrington, quoted in 'Monster Ink' by Tom Russo, *Entertainment Weekly*, 10 May 2002

Superman: The Movie

8 'They had prepared the picture for a year', he said, 'and not one bit of it was useful to me . . .' Richard Donner, quoted in 'Richard Donner on Superman' by Don Shay, *Cinefantastique*, Volume 8 Number 4, 1979

9 'They had things in there like a scene where Superman is looking for Lex Luthor . . .' Donner, ibid.

9 'They didn't buy Marlon Brando the actor . . .' Donner, ibid.

9 'I thought he was a little young for it . . .' Donner, ibid.

10 'It was the blind leading the blind, all experimentation . . .' Donner, ibid.

10 'So we decided to give everyone [on Krypton] a family crest . . .' Tom Mankiewicz, quoted in DVD commentary

10 'We noticed that the material lit up on its own . . .' Donner, ibid.

13 'a wonderful, chuckling, preposterously exciting fantasy . . .' quoted in 'Superman', uncredited, Variety.com

13 'by keeping the spectacular possibilities open . . .' quoted in 'Superman' by Martyn Auty, *Time Out Film Guide 11th Edition*, Penguin Books, 2002

13 'If you look at the pictures that were nominated . . .' Donner, quoted in 'Richard Donner on Superman' by Don Shay, *Cinefantastique*, Volume 8 Number 4, 1979

15 'Superman was going to leave Hackman and Beatty in the prison . . .' Donner, quoted in 'Richard Donner on Superman' by Don Shay, *Cinefantastique*, Volume 8 Number 4, 1979

17 'He literally dies as he professes his love to her . . .' Jonathan Lemkin, quoted in 'Super Duper' by Edward Gross, *Cinescape*, September/October 1997

17 'I thought it was terrible . . .' Kevin Smith, quoted in 'Cape Fear' by Rebecca Ascher-Walsh, *Entertainment Weekly*, 29 May 1988

18 'I really, really liked Kevin Smith's script . . .' Robert Rodriguez, quoted in 'I, Spy' by J Rentilly, *Cinescape*, March/April 2001

18 'With Tim Burton, hopefully we're going to bring a lot to it . . .' Nicolas Cage, quoted in *Premiere*, June 1997

19 'with eager anticipation, and a rising sense of bafflement . . .' and all other Wesley Strick quotes, AI.

20 '[Burton's] take on it was quite interesting . . .' and all other Sylvain Despretz quotes, AI.

20 'a freak, but a beautiful freak . . .' Nicolas Cage, quoted in *Premiere*, June 1997

21 'Attanasio will sift through the three or four *Superman* scripts . . .' quoted in 'Attanasio's 2 Scripts for WB to Net $3.4 mil' by Zorianna Kit, *Hollywood Reporter Online*, 19 April 2001

22 'JJ Abrams and Jon Peters were given the daunting task . . .' Jeff Robinov, quoted in Warner Bros press release dated 25 September 2002
23 'It was a trip I'll never forget . . .' Richard Donner, Director (Donner, quoted in DVD commentary

Akira

25 'All the movies were about leaving home . . .' Katsuhiro Otomo, quoted in DVD interview
26 'I met a lot of animators who were always complaining . . .' Otomo, quoted in 'Future Perfect' by Tony Rayns, *Monthly Film Bulletin*, March 1991
27 'Until now there was always a limit . . .' Otomo, quoted in Bandai's 2001
27 'was also dealing with beings with paranormal powers . . .' Archie Goodwin, quoted in 'Akira Production Report', on DVD
28 'any of the characters could be the lead of the story . . .' Otomo, quoted in DVD bonus materials
30 'a lavish animation extravaganza produced at a cost of $8 million . . .' quoted in 'Akira', uncredited, *Variety*, circa 1998
30 'over 1 billion yen . . .' quoted in 'Akira' by Richard Harrington, *Washington Post*, 25 December 1989
30 '*Akira* is very probably the first animated film . . .' quoted in 'Akira' by Tony Rayns, *Monthly Film Bulletin*, March 1991
30 'Otomo's first excursion into movies . . .' quoted in 'Akira' by Geoff Andrew, *Time Out Film Guide 11th Edition* edited by John Pym, Penguin Books, 2002
31 'I'd always felt that [the comic] would end . . .' (Otomo, quoted in 'Future Perfect' by Tony Rayns, *Monthly Film Bulletin*, March 1991
33 'It was the worst possible thing for me to make . . .' Otomo, ibid.

Batman

35 'I remember when I was 12 or 13 . . .' Bob Kane, quoted in 'Bob Kane, 83, Cartoonist Who Created Batman', *New York Times*, 7 November 1998
35 'Batman and Robin were always punning and wisecracking . . .' Kane, ibid.
36 'a definitive Batman movie . . .' Michael E Uslan, quoted in 'Batman' by Alan Jones, *Cinefantastique*, November 1989
36 'The first treatment of *Batman* . . .' Tim Burton, quoted in *Burton on Burton* edited by Mark Salisbury, revised edition, Faber and Faber, 2000
36 'The success of the graphic novel . . .' Burton, quoted in 'Batman' by Alan Jones, *Cinefantastique*, November 1989
37 'I tried to take the premise which had this . . .' Sam Hamm, quoted in 'Batman' by Taylor L White, *Cinefantastique*, June 1989
37 'I'd just meet Sam on weekends to discuss the early writing stages . . .' Burton, quoted in 'Batman' by Alan Jones, *Cinefantastique*, November 1989
37 'I see what they're doing . . .' Hamm, quoted in 'Batman' by Taylor L White, *Cinefantastique*, June 1989
37 'Why would this big, macho, Arnold Schwarzenegger-type . . .' Burton, quoted in *Burton on Burton* edited by Mark Salisbury, revised edition, Faber and Faber, 2000
38 'I don't think I've ever felt so naturally in tune with a director . . .' Anton Furst, quoted in 'Batman' by Alan Jones, *Cinefantastique*, November 1989
38 'Zoning and contruction was thought of . . .' Burton, ibid.
39 'The idea was to humanise Batman . . .' Burton, ibid.

39 '*Batman* doesn't have as blatant a soundtrack as, say, *Top Gun* . . .' Burton, quoted in 'Batman' by Alan Jones, *Cinefantastique*, November 1989

40 'We tried to put Robin in . . .' Burton, quoted in *Burton on Burton* edited by Mark Salisbury, revised edition, Faber and Faber, 2000

41 'The Gotham City created in *Batman* . . .' quoted in 'Batman' by Roger Ebert, *Chicago Sun-Times*, 23 June 1989

41 'plotless, unfocused, barely held together by mind-blowing sets . . .' quoted in 'Batman' by Dominic Wells, *Time Out Film Guide* 11th Edition, Penguin Books, 2002

42 'The fan reaction is a surface response . . .' Burton, quoted in 'Batman' by Alan Jones, *Cinefantastique*, November 1989

42 'came as a jolt . . .' Hamm, quoted in 'Batman' by Taylor L White, *Cinefantastique*, June 1989

42 'Hiring Kane was a very intelligent move . . .' Furst, quoted in 'Batman' by Alan Jones, *Cinefantastique*, November 1989

43 'I didn't want to do a little cameo and indemnify the picture . . .' Adam West, AI

43 'When I was hired to write *Batman Returns* (*Batman II* at the time) . . .' Welsey Strick, AI

45 'I told them I'd cast Clint Eastwood as Batman, and shoot it in Tokyo . . .' Darren Aronofsky, AI

46 'While I was never a big comic book fan, I loved Batman . . .' Tim Burton, Director (Burton, quoted in *Burton on Burton* edited by Mark Salisbury, revised edition, Faber and Faber, 2000

Dick Tracy

49 'I decided that if the police couldn't catch the gangsters . . .' Chester Gould, quoted in 'Strip Tease' by David Chute, *Empire*, July 1990

49 'Dick Tracy was my first enthusiasm as a kid . . .' and all other Max Allan Collins quotes, AI.

51 'Before we were brought on there were several failed scripts . . .' and all other Jack Epps Jr quotes, AI

52 'It's a naive kind of subject . . .' Warren Beatty, quoted in an interview with Barbara Walters, circa 1990

52 'There's something quaint about 1939/1940 crime fighting . . .' Beatty, quoted in *Dick Tracy: The Making of the Movie* by Mike Bonifer, London: Titan Books, 1990

52 'It never occurred to me to direct the movie . . .' Beatty, ibid.

53 'I really think that he looked to us to bring our discipline . . .' Jeffrey Katzenberg, quoted in 'Big Shot', uncredited, *Empire*, July 1990

53 'I think she's terrific . . .' Beatty, quoted in interview with Barbara Walters, circa 1990

53 'I wanted to work with Warren . . .' Madonna, quoted in *Dick Tracy: The Making of the Movie* by Mike Bonifer, London: Titan Books, 1990

53 'nobody's going to look like [the comic strip] Dick Tracy . . .' Beatty, ibid.

54 'To make movies is generally to create a reality . . .' Beatty, ibid.

54 'He loves to get these different forces out on the table . . .' Barrie M Osborne, ibid.

54 'All the things that Vittorio, Milena [Canonero, costume designer] and myself . . .' Richard Sylbert, ibid.

54 'These are not the kind of colours the audience is used to seeing . . .' Vittorio Storaro, ibid.

55 'He's a perfectionist . . .' Madonna, ibid.
55 'Warren is very aware that sometimes a look can carry the film . . .' Milena Canonero, quoted in *Dick Tracy: The Making of the Movie* by Mike Bonifer, London: Titan Books, 1990
56 'It was trial and error . . .' Madonna, ibid.
57 'though it looks ravishing, Warren Beatty's longtime pet project . . .' quoted in *Variety*, circa 1990
57 'a masterpiece of studio artificiality . . .' quoted in 'Dick Tracy' by Roger Ebert, *Chicago Sun-Times*, 15 June 1990
58 'wonderfully imaginative and carefully moderated . . .' quoted in 'Dick Tracy' by Colette Maud, *Time Out Film Guide 11th Edition* edited by John Pym, London: Penguin Books, 2002

Teenage Mutant Ninja Turtles
62 'When we created the Turtles, we wanted to spoof the world of superhero characters . . .' Peter Laird, quoted on ninjaturtles.com
62 'They're always willing to lend a helping hand . . .' Kevin Eastman, ibid.
63 'Gray mentioned *Teenage Mutant Ninja Turtles* . . .' David Chan, quoted in 'Teenage Mutant Ninja Turtles' by Daniel Schweiger, *Cinefantastique*, September 1990
63 'Bobby's [script] needed restructuring . . .' Todd W Langen, quoted in 'Teenage Mutant Ninja Turtles' by Daniel Schweiger, *Cinefantastique*, September 1990
63 'In a way, you have four different characters . . .' Langen, quoted in 'Teenage Mutant Ninja Turtles II' by Gary L Wood, *Cinefantastique*, April 1991
63 'When they approached me . . .' Steve Barron, quoted in *No Strings Attached* by Matt Bacon, Virgin Publishing, 1997
63 'Jim thought that family moves were the Henson tradition . . .' Barron, ibid.
64 '*Turtles* was pushing the edge of what my father thought . . .' Brian Henson, ibid.
64 'It's an unwritten law . . .' Barron, quoted in New Line press materials
64 'Making the Turtles and Splinter was a little tricky . . .' Jim Henson, ibid.
64 '*Turtles* was an outrageous effects film . . .' Brian Henson, ibid.
64 'We first made fibreglass body casts of each creature . . .' John Stephenson, ibid.
65 'To get motivation for the proper atmosphere in the designs . . .' Roy Forge Smith, ibid.
66 'While visually rough around the edges . . .' quoted in 'Teenage Mutant Ninja Turtles', uncredited, circa 1990
66 'did not walk into then screening with a light step . . .' quoted in 'Teenage Mutant Ninja Turtles' by Roger Ebert, *Chicago Sun-Times*, 30 March 1990
67 'though extra distinguishing marks between the Turtles . . .' quoted in 'Teenage Mutant Ninja Turtles' by Colette Maud, *Time Out Film Guide 11th Edition* edited by John Pym, Penguin Books, 2002
67 'someday, I'd like to tell the story behind the aborted fourth movie . . .' Peter Laird, quoted on mikeystmnt.com, 25 June 2001
67 'Rest assured, as long as I am alive and in charge of this ship . . .' Laird, quoted in 'An Interview with Peter Laird' by Dan Berger, ninjaturtles.com, circa 2001
68 'When we started to hear that the original rights owners . . .' Norman Grossfeld, quoted in 'Inside the (Fox) Box' by Chris Wyatt, *Cinescape*, January 2003

68 'John and I look forward to working with Peter [Laird] . . .' Terence Chang, quoted in 'Woo, Digital, Mirage on *Turtles* pic' by Tim Swanson, *Variety*, 20 June 2001
68 'I've always loved the *Teenage Mutant Ninja Turtles* . . .' John Woo, ibid.
68 'I [will] work on this project as a producer with my partner . . .' Woo, quoted on scifiwire.com, 3 June 2002
69 'It was a hard project, but satisfying . . .' (Brian Henson, Chief Puppeteer (Brian Henson, quoted in *No Strings Attached* by Matt Bacon, London: Virgin Publishing, 1997

The Crow
72 'I just wanted to stop thinking about it and have some structure in my life . . .' James O'Barr, quoted in 'Reliving the Pain' by Lisa Susser, 13 May 1994
72 'Writing *The Crow* didn't help at all . . .' O'Barr, ibid.
72 'James did this book because he died inside . . .' John Bergin, quoted in 'In A Lonely Place' by John Bergin, introduction to the collected edition of *The Crow*, Titan Books, 1995, 2002
72 'He remembers that *he* told *me* about it . . .' and all other John Shirley quotes, AI.
73 'We had promised James we would be faithful to the comic book . . .' Most, quoted in DVD commentary
74 'The first script they had pretty much had nothing to do with the comic . . .' O'Barr, quoted on kaos2000.net
74 'and immediately saw in his texturing and shading . . .' Most, quoted in DVD commentary
74 'John originally attacked the project . . .' and all other David J Schow quotes, AI.
75 'After I met him, I thought he was perfect . . .' O'Barr, quoted on kaos2000.net
75 'He is reacting to a terrible tragedy . . .' Brandon Lee, quoted in 'The Crow' by William Wilson Goodson Jr, *Imagi-Movies*, Summer 1994
76 'I think one of the most impressive things about the film . . .' Most, quoted in DVD commentary
77 'It was the encouragement of Brandon's mother . . .' Most, quoted in DVD commentary
77 'The music we ultimately wanted . . .' Most, quoted in DVD commentary
77 'It had never been done . . .' Most, ibid.
78 'I gave the producer a list of bands to approach . . .' O'Barr, quoted in interview with Rob M Gooze, *Arizona Daily Wildcat*, 4 May 1994
78 'At the time I was repeatedly told that the soundtrack would never sell . . .' Most, quoted in DVD commentary
80 'one of the most effective live-actioners ever derived from a comic strip . . .' quoted in 'The Crow' by Todd McCarthy, *Variety*, 29 April 1994
80 'a stunning work of visual style . . .' quoted in 'The Crow' by Roger Ebert, *Chicago Sun-Times*, 13 May 1994
80 'The sicko storyline has been softened . . .' quoted in 'The Crow' by Suzi Feay, *Time Out Film Guide 11th Edition* edited by John Pym, Penguin Books, 2002
82 'It thought [it] had a lot of possibilities . . .' O'Barr, quoted on kaos2000.net
82 'It was pretty good . . .' O'Barr, quoted on crowfans.com

82 'I saw the possibilities . . .' O'Barr quoted on kaos2000.net
83 'I think the way to go, to expand it, is animation . . .' O'Barr, ibid.
83 'Alex Proyas had never gone on the record with commentary . . .' Schow, quoted in 'DVD Stands for 'DiVideD',' gothic.net
84 'There's probably another hour and a half of interviews . . .' O'Barr, quoted on kaos2000.net
85 'It's impossible to separate the film from Brandon Lee's tragic death . . .' (Alex Proyas, Director (Alex Proyas, quoted on mysteryclock.com

Ghost in the Shell
89 'It was quickly apparent that there were few films . . .' Andy Frain, quoted in 'Global Vision' by A Osmond, *Imagine*, Spring 2002
89 'I remember suggesting an animated version of *Ghost in the Shell* . . .' Frain, ibid.
90 'We changed a few minor things here and there . . .' Mamoru Oshii, quoted in 'Cybernetic City: *Ghost in the Shell*', uncredited, *Newtype*, November 1995
90 'Although 'he' is a program without a real body to speak of . . .' Oshii, ibid.
91 'Working with computer graphics isn't like everyday work with animation cels . . .' Oshii, ibid.
91 'Because animation only exists in two dimensions . . .' Oshii, ibid.
94 '*Ghost in the Shell* is intended as a breakthrough film . . .' quoted in 'Ghost in the Shell' by Roger Ebert, *Chicago Sun-Times*, circa 1996
94 'A stunning work of speculative fiction . . .' quoted in Manga Video press materials
94 'While slick and visually dazzling . . .' quoted in 'Ghost in the Shell' by Kim Newman, *Sight and Sound*, January 1996
94 'Oshii's sci-fi anime conjures up a dazzling future cityscape . . .' quoted in 'Ghost in the Shell' by Nigel Floyd, *Time Out Film Guide 11th Edition*, Penguin Books, 2002
95 'a lot of my plans to pursue [other] co-productions . . .' (Frain, quoted in 'Global Vision' by A Osmond, *Imagine*, Spring 2002
95 'a real life version of the anime style . . .' Joel Silver, quoted in 'Schismatrix' by J Clarke, *Manga Max*, July 1999
98 'For a filmmaker, the most important question is . . .' (Oshii, quoted in the Sci-Fi Channel documentary *Out of His Shell: Mamoru Oshii* produced by A Gales, 2002

Judge Dredd
101 'a colourful and exciting take on a *Dirty Harry*-style cop hero . . .' and all other Edward R Pressman quotes, AI.
101 'It had a long history and there was a constituency . . .' Edward R Pressman, ibid.
101 'They spent over a year rewriting it . . .' Lippincott, quoted in 'Judge Dredd' by Alan Jones, *Cinefantastique*, August 1995
102 'The notion that in the future things are so grim . . .' William Wisher, quoted in *The Making of* Judge Dredd by Jane Killick, Boxtree, 1995
102 'catalysed the entire project . . .' Pressman, ibid.
102 'to create, within an imaginary world . . .' Andrew G Vajna, ibid.
103 'I even drew a poster of Judge Dredd and sent it into the comic', said Cannon. 'Imagine how thrilled I was when they actually published it!' Danny Cannon, quoted in 'Judge Dredd' by Alan Jones, *Cinefantastique*, August 1995

103 'What I didn't like were the mutants and aliens . . .' Cannon, quoted in *The Making of* Judge Dredd by Jane Killick, London: Boxtree, 1995
103 'In came this English guy who knew everything and more about Judge Dredd, carrying these mindboggling storyboards which visualised the atmosphere superbly.' Sylvester Stallone, quoted in 'Judge Dredd' by Alan Jones, *Cinefantastique*, August 1995
103 'The script dragged a great deal . . .' and all other Steven De Souza quotes, AI.
104 'the one and only person we showed the script to . . .' (Vajna, quoted in *The Making of* Judge Dredd by Jane Killick, Boxtree, 1995
104 'Julian Caldow, who drew the Batmobile on *Batman* . . .' Nigel Phelps, quoted in *Screencraft: Production Design & Art Direction* by Peter Ettedgui, Focal Press, 1999
105 'The exclusive top level of the city . . .' Phelps, ibid.
105 '[The uniform] is partially designed by Gianni Versace . . .' Sylvester Stallone, quoted in The Walt Disney Company documentary 'Stallone's Law: The Making of *Judge Dredd*', 1995
105 'at the same time it's vastly different to the comic book . . .' Phelps, quoted in *The Making of Judge Dredd* by Jane Killick, Boxtree: 1995
105 'because you can do anything in a drawing . . .' Emma Porteous, ibid.
106 'We have to play totally opposite to what is on the film . . .' Vajna, ibid.
107 'frankly acknowledges its source . . .' quoted in 'Judge Dredd' by Todd McCarthy, *Variety*, 30 June 1995
107 '[He] is ideal for a role like this because he's smart and funny . . .' quoted in 'Judge Dredd' by Roger Ebert, *Chicago Sun-Times*, 30 June 1995
107 'certainly has the square jaw-line and iconic presence . . .' quoted in 'Judge Dredd' by Nigel Floyd, *Time Out Film Guide 11th Edition* edited by John Pym, Penguin Books, 2002
108 'Sylvester Stallone looks fantastic . . .' Phelps, quoted in 'Production Design' by Alan Jones, *Cinefantastique*, August 1995
108 'he can take off his helmet . . .' and all other Jonathan Clements quotes, AI.
109 'We are reinventing the franchise . . .' Morris Ruskin, quoted in *Variety*, 23 October 2001
109 'They had got a few scripts written for them already . . .' and all other Chris Donaldson quotes, AI.
112 'There are layers in [*Judge Dredd*], because we cared to put them in . . .' Cannon, quoted in *The Making of Judge Dredd* by Jane Killick, Boxtree, 1995

The Phantom

114 'I think I created the first self-effacing hero . . .' and all other Lee Falk quotes, AI.
115 '*The Phantom* comics always had a kind of good old-fashioned adventure . . .' Simon Wincer, quoted in Paramount press materials
116 'Jeffrey Boam wrote the screenplay . . .' Wincer, ibid.
116 'For me, this guy was the end-all as far as role models and superheroes . . .' and all other Billy Zane quotes, AI.
116 'Billy had built himself physically into great shape . . .' and all other Simon Wincer quotes, AI.
116 'When I read the script for the first time . . .' Kristy Swanson, AI
116 'She's adventure-seeking [and] highly sexually charged . . .' Catherine Zeta Jones, AI

117 'a very wealthy New York businessman of the thirties . . .' Treat Williams, AI
119 'a pleasingly astute sense of its place . . .' quoted in 'The Phantom' by Godfrey Cheshire, *Variety*, 7 June 1996
119 'As far as straight-ahead, rip-roaring action goes . . .' Jonathan Ross, quoted on DVD sleeve
119 'Leading man Billy Zane [is] plastic and soulless . . .' quoted in 'The Phantom' by Trevor Johnston, *Time Out Film Guide 11th Edition*, Penguin Books, 2002
120 'There is a great history there . . .' Ashok Armitraj, quoted in 'The Phantom Menaced', uncredited, *Dreamwatch*, January 2003

Men in Black

122 'I always liked [this] because I thought it sets the tone . . .' and all other Barry Sonnenfeld quotes, AI.
123 'I first heard about the 'Men in Black' . . .' Lowell Cunningham, quoted in 'Metamorphosis of *Men in Black*' featurette, *Men in Black* DVD
123 'But I knew people who had gotten into the comics industry . . .' Cunningham, quoted in Columbia press materials
123 'There really isn't anyone else like Barry . . .' Laurie MacDonald, quoted in Columbia press materials
124 'a very Kennedyesque period in history . . .' Bo Welch, quoted in Columbia press materials
124 'I looked at the headquarters as a sort of alien Ellis Island . . .' Welch, ibid.
126 'We made this giant 'Edgar bug' for the end sequence . . .' Rick Baker, AI
129 'A witty and sometimes surreal sci-fi comedy . . .' quoted in 'Men in Black' by Todd McCarthy, *Variety*, 29 June 1997
130 'a comedy of facetiousness . . .' quoted in 'Men in Black' by Owen Gleiberman, *Entertainment Weekly*, 18 July 1997
130 'so much fun . . .' quoted in 'Men in Black' by Tom Charity, *Time Out Film Guide 11th Edition*, edited by John Pym, Penguin Books, 2002
132 'I've discovered Hollywood likes to take things one at a time . . .' Cunningham, quoted in 'Men in Black's Lowell Cunningham' by Rob Allstetter, www.comicscontinuum.com, 17 June 2002
132 'I'm going to be optimistic about the possibility . . .' Will Smith, quoted in 'Q&A: Will Smith and co-stars talk *Men in Black II* (Pt 1)' by Luisa Sanders, www.playstation.com, 22 July 2002

Spawn

136 'Back then it was set in more of a *Star Wars* environment . . .' Todd McFarlane, AI
136 'Spawn makes Batman look like a pussy . . .' McFarlane, AI
137 'It was kind of odd that they put me in charge . . .' McFarlane, AI
137 'Ninety per cent of episodes seven through twelve . . .' McFarlane, AI
138 'They just assume that because they're going to spend . . .' McFarlane, quoted in 'Todd McFarlane' by James Van Hise, *Cinefantastique*, September 1997
138 '[They] were around when we were doing the original pitches . . .' McFarlane, ibid.
138 'It's not like they gave us Tom Cruise . . .' McFarlane, AI
138 'We had a good story and a lot of interesting designs . . .' Mark A Z Dippé, quoted in 'Spawn' by James Van Hise, *Cinefantastique*, September 1997

139 'The actual making of the show is a slow, tedious process . . .' McFarlane, ibid.
139 'A big part of the film is visual effects . . .' Dippé, quoted in 'Mark Dippé, Director' by James Van Hise, *Cinefantastique*, September 1997
139 'It's a film. It's not the comic book. There are differences . . .' Dippé, quoted in 'Spawn' by James Van Hise, *Cinefantastique*, September 1997
139 'The biggest things were how to make a cape forty feet long . . .' McFarlane, AI
141 'narratively knuckleheaded [but] visually teeming . . .' quoted in 'Spawn' by Todd McCarthy, *Variety*, 30 July 1997
141 'makes a powerful Spawn . . .' quoted in 'Spawn' by Roger Ebert, *Chicago Sun-Times*, 1 August 1997
141 'In future, Dippé, an old SFX hand, needs to think about . . .' quoted in 'Spawn' by Nick Bradshaw, *Time Out Film Guide 11th Edition* edited by John Pym, Penguin Books, 2002
142 '[movie offers] came out of the woodwork . . .' McFarlane, quoted in 'Todd McFarlane' by James Van Hise, *Cinefantastique*, September 1997
142 'The largest hurdle was attempting to convince Hollywood . . .' McFarlane, quoted in DVD sleeve notes
142 'more like *Se7en* than the *Spawn* movie . . .' Michael De Luca, quoted on corona.bc.ca, *21 June 1999*
142 'I think the biggest surprise will be how different this film will be from the first . . .' Steve Niles, quoted on comicscontinuum.com, 26 February 2002
142 'I'd like this one to be really as 'R' [rated] as it should be, as the comic was', he added. John Leguizamo, quoted on scifi.com/scifiwire, 5 March 2002
142 'In some ways the first movies of a comic book . . .' McFarlane, AI
143 'One of the things Niles and Todd did with the last draft . . .' Hans Rodionoff, quoted on comics2film.com, 3 December 2002
144 'I don't think a movie's any different to a comic book . . .' McFarlane, AI

Blade

146 'The prologue is, in a sense, Blade's origin . . .' David S Goyer, quoted in DVD commentary
148 'I went in and pitched a trilogy of big-budget films . . .' David S Goyer, quoted in interview with www.comics2film.com, 27 February 2002
148 'I wanted to do a post-modernist vampire film . . .' Goyer, quoted in 'Blade' by Dale Kutzera, *Cinefantastique*, February 1998
149 'There have been something like 350 vampire films made . . .' Goyer, quoted in DVD commentary
149 'I had played a lot of cops and the good guy stuff . . .' Wesley Snipes, quoted in 'Blade' by Dale Kutzera, *Cinefantastique*, February 1998
149 'From the very first draft he wanted to be Blade . . .' Goyer, ibid.
150 'Steve Norrington was the one that made me feel like this was one to go for . . .' Stephen Dorff, quoted in New Line press materials
150 'We decided on Traci pretty late in the game . . .' Peter Frankfurt, quoted in DVD commentary
150 'The vampire world is angular . . .' Kirk M Petruccelli, quoted in New Line press materials
150 'You can count on the fingers of one hand . . .' Goyer, quoted in DVD commentary

150 'It made the shoot a lot easier . . .' Snipes, quoted in New Line press materials
151 'Pearl started out fat, androgynous and Asian . . .' Miles Teves, AI
151 'I thought Blade would have a sort of . . .' Sanja Milkovic Hays, ibid.
151 'Action pictures can be a lot of fun because of the adrenaline . . .' Mark Isham, quoted in DVD commentary
153 'After Karen tries to pick up Blade's sword . . .' Goyer, ibid.
153 'Originally, Pearl had a number of dead children laying about him . . .' Goyer, ibid.
154 'We had always had trouble with the last twenty minutes . . .' Goyer, ibid.
154 'It read great on the page . . .' Goyer, ibid.
154 'We tested the movie with that ending . . .' Peter Frankfurt, ibid.
154 'There was also another ending . . .' Goyer, ibid.
154 'You don't see Whistler's face . . .' Goyer, ibid.
155 'anyone patiently attending the film . . .' quoted in 'Blade' by Roger Ebert, *Chicago Sun-Times*, 21 August 1998
155 'The dark ooze that even tinges *Blade*'s daylight sequences . . .' quoted in 'Blade' by Gene Seymour, *Los Angeles Times*, 21 August 1998
155 'An attempt to redefine cutting edge horror.' quoted in 'Blade' by Nigel Floyd, *Time Out Film Guide 11th Edition* edited by John Pym, Penguin Books, 2002
156 'On *Blade*'s opening weekend, Michael De Luca called me . . .' Goyer, quoted in 'Staking Out New Territory' by Den Shewman, *Creative Screenwriting*, March/April 2002
157 'I made some comments about some of the parts . . .' Guillermo del Toro, quoted on www.comics2film.com, 20 March 2002
157 'What I really want to do for the third one . . .' Goyer, quoted on www.comics2film.com, 27 February 2002
157 'I would love to be involved in that one . . .' Del Toro, quoted on www.comics2film.com, 20 March 2002
157 'It's been modified somewhat . . .' Goyer, quoted in 'Which Blade?' by Rod Edgar, *DreamWatch*, July 2002
157 'I was very disappointed with the *Batman* films . . .' Goyer, quoted in New Line press materials
158 'a separate entity from the *Blade* films . . .' Goyer, quoted in 'Which Blade?' by Rod Edgar, *DreamWatch*, July 2002
158 'I would love to see it done CG . . .' Goyer, quoted on www.comics2film.com, 27 February 2002
159 'I loved the first Blade movie . . .' (Marv Wolfman, quoted on www.silverbulletcomics.com, 2002

Mystery Men

161 'In making *Mystery Men* I really wanted to make it feel like . . .' Kinka Usher, quoted in DVD commentary
162 'Flaming Carrot is a second-string, mill town, blue collar superhero . . .' Burden, quoted in 'Bob Burden Interview' by Roger A Ash, westfieldcomics.com, March 1997
162 'just too weird . . .' Bob Burden, quoted on www.flamingcarrot.com
162 'a bizarre collection of oddball costumed adventurers . . .' Burden, ibid.
163 'The Mysterymen is a departure . . .' Burden, ibid.
163 'I could see that *Mystery Men* had a much better shot . . .' Mike

Richardson, quoted in 'Drawn to the Odd' by Michele Botwin, *Los Angeles Times*, 2 August 1999

163 'What really attracted us to *The Mysterymen* were the characters . . .' Lloyd Levin, quoted in Universal press materials

164 'included forty descriptions of heroes and villains . . .' Levin, ibid.

164 'Basically what they did was . . .' Burden, quoted in unedited transcript of *Mean Magazine* interview, 18 June 1999

164 'Neil wrote from the point of view of genuine heart . . .' Levin, quoted in Universal press materials

164 'I didn't really have any desire to make movies . . .' Kinka Usher, ibid.

164 'Originally, as I envisioned them, the Mysterymen . . .' Burden, quoted in 'Origin of the *Mystery Men* Comic Book Characters', *Mystery Men* DVD

165 'The relationship between Geoffrey and Greg . . .' Usher, quoted in director's commentary, *Mystery Men* DVD

165 'I had heard about some of the other actors . . .' Janeane Garofalo, quoted in Universal press materials

165 'I called Ben up and said . . .' Garofalo, ibid.

165 'We were after Ben for this project for quite a while . . .' Levin, ibid.

165 'the combination of the cast and the story . . .' Ben Stiller, ibid.

166 'When you have a cast this size . . .' Garofalo, ibid.

166 'I didn't quite realise going into this movie . . .' Usher, ibid.

166 'There were times when we were kind of stumped . . .' Levin, quoted in 'Drawn to the Odd' by Michele Botwin, *Los Angeles Times*, 2 August 1999

166 'We wanted to create a retro European . . .' Kirk M Petruccelli, quoted in Universal press materials

166 'I wanted the city's exterior to feel like a Hong Kong harbour . . .' Usher, ibid.

166 'A lot of the design was actually more European . . .' Usher, quoted in director's commentary, *Mystery Men* DVD

167 'We talked about the background of each character . . .' Marilyn Vance, quoted in Universal press materials

167 '[It was] a breakthrough for us . . .' Vance, quoted in Universal Home Video's 'Spotlight on Location', *Mystery Men* DVD

170 'Originally [Casanova] gets thrown off . . .' Usher, quoted in director's commentary, *Mystery Men* DVD

170 'We actually had another scene . . .' Usher, ibid.

171 'An amiable spoof of comic book heroes . . .' (quoted in 'Mystery Men' by Godfrey Cheshire, *Variety*, 2 August 1999

171 'an amiable spoof of superhero movies . . .' quoted in 'Mystery Men' by Nigel Floyd, *Time Out Film Guide 11th Edition*, Penguin Books, 2002

173 'We were hoping maybe we could do what *Scream* did . . .'(Levin, quoted in Universal press materials

X-Men

176 'With every superhero story . . .' Stan Lee, quoted in Fox press materials

177 'At first, Bryan said, 'Oh, leave me alone . . ."' Tom DeSanto, quoted in 'Meet The X-Men . . . and Women' by Emma Cochrane, *Empire*, September 2000

177 'watching all 70 episodes of the animated series . . .' Bryan Singer, quoted in 'The Uncanny Suspects' by Andy Mangels, *SFX*, September 2000

177 'The first two scripts I read were not taking it seriously . . .' DeSanto, quoted in 'X-Men' by Paul Wardle, *Cinefantastique*, August 2000

177 'I always try and remain respectful . . .' Singer, quoted in Fox press materials
178 'She's not the Rogue most of [the fans] know . . .' Singer, quoted in 'X-Men' by Paul Wardle, *Cinefantastique*, August 2000
178 '[I was] worried about the fans to some degree . . .' Singer, quoted on *The Charlie Rose Show*, circa July 2000
179 'The budget of the film . . .' Singer, ibid.
180 'I was the number one champion . . .' DeSanto, quoted in 'Meet The X-Men . . . And Women' by Emma Cochrane, *Empire*, September 2000
180 'Imagine them wearing suits of any other colour . . .' Singer, quoted in 'The Uncanny Suspects' by Andy Mangels, *SFX*, September 2000
180 'We used the comic books as much as we possibly could . . .' Gordon Smith, quoted in Fox press materials
180 'My goal was . . .' Singer, quoted in 'Meet The X-Men . . . And Women' by Emma Cochrane, *Empire*, September 2000
183 'That's an example of something we toyed with early on . . .' Singer, quoted in 'X-Men' by Paul Wardle, *Cinefantastique*, August 2000
185 'X is for X-Men . . .' quoted in 'X-Men' by Brian Harvey, *Variety*, 14 July 2000
185 'at the halfway mark . . .' quoted in 'X-Men' by Roger Ebert, *Chicago Sun-Times*, circa July 2000
185 'If the climax leaves you feeling short changed . . .' quoted in 'X-Men' by Colin Kennedy, *Empire*, August 2000
185 'The conflict between Xavier and Magneto . . .' quoted in 'X-Men' by Trevor Johnston, *Time Out Film Guide 11th Edition* edited by John Pym, Penguin Books, 2002
186 'If people want to see a sequel, they want to see an evolution . . .' Singer, quoted at Internet press conference, www.x-men-the-movie.com
186 'We very much see it as a franchise . . .' Lauren Shuler-Donner, quoted in 'Meet The X-Men . . . And Women' by Emma Cochrane, *Empire*, September 2000
188 'I viewed *X-Men* as an SF film . . .' Singer, quoted in 'The Uncanny Suspects' by Andy Mangels, *SFX*, September 2000

From Hell

191 'The idea was to do a documentary comic about a murder . . .' Alan Moore, quoted in 'Hellraiser' by Danny Graydon, *Empire*, February 2002
191 'Five murders is nothing . . .' Moore, quoted in 'Mad Man' by Brad Stone, *Newsweek*, October 18 2001
191 'It was interesting in parts but really Hollywood-corny . . .' Allen Hughes, quoted in DVD commentary
192 'For me, as a writer, [*From Hell*] is about . . .' Rafael Yglesias, ibid.
192 'The original graphic novel is very much . . .' Don Murphy, quoted in the Fox documentary 'Graphic Novel', circa 2001
192 'Basically I eliminated the character of the clairvoyant . . .' Yglesias, ibid.
193 'He wasn't our first choice . . .' Albert Hughes, quoted in 'Albert and Allen Hughes' by Damon Wise, *Total Film*, October 2001
193 'I've always been fascinated by it . . .' Johnny Depp, quoted in 'New Jack City' by Ian Freer, *Empire*, February 2002
193 'We saw a lotta, lotta girls . . .' Allen Hughes, ibid.
193 'If you go to [Whitechapel] now . . .' Martin Childs, quoted on DVD commentary

194 'It looked spectacular . . .' Moore, quoted in 'Mad Man' by Brad Stone, *Newsweek*, October 18 2001
194 'A lot of the JtR story takes place at night . . .' Deming, quoted in DVD commentary
194 'This is a ghetto story . . .' Albert Hughes, quoted in 'From Hell' by Ian Freer, *Empire*, December 2001
194 'We would just listen to rap music . . .' Heather Graham, quoted in 'New Jack City' by Ian Freer, *Empire*, February 2002
196 'A fraction of what we shot is in the movie . . .' Deming, quoted in DVD commentary
196 'When Abberline and she finally kiss . . .' Yglesias, ibid.
196 'I felt you needed to see that . . .' Yglesias, ibid.
197 'The graphic novel has him going along with it . . .' Allen Hughes, ibid.
198 'more amped-up Hammer Horror than genuinely *From Hell* . . .' quoted in 'From Hell' by Derek Elley, *Variety*, 10 September 2001
198 'The movie feels dark, clammy and exhilarating . . .' quoted in 'From Hell' by Roger Ebert, *Chicago Sun-Times*, 19 October 2001
198 'The first 20 minutes are grim . . .' quoted in 'From Hell' by Tom Charity, *Time Out Film Guide 11th Edition* edited by John Pym, Penguin Books, 2002
199 'it is more visual than the alcohol . . .' Don Murphy, quoted on sfx.co.uk
199 'of absolutely no evidence whatsoever . . .' Paul Begg, ibid.
199 'I thought that Abberline being portrayed as an opium abuser . . .' Begg, quoted on Comics2Film.com, 7 February 2002
200 'I was not at all interested in who Jack the Ripper was . . .' Moore, quoted in 'Mad Man' by Brad Stone, *Newsweek*, October 18 2001
201 'The thing we took [from the comic book] . . .' Albert Hughes, quoted in 'Albert and Allen Hughes' by Damon Wise, *Total Film*, October 2001

Ghost World

204 'I was once walking around Chicago . . .' Daniel Clowes, quoted in MGM press materials
204 'Films of comics are usually a bad idea . . .' Terry Zwigoff, quoted in 'The Misfits of Zwigoff' by SF Said, *Sight and Sound*, August 2000
204 'She was a big fan of it . . .' Zwigoff, quoted in the MGM documentary '*Ghost World*: A Comic Book Comes To Life', 2000
205 'Terry and I were the two worst pitch-men . . .' Clowes, quoted in 'The Misfits of Zwigoff' by SF Said, *Sight and Sound*, August 2000
205 'three hundred scripts a month . . .' Zwigoff, ibid.
205 'because then we could say . . .' Clowes, ibid.
205 'She's a very accomplished actress . . .' Zwigoff, quoted in MGM press materials
205 'Scarlett's 15 going on 35 – wise beyond her years . . .' Zwigoff, ibid.
205 'They're very close . . .' Clowes, ibid.
205 'We had some wacky, wacky times . . .' Scarlett Johansson, quoted in *Index*, April/May 2001
205 'I could never picture anybody else . . .' Zwigoff, quoted in the MGM documentary '*Ghost World*: A Comic Book Comes To Life', 2001
205 'We got lucky with every single person we hired . . .' Zwigoff, ibid.
206 'it looks like any place in modern America . . .' Clowes, quoted in MGM press materials

206 'Directors and producers usually expect to see . . .' Edward T McAvoy, quoted in 'The Misfits of Zwigoff' by SF Said, *Sight and Sound*, August 2000
206 'I guess most screenwriters aren't allowed anywhere near the set . . .' Clowes, ibid.
206 'When I saw Affonso's work on *All About My Mother* . . .' Zwigoff, ibid.
206 'The colours are enhanced and co-ordinated, as in comics . . .' Affonso Beato, ibid.
206 'I'm trying to make a film the way I see the modern world . . .' Terry Zwigoff, ibid.
207 'She knows everything about who she doesn't like . . .' Thora Birch, quoted in the MGM documentary '*Ghost World*: A Comic Book Comes To Life', 2001
209 'By sharp turns poignant, disturbing and hysterically funny . . .' quoted in 'Ghost World' by Ken Eisner, *Variety*, 21 June 2001
210 'a film like no other, an artful spellbinder that cuts deep . . .' quoted in 'Ghost World' by Peter Travers, *Rolling Stone*, 24 May 2001
210 'what makes the film special is how . . .' quoted in 'Ghost World' by Tom Charity, *Time Out Film Guide 11th Edition* edited by John Pym, Penguin Books, 2002
212 'It has something to do with the decline of Western civilisation . . .' Zwigoff, quoted in the MGM documentary '*Ghost World*: A Comic Book Comes To Life', 2000

Road to Perdition
215 'Conner was the heir apparent, but he was flawed . . .' and all other Max Allan Collins quotes, AI.
215 'The father and son story had a powerful emotional impact . . .' Dean Zanuck, quoted in DreamWorks press materials
216 'It had wonderful action and colourful characters . . .' Richard Zanuck, ibid.
216 'The graphic novel is one step closer to a film . . .' and all other David Self quotes are from 'A Writer's Road to Perdition' by Den Shewman, *Creative Screenwriting*, July/August 2002
218 'The graphic novel was told in pictures and images . . .' Richard Zanuck, quoted in DreamWorks press materials
219 'I thought this would be the kind of genre movie . . .' Tom Hanks, ibid.
219 'I read the script first . . .' Sam Mendes, quoted in 'Everyone Loves Uncle Sam' by Colin Kennedy, *Empire*, October 2002
219 'When the first sent it to me . . .' Mendes, quoted in 'Play It Again Sam' by Quentin Falk, *Academy*, October 2002
219 'I turned up to his apartment . . .' Sam Mendes, quoted in 'Everyone Loves Uncle Sam' by Colin Kennedy, *Empire*, October 2002
220 'When Sam told me where it was set . . .' Daniel Craig, quoted in 'Gang Related' by Steve Rose, *The Guide*, 14–20 September 2002
220 'It's what you hope for . . .' Mendes, quoted in DreamWorks press materials
220 'We had four generations of great actors . . .' Richard Zanuck, ibid.
220 'It was like having an entire engine room of ideas . . .' Mendes, ibid.
220 'I wanted to shoot on location . . .' Mendes, ibid.
220 'a kind of Oz in the middle of the movie' Mendes, ibid.)

221 'The film shouldn't be colourful . . .' Conrad L Hall, ibid.
221 'The reason there is snow and ice . . .' Mendes, ibid.
221 'Once Michael Sullivan and his son are on the road . . .' Albert Wolsky, ibid.
223 'Moody, methodical and measured . . .' quoted in '*Road* Will Give Summer Auds a Beautiful Detour' by Todd McCarthy, *Variety*, 1–14 July 2002
223 '[I]mprobably trapped inside a villanous role . . .' quoted in 'Too Much Mr Nice Guy' by Peter Bradshaw, *The Guardian*, 20 November 2002
224 'autumnal feel and A-plus awards-season pedigree . . .' quoted in '*Road* Will Give Summer Auds a Beautiful Detour' by Todd McCarthy, *Variety*, 1–14 July 2002
225 'In a sense, I realise now, I chose to direct *Road to Perdition* . . .' Mendes, quoted in 'One of the Few Genuine Artists I Have Known' by Sam Mendes, *The Guardian*, 17 January 2003
227 '*Road to Perdition* was everything that *American Beauty* wasn't . . .' Sam Mendes, Director (Mendes, quoted in 'Play It Again Sam' by Quentin Falk, *Academy*, October 2002

Spider-Man

228 'We really didn't want to show Spider-Man . . .' Sam Raimi, quoted in DVD commentary
231 'I couldn't think of a better director for that movie . . .' Stan Lee, quoted in 'Marvel Comics' by Frank Garcia and David Evans, *Cinefantastique*, February 1998
231 'What Jim managed to do . . .' Lee, quoted in 'Tangled Web' by John Horn, *Premiere*, September 1998
232 'I'm doing the origin story . . .' James Cameron, quoted in 'Truth or Dare' by Iain Blair, *Platinum*, February 1995
233 'One of the things that really interests me . . .' Cameron, ibid.
234 'It's a tangled web . . .' Sam Perlmutter, quoted in 'Tangled Web' by John Horn, *Premiere*, September 1998
234 'Jim's a big fan and has the utmost respect for Stan Lee . . .' Rae Sanchini, ibid.
234 'For years now, lawyers have been working on this . . .' Lee, quoted in 'Spidey Swings Into Action', uncredited, *Dreamwatch*, April 1999
235 'Here's where I am philosophically . . .' Cameron, quoted in *Premiere*, November 1998
235 'I wanted to do the character's genesis only . . .' David Fincher, quoted in 'Swing Time' by Tom Russo, *Entertainment Weekly*, 26 April 20202
235 'The thing that sold me . . .' Amy Pascal, quoted in *Behind the Mask of Spider-Man* by Mark Cotta Vaz, Boxtree, 2002
235 'It just made sense . . .' John Calley, ibid.
235 'Because the Goblin is the father of Harry Osborn . . .' Sam Raimi, interviewed by Bill Warren, *Fangoria*, January 2001
236 'Freddie Prinze Jr won't even be allowed to buy a ticket . . .' Raimi, quoted in 'Spin City' by Kim Newman, *Sight and Sound*, July 2002
237 'I called up John Calley and Amy Pascal . . .' Laura Ziskin, quoted in *Behind the Mask of Spider-Man* by Mark Cotta Vaz, Boxtree, 2002
237 'The Times Square sequence was the single . . .' Ian Bryce, ibid.
238 'Spider-Man started off far more experimental and creative . . .' and all other Miles Teves quotes, AI

238 'After this very elaborate journey . . .' James Acheson, quoted in *Behind the Mask of Spider-Man* by Mark Cotta Vaz, Boxtree, 2002
239 'The core of the orchestra might be the same . . .' Danny Elfman, quoted in the DVD documentary *Composer Profile: Danny Elfman*
240 'We were really pleased with [the footage] and included it . . .' Ziskin, quoted in 'Arac Attack' by Adam Smith, *Empire*, July 2002
241 'a perfectly serviceable early summer popcorn picture . . .' quoted in '*Spider-Man* Spins Huge Box Office Web' by Todd McCarthy, *Variety*, April 22–28 2002
242 'like too many first films in superhero franchises . . .' quoted in 'Spin City' by Kim Newman, *Sight and Sound*, July 2002
242 'raised the game . . .' Jonathan Ross, quoted on DVD sleeve
243 'David had an idea . . .' Pascal, quoted in *Variety*, 10 June 2002
244 'I'm completely the man for the job . . .' Michael Chabon, quoted in 'An Author They Can't Refuse' by Nicholas Fonseca, *Entertainment Weekly*, 27 September 2002
244 'more or less rocked . . .' Chabon, quoted in 'Michael Chabon Gives An Update', www.countingdown.com by 'Scooby', 4 January 2003
244 'The series is being created in a unique computer-animated style . . .' Brett Gannon, quoted in press release, 29 July 2002
246 'When I came to make the film . . .' Raimi, quoted in 'Arac Attack' by Adam Smith, *Empire*, July 2002

Daredevil

248 'I had just run into the legendary Bill Everett . . .' Stan Lee, quoted in the introduction to *Marvel Masterworks: Daredevil* by Stan Lee, et al; New York: Marvel Comics, 1999
249 'He's got all the makings of a villain . . .' Frank Miller, quoted in the introduction to *Daredevil: The Man Without Fear* by Frank Miller, et al; Marvel Books, 1994
250 'I called up Bob and Harvey [Weinstein] . . .' Kevin Smith, quoted in interview with Elston Gunn, aint-it-cool-news.com, circa 1998
250 'All I wanted in the third grade was to be Matt Murdock . . .' Johnson, quoted in '*Daredevil* Dedication Pays Dividends' by Michael Fleming, *Daily Variety*, 6 February 2003
250 'He's a real guy with real problems . . .' Mark Steven Johnson, quoted in Fox press materials
250 'I read their draft, wrote meticulous notes . . .' Mark Steven Johnson, quoted in '*Daredevil* Dedication Pays Dividends' by Michael Fleming, *Daily Variety*, 6 February 2003
250 'Gary truly drove me crazy . . .' Avi Arad, ibid.
251 'I always believed in it . . .' Johnson, quoted in 'Better the Devil You Know' by Ed Gross, *SFX*, February 2003
251 'I did a bunch of drawings . . .' Johnson, ibid.
251 'He was not the logical choice for this.' Gary Foster, quoted in 'Speak of *DareDevil*' by Steve Daly, *Entertainment Weekly*, 7 February 2002
251 'He was decisive . . .' Arad, ibid.
251 'That's more of the untouchable superhero . . .' Johnson, quoted in 'Speak of *Daredevil*' by Steve Daly, *Entertainment Weekly*, 7 February 2002
251 'That saga (now known famously to those in the comics world as the 'Frank Miller Daredevils') . . .' quoted in 'Introduction' by Ben Affleck, *Marvel Visionaries: Daredevil* by Kevin Smith, et al. Marvel Comics, 1998

251 'I said, 'Look, I've got to be honest right away . . .'' Johnson, quoted in 'Speak of *DareDevil*' by Steve Daly, *Entertainment Weekly*, 7 February 2002
252 'A lot of people were clamouring for the part . . .' Foster, quoted in Fox press materials
252 'Jennifer has an ability to be so sweet . . .' Arad, ibid.
252 'The spirit of the character . . .' Johnson, ibid.
252 'Mark Steven Johnson was goodly enough to offer a brother a cameo . . .' Smith, quoted on ViewAskew.com, 28 March 2002
252 'Kevin is the reason I'm back into Daredevil . . .' Johnson, quoted on Comics2Film.com, 4 April 2002
253 'It was a new training regimen for Ben . . .' Dave Lea, quoted in Fox press materials
253 'We have more stunt guys than actors . . .' Affleck, quoted in 'Speak of *Daredevil*' by Steve Daly, *Entertainment Weekly*, 7 February 2002
253 'I feel so ignorant and behind . . .' Garner, ibid.
253 'She's fabulous . . .' Affleck, quoted in 'Devil May Care' by Tom Baxter, *Dreamwatch*, March 2003
253 'We tried to set up a situation . . .' Tom Sullivan, quoted in Fox press materials
254 'Right now, *Spider-Man* is kind of a blessing and a curse . . .' Johnson, quoted in 'A Film Without Fear' by Ed Gross, *Cinefantastique*, February/March 2003
254 'You don't make a movie like *Daredevil* and change the costume . . .' Johnson, quoted in 'Speak of *Daredevil*' by Steve Daly, *Entertainment Weekly*, 7 February 2002
254 'We didn't want to do a spandex costume . . .' Foster, quoted in Fox press materials
254 'Apparently the studio felt like . . .' Smith, quoted in 'Speak of *Daredevil*' by Steve Daly, *Entertainment Weekly*, 7 February 2002
255 'On the Internet, people hated the *X-Men* idea . . .' Affleck, quoted in '*Daredevil* Doodles', uncredited, *Empire*, October 2003
255 'Jim Acheson has done an incredible job of making Elektra's costumes as cool as possible . . .' Affleck, ibid.
257 '*Daredevil* is a pretender in the realm . . .' quoted in 'Somber Superhero Aims at Super Bow' by Todd McCarthy, *Variety*, 14 February 2003
257 'The movie is actually pretty good . . .' quoted in 'Daredevil' by Roger Ebert, *Chicago Sun-Times*, 14 February 2003
258 'since the storyline lays out confrontations . . .' quoted in '*DareDevil*' by Trevor Johnston, *Time Out*, 12–19 February 2003
258 'The good thing about a Marvel property . . .' Avid Arad, quoted in 'Flying Blind' by Liane Bonin, *Entertainment Weekly*, 4 July 2002
259 'In the comic books, you know, Spider-Man and Daredevil have been at it . . .' Michael Clarke Duncan, quoted in 'Speak of *Daredevil*' by Steve Daly, *Entertainment Weekly*, 7 February 2002
259 'The thing that's fucked up, actually . . .' Affleck, ibid.
259 'From the minute Ben showed up to get a plaster cast . . .' Johnson, quoted in 'Flying Blind' by Liane Bonin, *Entertainment Weekly*, 4 July 2002
260 'The movie's heavy. The movie's dark . . .' Johnson, quoted in 'Better the Devil You Know' by Ed Gross, *SFX*, February 2003

Hulk

262 'My grandmother had know idea who The X-Men were . . .' Kevin Feige, quoted in 'Hulk Smash' by ed Gross, *Cinefantastique*, February/March 2003

262 'I think the main reason The Hulk has survived . . .' and all other Michael France quotes, AI.

263 'It is odd, isn't it, that with all the feature [film] writers . . .' and all other Kenneth Johnson quotes, AI.

264 'It was done by Kenneth Johnson . . .' (Stan Lee, quoted in 'Interview with Stan Lee' by Kenneth Plume, filmforce.ign.com, 28 June 2000

264 'Hulk is the antithesis of a superhero . . .' Gale Anne Hurd, quoted in 'Hulk Smash' by Ed Gross, *Cinefantastique*, February/March 2003

265 'They knew the budget for the last six months . . .' Hensleigh, quoted in 'Hey, Big Spender' by Oliver Jones, *Premiere*, June 1998

266 'David Hayter did a kick-ass job on the script . . .' Feige, quoted on comics2film.com, 24 November 2000

266 'David [Hayter]'s script was the inspiration . . .' James Schamus, quoted in 'Schamus Talks *Hulk*' by Typhon24, cinescape.com, 27 April 2002

267 'I think The Hulk is the only reluctant superhero . . .' Eric Bana, quoted in 'The Green Machine', uncredited, *Empire*, April 2002

267 'It's really interesting and ambitious . . .' Jennifer Connelly, quoted on scifi.com/scifiwire, 11 December 2001

268 'I'm a hands-on kind of person . . .' Ang Lee, quoted in 'How to Make a Hulk', uncredited, *Entertainment Weekly*, 24–31 January 2003

268 'his attention to detail, his attention to the emotional element . . .' Hurd, quoted in 'Hulk Smash' by Ed Gross, *Cinefantastique*, February/March 2003

268 'I can absolutely vouch that Ang Lee has preserved the Hulk . . .' Gale Ann Hurd, quoted on comics2film.com, 6 August 2002

269 'I believe Hulk is the first Marvel creature . . .' Ang Lee, quoted on cinescape.com, 26 April 2002

Index